Information
in Business and Administrative Systems

Information
in Business and
Administrative
Systems

Ronald Stamper

A HALSTED PRESS BOOK

JOHN WILEY & SONS
New York

Published in the U.S.A., Philippines & South America
by Halsted Press, a Division
of John Wiley & Sons, Inc.
New York, 1973.
ISBN: 0 471-82045-8

Library of Congress Catalog Card No.: 73-176408

Contents

Preface

The explosive growth of information technology has not been accompanied by a commensurate improvement in the understanding of information. It is undoubtedly easier to manufacture and distribute electronic hardware than to refine our concepts of information and disseminate them to the hard-pressed men and women who are trying to put the new technology to work in government, industry and commerce. Too often the computer has either had a muffled impact or caused unexpected damage when introduced by technicians who do not understand how information functions in organisations. The application of information technology to organisations demands a wider knowledge than many of its specialists now display. It calls for an understanding of both machine and human information systems.

Society is a fabric woven from threads of communication. Organisations occupy a significant area of that fabric and increasingly they affect the texture and tensions of the life of every individual. The products of technologies have had a profound effect upon society, which has adapted its contours to accommodate them as though they were objects underneath and external to it. But information technology is different. It can be woven into the fabric itself and, by making possible new patterns of communication among people, it can allow us to create new kinds of organisation and, therefore, in some respects a new kind of society.

The problem area is large and its urgency is only now being recognised. This book tackles one important part by showing how we can untie the loose bundle of concepts we call 'information' to reveal a range of more precise tools which we can use for investigating organisational systems.

The book is written for members of various old and new professions in business and administration: they may be accountants, statisticians, company secretaries, organisation and methods or systems and procedures specialists, systems analysts, computer specialists, operational research scientists, personnel specialists, as well as managers and administrators themselves. The book is not addressed to all these categories of people indiscriminately. It is addressed to those who recognise that they must understand what their organisations do with information. Whatever their professional backgrounds, it will be a convenient shorthand to refer to all those who adopt this analytical role as 'information specialists'.

The scope of the problem has made it necessary to cull ideas from many subjects which can contribute to our understanding of how information is used in organisations. These disciplines include: anthropology, social psychology, psycholinguistics, philosophy, measurement theory, statistics, probability theory, logic, formal linguistics, computer science, communication and control engineering and experimental psychology.

A consequence of the variety of ideas explored is that the reader will almost certainly experience some unevenness in the difficulty of the material. I am sure that he will find that some topics are commonplace to him while others appear esoteric; I am equally sure that what seems esoteric to one reader will be commonplace to another. I hope that each will be patient when I am spelling out for other readers what seems obvious to him and that he will tackle patiently the less familiar topics.

The reader should not expect the book to lead him through a progression of ideas towards a portentous conclusion; it will not do so. If there is one key idea to look for it will not be found in any sentence or paragraph but in the overall arrangement of ideas to provide a coherent framework of concepts broad enough to help in the analysis of many organisational problems which, in practice, are very complicated. Neither should the reader expect another cookery book of methods for solving the familiar problems of information systems design. Instead, I have attempted to provide some conceptual tools which enable problems, even unfamiliar ones, to be understood and which might lead to new methods of solution. There are plenty of brief illustrations and hints of how to apply these concepts but it would require at least one more book, the size of this, to deal with applications thoroughly. (In fact, this book started life as a preparatory section for exactly such another book on methods of systems design and the temptation has been to digress into that wider subject).

Only recently has it become necessary for many people to discuss information with rigour in a context that does not fall conveniently into the framework of a single discipline such as psychology or communications engineering. How to use information technology to solve organisational problems is a question which cannot be answered within the confines of any single established discipline, hence the need for a new framework such as the one offered in this book. This change to a new point of view on a subject which has been studied by many specialists with their own standpoints makes necessary many changes of emphasis. Features in the conceptual landscape which are distinguished clearly by one group of specialists can be treated relatively crudely for our purposes, while other features must be differentiated into their components. In these circumstances there is a great temptation to coin many new words or assign technical interpretations to familiar words, but I think that to do so would only be to lay another course of bricks on the Tower of Babel. A few well-established specialist terms are used where they are appropriate, otherwise commonplace words are given qualifiers or are used in a reasonably exact way which should be clear from the context. Remaining difficulties may be resolvable using the index in lieu of a glossary.

In any discussion of organisational information systems, difficulties abound. Some are intellectual—caused by familiarity with only one side of the subject. Some are philosophical—caused by the very nature of information. Others are methodological—caused by the relationship between the information system and the investigator.

Intellectual difficulties may be experienced by anyone brought up on the social sciences or in the literary tradition because of the temptation to dismiss the potential impact of information technology on the organs of society. They see devices such as computers and micro-wave networks as mere extensions of the typewriter and the penny post. This pre-judgement will be self-realising if it is the only one current among the senior decision-makers in our society, but it will lose society the benefits of the greatest possible innovations of our age. Similarly, the person brought up with an academic engineer's or natural scientist's outlook will experience the difficulty of acknowledging the inadequacy of his rigorous methods of decision-making in administration and business. Lack of time or money often excludes the luxuries of building and testing models even when they would be relevant. The administrator or manager must normally operate with information which is highly subjective, often unreliable and quite unlike the data used by the engineer or scientist.

Philosophical difficulties are inevitable when discussing information. There is the incestuous relationship between the subject of discussion and the medium of discussion which is also information—this is not embarrassing once you get used to it. Philosophy has been the womb of all the sciences and nearly all other branches of learning. Not surprisingly, therefore, when we are facing a new and urgent set of problems we can turn to mother philosophy and find a member of her brood almost prepared for the work. Hence parts of this subject may still be regarded as essentially philosophical.

Methodological difficulties in developing information systems are ones shared by all 'social engineers'. Organisations, because of their size, complexity and uniqueness are difficult to describe and theorise about except at a general level and, because they are in constant flux, their study often does not permit repeated observation and experiment. Also, the organisation must absorb the information specialist, at least at a social level, before it can be observed and then changed by him; this presents a marked practical difficulty which the mechanical engineer does not experience vis-à-vis the systems he works upon.

There is one way of escaping from these difficulties and that is by changing our expectations. We should not imagine that our knowledge of information and information systems can become an additional science with its associated field of engineering. Only to a limited extent can the 'social engineer' mimic his mechanical engineering colleague by designing, modelling and making prototype versions of organisational systems because he, unlike his colleague, can neither describe in detail nor detach himself entirely from the object he is studying. But he does have the advantage that organisations create their òwn information systems according to the ways in which their members perceive their relationships with one another, their tasks and the tools at their disposal. The role of the information specialist should be that of the critical analyst, his task being not to impose fully designed systems on people but to reveal malfunctioning in the system caused by misuse of information and to provide improved facilities for handling information where appropriate. The organisation can then respond by restructuring itself in response to its improved perception of the information at its disposal and its improved facilities for handling information. The concepts outlined in this book are among those which the information specialist will need to carry out his task.

RONALD STAMPER

Acknowledgements

The stimulus for writing this book came initially from my work on systems analysis at Ashorne Hill College and has subsequently been sustained by my colleagues Frank Land, Sam Waters and Colin Tully in the Systems Analysis Group at the London School of Economics and Political Science. Without the help which they have given me in reading and commenting upon its several drafts, this book would have had many more defects. I must thank many others who have helped me in the same way, including: Peter Wakeford, Douglas Campbell, Alan Lees, Professor Tom Singleton, Michael Luck, David Park, Thomas Easterfield, Robert Fairthorne, Philip Buckerfield.

Four ladies have between them covered a mountain of paper with typescript, deciphering my writing and making order from my dictation with patience and charm: Shirley Harden, Betty Johnson, Janet Appleby and Kay Cooper. I thank them most warmly.

My wife, Grace, has earned my thanks not only for sharing the typing, reading every draft and insisting that I write English, but also for tolerating my preoccupation with this task.

Part One

Orientation

These two chapters examine some of the problems that make the study of information important.

Organisation entails working with information instead of the actual resources being organised. Machines are taking over much of the direct productive effort, leaving people the tasks of planning, organising and controlling. We are also discovering the benefits and disadvantages of organising our resources more tightly and on a larger scale. The increasing complexity of products, services and government all add to the importance of information, which can no longer be regarded as a relatively unimportant or secondary economic factor.

Information is a word used very loosely, especially in the context of business studies, to identify a mixed bundle of concepts. The time has come for us to use these concepts with greater precision. We shall need them if we are to employ the rich technology of information-processing with more success than we have attained so far. They will be essential if we are to understand how to make colossal organisations responsive to human needs and economical in performing their tasks.

Part Seven, which contains a summary, may also help to orientate the reader.

1 Organisation

New millions of participants in the control of general affairs must now attempt to form personal opinions on matters that were once left to the few. At the same time, the complexity of these matters has immensely increased.

C. K. Ogden and I. A. Richards, *The Meaning of Meaning*

The fabric of our society is changing and, in one particular respect – the evolution of large and complex organisations – that change is very rapid indeed. The wealth of our society is largely a product of our ability to organise. By co-ordinating a multitude of activities widely separated in time and space, we can employ physical resources with greater economy and create artefacts of a size and complexity previously beyond our ambitions; by pooling our resources we may reduce dramatically the risks which individuals face and increase amazingly the wealth and variety of satisfactions which each person can obtain. The benefits of organisation are great but the work it involves is often regarded as wasteful.

No wonder! because organisation is achieved not by doing things but by talking and writing about them: transmitting and processing information.

Instead of working with materials or performing services directly for people, many are employed to sit at desks and work with drawings, numbers, words and other *signs* which represent materials and the productive activities of others. Instead of selling goods and services which will immediately satisfy people's requirements, many are engaged in discovering the needs, priorities and values of others so that, after more talking and data-processing, these hypothetical desires will one day be satisfied.

An organisation comes into being whenever a group of people work together on a shared task. As the task and the organisation grow, it may be necessary to supplement the natural channels of personal communication. Codes may have to be designed to make communication economical. Formal systems may have to be imposed upon the natural use of language, to preserve the uniformity of action and standardisation of meaning essential for coordinating parts of the task performed in widely separated times and places. Organisers are gradually removed, by the increasing scale of their activities, from the physical resources they employ and the people with whom they deal; as the information they use becomes more abstract, there is a growing danger that it becomes meaningless. The volume of information used by a large organisation is also so vast that it becomes difficult to process and store it for future use.

Size of organisations

We need large organisations. They give us economy of scale, as in making steel and chemicals, for example. Some things we have discovered, such as the use of nuclear power, can only be attempted on a vast scale. In commerce, increased scale of operation can translate many similar, unpredictable risks into the statistical predictability of insurance. It can also reduce to predictable proportions the risks of managing a diversity of enterprises, by organising them around a central financial pool, as a conglomerate business. The unavoidably large scale of some research and development would be impossible outside a large organisation, as in the electronics industry. Distribution and transport, when organised over a wide geographical area, can be made far more efficient and flexible. And, as the scale of all these activities increases, administration and government must also grow to provide a framework to facilitate their operations and to serve as a counterpoise to the increasing concentration of power.

Whatever its cause, large-scale organisation gives rise to problems in the use of information. Obviously there will be a need to gather, store and process data on a vast scale. Large staffs of clerks, often aided by computer systems, will be needed. The increase in the proportion of the working population engaged in clerical activities is probably symptomatic of the growth in scale of organisation. This increase would probably have been greater still in the absence of computing power which has been growing at a dramatic, exponential rate. Technical skills of a new and important kind are necessary for handling vast amounts of data, but it is only one of the problems concerning information in large organisations.

From the market economy to the administered economy

As the scale of organisation increases and the products and services which we require also become vast in scale, it is clear that a market economy is incapable of exercising adequate control over many crucial economic decisions because of their complexity. A market is an informal message system which can transmit financial messages from the individuals in the community about the relative desirability of simple commodities, such as butter or bananas, umbrellas or underclothes; it will not function in the same way when the choices involve the building of a chemical plant or the construction of a motorway. In simple situations the nature of a commodity can be discerned fairly accurately by a consumer; he can estimate the consequences of his choice moderately accurately and he can learn from his mistakes because he makes these simple decisions very often. It would be naive to expect the same market mechanism to regulate the supply of many of the more elaborate artefacts and services that we demand. Firstly, there is often no single consumer – a whole community is involved. Secondly, the output includes more than its obvious primary consequences: a chemical plant produces not only chemicals but more job opportunities, and a motorway, whilst reducing journey times, causes pollution and noise. In such circumstances, the market mechanism is not sufficient to force the decision-maker to consider the secondary effects of his action.

The great advantage which can be claimed for a market economy is that the key economic decision-makers are exposed to the force of the aggregate desires of many individuals. The large organisation, however, can shield its decision-makers from the harsh climate of an open market. Administrative organisations, which provide many of the most complex services and artefacts which we consume, are able to frustrate nearly all external pressures by exposing just the narrowest of crevices in their façades, through which only the most persistent can make themselves felt. It is also possible for the large organisation to devote resources to advertising and public relations on a scale sufficient to temper the opinions which would otherwise be expressed.

As we move into the era of large corporations and vast government departments, the market economy gives way increasingly to the administered economy. Managers in large organisations must still be aware of the market pressure upon the organisation. This is achieved by the financial constraints which are imposed by the cost accountant: standards, budget figures, variances and transfer prices. These accounting figures are not always easy to justify; they may give to the manager in a large organisation a completely distorted representation of the kind of market pressures to which a manager in a small organisation is subjected. The artificiality of these costing methods is no bad thing because it allows the managers of large corporations to organise resources in ways that are far more economical than a market mechanism would permit. A market rewards those who pursue local and short-term advantages; by taking decisions in a larger organisational framework, a number of departments may yield a higher overall performance than they could by working independently. Whether central administrative decisions can improve upon decentralised decision-making by a market depends upon the quality of the information available, among other things.

When administrative decisions affect a whole community they should be made responsive to the value-judgements of the many people affected. This is another problem in the supply and processing of information. It may be sufficient to rely upon our elected representatives and a few consultative bodies. Perhaps we should be trying to develop ways to supplement these channels.

Decisions which lead to large-scale innovations pose severe problems about knowing what alternatives are offered. How do you examine a plan or proposal in order to discover its consequences with sufficient accuracy for anyone to say whether he likes them or not? This is a problem in the use of *information* as a substitute for *things*. The scale of the innovation rules out the use of trial and error.

These problems, associated with the scale of an organisation and the scale of its activities, are fundamentally about the use of information. A market transmits information in two directions: the goods and services themselves or samples of them inform the consumers about what they may have; a flow of orders and money in the opposite direction transmits information to the suppliers about the actual demand. The market mechanism, which diffuses messages about simple commodities to many individuals and, with equal efficiency, aggregates their many small decisions, is no longer adequate. Increasingly, we need to take decisions collectively about vast, complex products and services while they are still plans or proposals. The market mechanism must be supplemented by a growing sector of administered economy if these larger decisions, requiring so much more information, are to be made correctly.

The role of information technology

To make the new kinds of economic decisions and to run our large organisations, vast bodies of data must be transmitted, stored, processed and communicated to many people. Fortunately the modern technology of information-processing can facilitate this work. We are familiar with the telephone, radio and television and soon we shall treat communication by satellite and modulated laser beam as equally commonplace. Added to the printed word and the punched card, we now have data stored magnetically and available to a computer in a tenth of a second; soon we shall be able to store a million erasable characters on a square inch of film and have access to any of them by laser optics in a millionth of a second. We have evolved from the abacus and slide rule, through the desk-top calculating machine, to the computer which can now perform a million additions per second, and there are still prospects of a hundred-fold improvement.

Information technology is not being used effectively to solve organisational problems. On the one side stand the technologists, most of whom have no idea of the complexity of organisations; on the other side stand the managers and administrators, unable to translate their problems into feasible demands upon technology; between them a river of mistrust flows through the chasm of misunderstanding. Distressingly often, I hear computer specialists talk of 'mere O. & M.' and dismiss management as either common sense or a waste of time; and, with equal frequency, I hear managers call computer science a 'mere technicality' and then chafe about their difficult problems that have simple technical solutions which they fail to perceive. These two extremes have quite different intellectual climates. It is often difficult to work comfortably in the zone between because one needs to understand both the intrinsically exact problems of the computer specialist and the intrinsically vague problems of the manager. They can all be regarded as problems in the use of information and I believe that a wide-ranging understanding of the nature of information can be of the greatest help in bridging the gap between organisational problems and their technological solutions. This is not to suggest that other views are invalid.

We should be prepared to make full use of information technology by designing organisations that are markedly different from the familiar ones that have evolved within the limits of clerical data-processing methods. The computer can centralise the information needed for running an organisation but data transmission networks can decentralise the decision-making. The elaborate, formal rules which are the foundation of bureaucracy can be administered by computers; depending upon the way this is done, they can be made even more inscrutable to the victim or their inner mysteries can be exposed with the aid of the computer itself. Large organisations, public and private, can have instant access to intimate details about millions of people through a system of data banks; conversely a whole citizenry can be kept better informed about the conduct of the large organisations which so vitally affect their lives because work done on computers is open to closer scrutiny than ever before. The technological alternatives can be bewildering. We are entering a new era in society; the power of steam and gasoline is being overlaid by the power of information.

The information specialist

Technology was once very limited. Organisations were then driven slowly down the one, narrow track of progress. Suddenly, technology has broadened out – acres of tarmac stretching unimpeded towards almost everything we desire. We should like to go in all directions at once but we have limited resources for the organisations to take us there. The old organisational dray-horses, that were bred over many years to match their heavy work, have now been supplemented by many larger, more mechanical organisations; but travelling on them can be very disappointing. They are hastily assembled and usually badly made. Some move off in many directions simultaneously and fall apart. Some are run by the technologists themselves; they procure vast resources and drive off where no one wishes to go. Others, some of the largest, just whirr and clank. Some move ponderously round in circles but the driver is happy provided he remains at the wheel and stays in familiar surroundings. There is a fashion for merging them together or hiving pieces off in order to provide an illusion of movement. Some do very well, perhaps as much through luck as judgement; but all are hampered by a lack of 'engineers'.

The demands of society and the opportunities of technology are now changing so quickly that we must learn to construct organisations that are responsive to our needs. Organisations cannot be left to evolve; as far as it is possible they must be designed. Many people are working on these problems: managers, administrators and staff specialists. In one way or another they are all trying to make organisations use information effectively. It is information that holds organisations together and drives them along. What we urgently need, therefore, are information specialists who are as thoroughly acquainted with the information needs of organisations as they are with the capabilities of modern information technology.

Perhaps the genuine information specialists will emerge from the ranks of the systems analysts. These people are expected to be able to harness the power of the computer to the problems of the organisation. Their new profession was brought into existence by the development of the computer and they tend to regard themselves as computer experts of a kind. Many of them are so interested in this engine that they devote their energies to getting the maximum 'revs' out of the computer, without its serving to drive the organisation anywhere. If systems analysts are to play a leading role in developing the new generation of organisations which make effective use of information technology they must realise that they need to be as expert on the problems of organisation as upon the capabilities of the computer.

Information specialists, under whatever title they are operating, need to have a balanced view; they need an intellectual framework that encompasses the whole range of their problems and the available methods of solution. A wide-ranging study of the nature of information can help to provide that framework.

2 Information

There are some who find difficulty in considering any matter unless they can recognise it as belonging to what is called 'a subject'. . . . These need only be reminded that at one time there were no subjects and until recently only five. But the discomfort experienced in entering the less familiar fields of inquiry is genuine.

C. K. Ogden and I. A. Richards, *The Meaning of Meaning*

We take information for granted. We think of it simply as the way of getting to know about 'real things', things that matter, like what is happening in Paris, who owes us money, the price of zinc, facts about aeroplanes and reports about people's attitudes. Problems about information – its nature, the processes whereby it is communicated and stored, and the ways in which it reveals its meaning, are regarded as either technical problems for the telephone engineer, or philosophical problems having little to do with practical matters. This is a mistaken view. There is little we can do without information. There is no organisation controlling the flows of materials and energy, or the work of people and machines, which does not make elaborate use of information; so why has its study been neglected?

One reason is that, until recently, information has presented us with few technical difficulties. Until the days of the telegraph, communication was always either direct over short distances, or by some physical form of transport over longer distances, and therefore if the physical problems of contact or transport could be solved, problems of transferring information took care of themselves. Until the computer came along there existed no creature or machine which could seriously challenge the ability of a human being to handle information. It is also true to say that, until recently, co-operative human endeavour has been on a small scale, or very simple or slow, these limitations being imposed by the speeds at which physical communication could be accomplished.

The kind of world we live in today probably owes more to our newly-found ability to transmit information accurately by electro-magnetic impulses at the speed of light rather than by messenger at the speed of a horse or steam locomotive than to any other innovation. We are at last being forced, by the way our society is developing, to make a thorough study of information.

It is common to distinguish two extreme kinds of information systems within an organisation. Let us examine each of them briefly in order to establish the context of our enquiry.

Formal information systems

Most people, if asked to describe an organisational information system, would talk about a formal system, embracing the kinds of activities shown in fig. 1. Starting at the bottom of the picture, you can trace the flow of information.

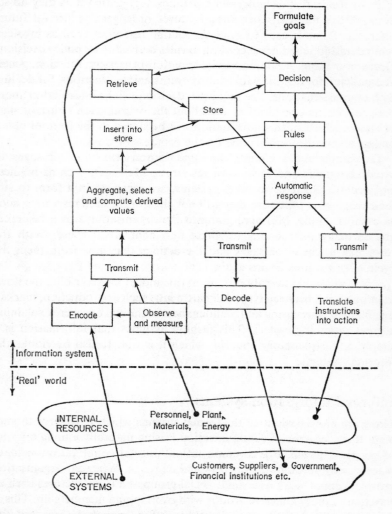

Fig. 1. Major formal information functions in an organisation.

Messages from external systems, such as customers, suppliers, government agencies, and financial institutions, normally arrive in a perfectly explicit form of words and numbers. Occasionally this information must be transcribed or coded into a standard form which is used within the organisation. The organisation also derives information from its own resources: the people, machines, materials and sources of energy with which it performs its tasks. These do not submit information about themselves in a convenient form. They must be observed and measured.

The incoming information is transmitted to people who select some of it for use in further processing, perhaps aggregating it as they do so. Some of this filtered information is stored in ledgers or files for future reference. Some is used to generate routine responses such as invoices, reminders and schedules according to rules derived from policy decisions. Decision-making, itself another information-processing function, generates policies, for dealing with routine events and instructions, for dealing with unique situations. The input to a decision will be information about the goals of the organisation and about the organisation's current state of affairs. Much of this information will be stored in the form of plans, budget statements and reports on the progress of work.

To complete the circuit, the organisation transmits messages to external systems and to its own resources. Messages, such as invoices and orders, which go to other systems, are recorded in a form to suit their recipients; otherwise they will not elicit the desired responses, such as cash or goods. Messages going to the organisation's own resources are normally instructions to direct and control their use. With the responses to these messages and the actions that flow from them the cycle of operations begins again.

It is fashionable to elaborate upon this model by describing the flows of information between typical departments, such as production, marketing, finance, purchasing and maintenance, as though one were explaining a great plumbing system. This fashion assumes that information is a simple, self-explanatory concept, which it is not. It also overlooks the informal systems.

Informal information systems

These are more basic than the formal systems which only serve to augment those systems of communication arising naturally among a group of people engaged in a common task. Informal communication takes place mostly through direct, personal contacts. When an organisation grows it cannot work as a single social group and it restructures itself as a system of fairly cohesive groups with overlapping membership. This is depicted in fig. 2. Each group is held together through the constant flux

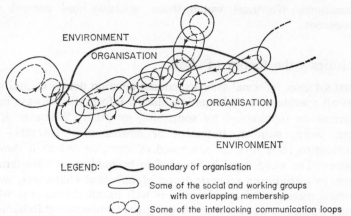

ENVIRONMENT

ORGANISATION

ORGANISATION

ENVIRONMENT

LEGEND: 〰 Boundary of organisation

⬭ Some of the social and working groups
with overlapping membership

⬭⬭ Some of the interlocking communication loops

Fig. 2. Informal information structure based on social groupings and 'natural'
communications.

of social intercourse. Each group has its own minute variations on the
prevailing culture of the organisation helping to differentiate it from
other groups. Members who belong to more than one group are aware
of differences of attitudes and goals between the groups; sometimes
these differences are the cause of psychological tensions which the link-
members will attempt to remove by persuading one or perhaps each
group to adjust its views. This mechanism enables attitudes to be communicated through a chain of overlapping groups.

There will also be tension between the formal and informal systems.
They interact whenever a person has to obey the rules of some formal
system. Formal systems are intended to operate in a uniform way,
throughout time and over the whole of the wide territory across which
the organisation may be spread. Formal systems are insensitive to local
problems which are the major concern of the informal systems. When a
formal system seems to impose an inappropriate procedure or a way of
thinking it will be resented and its operation will perhaps be distorted.

There is an analogy between organisational systems and biological
systems in which messages are sometimes carried by chemicals, sometimes by nerves. Creatures low down the scale of evolution rely upon
endocrine systems which communicate slowly by diffusing chemicals
throughout the organism. The higher orders have evolved nervous
systems carrying messages very quickly between specific sense-organs
and specific effector-organs. Nervous systems evolved in two stages:
first the nerve-fibres for carrying the signals and, later, the brain where
messages are processed and exchanged. Is there not a parallel in the
evolution of organisations? With the arrival of the computer, the
analogue of a rudimentary brain, we are likely to see rapid changes in

organisations. We must watch them zealously and control their development.

Semiotics – the theory of signs

Formal systems, informal systems, communication networks and computers all operate upon information but the information always has to be carried or represented by something or other. Whatever it is – gesture, word, number, statement or mathematical formula – it is convenient to refer to it as composed of *signs*, or *signals* if they are transitory. The word 'sign' is intended to be used in an all-embracing manner to include the numerical and alphabetical characters, words, sentences, messages of any length, as well as all the actions which, through custom or convention, have acquired some recognisable interpretation. A major proposition of this book is that almost anything can be regarded as a sign. We should be accustomed enough to this kind of general use of terms. We talk about 'matter' and 'energy' which apply to virtually anything. When we use very general terms of this kind we are, in effect, directing attention to certain very specific properties of things.

As physics is concerned with some special physical properties of things, so semiotics, the theory of signs, is concerned with the properties of things in their capacity as signs. Physics is concerned with mass and energy. Semiotics is concerned with the properties which we are accustomed to lump together under the title 'information'.

The word 'semiotics' comes from the Greek for 'symptom'. It was used by the Stoic philosophers and, in modern times, by John Locke in his *Essay Concerning Human Understanding*. It is now used to designate the unified theory of signs which was probably initiated by C. S. Peirce (1839–1914), who was primarily a logician. More recently, Charles Morris has made many important contributions, largely from a behavioural standpoint. This book adopts a point of view determined by the need to solve organisational problems.

(Incidentally, 'semiotic' is the traditional form of the word. However, this strikes so many people as archaic that I shall add a final s.)

The problems of semiotics are usually classified under three major headings: *pragmatics*, *semantics* and *syntactics*; to these I shall add a fourth: *empirics*. They represent very different ways of understanding signs and measuring their properties. Each one has associated with it a group of established disciplines. Semiotics is not so much a new subject, as a regrouping of ideas from many disciplines having their own private jargons, and little intercommunication.

To gain an overall impression of the field to be surveyed, consider the important function of decision-making. Fig. 3 shows a group of people

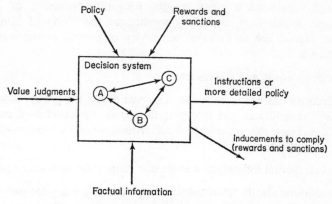

Fig. 3. Information aspects of a decision process.

making a decision; they have to acquire information of a number of different kinds, communicate among themselves until they decide what to do, and then they must transmit their decision to other people who will give effect to it. The questions one might ask about the use of information for making the decision can be grouped under the headings of the main parts of this book: pragmatics, semantics of words and statements, semantics of numbers, syntactics and empirics.

Pragmatics

This branch of semiotics is concerned with the relationships between signs and behaviour. It draws upon the social sciences and upon the humanities. In the decision-making situation it examines questions such as:

What signs can be used to inform the decision-makers about facts, policies, value judgments, rewards and sanctions?

How sensitive are people to these signs?

How do they exchange information in a way that will lead to their reaching a consensus?

How can a member of the decision-making group exert his influence?

As a participant in the process, experience of similar problems, skill in communicating and judgment are most important for guiding one quickly and intuitively to the right answers. Experience and study of the humanities constitute a good training.

The social sciences can aid the critical assimilation of experience and theirs is the point of view adopted in this book. Anthropology deals with the important question about what people use as signs. Social psychology gives us a clear insight into the processes of group behaviour. Psychology, especially applied to the study of language, helps to expose the remarkable sensitivity of people to the messages they receive.

Semantics of words and statements

If the decision has not to be made in a great hurry, the group, who have to weigh the evidence and interpret the views presented to them, will want to subject the information to critical analysis. They will ask questions such as:

How can factual information and value judgments be disentangled?

How can one clarify what the words used in reports refer to?

When someone puts forward a plan or proposal, how is it possible to make sure that it is meaningful?

When large, crucial and complex decisions are to be made, there will nearly always be time for critical analysis of the data, but it is often done rather badly.

Philosophy is the major source of material for this branch of semiotics. It cannot provide clear-cut answers to most business problems because there is always an interplay between the linguistic signs we use and our thought processes, especially at the very high level of abstraction at which most important organisational problems must be formulated. Philosophy provides methods of analysis which can protect us from the worst errors of reacting unthinkingly to what we have been told without making sure that we are justified in doing so.

Semantics of numerical information

It would be unusual if managerial and administrative decision-makers were not assailed by volumes of numerical information. Starting from the critical methods applied to words and statements, another kind of criticism can be developed to ensure that numerical information is meaningful. We shall want to know:

What is a satisfactory measurement?

What kinds of arithmetical operations can justifiably be performed on various measurements?

How are the results to be interpreted?

The theory of measurement (which is shown in chapter 9 to be a branch of semantics, *not* mathematics) and some aspects of statistics are disciplines relevant to these questions.

Prompted by the discussion of measurement, it would be appropriate to ask:

Can we measure the signs, conveying information to the decision-makers?

Is it possible from these measurements to determine how far the decision-makers should alter their views?

Are there any objective ways of measuring signs that can be used to 'compel' reasonable people to reach agreement?

Questions of this kind lead directly to the measurement of information and its use in models of how decision-makers should behave. The theories of subjective probability and statistics are the disciplines to which we must turn for guidance.

Syntactics

A decision may be one which can be embodied in a system of rules and regulations, or it may require information which should be available in the organisation's files. It is natural to ask:

How can formal rules be expressed economically?

Can they be applied to individual cases by a computer?

If information is to be stored in large quantities, using a computer, how should it be organised?

What kinds of question can the computer be made to answer automatically?

These are all questions which can be answered without any further concern for problems of semantics.

The study of formal language structures is a very new subject and essential to this branch of semiotics. It extends into logic which leads to various aspects of file design, a very new subject indeed. One aspect of logic has an application to the measuring of information. However little an information specialist serving decision-makers knows about computers, he should know some parts of syntactics.

Empirics

Decisions are often made repeatedly in order to control a process or activity. These tend to be relatively simple decisions but they pose some problems of their own:

Is it possible to obtain enough information from the process being controlled?

How can we measure the degree of control?

What are the effects of applying control less frequently or of using out-dated information?

All these questions relate to communication channels or to the statistical behaviour of the control system.

Communications engineering has a highly developed theory for the analysis of these problems. Their theory has also been applied by experimental psychologists to the study of routine human behaviour, so the methods can apply to organisational problems, not only to telephone lines.

Conclusion

This brief, introductory pair of chapters has presented a number of issues which make the study of information important. It is true to say that information has been examined in a variety of ways by many established disciplines but it is not yet common to find the whole spectrum of the subject drawn together under the single heading of 'semiotics'. The reader may find it helpful, in keeping the whole subject in perspective as he goes through the book, to turn occasionally to the summary in Part Seven. This may also serve to augment the introduction if the reader needs more orientation.

One day, when we train information specialists as we train engineers today, this subject will appear in their courses. At least it is worth having a name for a set of related problems. It is useful in industry or commerce or administration to be able to talk about 'economic problems' or 'industrial relations problems' or 'engineering difficulties' or 'financial headaches'. There may also be some value in being able to refer to one's 'problems of semiotics'. There is nothing like having a name for a collection of problems to help you remember to do something about them.

Part Two

Pragmatics

The next three chapters examine information from a behavioural point of view. We exchange information in order to influence the behaviour of one another. This is certainly true of information used in organisations. To convey information we have recourse to verbal and other 'signs'. The essential property of a sign is that it is capable of referring to something else so that behaviour, towards whatever is referred to, can be influenced. Thus if you tell me in words or by displaying a road sign that a certain bridge is too low for my lorry to go underneath it, I can behave appropriately, by not trying to drive my lorry underneath it, although I may never see the bridge.

It is important to be clear what can act as a sign. Chapter 3 examines this question and shows that any pattern of behaviour, or any object which is associated with the pattern of behaviour, can acquire the status of a sign and so be capable of carrying information.

The way in which signs acquire their meanings is rooted in human behaviour. There is an important social mechanism of norm formation that creates the necessary stability in behaviour, including the usage of signs. This is the subject of chapter 4.

The most important signs we employ are words. Verbal signs can be used to denote things but they are also used to indicate what we feel about them. The ability of words to carry both kinds of information depends upon our sensitivity to them. The third chapter of this Part concentrates upon verbal signs, especially our sensitivity to them, which enables words to use us, as surely as we use them.

3 Communication and Culture

Here the face, the arms, the hat, the stick, the body throughout spoke equally with the tongue. To express satisfaction the Casterbridge market-man added to his utterance a broadening of the cheeks, a crevicing of the eyes, a throwing back of the shoulders, which was intelligible from the other end of the street. . . . Deliberation caused sundry attacks on the moss of adjoining walls with the end of his stick, a change of his hat from the horizontal to the less so; a sense of tediousness announced itself in a lowering of the person by spreading the knees to a lozenge-shaped aperture and contorting the arms.

Thomas Hardy, *The Mayor of Casterbridge*

It is worthwhile, very early in a book on information, to take note of the full spectrum of signs that we human beings use to influence one another. The anthropologist, more than any other specialist, has drawn our attention to the rich and complex ways in which human communication takes place. Social behaviour and communication are opposite faces of the same coin. All uses of signs can ultimately be justified only in terms of patterns of behaviour. Special kinds of social behaviour, such as those displayed by people working in organisations, demand special kinds of communication – for example, the jargons of various trades and professions and the highly formalised languages that enable computers to be employed by an organisation. Even with the most technical uses of signs (such as in mathematics, logic and computer programming), we must never lose sight of the fact that these activities are founded upon social behaviour.

Technical people too easily forget the social context which justifies all technical activities and provides every worthwhile yard-stick of technical performance. Machines are a part of human affairs: they serve us; we make them; we operate them and maintain them. Therefore their design should start from an understanding of human characteristics. This self-evident premise does not appear to be given the weight it deserves, judging by the number of articles whose design contradicts it. For example, my car has a battery that cannot be inspected unless a pocket torch and a mirror are used and then one has to kneel down on the road; the seats in first-class railway carriages have a dimension from front to back that is uncomfortable for the 50 % of the population of less than median height (presumably this is an attempt to give value for money!). We often see the needs of the human users brushed aside through considerations of engineering, aesthetics, or apparent economy. The user is expected, by contortion, agility or ingenuity, to adjust himself to a piece of bad design. The same is true about the use of computers. Except merely as adjuncts of other machines, successful computer systems cannot be devised without regard for the characteristics of the people and the society which they are to serve. Many bad computer systems serve to underline this assertion.

These strictures upon the importance of human factors in the design of machines apply with even greater force to the construction of organisations. Organisations are machines for achieving human goals, although one sometimes hears talk which suggests that a business is a machine for producing money as an end in itself, or that the efficiency of an administrative arm of government is justification enough. It should also be remembered that the components of organisations are whole human beings, but quite often one hears the people in an organisation being talked about as though each brought with him some isolated faculty – the strength of his right arm or his ability to do sums – which the organisation required, leaving behind his other human characteristics. This idea is dangerously misleading because we employ the whole man with all his faculties. The problem is even more complicated because we cannot employ one person in isolation. He and his colleagues bring with them all the cultural patterns of the social groupings of which they are members. Most experienced businessmen and administrators are aware of this, although some accept the idea grudgingly. However, many of their advisers with technical backgrounds in engineering, accounting, operational research, organisation and methods, work study, computer system-design, and so on, display a rather disturbing insensitivity to the human problems of organisation.

Culture

Culture, in the anthropologist's sense, should interest the designer of organisations; it is *the totality of patterns of behaviour that are shared by members of a society so that they may understand one another and behave in a coordinated fashion.* Without a common culture, people would not be able to act together to form any kind of organisation.

Organisational failure, more often than not, can be explained by a breakdown in communication. Because we tend to think of communication in terms of speaking to people, writing reports, holding committee meetings, distributing company newspapers and so on, we are blinkered and fail to give our non-verbal means of communication the attention they deserve. A study of culture, in its widest sense, should help to correct this mistaken bias.

The important thing about culture is that it is *shared*. When we are with people who share the same cultural background as ourselves, we are unaware of the way in which it facilitates our mutual understanding. We take for granted our common beliefs and knowledge, common expectations and values. Only when we enter another society do we experience the play of cultural forces; we then feel the disequilibrium between what is expected of us and our customary behaviour.

Consider how you felt and behaved when you first visited another country; or when you had just joined the organisation you are working with now; or when, as an adolescent, you were being invited to participate for the first time in some adult activity. You must have been aware of the difficulty of knowing what to expect of others and what they expected of you. In those new circumstances you would have been alert to all the indications given to you about how to behave. You would not only have listened to advice, but you would also have been attentive to the signs of approval and disapproval which established members of the group displayed towards your own and other people's behaviour.

Consciously or unconsciously, in response to real or imagined social pressures from the people around you, you would have reduced the incongruities in your dress, tone of voice, choice of words, your stance, even what you considered to be funny. Because of your sensitivity, heightened by your desire to become acceptable in the particular social group, you would have acquired a repertoire of skills ranging from some needed for survival down to mere social affectations. In this manner you would have received the cultural 'message' and, in your turn, you could begin to play your part in transmitting that culture to others.

Another consequence of your learning the patterns of a culture would have been your ability to communicate quite complicated messages without recourse to language. You would have learnt to use nuances of behaviour to express yourself and to read in them fine shades of meaning in the behaviour of others. Once you had absorbed the new culture thoroughly, you would have been able to receive accurate and detailed messages conveyed by all kinds of commonplace actions; for example, the way a person offered you a chair or the way two people stood whilst conversing, or the time that you were kept waiting in an outer office. Until you appreciated these minutiae of cultural difference you may easily have applied, subconsciously and mistakenly, the standards appropriate to a more familiar culture.

Culture can be understood in terms of these many subtle, silent message systems. An insensitivity to these messages is a serious failing if found among those who create and operate organisations. It is often seen in a young person recently recruited into business or industry. He may talk sound sense most of the time, but he can often forget the endless silent messages that he is sending to people by his manner and appearance, preparing them to accept or reject whatever he will say.

It is possible to classify the kinds of message which people exchange in a variety of ways.* It is convenient, here, to adopt a scheme of classification proposed by E. T. Hall (1957): he defines ten areas of human activity in which there exist conventions of knowledge, belief, evaluation and behaviour. It is worth listing each of these and looking at circumstances in which they might affect the work of someone trying to investigate an organisational problem and implement his solution. In such circumstances some readers might already have had sharp encounters with cultural influences.

Ten streams of cultural messages

Culturally determined patterns of behaviour can be regarded as messages communicated to all newcomers by the existing members of a group. This mechanism transmits information from generation to generation, thereby preserving the skills, the opinions and the attitudes of a group of people, for instance those who regularly work together.

It is also important to understand cultural patterns of behaviour in quite another sense as a communication mechanism. The rich repertoire of behaviour which the anthropologist refers to as a 'culture' can be used as a 'silent language' (to use Hall's expression), with a 'silent dialect' for each sub-cultural group. Variations upon one kind of behaviour (e.g. dress) can be used to convey messages about other aspects of our behaviour and what other people should expect of us (e.g. clothes reserved for certain groups of people, for certain trades or to distinguish the sexes, clothes to be worn in certain places or at certain times, clothes as a mark of learning, etc.). In the following pages there are many examples illustrating the variety and eloquence of the non-verbal messages which we encode by subtly modulating our cultural behaviour patterns.

Of course, much of our behaviour is determined biologically and physically by the nature of the human animal and the world he lives in. In this sense, we behave as we do because there is no alternative but surprisingly little of our complex behaviour is so inevitable. We formalise and refine the biological and physical necessities to create a rich environment of signs which is the social side of human behaviour. For many people, one and only one social environment is so familiar that a compelling logic appears to govern what are really quite artificial *social*

* See Malinowski, 1944, Lévi-Strauss, 1963.

B

patterns of behaviour, just as though they were determined by biological forces. Too often, as a result of this narrow outlook, the equally elaborate and equally justifiable cultural patterns of other communities are dismissed as barbaric or uncouth. To a lesser degree this lack of understanding is even found to stand between the sub-cultural groupings in a single large organisation. Hall's classification helps one to perceive the cultural differences between groups and to recognise their importance.

1. *Association* Conventions that govern the groupings of people and the roles that people play are included under this heading. Rank and hierarchy, class and formal organisation are all phenomena of association.

To disturb established patterns of association can be to provoke strong emotional reactions to change. For example, there is often a basic harmony between patterns of authority, responsibility and skill and the age-structure of a mature organisation. Today, innovations may call for skills which are not so readily found among the older members of the community, as in data-processing, and consequently a new hierarchy has to develop, conflicting with the relationships that people have come to expect between age and authority.

One common mistake is to imagine that the ethics of association, appropriate in a mobile and competitive managerial middle-class, are equally relevant in a stable community of workmen. In industry it is no good introducing an incentive scheme for individuals, in the hope of exploiting a competitive spirit among members of a working group who regard unfavourably any marked deviation from what the members consider a normal rate of working. This tendency to regulate the pace of work is natural among a group of men who expect to work together for many years. Much the same can be said of other stable working groups such as a team of consultants in a hospital. Competition is not rewarding in these circumstances, solidarity is more important.

2. *Subsistence* This is a label for the processes by which a society satisfies the basic physical needs of daily life and the attitudes displayed towards such matters as food, drink, work.

Anyone contemplating a change of meal-times or eating facilities for any group of people in an organisation will obviously watch his step over such a basic matter. The way in which canteen facilities are organised within a firm is one of the clearest indicators of how it regards its employees; there is no more potent way of drawing hierarchical lines among management than by using carefully graded, segregated places where they perform basic human functions such as eating. (This example, of how subsistence behaviour can convey messages about a person's position in a hierarchy of association, is just one instance of how cultural message streams interact. You will notice that all the other categories of behaviour are also used to support the hierarchical framework of an organisation.)

Attitudes to work can present cultural obstacles to innovation. Jobs are status labels. Anyone proposing changes in an organisation will need to think about how changes in jobs will affect status.

Occupational groupings have their roots not only in a specialisation of skills but also in the need to influence the distribution of wealth. When changes of technology lead to the overlapping of skills or when organisational economy dictates the sharing of skills, then one can reasonably expect the release of strong emotional forces over the problems of how to redistribute the work and the income. This kind of cultural difficulty probably lies at the root of such varied problems as the legendary dispute in the shipbuilding industry between wood-workers and metal-workers over who should drill holes in metal/wood laminates, and the disapprobation given to any suggestion to amalgamate the professions of barrister and solicitor.

3. *Bisexuality* The ways in which the sexes are distinguished and the relationships which are permitted between them are fundamental to society.

The kinds of work that people may do are commonly influenced by sex and these differences help to emphasise sexuality. It is not surprising, therefore, that in countries where engineering is regarded as a masculine occupation, women are not attracted to it, despite potentially high financial rewards.

4. *Territoriality* There are conventions which govern the division of space between people and its allocation for different purposes.

Territorial rights accorded to a person indicate his position in the hierarchy; these rights may be strictly formalised, as in civil service regulations. This cultural factor generates strong feelings, as was demonstrated on the railways when the footplatemen vigorously resisted attempts to locate the guard in the cabin of the locomotive, their holy of holies.

Anyone who has had practical experience of gathering the facts about how a part of an organisation works will have spent a lot of his time interviewing people. He will have acquired some feeling for the way in which space affects his relations with the people he is interviewing. A person who is interviewed on his own territory will be much more at his ease than one who is interviewed in alien surroundings. The reverse of this is the problem encountered by the person new to interviewing, who is reluctant to leave his cosy office to encounter people in their alien preserves. Communication may be easier if each knows the other's territory. It may be important, therefore, deliberately to make the other man feel at home when he is on your domain. In many ways you can use the territory over which you have control to indicate your attitude to someone by the degree of access you give to him.

5. *Temporality* These conventions govern *when* we do things, the times of the day, month or year that are appropriate, and the amount of time that may elapse between doing things.

Cycles of community activity are at the root of some organisational difficulties in service industries. It suits those industries which must deal with the general public to be very active commercially at times during the day or week when the majority of people are at leisure. Shop assistants would obviously prefer to be in step with the rest of the community and not be working at those times. Patterns of organisation which lead to the lives of employees being disjointed from those of the rest of the community are likely to cause some tension.

Lateness for a meeting may be accidental, but it can easily be construed as lack of regard for the person kept waiting.

6. *Learning* Most behaviour must be learnt. The conventions that govern such things as the time, the place and the manner of learning or of teaching are themselves a vital part of a culture.

The growing need to innovate in industry will force us to revise our own cultural prejudice against a person entering any kind of full-time education after the age of about 25. People in management have already overcome much of this resentment but other groups certainly do not regard extensive retraining as a natural part of their working lives.

There are three basically different ways in which people learn from others: through *technical* instruction; from *formal* prescriptions and from the informal example given by the behaviour of others. Different groups make quite different uses of these modes of learning. The technical man can, too easily, over-value the medium of reasoned explanation as a method of imparting new skills to people; although they may understand an explanation they may fail to use it in modifying their behaviour unless they are well practised in translating the world of descriptions into the world of actions. It is customary to supplement or replace technical instruction by giving a person a task to perform and then correcting his mistakes – that is to exploit the formal method of learning. However, in our society, most patterns of behaviour are transmitted informally: we do as others do, not as they say. Although some specific tasks in organisations can be specified and analysed, so that they can be taught technically or formally, many aspects of behaviour, vital to organisational effectiveness, such as enthusiasm, frankness, willingness to cooperate with others, tolerance of difficult working conditions, can only be communicated by example.

7. *Recreation and Humour* This is 'culture' in the popular sense but only a part of culture in the anthropologist's sense. Painting, music, literature — plus sports, games and what a society regards as funny – are very sensitive indices of a culture, perhaps because they are further removed

from the influence of biological necessities than the other cultural message-streams.

There are marked differences between social classes in their notions about deriving pleasure from work. For most people today, work is indeed hard if there is no fun in it. Pleasure is derived by some people from the intrinsic interest of the problems that they are working on; by others, from a measure of freedom to organise the pattern and tempo of their work to suit themselves, while perhaps for most people the satisfaction is provided by social contact within the working group. Organisational changes which affect any of these factors must be treated cautiously. The introduction of a computer into administration can often introduce into the work of a clerical section the kind of rigidity and pacing of tempo associated with factory life. Some adjustment has then to take place to enable the working group to accommodate its social contacts within a more rigid framework. Similar problems are likely to arise when changes in working practice reduce the opportunities for social contact, especially if, as a result, the men are fairly isolated in a large plant.

When you are getting to know, or be known by, an organisation, you must pay attention to this aspect of culture: always display a cautious sense of what is amusing until you know what is accepted; be sure you are not inappropriately labelled by those recreations you are known to enjoy (golf or ballet? football or painting?). Observe, also, the degree to which people label others; it varies from group to group and probably increases with narrowness of outlook.

8. *Defence* Techniques of defence are needed by the individual and by the community. Clothing and building materials for protection against the elements, medicine for protection against disease, military techniques for protection against hostile societies, and religious practices for protection against supernatural evil all fall into this category.

Any manager in this country who is trying to improve safety is bound to find himself rowing against this stream of the cultural tide. Because of the different roles men and women play in defending society, there is a close interaction between the defence mechanisms which are culturally accepted and the manner in which sexuality is indicated: two important cultural means of expressing one's sexuality – clothing and the degree of caution a person may exhibit – are also important in safety. As a result, a woman may run unnecessary risks by refusing to wear unfeminine but safe clothes, while a young man may feel that to wear a safety device such as a safety belt in a car is to admit a lack of courage and so detract from his masculinity.

9. *Exploitation* Knowledge of how to make and use tools and how to exploit materials is a part of our cultural awareness.

In the exploitation of our environment, current developments are very rapid. It is not sufficient that new materials and techniques should be discovered: people must know how to use them. In other words they must become absorbed by our culture. Partly this can be achieved by disseminating technical knowledge about the new methods, but the benefits of many of our discoveries can only be realised when people in general have adjusted their attitudes towards the materials they consume and the services they employ. Advertising is one important instrument for inducing this change. The materials and tools we use have immense significance as a part of our cultural language. The commercial exploitation of materials may succeed or fail, not on account of any technical reasons but on account of their cultural acceptability. The success of advertising in changing attitudes towards materials is obvious. In doing this, advertising has enormously extended and refined our wordless vocabulary of material possessions. We may now exhibit our personalities in such a way that the brash may be distinguished from the modest by a glance at a thousand yards.

10. *Interaction* The mechanisms for explicit communication – symbols, conventional signs, language, money and procedures for exchanging goods – are all culturally determined.

This is the subject of most of the remainder of this book so there is no need, here, to examine this aspect of culture in the way that the other nine aspects have been treated. However, I can use this tenth heading to summarise the ideas about the cultural message-streams listed above by indicating how each one interacts with our explicit modes of communication.

Language both determines and is determined by patterns of *association*. In England, but not in all countries, pronunciation is the most obvious label of a social class. Professions have their jargons and indeed every group has its 'in-words'. Our means of *subsistence* would not be so advanced if it were not for the explicit means of exchanging the products of our labour made possible by the evolution of the concept of money. Our use of spoken language is very strongly influenced by the situation: for example, the *sexes* of those taking part in the conversation and the *place* and *time*. The arts and indoor games, as representative of our *recreations*, are almost entirely dependent on language and the elaborate formal use of signs. In *defence* words play a very special role; they can be used to display aggressive postures between nations or members of a family. Languages, especially mathematics and logic, are becoming most important tools for the *exploitation* of our material world. Finally, we should notice the relationships between *learning* and language. These are important enough to warrant more than a passing comment, so the next section will be devoted to elaborating upon some ideas about learning.

The transmission of culture

Culture is the sum total of all our shared patterns of behaviour. It is the fabric from which our social existence is derived, just as our biological existence depends upon the physical material of our world.

An organisation is social; its existence depends upon the maintenance of cultural patterns within a changing group. Individuals enter and leave its ranks just as chemical elements pass through our bodies and for a while serve some vital function there. It is obviously important, therefore, that anyone concerned with the creation, change or preservation of an organisation should understand how cultural patterns are transmitted to individuals, so that these can be maintained by the group as a whole. An organisation is a sub-cultural grouping within the context of a wider culture, which it usually serves by performing some special, socially necessary functions. Therefore, what the individual in the organisation must learn will depend upon how far he is expected to depart, in his organisational role, from the patterns of behaviour established in his normal cultural background. How he *learns* will depend on how he is accustomed to absorbing cultural patterns.

It is useful to distinguish three different ways of communicating to people how to behave. Hall labels the *first* of these the *formal* mode of learning. Without adducing any reasons why, a person is told what he should or should not do under various circumstances: 'You must start work exactly at 6 o'clock and not finish until the whistle at 2 o'clock.' Characteristic of this mode of learning is the use of quite explicit prescriptive statements, especially negative ones, to direct a person's behaviour. The emphasis on prohibitions and the lack of any supporting explanation means that formal learning is inappropriate when people have to react to changing conditions. Learning at the formal level is supported by a system of explicit rewards and punishments. These may be a part of a legalistic system as, for example, rules about forfeiture of pay, or they may be embodied in a training scheme in which performance is explicitly appraised by someone as 'good' or 'bad'. The answer to a question about why we should behave in one way rather than another would be characterised at the formal level by the formula: 'You do A in order to obtain the reward x and you do not do B in order to avoid the token of disapproval y', or by making a distinction, heavily charged with emotional overtones, between A being 'right' and B being 'wrong'. Consequently, when a patttern of behaviour has been imbued through the formal mode of learning, it cannot normally be changed without some emotional effort.

A *second* mechanism by which patterns of behaviour can be transmitted to a person new to a cultural grouping is by *informal example*.

Such communication of cultural patterns may never be made explicit. It depends upon the newcomer copying the behaviour of those around him. Conformity brings approval from the group, whilst non-conformity attracts signs of resentment, so this kind of learning is also supported by a system of rewards and punishments, although the signs of approval or disapproval may not be recognised consciously by those concerned. Effective team-work depends upon the group evolving and retaining methods of working which are never formalised, and which are transmitted to the new member of the team by this process of imitation. The importance of these informal patterns of behaviour is clearly underlined when they are abandoned in the form of industrial action known as 'working to rule' in which the explicit rules of the formal system are reinstated. At the informal imitative level, people do not normally ask questions about behaving in one way rather than another, but they might acknowledge a distinction between normal and eccentric behaviour, or they might go so far as to say 'do it this way' and give a demonstration. Informal behaviour can be changed without exciting much emotion – only feelings of self-consciousness.

At the *third* level we communicate how to behave in a *technical* way, not by the use of prescriptive statements which say 'do this' or 'do that' but by giving reasoned and analysed descriptions of the way things are, and of the consequences of acting in various ways. This mode of transmitting our cultural heritage is quite explicit and frequently embodied in writing. Schools and universities are largely concerned with imparting culture in a technical mode. When a question about behaviour is answered at a technical level, reasoned analyses are given in an emotionally neutral way, with recourse neither to the right/wrong distinction of the formal, prescriptive mode of learning nor to the normal/eccentric distinction at the informal, imitative level. The technical transmission of culture is easier in a highly literate society, perhaps because written communication tends to be far less permeable to emotion than face-to-face communication. One consequence is that change is easier in a society which transmits much of its culture at the technical level, because it can adopt new ways of behaving without exciting emotive responses: consider the difficulties of introducing new methods of husbandry and use of animals in countries like India where the cow is a potent religious symbol and its treatment is explicitly prescribed.

Information and the Corporate Structure

To understand an organisation we must recognise three layers corresponding to the formal, informal and technical levels at which culture is transmitted and behaviour determined. At the formal level are the explicitly recognised precepts of behaviour which may be a part of the wider culture in which the organisation operates; on the other hand they may be expressed in the rules, regulations, and the official structure of authority. At the informal imitative level, an organisation will gradually evolve complex patterns of behaviour which are never formulated, but which must be learnt by newcomers. This informal culture will be vital to the effectiveness of the organisation; in some respects it may aid, and in others impede, the attainment of organisational objectives, but, even at its most neutral, the informal culture will affect the satisfactions people derive from working in the organisation, and hence their morale. At the technical level an organisation must be described in terms of its flows of messages about the transactions performed, plans made, problems investigated, and in terms of the data-processing activities necessary to accomplish organisational tasks. Management must be concerned with the maintenance of all three levels of the organisational fabric.

The information specialist must give attention to the formal (prescriptive) and informal (imitative) as well as the technical layers of an organisation. He is very likely to exaggerate the importance of written information compared with face-to-face conversation, and ignore the messages which are transmitted non-verbally. Take one example of a term frequently used by information specialists: 'corporate memory'. It is normally used to denote the bodies of written information stored in the organisation's files. This ignores the vast repository of skills, expertise and attitudes which are preserved by the members of the organisation within their working groups. Methods of performing complex tasks may be sustained solely through their constant rehearsal by the working group. This is particularly true of many managerial skills and attitudes. If the group of people who preserve a cultural memory-trace of this kind is disbanded, or diluted too much or too quickly, then the information circuit is broken and the skill or attitude will die away. This may or may not be desirable. When bringing about change in an organisation it is essential to do so with an awareness of these cultural processes.

In creating an organisation, the use of the formal, informal and technical means of establishing the desired patterns of behaviour must be judged carefully. The ways in which the people concerned are accustomed to learning must be taken into account. Over-emphasis on formal rules will be resented by people accustomed to a cultural background in which behaviour is usually determined informally, whereas a very informal organisation will leave people used to being told what to do feeling rather disorientated. Changing an organisation will usually be simpler in one where behaviour is determined informally and technically than in one based upon emotionally charged, formal rules of right and wrong conduct.

There is not space here, nor would it be apposite to the theme of this book, to do more than draw attention to these considerations and state that they deserve to be studied by anyone interested in understanding and designing organisational information systems.

A Few Conclusions

The way information operates within organisations, causing things to happen, cannot possibly be understood without an awareness of the full gamut of signs, verbal and non-verbal, through which a shared culture enables us to communicate. Language depends for its meaning upon all the streams of culture. The effect that a communication will have on a person can only be predicted accurately by reference to his cultural background. It is unfortunate that many people, trained in technical skills, who are able innovators in the technical sense, never learn to overcome the cultural obstacles to innovation. Some people are fortunate enough to have sensitive powers of observation that enable them to see things from the point of view of others who, for reasons such as age, sex, or social class, possess different cultural backgrounds. If you are not fortunate enough to possess this empathy (and no one can find it in him in all situations), then a first step towards overcoming the communication barrier is to realise that the attitudes, beliefs and patterns of behaviour which may seem eternally true to yourself are a product of the culture to which you belong. Perhaps you can then achieve an intellectual, if not an emotional, detachment, enabling you to make allowances for the cultural determinants of other people's behaviour. It should be an object of management education to enable a man to do this. (This is an example of how we can turn an appreciation of social skills, which everyone normally acquires informally, into an analytical study which can be communicated technically.)

The information specialist, often working as an innovator in organisations, must have an appreciation of the cultural forces which his work is bound to release. He also needs to understand the cultural origin of *all* informative signs in order to appreciate fully the nature of information.

In the next chapter we shall examine the social mechanism which enables stable patterns of behaviour, belief, perception and evaluation to be formed and maintained. This is the foundation upon which the human use of information is built.

4 The Social Mechanism and the Meaning of Signs

In a highly developed culture we have a whole set of specific devices to insure the adherence to our scientific tradition, to our economic organisation and to the accuracy of our symbolic transmission of ideas and principles.

Malinowski, *The Scientific Study of Culture*

You can make a person go through a door by opening the door, taking the person by the shoulders and propelling him in the right direction. This is an example of human behaviour having desired consequences by virtue of primary or physical effects. It is more usual to achieve roughly the same result by opening the door, smiling at the person and giving a particular movement and inclination to the head. This is an example of human behaviour having consequences by virtue of its secondary effects as a sign-process. The molecules of a gas achieve equilibrium through the interplay of physical forces. The members of a human society, or an organisation within it, attain their stable patterns of collective behaviour through the interplay of sign-processes, that is, by the transmission of information rather than physical energy.

As we have seen, any pattern of human behaviour or any artefact or natural token (the clothes we wear or the land we own) which becomes involved in human behaviour, can be used as a sign. It affects a person's behaviour indirectly by conveying information to him, either consciously or unconsciously. The effect of a sign is not random or unpredictable; only when the token object or behaviour pattern can elicit some uniformity of response are we able to talk of it as a sign. An individual may develop his own idiosyncratic way of responding consistently to some stimulus which may then be regarded as a sign for him, but, unless he can induce others to share his behaviour pattern, this kind of personal sign will not help him to communicate with others. Some patterns of response we all share because of our identical biological natures, but most of our finely discriminating responses to signs are acquired through a social mechanism which is the subject of this chapter.

By the meaning of a sign we usually imply a relationship between a sign and what it refers to. This is its *referential meaning*. In this chapter 'meaning' is a relationship between a sign and the response it elicits in a given social setting. This is its *behavioural meaning*. Only those signs to which a person consciously responds can have a referential meaning for him but other signs, acting subconsciously, reveal their behavioural meaning to an observer. (The observer may give these signs additional second-order meanings by imputing to them references of which the respondent is unaware.)

The meaning of all the signs used for communication among a group of people are found in the stable patterns of behaviour which are shared by the group members. The behaviour patterns are established and sustained through a social mechanism which depends upon close, personal contacts with frequent face-to-face encounters.

It is essential, therefore, to examine face-to-face conversation, the channel through which most information is transmitted in organisations. This channel employs nearly the whole range of our cultural message systems. People are highly sensitive to information transmitted this way. One of the consequences, as we shall see, is that a group of people can develop stable behaviour patterns which define the meanings of signs by their use in a social context. Formal definitions of words and other signs and symbols serve only to indicate very special refinements upon the socially established uses of signs. Many information specialists become so engrossed in these refinements that they lose sight of the foundations upon which all information systems are built: the cultural infrastructure. The result is often that systems are designed that are unworkable in human terms, although they may be technically perfect.

What happens in a conversation?

Business is very largely performed through people conducting myriad conversations every day. Even the least important of them may contribute towards the organisation's performance, if only by helping to weld together a working group. Some conversations are crucially important, such as those which may lead to an important contract or win a large donation of funds, or the discussions between an innovating team and the people in a department to be affected. Some preparation can be made for such vital encounters, but much rests upon the conduct of the actual conversation, which is a complex process of interaction on many levels. Consider only a very simple case, by way of illustration.

Imagine two strangers who happen to meet by chance on some quite neutral ground. The place is equally unfamiliar to both of them; there is no one else present and neither belongs to any group of people who might expect them to behave in any special way towards a stranger. They are subject only to the forces that arise out of the images they present to each other, and what passes between them in word and gesture.

Conversation will soon begin, provided that the two people are not abnormally inhibited about speaking to strangers, and provided that there exists no social convention that conversation is frowned upon in the place where they happen to be (for example, in an English railway compartment).

Trivia will first be exchanged: talk about the weather or about something that is happening nearby, anything, provided that it is so commonplace that there is no chance of its being misconstrued. These preliminaries will supply hints of other conversational topics which may be ventured upon at a later stage. In these early rounds of the conversation, each will be looking for clues about the personality and background of the other. As they become armed with better means of predicting each other's reactions, they will embark upon topics of deeper interest. As they do so, each will try to keep his remarks within the bounds of what he guesses will be acceptable to the other.

As they talk, they will tend to be drawn into a closer relationship, provided that each is sensitive to the other's reactions. They will modify their own behaviour in response to the hints of approval and disapproval supplied by the other. The process is a very subtle one, with a mechanism that is as yet far from clearly understood. It depends upon the choice of words, the course of the conversation and upon the modulation of the voice, but also upon the way each person directs his gaze and how he meets the regard of the other when speaking and listening; it depends upon signals given by smiles, frowns, pursing of the lips, inclination of the head, direction of the body, distance at which the speakers place themselves apart, use of hand, arm and shoulder movements. . . . The range of signals is very wide.

There is good reason to consider that the verbal protocol of a conversation constitutes only a small part of the exchange, which should be regarded as being conducted in an extended language far richer than the verbal skeleton. The inescapability of non-verbal messages in face-to-face encounters has been demonstrated in an interesting experiment: students, already experienced in conducting psychological experiments, were given a practical project to reproduce what they were led to understand to be the established results of a classical experiment. They had identical instructions to read to the subjects, identical instructions on how to conduct the experiment and were specifically cautioned not to deviate from them. *But* half the students were told to expect one result and the other half the opposite result. In fact, the experiment should have confirmed neither. However, the actual results showed that *each group of student experimenters had quite unconsciously induced its subjects to behave in a manner which confirmed the results which the experimenters had been led to expect.**

* See Rosenthal, 1966, 1968.

This experiment seems to support the subjective impression we so often have, that people tend to behave as we expect them to behave. No doubt, in face-to-face conversation we constantly apply subtle emotional pressures, sending a stream of affective messages to which people are very sensitive. Should these ideas, then, add up to the conclusion that affective communication is easy? No: for two reasons.

In the first place, although it is easy to make some emotional impact upon one's listeners, it is extremely difficult, except in very familiar situations, to control the effect one has. A minor conversational mannerism can be a major blot upon a public speaker's performance; a manager and a machine operator, because of their social backgrounds, may place very different interpretations upon the same words and behaviour of a work-study engineer. To impart and receive the right impression calls for constant awareness of the cultural forces at play in personal relationships.

Given this awareness, it is still very difficult to communicate feelings that are not sincere; there are so many non-verbal channels of communication over which we have no conscious control that anyone but the most accomplished actor will give his listener hints of his lack of conviction. Avoidance of the complexities of face-to-face encounter is no solution, as such evasion is usually given an unfavourable interpretation.

In the second place, our power to alter the values by which people judge things, their attitudes or their actual behaviour, is limited by the countervailing forces exerted by other people with whom they are in social contact. The group as a whole makes sure that its individual members do not deviate too far without being made to feel ill at ease. It is this sensitivity of the individual towards affective messages which can account for the great stability of attitudes, beliefs and behaviour among the members of a group. This idea is important in understanding the nature of all human communication, and we need to look at it more closely.

Groups of people – communication and cohesion

Although there is no single name for it, the totality of the means of communication which people use when face-to-face generates the force of social cohesion. Experiments in social psychology have revealed some of the nature and power of this cohesive force. The mechanism of group behaviour can be understood in terms of group 'norms,' which are the stable positions of equilibrium in group behaviour and thought. The stability of a norm is guaranteed, because a person who starts to diverge from the accepted equilibrium of the group will find himself exposed to pressures to conform. These pressures can be understood in terms of individual sensitivity to our extended language. A person who does not wish to expose himself to the adverse judgements of others will tend to behave as he is expected to behave; he will adopt their beliefs and may even *see* what the others say he should see, like the emperor in the fairy story.

One of the first classic experiments to demonstrate the mechanism of group dynamics was conducted by Muzafer Sherif.* Subjects were brought into a darkened room and asked to observe a stationary pinpoint of light at some distance from them. In these circumstances, because of an optical illusion, the light appears to move. Individuals were asked to gauge this apparent movement in many different trials. Each person settled on his own 'individual norm'. These varied between 2 and 10 inches. The experiment was then repeated with groups of people who were able to hear one another's judgements about the movement of the light. Groups that were formed of people who had already been allowed to develop individual norms gradually reached agreement in the course of several trials, establishing a 'group norm'. Other groups of people, who had not encountered the experiment before, established a norm on the first trial which, in succeeding trials, they modified, but from which no individual diverged significantly. This experiment demonstrated the formation of *perceptual norms*.

The powerful effect of opinion upon a person's judgement has been demonstrated rather dramatically in another experiment, by Asch.† He required subjects to match the length of a line with one of three standard lines of clearly unequal lengths. Each trial was performed by a group of people all but one of whom were 'in the know'. All was perfectly normal except that on certain occasions the odd man out found himself confronted by a unanimous opinion that quite contradicted the evidence of his own eyes. In one third of all the judgements made by 50 such subjects, errors were made in the direction of this artificial norm. Fifteen of the subjects yielded at least half of the time to the majority opinion. For a few, their perception seems to have been distorted, and they actually saw the wrong thing. Most of those who accepted the majority view did so because they concluded that their perception must be mistaken. A few others abandoned the evidence before them simply in order not to appear different from the rest of the group. Evidently the forces directing us to accede to the norms of the group appear to be extremely powerful.

The persistence of a norm was demonstrated by Jacobs and Campbell

* Sherif, 1935.
† Asch, 1957.

using the same phenomenon of the moving light which Sherif used in his experiment.* They arranged that three confederates should declare that the light was moving 15 or 16 inches before the first subject gave his judgement. In each of the following trials, an uninitiated subject replaced an experienced group member; first the confederates dropped out and then the others in order of seniority. The effect of the artificially created norm persisted until about the 11th generation. A generation was the period in which the composition of the group remained the same; each of these involved 30 trials in which each person gave his judgement. Control data were obtained from subjects who made judgements about the movement of another light when alone. These were fairly unanimous on an apparent movement of three to four inches. As an application of this idea, be sure to inaugurate a training programme with high but realistic norms, since they are likely to persist.

Relevance for the information specialist

I have mentioned these experiments because they speak for themselves. This is not the place to discuss their implications in detail.† However, a number of simple conclusions may clearly be drawn. The behaviour of a group of people tends to settle down towards points of equilibrium, the group's norms. An individual is powerfully induced to conform to apparent norms, sometimes even against the judgement of his own senses. It is this sensitivity of each member which accounts for the formation of norms which are highly stable and persist within a group through many changes in its membership.

Evidently, anyone who has the task of changing the accustomed patterns of group behaviour has to overcome very powerful social forces. This is commonly enough a problem encountered by an information specialist. To change the ways in which information is handled by an organisation frequently has profound repercussions on the activities of working groups and relationships between them. From a severely practical point of view, the information specialist must appreciate the nature of the forces unleashed by his innovative programme. If his particular responsibility is to design and create new *formal* information systems, he must not lose sight of the informal system with which his new system must coexist. His success will depend as much upon the way he tries to induce the necessary changes in the working community as upon the technical excellence of his designs. There should be cooperation between those information specialists concerned with formal systems

* Jacobs and Campbell, 1961.

† See Newcombe, Turner and Converse, or Hollander, or Hartley and Hartley for such a discussion.

and those with particular understanding of informal systems. Ideally, the systems designer must have a balanced knowledge of both the social and the mechanical aspects of information systems.

Knowledge of the social mechanisms which operate within human groups is needed by any information specialist, not only so that he should be a successful innovator, but also to enable him to appreciate fully the nature of information. It is a key theoretical idea to recognise that, in the ultimate analysis, all informative signs must be defined not by any logical or philosophical formulation but by their *use* within a social context, and that the reliability of the social definition is ensured by the mechanism of norm-formation. The practical consequences of th is idea are valuable. It should be a constant reminder to check that an adequate informal system embraces those people who need to communicate with one another. Only an informal system, permeable to affective messages, can provide a stable basis for reliable human use of signs in an unselfconscious way. Notice the emphasis here on the normal unselfconscious use of signs. There are circumstances where a highly conscious and analytical use of signs is necessary, e.g. in making crucial decisions and in designing formal information systems. This analytical approach will be examined in Part Three, but it has no relevance at all to most of the everyday communications in any organisation. This is especially true of communications about attitudes, goals, priorities, judgements of value, so important to any cooperative human endeavour. It is true also of communication about factual matters: a thicket of jargon swiftly grows between separated communities of specialists, even when they may be engaged on very similar problems.

Kinds of norms

We have looked briefly at the machinery whereby norms are developed and maintained. For man, a social animal, these norms are a biological necessity. It is sometimes useful to classify norms into four types: perceptual, cognitive, evaluative and behavioural.

Without the *perceptual* norms, which are tacitly agreed ways of seeing the world, words themselves would be unable to acquire the standard meanings that enable them to act as labels on the things around us, so that we can code the messages picked up by our own eyes and ears in a way that is useful to other people. This powerful tendency to see the world in a way which is determined by the people around us has dangers, but they can be overcome to some extent if we are aware of them. When a manager moves from one department to another or into a higher echelon, he must learn to view the world in a new way. The same problem is encountered in acquiring scientific knowledge or in transferring from programming or accounting, for example, into systems analysis. It involves recognising patterns that we have not used previously and attaching labels to them. In order to achieve this, we sometimes have a difficult struggle against the prison bars of our current perceptual norms. The process can be uncomfortable because, in effect, we have to get used to living in a world that looks rather different. For example, the concept of a group norm is itself something that we can perceive in people's behaviour readily enough once our attention has been drawn to it, but some people may be very reluctant to accept the idea, because it may, perhaps, throw suspicion upon their cherished stereotyped ideas of unfamiliar things and especially of people different from themselves.

Perceptual norms are greatly influenced by our *cognitive* norms. These are the standardised beliefs and knowledge possessed by a group. From a biological point of view they ensure that we acquire the knowledge and expectations about the world which have been accumulated by other members of our culture. This type of norm can impede the growth of rational knowledge, because it imprisons our minds in an orthodoxy. Our orthodox views, even when they are scientific in origin, may be more like group norms than objective knowledge, once they have become habitual ways of thinking and are no longer subjected to criticism.

Evaluative norms serve the biological function of directing the group towards common ends. At least they provide a framework within which agreement about objectives is more likely to be reached. In the next chapter we shall examine a method of characterising the evaluative norms that surround the words we use (Osgood's semantic differential).

Finally, *behavioural* norms govern our simple, often subconscious, reactions towards one another – when to say 'please' or 'thank you' or to shake a person by the hand, or to offer someone a seat or a meal. Behavioural norms make human actions predictable.

The process of acquiring a national culture, or of learning the special variations of behaviour of a group we are going to work with, is basically this process of discovering the appropriate norms. They give pattern, regularity and *meaning* to many aspects of our lives. Even language of the most abstract or technical form ultimately depends upon the social mechanism for its correct interpretation.

Organisational relevance – the establishment of an informal communication system

To organise in business or administration is to set up an appropriate communication system, keep it in repair and change it when necessary; or, better still, design it so that it keeps itself in repair and changes itself as necessary. Informal systems based upon the social mechanism will do that: they will adapt to a changing environment or to changes in the group task, they will evolve refinements of operation, and they can be handed on to new personnel with a minimum of training. For an informal system to work at all, face-to-face communication is almost indispensable. The actual communications which take place will depend upon the nature of the work being done, and they will be prompted by the problems facing the organisation and the individual members, at any time. There are certain prerequisites for an organic and self-adapting informal system to exist.

The first prerequisite is the physical opportunity to communicate. If circumstances of geography or timing do not bring people face to face, then informal communication will not even be possible. All too often, companies fail to exploit the location of offices, work places, dining rooms and other means of achieving casual contact between people; instead these physical facilities are used to establish and maintain social distance. This is not to appeal for a falsely democratic attempt to get everyone to 'muck in together', but to advocate the intelligent use of natural opportunities to increase the chance of spontaneous communication when this may be potentially valuable to the organisation. It is better that a manager should have his attention drawn by a few pointed remarks to some dissatisfaction which can be settled informally, than that matters should reach serious proportions before he learns about the problem. It is better that two people interested in solving related problems learn of their common interest from casually overheard conversation than by each reading the other's expensively produced report.

The second prerequisite is the psychological opportunity to communicate. In our everyday concerns, social convention compels us to keep open many possible lines of contact with comparative strangers. Malinowski has drawn our attention to a process that he labels 'phatic communion'. The commonplace phrases such as 'How do you do?', 'Good morning', the nods and smiles of mutual recognition, our talk about the weather, and much gossip that would otherwise be devoid of interest, are all examples of this type of social and linguistic behaviour. Such communication, Malinowski says, 'serves to establish bonds of personal union between people brought together by the mere need of companionship, and does not serve any purpose of communicating ideas' (see Malinowski, 1923). This atmosphere of polite social intercourse does facilitate more serious exchanges of words, should the need arise. The mechanism of phatic communion does seem to be a powerful force in our society, judging by the quite strong emotive reactions which may be felt on the failure of someone to return a simple greeting. A failure of contact between people at even this banal level can have unfortunate consequences for an organisation: for example, the flow of factual information is less reliable, because people do not volunteer information if they fear a rebuff.

The physical and psychological opportunity to communicate freely constitutes the foundation upon which a robust informal system can develop in an organisation. The foundation must be firm, however. Sometimes one encounters organisations which aspire to achieve the necessary psychological conditions by imposing the outward show of bonhomie (by insisting upon the use of familiar forms of address, for example) while simultaneously making the insincerity of the relationships clear by a host of other cultural indicators. Social distance is not only dependent upon differences of status; perhaps more fundamental is the psychological separation which is caused by the perception of a conflict of objectives or values. These differences are likely to be larger when there is an absence of informal, face-to-face contact. The interaction of these contrary forces prevents the instantaneous creation of the conditions in which informal organisation can flourish. A failure to recognise this complexity has led to disillusion with informal organisation by those who have suddenly relaxed the grip of authority, only to find that the immediate response is the unleashing of those disorderly forces which the authoritarian structure has held at bay. There must necessarily intervene a period of social adjustment during which the group can learn to impose the necessary discipline within itself. The process of creating an informal information system is quite different from that of creating a formal system. One may issue no *fiat* that people in an organisation should behave informally, as one might issue a new form with instructions on how to fill it up. The social mechanism must operate to enable the new patterns of behaviour and expectation to arise.

This adjustment will not necessarily take place unaided. The leadership of the group is bound to exert great influence upon the learning process within the group. Positive intervention is possible; for example people might be trained to use an enlarged degree of freedom of contact between members of the organisation. There are very severe obstacles to be overcome when trying to produce new patterns of behaviour in a group. The social control mechanism ensures that a group as a whole will be reluctant to change, although the members individually may be quite tractable.

Advantages of informal organisation

An organisation in which enough of the members meet one another, behave in a generally friendly manner, and speak in the same terms, will normally be permeable to the inevitably conflicting views of its many working groups. This permeability will enable a resolution of conflicts of values or priorities to take place without the exercise of overt power. If, in an impermeable organisation, a particular sub-group feels that its point of view is not understood nor responded to by others, it will restrict or threaten to restrict the resources it controls, that is, it will exercise its power. To say that decisions can be made on the basis of a consensus if there are adequate channels of affective communication is, therefore, to raise other questions about the extent to which power must be diffused among the separate parties before they will be prepared to listen to one another's opinions. However, leaving aside such awkward questions, it does seem reasonable to expect greater effectiveness in those organisations where the members have a commonly agreed set of objectives which they have all helped to select. Experiment and observation* tend to support this hypothesis which should not be ignored by anyone trying to change an organisation.

The informal system is always present wherever a group of people is employed. It may exist side by side with a formal system but it will be there because it is indispensable to human nature. You cannot employ a man merely for his mechanical skills at manipulating information in a formal clerical system without engaging also the social aspects of the same person. If you have the informal system, you might as well have it playing an effective part in the organisation. In circumstances of change, the informal system will be of overwhelming importance. A working team, all of whose members are committed to the same goal, will cope with unusual problems and, by supporting one another, find solutions to problems that could never be anticipated in the design of any formal system. This is only to acknowledge that human beings use information (signs) in fundamentally different ways from those suited to machinery (which are essentially the formal processes described in Part Five). A well-designed business information-system will use this complex, flexible and robust social mechanism as one of its components. Failure to do so may stimulate resistance to the imposition of the system, especially if it is conceived only in formal terms, which conspicuously and offensively disregard the people who must operate it.

Obviously, there are limits beyond which an informal system breaks down. If a high volume of exact factual data must be gathered from a wide area, an informal system will not succeed. Attempts to create a company-wide informal system, if not carefully controlled, may result in the holding of many committee meetings; in the long term, these may become an excuse for unnecessary, status-providing formalities, rather than the occasion for useful personal contact. The informal organisation is most apt when the people being organised are, by the nature of their

* See Likert.

task, in fairly close and regular contact. To impose a formal system in these circumstances can be very wasteful.

Inducing change in an informal structure

Finally we should note that the process of change in an organisation is likely to be very sensitive to the network of informal communications. At such times, the cultural fabric will be subjected to stresses which call into play the forces of reaction that have served earlier to maintain stability. Organisational change must, therefore, take account of this group response.

Our cultural systems enable us, as individuals, to learn, and as a society to remember our accumulated wisdom. Within a sub-culture, such as a working group or an organisation, a great deal of information is stored in its structure and its established patterns of behaviour. As pointed out earlier, a culture stores information dynamically by the constant flow of action and reaction. Changing an organisation may entail moving some people right away from their former positions of influence, so that the wrong patterns of behaviour may more readily be forgotten. It may be possible to achieve the same effect by attenuating the old cultural network. To change an organisation rapidly it is probably necessary to attack the cultural memory, but it should be remembered that when undesirable organisational habits are cut out, desirable group skills may be lost in the process. These skills, being inherent in the structure and functioning of the organisation, cannot be taken elsewhere by individuals.

To change the behaviour or value patterns of a working group without recourse to 'surgery' requires the group as a whole to learn. As the classical experiments on group behaviour reveal, it is likely to avail us little to influence an individual (for example, by a special training course) if the group as a whole, and more particularly the senior and most influential members of the group, are going to expect him to retain his old behaviour patterns. It would seem to be a sensible rule of thumb to try to influence an organisation from the top down.

This conjecture is supported by research such as that of Katz and Lazarsfeld (1955). In studying the effects of mass communications, they discovered that people were not decisively affected by direct communication. They were more strongly influenced by the communications that took place via their reference groups, that is, those people with whom the individuals enjoyed personal relationships. It was found that the changes of attitude within the reference group depended very largely upon particular individuals who played the role of 'opinion leader'. In the organisational setting, the change will come about more smoothly if it can be transmitted through the acknowledged opinion leaders of the working groups. Ideally these would be the same people as the formal leaders of the groups.

Communication between managers and management scientists

As an example of how the lack of contact between communities of people causes failures of communication, consider the lack of trust and mutual comprehension that often separates managers and the various groups of management scientists and specialist advisers. All the problems are exemplified.

Even the lowest common denominator of communication, a shared vocabulary, demands not only the opportunity, physical and psychological, to communicate, but also a positive working relationship. Today's businesses are alive with small groups dedicated to advancing some special technology aimed at improving organisational efficiency: systems analysis, operational research, organisation and methods, work study, cost accounting, manpower planning and a dozen more. They tend to be farther apart, socially, geographically and intellectually in many companies than is either necessary or desirable. Their members belong to professional or quasi-professional societies that aim to be fairly exclusive, and they often have closer relationships with fellow specialists in other companies than with the managers with whose problems they will be concerned. If companies themselves do not organise their management services' structure in order to minimise the effect of this divisive influence, they will have a number of groups that find communication difficult, even when they realise it would be useful or stimulating, and, in the worst cases, they will have open rivalry between groups.

More serious still is the gulf between the manager and the management services specialist. The gap has widened as a result of the views expressed by some writers on management such as Peter Drucker, that managers should manage and management services people should serve. Such an organisational policy is not conducive to frank, cooperative teamwork. It is no good, of course, relying upon a few bland 'appreciation' courses for managers to enable them to make use of the knowledge of specialists. Regular contact and mutual respect at a personal level are necessary before people with very different training and backgrounds can learn to benefit from one another's knowledge and approach to problems. Too often one hears a group of managers swap stories to support their belief that these bands of specialists are naive or harebrained and, just as often, a group of management scientists will hold up to ridicule their images of the dull, over-cautious 'dependable' manager and his opposite – the erratic 'dynamic decision-maker'.

To alleviate the problem, closer everyday contact and a harmonious working relationship must be engineered. This is not simple, because at the present time the typical manager or administrator is older, therefore more mature, and differently trained (but usually with less full-time education behind him) than the typical management scientist. The social gulf is hard to bridge. Perhaps it would be easier if career planning were directed to achieving more mobility between the two sides, and if organisational structures helped more to emphasise the mutual dependence of line and staff. The very same could be said of other groups in business (such as marketing and production, or management and labour) which tend to have their identities too strongly marked out.

Summary

Communication of all kinds among people is rooted in the totality of their shared patterns of behaviour – their culture. Language and the other explicit uses of symbols constitute only a part of our culture, and we must not overlook the other facets of human behaviour as vehicles of communication. In particular, our non-linguistic modes of communication are powerful means of conveying messages of approval or disapproval of another person's behaviour. However, we are normally not conscious of using the full range of cultural signs, though they are essential to the interplay between individuals which gives rise to social norms and the differentiation of social groups.

It is our sensitivity to language and its non-verbal accompaniments that ensures stability for patterns of perceptions, beliefs, values and behaviour. If conflicts between the groups in an organisation are to be resolved there must be a ready exchange of value judgements and the pressures of opinion must be easy to transmit. We are able to communicate these affective messages fluently and accurately in face-to-face encounters but in writing only with difficulty and danger of misunderstanding. The informal information system can be partly controlled by adjusting the network of personal contacts. It is at times of rapid change, when the potential level of conflict is high, that an organisation must ensure that it is permeable to affective information. The systems analyst, as an agent of change, therefore has a special responsibility in his face-to-face encounters with the people whose jobs he will be changing.

In the next chapter we shall discover more about the ways in which language transmits feelings and reveals attitudes, by looking at the work of the experimental psychologist. One branch of this subject – psycholinguistics – provides valuable insight into our sensitivity to linguistic signs, and indicates some ways in which we can begin to measure the capacity of a sign to inform.

5 Sensitivity to Words

My language is the sum total of myself; for the man is the thought.

C. S. Peirce, *Collected Papers*

A popular definition of a manager is 'someone who gets things done through people'. This definition serves to draw attention to the difficult, human-relations part of the job and away from the technicalities of manufacturing and distribution. I suggest that it is worth focusing attention upon some other, neglected areas of a manager's job by proposing the definition that a manager is 'someone who gets things done through language'.

Certainly you never get anything done 'through' a person without communicating with him. The proposed new definition, besides embracing the old one, has a further advantage. In future a manager will also get things done through the computer and, as we shall see in later chapters, getting things done through computers also entails the use of language. Very few problems about information can be solved without reference to language. Some urgent, practical problems in the use of computers can only be understood in terms of the differences between the formal languages used by machines and the natural languages used by people. Let us therefore turn our attention to this most important of our cultural message systems.

Language-signs are physically insubstantial, easily reproducible symbols capable of an independent existence. It is this characteristic which makes them unlike most non-verbal signs, which cannot be abstracted from the social and physical context in which they are used. From words and numbers we are able to construct a symbolic model of a situation and then record it at a distant place, perhaps as a part of a much larger model; these models, manipulated according to the rules of logic, can help us to predict the results of our contemplated actions. Language also enables us, at a further level of abstraction, to step outside the situations in which we use signs and signs use us and, by reasoning, to remedy misunderstanding and other faults or inadequacies, in our information systems. Such is the standpoint of the information analyst.

Modes of language

We use language in many different modes which we may attempt to classify and label.* Four useful modes to recognise are: the 'affective', the 'denotative', the 'ritual' and the 'formal'. The first three of these are readily associated with the social norms described in the previous chapter. The affective use of language is associated with evaluative norms; the denotative use of language, concerned with both conveying statements about things and labelling the things we perceive, is associated with both cognitive and perceptual norms, whilst the ritual use of language is supported by behavioural norms. The fourth mode – formal usage – has probably more affinity with machine behaviour.

Usually, ordinary communications between people, whether written or spoken, operate in both the affective and denotative modes simultaneously. The mixture may vary from the almost purely emotive, as in some poetry, to the almost purely denotative as in a railway timetable. Spoken language tends to be largely affective, whereas written language is more commonly used denotatively. To be either very rational in speech or highly emotive in writing requires great skill. Affective language, as its name might suggest, plays upon its hearer's or reader's feelings as a finger plays upon a delicate instrument. It conveys judgements of value. Denotative language is used by one person to point out things to another person. It is the language of fact, science and evidence. Language used in the ritual mode may appear, superficially, to be affective or denotative, in the sense that it appears to convey judgements or facts; but, on closer inspection, it turns out to be little more than verbal habit.† Much of our everyday discourse is on this level; those conversational gambits which elicit some standard response may be regarded as ritual. The 'buzz-word' and the cliché and some sterile forms of philosophy and criticism are in this category; it is possible that the ritual forms may serve to mark their user as belonging to some in-group, but it cannot be demonstrated that they refer either to fact or any genuine feelings. This ritual quality is a matter of degree, of course; it is neither good nor bad except as circumstances make it so: it may help us coordinate our routine activities in an easy, unselfconscious way but, at the other extreme, it may lead us to make decisions on the basis of verbal habits which embody stereotypes that have nothing to do with the facts.

What then is the 'formal' mode? This is a way of using language neither to influence a person's feelings nor to tell him about anything but is a part of a 'game'. Formal signs are used as tokens. They are important in practice for making models with signs as components. Card games, chess, pure mathematics and symbolic logic are in this

---

* For a quite elaborate classification see the writings of Charles Morris.

† Ogden and Richards have dubbed this parrot-like use of language 'psittacism' or 'the use of words without reference'.

category. The characteristic of formal language is that *it employs the signs as objects in their own right.* They need excite no one, refer to nothing, nor trigger any behavioural response. The signs in a formal language are merely cheap and easily reproducible objects which can be employed to build elaborate structures that bear a closer resemblance to machinery than to natural language.

Distinctions between these modes of language are valuable for understanding the different uses of information in a business. A manager should be able to discern the affective force and the denotative significance of whatever he is told. He should be on his guard against being misled by the ritual use of language either by himself or his colleagues. He should also be able to recognise when an accountant, a management scientist or a computer specialist is using one of his formal 'models' without the numbers, equations or computer programs being made to refer to anything.

Language must be used in all four modes when running an organisation. To respond to its physical environment and to employ its physical resources effectively, an organisation must use signs which accurately denote the world in which it operates. If it does not, it will give instructions which cannot be carried out or which lead to unintended consequences. Accurate instructions alone will not get people to do things – to be cooperative citizens, to buy certain goods, to work as an effective team; affective communication is also needed to persuade, tempt or inspire people to follow the instructions. The formal methods of mathematics, logic and computer science can be used to organise, coordinate, balance, schedule and allocate resources more effectively than is possible without their analytical aid. The ritual use of language enables people in an organisation to perform their routine work in an effective, semi-automatic way.

Behavioural model of language

Information often acts upon a human being by producing some observable response. A prick on the finger will cause its withdrawal; a question may provoke an answer; an order an action or a picture a blush. If there is no spontaneous detectable response, it may be possible to provoke one by asking the person what he felt, or heard, or saw. This approach to human behaviour through the study of stimulus and response is that of the behavioural psychologist. It is an objective, scientific approach which is well suited to the understanding of communications that take place at the level of simple, immediate responses.

Everyone is familiar with the classic experiment of Pavlov, who taught a dog to salivate at the sound of a bell. He presented the dog with two stimuli at the same time: some food and the sound of a bell. The dog responded to the food by salivating and eating it. After repeatedly hearing the bell when his food was given him, the dog became 'conditioned' to respond to the bell alone, also by salivating, but at a reduced level compared with its unconditioned response to the food.

Many generalisations of this conditioning process have been conjectured and they have been used in attempts to explain the acquisitions of language.* Experiments have shown not only that direct responses to stimuli can be conditioned:

$$\text{Stimulus} \rightarrow \text{Response}$$
$$\text{or } S \rightarrow R$$

but that conditioned responses can also occur indirectly through a kind of chain reaction:

$$S \rightarrow R° = S° \rightarrow R°° = S°° \rightarrow R$$
$$S \rightarrow \ \ M° \ \ \rightarrow \ \ M°° \ \ \rightarrow R$$

Stimulus S produces a response $R°$, which itself acts as a stimulus ($S°$) to produce the response $R°°$ which, as stimulus $S°°$, produces the overt response, R. The intermediate stages $M°$ and $M°°$ are called 'mediating responses'. This mechanism shows how one word can evoke echoes of other words or suggest associated ideas which contribute to the word's affective meaning. This is often referred to as the 'connotation' or 'connotative meaning' of a word.†

Some of the earliest experiments to discover what words 'mean' to people were word-association tests. A person is given a stimulus word and asked to respond with the first word he thinks of. Interesting differences of verbal behaviour are displayed between the patterns of responses made by different groups of people, for example between those of children and adults. Whilst children tend to give a response that adumbrates the meaning of the stimulus word, adults tend to give a quite different but abstractly related word. For example, a child might respond to an adjective by giving a noun with that property (deep: hole, soft: bed, black: dress), or by giving a verb related to the stimulus word (table: eat, dark: see, music: play), or by naming something which is physically related (table: dish, dark: night, sickness: doctor). Adult responses tend to be based on a classification (table: chair, deep: low, house: barn), or a contrast (dark: light, sickness: health, deep: shallow), or a similarity

---

* See Skinner, 1957, and Mowrer, 1954.

† 'Connotation' sometimes is given another meaning which is strictly confined to the denotative use of language, as J. S. Mill does in his logic. He calls the collection of properties connoted by a term, and necessary for its definition, its 'connotation.'

(dark: black, sickness: illness, mountain: hill). These differences between the behaviour of children and adults suggest that word-association experiments are capable of uncovering some relationships between thought and word.

One of the difficulties about the word-association method is that it may be confused by complicated, conscious mediating responses which cannot be observed. The responses may be very far-fetched and almost impossible to interpret. To overcome this difficulty experiments were conducted using responses over which a subject had no conscious control. One such experiment (see Riess, 1940) used the 'galvanic skin reflex', a change in the electrical resistance of the skin which is the basis of the infamous lie-detector. The reflex can be produced by startling a subject with a loud buzzer. This was done whilst showing the subject a word. In this way, the reflex could be made a conditioned response to the word. It was found that the subject would also respond to associated words. Thus conditioned to 'urn', a response could also be obtained for the synonym 'vase' and for the homophone 'earn'.

In a similar experiment (see Razran, 1949), subjects were conditioned to salivate in response to certain words which they were shown whilst eating. Once a salivatory response had been established, it was found that words of related meaning would also elicit some fraction of the conditioned response. The percentage response to the associated word was then taken as measure of the 'stimulus generalisation'. This suggests the possibility of measuring the 'distances' between the affective meanings of words.

The interesting point is that these experiments suggest that we might develop quite sensitive and objective techniques for measuring the affective 'information' in a word. The experimental methods referred to above are either unreliable or very difficult to administer, because of the need to establish conditioned responses to the words being investigated. If convenient measuring techniques were available they could be used

(a) to show how different cultural groups respond to the same words;
(b) to measure individual deviations from the pattern displayed by a person's cultural group;
(c) to assess the affective response of a person towards some communication (e.g. an advertisement or an instruction).

Fortunately, we have a method which is both sensitive and, compared with the techniques mentioned above, relatively easy to apply. This method assumes that people from the same culture are already conditioned by the social mechanism of norm-formation to respond to words in much the same way.

The method was devised by Osgood and others (see Osgood *et al.*, 1957 and Osgood, 1964). They call the resulting measurements 'Semantic Differentials'. The method is to ask people to classify words on a variety of scales. Scales are defined by verbal opposites, such as 'good/bad', 'strong/weak', 'fast/slow', 'hot/cold', 'fair/unfair', and so on. For each of these attributes, the scale is given seven different values. For example, the first of those scales might have the values $+3$ = extremely good, $+2$ = quite good, $+1$ = slightly good, 0 = equally good and bad or neither, -1 = slightly bad, -2 = quite bad, and -3 = extremely bad. Obviously a very large number of scales could be used and many of them would tend to produce the same results as one another. For example, a very close correlation would be expected between the ratings of words on the scales 'good/bad', 'fair/unfair', 'right/wrong'.

The resulting questionnaires are subjected to *factor analysis*, which is probably familiar to readers through its use in measuring intelligence and aptitudes. In educational psychology many children are given tests; some of the test scores will be highly correlated, such as those for English and History, others less so, such as those for English and Mathematics. Factor analysis enables the variations among the children to be summarised, using relatively few hypothetical factors of which the three most important are called G, the general intelligence factor, V, verbal ability factor, and S, spatial ability factor.

Similarly, by substituting in the above paragraph 'words' for 'children' and 'quality scales' for the 'psychological tests' we have a description of Osgood's method. The question becomes: can the variations in the scores of the words be explained by only a few hypothetical factors? The analysis shows that this is so and that most of the variations can be explained by three factors. For the analysis of American English these factors and the quality scales most nearly corresponding to them were as follows:

Factor	Quality scales
EVALUATION:	Nice/awful, sweet/sour, heavenly/hellish, good/bad, mild/harsh, happy/sad.
POTENCY:	Big/little, powerful/powerless, deep/shallow, strong/weak, high/low, long/short.
ACTIVITY:	Fast/slow, noisy/quiet, young/old, alive/dead, known/unknown, burning/freezing.

These three, unrelated factors accounted for about 63·1% of all the variability in the 'meanings' of the words used in one of Osgood's experiments.*

* See Osgood, 1964.

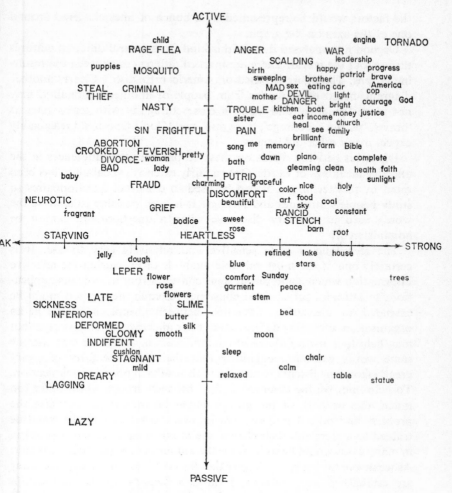

Third scale is indicated thus: good/BAD

Fig. 4. Semantic differentials on three scales: weak/strong; active/passive; good/bad.

Typical results are illustrated in fig. 4. The actual words which people were asked to evaluate are displayed on a graph which uses the Potency and Activity factors as the abscissa and ordinate. The Evaluation factor can be imagined to pass through the plane of the paper at right angles to these; the words evaluated favourably are written in lower-case letters and those evaluated unfavourably in upper-case. You can imagine the quality scales on which people assessed the words as straight lines passing through the origin. The scales corresponding closely to one of the factors would be represented by a bunch of lines clustered around one of the axes on the graph.

Osgood has analysed data of this kind from several different cultures throughout the world. There are marked differences between the resulting graphs. The figure is based on American English.* Clearly another diagram, based upon replies from people of another nationality, may not place 'America' and 'cop' in close contiguity with terms such as 'brave', 'patriot', 'courage', 'progress', and 'God'! One could reasonably expect many other differences.

Distances between words on these graphs measure differences in the affective meanings of words. Once a fairly extensive vocabulary has been rated by this technique, it can be used to construct questionnaires to study people's attitudes and feelings. It is even possible to analyse the words used in ordinary discourse when a questionnaire cannot be administered.†

The technique is quite sensitive and relatively easy to use. It is certainly one of the most valuable methods of measuring the affective information which some verbal signs convey. From its obvious applications to attitudes surveys and consumer research the method might be extended to measuring differences between groups of people in an organisation, including differences in their affective use of language that may help to explain failures of communication. A person may use the same words without recognising that their affective force can vary greatly from one listener to another; this results in poor communication. To help improve the communications between groups which differ too much, one or both of the groups might be trained to recognise the problem and take it into account (new social security clerks could be trained to understand their clients' use of language). A simpler solution in many cases would be to increase the amount of regular social contact. As we saw in the previous chapter the effects of language upon behaviour are established and maintained through face-to-face contacts within social groups. Physically and socially separated groups of people will tend to use language in rather different ways – just consider managers, shop-floor workers and technical staff.

It is a great over-simplification to treat organisational problems as problems of communication but, at least, the language that people use is easy to observe and open to analysis. To provide such analyses may become a routine activity for the department which specialises in the management of a company's information resources. And, just as the analyses provided by a pathology laboratory are used to guide a doctor

---

* The diagram is taken, with permission, from *Language and Thought* by J. P. Carroll and is based on the data of J. J. Jenkins and W. A. Russell (q.v.).

† See Dunphy and Stone on applying computers to 'content analysis'.

in diagnosis and treatment of physical ailments, so might the analyses of language serve the management and personnel specialists in an organisation.

Sensitivity to verbal stimuli

So far in this chapter we have seen how some of the effects of words upon people can be measured objectively. The methods of the behavioural psychologist are useful, but in their current state of development they are still extremely crude compared with our personal, subjective assessments of language. You only have to think of employing statistical analyses as a substitute for literary criticism to realise that this is so. Yet these rough methods have the virtue of being objective. The experiments described above serve to show that we make discriminations and establish relationships between words in a stable manner, and they also show something of the structure of these discriminations and relationships. However, they do not show how sensitively people respond to verbal stimuli or how sensitive are their verbal responses to other stimuli. As we saw in the previous chapter, the mechanism which maintains stable social patterns depends upon our ability to recognise and respond to very subtle signs. This was taken for granted in the earlier discussion of the social mechanism, but it can be demonstrated quite clearly with respect to language.

We are extremely sensitive to the verbal stimuli we receive and we are very receptive to the conditioning processes that govern our patterns of verbal reaction. In one experiment six different nonsense syllables were presented to subjects at random in a series of ordinary words.* There was nothing special about the treatment of four of the nonsense syllables. However, two were associated with different groups of related words. Thus XEH appeared with words like 'thief', 'bitter', 'ugly', 'sap', 'worthless', 'sour', whilst YOF was associated with words like 'beauty', 'win', 'gift', 'sweet', 'honest', 'smart'. Subjects were then asked to rate the various nonsense syllables on semantic differential scales. It was found that the syllables that were given special treatment were rated significantly differently, although most of the subjects were not consciously aware of the associations created during the conditioning process. The experiment indicates that we can learn very quickly to attach some emotive colouring to even the most neutral of words.

Our sensitivity to words is not only exhibited in our verbal behaviour. Words can affect our beliefs, our actions and even our perception of things. One experiment employed a recording of a voice so muffled by

* See Staats and Staats, 1957.

random noise that it was impossible to hear what was being said. Subjects were then told that they would hear a voice talking about some specific, named topic and were asked to report what they heard. The same recording of obscured speech was used in a number of trials with the same subjects, but they were told each time that they would hear about a different topic. The subjects usually heard the speaker talking on the topic which they had been primed to expect and were astonished to learn that they had heard the same recording each time. (Perhaps Hamlet was playing a similar trick on Rosencrantz and Guildenstern in their conversation about images in the clouds.) We tend to perceive what we expect to perceive. The manager who is making decisions based upon facts which tend to be obscured by a great deal of random interference must be careful not to fall into the same perceptual error, self-deceptively reading into the facts what he is predisposed to see there.*

Not only are we highly sensitive to verbal stimuli but, reciprocally, our use of language is very sensitive to non-verbal stimuli. This was demonstrated in experiments by L. Krasner (1958), who revealed the sensitivity of a speaker to the reactions of the person he is talking to. In one experiment the subject was told that the experimenter was interested in the free flow of ideas. He was asked to produce a stream of words just as they came into his mind. The experimenter then responded to any plural noun by saying 'good' or grunting 'aha!' in some affirmative manner; by this simple means the experimenter was able to direct the course of the subject's stream of words, leading him unconsciously to produce a higher proportion of plural nouns than was otherwise the case. In another experiment by Verplanck (1955), experimenters systematically agreed to the opinions offered by other people in a conversation. The effect of this conditioning was to cause a significant increase in the proportion of statements of opinion from the subjects.

These experiments serve to clarify the process whereby an individual is conditioned by a group, a process which underlies the social mechanism of norm formation. They also prompt one to enquire about the ability of people to transmit messages, which is a problem of great importance in the design of organisational information systems. We shall now examine two communication problems: first, how accurately people can transmit factual information and second, how we transmit the affective messages which influence people's judgements, choice of goals and degree of motivation.

Accuracy of human transmission of factual messages

As we have noted, words can predispose a person to interpret what he

* See also Rosenthal, 1966.

actually sees or hears in one way or another. Conversely, this predisposition of the mind (or mental 'set' as it is sometimes called) also determines how words are interpreted and remembered and recalled later. Pertinent experiments were carried out by Allport and Postman (1947) in their study of the psychology of rumour. A person was shown a picture and, while looking at it, was asked to describe it to a second person. He was asked in turn to pass on this description, as accurately as possible, to a third person who had not seen the picture, and he in turn to a fourth person, and so on. The experiment showed how the interest, attitudes and stereotypes of the particular group of subjects influenced what was reported. When the original picture contained a policeman, the retelling of the story tended to centre around that figure when the subjects were themselves police officers. Details about dresses became of major importance when the reporters were women, but not when they were men.

One picture used by the experimenters depicted the carriage of an overhead train in which five people sat, one of them being a woman carrying a child, another a bearded Rabbi reading a book, another a fat man asleep, the fourth a man reading a newspaper, and the fifth a respectable woman with a shopping bag. Standing in the gangway were two characters, the taller a negro, the shorter a white man. These two were apparently arguing and the white man carried an open, cut-throat razor. As the descriptions of this scene were retold errors were introduced, some details were omitted; those that were preserved were given more importance, and all these changes were clearly influenced by the stereotyped views of the subjects. Typical changes that occurred in the description transferred the scene to an underground railway with the woman holding the baby now standing; omitted all but one of the advertisements in the train making that one more important by converting it from a local to a national election poster; and shifted the razor from the hand of the white man to the hand of the negro. Changes of this kind occurred although the subjects were asked to report the descriptions as accurately as possible, and were aware that the experimenter and the class knew the original version. (Longer and less distorted reports were given, however, when there was no audience.) How reliable then is verbal reporting in less controlled conditions? It does suggest that information which is not based upon a report written when the observation was made is liable to very serious error. This experiment does reveal how reports which supposedly deal with facts and with objective descriptions of the world around us can rapidly lose their denotative meaning and become simply a vehicle for affective judgements, serving mainly to reinforce the attitudes and stereotyped views of the people transmitting them. For the information systems designer the lesson is clear. Facts must be recorded at their time and place of origin, and transmitted in a written or mechanical medium with an absolute minimum of opportunity for subjective interpretation.

The directions in which attitudes can be influenced by words

There have been references on earlier pages to the means by which we convey approval and disapproval. These subtle channels of affective communication are largely extra-linguistic. Language, to which we are so sensitive, also has many facilities for embodying emotive overtones; by choice of words:

> Albert walked up to Mr Thompson;
> Our Albert crept up to the gaffer;

or by grammatical structure:

> After two minutes the engine broke down;
> The engine broke down after two minutes.

In written language, these, with the use of typography, italics and the lengths of sentences or paragraphs, are the only affective devices available. In face-to-face conversation, gestures of the hands, facial expression, body posture, distance from the listener, touch and, of course, vocal tempo and inflection all add their emotive overtones to the words that are uttered. In a face-to-face encounter, the speaker is able to influence the attitudes of whoever he is addressing, far more powerfully than in writing.

It is useful to classify the attitudes that are influenced during communication as in fig. 5. The solid line from the speaker to the listener

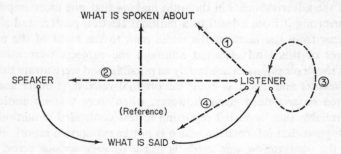

Fig. 5. Four attitudes influenced by a communication.

indicates the signal which is actually transmitted. The words 'What is said', are related to 'What is spoken about' by a reference relationship shown by a line of dashes. The remaining broken lines in the diagram correspond to the main categories of attitudes which are influenced. Most obviously the speaker will attempt (1) to influence his listener's attitude towards the subject being spoken about: he may be trying to persuade a client to buy something. He will also (2) tend to cause the listener to adjust his attitude towards him, the speaker: as an interviewee for a new post this may be his major aim. These are the most common and the most obvious kinds of influence that we try to exert when we are talking to someone.

Less consciously we influence the attitude of the listener towards himself (3). This can be deliberate, as when one speaks to a person in order to raise his morale or self-confidence or, on the contrary, to induce a feeling of self-criticism or even of shame. If the listener has some preconception of what the speaker might wish to convey to him in this respect, then the fact that he has been spoken to at all can have quite enough influence upon the listener, regardless of the content of the message.

The attitude of the listener towards the message itself (4) is very interesting in the context of communications among decision-makers. It is important that the listener should judge the reliability or credibility of what he hears. The speaker, perhaps unintentionally, but often deliberately, will provide clues to guide the listener in the attitude he should adopt. We may 'label' a figure of speech, such as a metaphor, by using a rather less matter-of-fact tone of voice. Sarcasm and ironical use of language we might indicate by facial expressions that are sneering or are exaggeratedly deadpan. Perhaps most interesting of all is that with every statement we tend to convey some measure of the confidence that should be placed in it. We can do this by our emphasis and expression but we also have a range of phrases to help us. Examples are: 'in all probability', 'I should think that', 'you wouldn't believe it, but', ranging to the 'did you hear the one about', which also manages to convey the idea that the speaker will be offended if the listener isn't amused! Many forms of written communication fail to convey this important information about the reliability of the messages. This can be overcome in some special situations by attaching estimates of probability to some statements. It is as well to remember that without face-to-face communication the decision-maker can be deprived of vital information about the reliability of his data.

In a conversation, there are always two people listening, one of them being the speaker. Therefore, the words can also influence the speaker's own attitudes. A person tends to be better disposed towards those sentiments he has uttered himself; in the pathological extreme you find the bigot who convinces himself of the rectitude of his own views by listening to no others. We also speak, sometimes, to convince ourselves of our own worthiness; the bore is the pathological instance.

The analysis of the emotive force of language can be carried to degrees of very great refinement. Dramatic and literary critics do so, while art and music critics analyse some of our non-verbal 'languages'. The affective use of language requires a far more delicate choice of words than the scientific. Whereas our denotative use of language generally admits the substitution of one word for another without any change of 'meaning' in the sense of what is referred to, it is very much more difficult to change one word for another without changing the emotive force of what is being said and therefore changing the 'affective' meaning.

A manager with well-defined objectives who does not achieve emotional rapport with the people he directs will be left with a handful of well-written and tidily formulated proposals, but he will fail in action. The manager who is *en rapport* with his men, with his peers, with his boss, will promote a great deal of enthusiastic activity and may indeed promote himself. But he may not achieve any organisational, as opposed to personal, goals. To create an effective organisation both these extremes must be avoided.

Affective communication in an organisation

Business information systems must transmit denotative information, for example data about movements of goods and who has paid money, etc. Equally vital to an organisation is the affective information about the values that people hold, the goals they seek and their attitudes to what is expected of them. Fear and resentment or enthusiasm and confidence are the messages carried by the channels for affective communication. Managers can be receptive to this information if they choose. In particular they may increase the amount of face-to-face contact, the appropriate channel for affective signals, and may also create, in such direct encounters, a psychological climate which does not inhibit openness of expression. Communication of affective messages in the reverse direction – from the individual manager to the group he leads – is less easy to control.

Although one individual is very susceptible to affective communication, the attitude of a whole group is an evaluative norm which can be very difficult to change. As it was pointed out in the previous chapter, a group is little influenced from outside except through the mediation of 'opinion leaders', in a two-step process. It has been found that effective opinion leaders:

(a) adhere more closely than others to the norms of the group;
(b) are regarded by the group as competent in the light of their previous performance;
(c) are strategically located for communication within the group.

These distinguishing features are derived from experimental observation (see Katz, 1965). Conformity and competence underlie the credibility of the opinion leader and hence the acceptability of his views, whilst the third feature ensures that he has adequate opportunity to communicate with the members of the group.

Now consider the role of the manager or of the organisational innovator who stands outside the group membership. In some circumstances, he may be free to choose a strategic location which enables him to communicate with all the group members but he will not so easily establish his credibility in a short time. He may be so different in his behaviour from the norms of the group that he may never be accepted. In these circumstances, opinion leaders who are already within the group will govern reactions. The organisational structure, especially during phases of innovation, should make use of the natural opinion leaders – for example by the careful appointment of 'link-men' to systems analysis teams from the departments to be affected by change.

Relevance to organisational design

The effectiveness of any organisation is highly dependent upon the attitudes of its own members, and of those outside who consume its products or supply its resources. By deciding whether to buy this or that, whether to give to this cause or that, whether to do this job now or leave it till tomorrow, they determine the behaviour of the organisation. Each individual will decide how much or little he likes the goals of an organisation as he perceives them; an organisation whose members do not largely accept its goals can only operate under authoritarian management with inevitable social tensions and consequent inefficiencies, compared with the organisation in which all the members are pulling willingly in the same direction. The communication of attitudes concerning the work being done is vital to any organisation. For an organisation to function well, adequate channels of affective communication must be open. They should enable a degree of consensus to form about the goals of working teams of all sizes, including the whole organisation. They should be capable of transmitting the motivating energy of leaders and of generating commitment to the task. This is becoming more important in our society which is less prepared to accept financial rewards and the threat of authority as the only inducements to work.

The emotive forces of language are much attenuated when communication is in a written form and not face to face, because nearly all the non-verbal messages are stripped away. The written word is not a reliable way of conveying affective messages. The advertiser can do it using pictures and music in addition to words but it can best be done in personal encounter. Hence the major obstacle to providing adequate channels for communicating affective messages in an organisation is the cost of relatively expensive, regular personal contacts. Perhaps there is scope for extending the analysis of information systems to the affective communication channels within an organisation. Surely a company would benefit as much from a knowledge of the volumes and types of internal, face-to-face contacts between the members of groups which need to cooperate as they benefit from a knowledge of the numbers of invoices processed.

Too many of those who are engaged in the design of so-called 'management information systems' forget that the information which a manager requires in order to make good decisions has two aspects. He needs both denotative information to provide the factual basis for his decisions and also affective information to guide his judgements of value. Information specialists who are mostly concerned with computer operations or with the efficiency of bureaucratic activities frequently disregard the second type of communication. The techniques of information-systems analysis and organisational design will not reach maturity until they include consideration of affective communication.

Relevance to the study of information

In this chapter and the two preceding ones we have explored the use of signs by people. This subject is not only important in the conduct of practical work of an information specialist but it is also essential as the foundation of any comprehensive theory of information. 'Information' is a vague term synonymous with 'signs and the properties of signs'. We have seen that what constitutes a sign depends upon human behaviour and that social interactions employing a sign are essential for establishing and maintaining its 'meaning'. 'Meaning' in this sense is a relationship between sign and behaviour. Our ability to communicate with one another does not rest upon the fictions of logical absolutes but upon the slowly shifting sands of human culture. This must always be our ultimate point of reference in the study of information.

Part Three

Semantics of Verbal Information

Not only are we sensitive to words but we use them very effectively in all commonplace situations. However, words referring to things that are neither near to us in time and space nor readily observable are the commonest cause of misunderstanding. We must be constantly vigilant and critical about the words we are using or there is a danger that they merely become a part of a reassuring ritual.

If we want to do things in an organised way, operations must first be carried out upon the names of things by making plans, evaluating them, and setting out instructions. Only then can someone be set to work, upon the real things, in a systematic way. This is what management is about. If it is to be successful, then we must make sure that there is a justifiable relationship between the things and events we want to operate upon and the verbal labels we attach to them. The whole of this part is concerned with the problem of critically appraising verbal information. It examines the relationships not only between things and their names but between statements and the 'real' states of affairs that they describe.

6 The Critical Appraisal of Language

Philosophy is the battle against the bewitchment of our intelligence by means of language.

Wittgenstein, *Philosophical Investigations*

An animal lives in a physical environment, to which it reacts directly, and from which it derives directly the means to satisfy its needs. The human being lives also in a rich environment of sign processes, which serve to extend his control over his physical environment by endowing him with the ability to organise and cooperate with his fellows. His rich use of signs also creates desires and gives satisfactions of quite a different kind: the need to explain, the creation of beauty, the pleasure of laughter, the enjoyment of fictional experience. Human culture is composed of this secondary environment of signs, which embellish and elaborate upon every detail of our basic, biological necessities. Civilisation arrives when the secondary, cultural environment becomes of greater concern to the individual than his primary, biological environment. It is possible to be sensitive and discriminating both in using and in responding to signs, and therefore highly civilised in one sense, without questioning the ways in which words and other signs are used. Indeed, most of the time we take the cultural messages we receive at their face value. The process of communication would be impossibly laboured if we did not.

Critical awareness of how signs are used

At some stage in the evolution of civilisation there develops a self-conscious awareness of the sign processes. Instead of accepting signs, words and statements at their face value, questions are asked about their purposes, their justification and just what kinds of messages they are intended to convey and what their consequences might be. Questions like these are posed by lawyers and historians who wish to clarify the value of different kinds of evidence, by theologians concerned with revelations and miraculous signs, by philosophers enquiring into the nature of knowledge (epistemology) or hoping to discover what really exists (ontology), by scientists who need to understand the relationship between hypothesis and observation, by critics and moral philosophers who seek elucidation of the language of aesthetic and ethical judgement. Parts of their enquiries may be usefully construed as a search for an understanding of how signs are used and how they *do*, or *should*, affect our actions.

Part Two of this book has presented some scientific findings about human reactions to signs. Anthropology draws attention to the wealth of signs we employ; social psychology indicates how the group establishes stable patterns of behaviour, beliefs, evaluations and even perceptions, and experimental psychology reveals how sensitive we are to signs, verbal or otherwise. This knowledge helps to sharpen our intuitive grasp of the effects of signs upon ourselves and others. In the ultimate analysis, the meanings of all signs rest upon a social mechanism that gives them what stability they have; to recognise this is to acknowledge the futility of asking questions that demand *absolute* answers about *the* meaning of any word. It forces us to relate such questions to the people among whom the word is used. It indicates a healthy lack of dogmatism and encourages one to inspect one's prejudices. The behavioural sciences will pin down more and more of the problems of pragmatics, the relationships between signs and behaviour, but they will never capture them all.

A manager or administrator must be critically aware of how he reacts to the signs which convey the information he needs for making decisions. He has to solve a series of unique and complex problems; often under severe time pressure he must take some action or issue a directive to others. Sometimes decisions can be made on a scientific basis, particularly when the same decision-situation is encountered repeatedly, or when time permits empirical knowledge to be applied to his problem. Very frequently the uniqueness of the problem, and the lack of time, remove the decision procedure entirely from the sphere in which empirical science has any competence. A manager must learn to read with discrimination, sensitivity and accuracy the multiplicity of signs to which he is exposed. This skill can be acquired through personal experience which is encountered with an open mind, but it can be augmented by training. One possible method is through the discussion of suitable case-studies, whilst another method sometimes used in management education is the sensitivity Training Group. In the T-Group, as it is called, about ten people are brought together for a period of about a week; they spend their time coming to terms with one another and analysing how they do it; the training concentrates upon the interpersonal sign-situation. Expert guidance is necessary because the members can reveal with traumatic frankness how they interpret one another's behaviour.

The decision-maker does not have to rely unaided upon a well-trained intuition. He can employ methods of analysis developed by the philosopher, the critic, the historian and the lawyer, for example. Their critical techniques can be used for discovering the full import of language, and appraising the standing of evidence and opinion. The methods are not scientific but are just as basic to science as they are to any other disciplined way of thinking: 'scientific method' is the name given to the critical principles used to gauge the fitness of scientific information; it is a body of philosophical, not scientific knowledge. A manager can also benefit by the acquisition of some of those analytical skills which can help him to gauge the fitness of information for his managerial tasks.

Methods of appraising the use of words, numbers and other signs should be regarded as highly relevant to the professional information specialist. If his responsibilities extend to judging the *quality* of the information used in an organisation for making decisions, then he will have to use these methods. He ignores them at his peril if he wishes to construct a system for providing information to decision-makers, and they form the basis of methods of diagnosing failures of organisational performance caused by the misinterpretation of information, or the misjudgement of its reliability. This concern with what signs signify is the province of semantics. The chapters in this part are mainly about aspects of the semantics of words while, in the following part, they are about the semantics of numerical information.

'Mere semantics'

It is unfortunate that the word 'semantics' is used most often as a part of the above pejorative cliché. Semantics is concerned with problems of relationships between words and things, especially those problems of making relationships stable and reliable enough for us to communicate with one another accurately on matters of fact and judgement. In discussion it may be wise to regard with mistrust anyone who makes much use of this cliché: either he is incapable of appreciating that someone else may have a valid reason for viewing a subject differently, or he wishes to blur a distinction in order to uphold his own view; in neither case would further discussion prove fruitful.

Semantics is concerned with clarifying how signs are used. We have seen in chapter 4 how signs can be used in conjunction with cognitive and perceptual norms to *denote* things, and in conjunction with evaluative norms to convey *affective* messages. Semantic analysis is complicated because signs can have significance in both these modes simultaneously. This is especially true of face-to-face discourse which, as noted in chapter 5, can refer to some object and simultaneously convey a judgement about it. Written language can be slightly easier to disentangle. Mathematical formulations can deceive one into believing that they separate the denotative information from the affective; a mathematical model for a business decision usually includes a set of equations describing the physical constraints, and an 'objective function' which enables any course of action to be evaluated. On closer inspection, this, or any other kind of mathematical formulation of an organisational problem, will yield its quota of dubious value-judgements lurking in the supposedly objective choice of variables and equations.

The essential problem is how to discriminate references to matters of fact from expressions of opinion, and how to justify their implied claim to describe the way things are. The obstacle which anyone faces when he raises the question of semantics is that people are unwilling to concede that their intelligence is in danger of being bewitched by language—the ritual quality of quite meaningless language makes its use seem familiar, a matter of common sense and, therefore, safe.

We all have a natural resistance to adopting philosophical procedures for the analysis of what we are told or what we believe. This is because an individual, from his own position firmly rooted in the culture to which he belongs, believes himself to be looking out upon a world that seems to be the same as the one that other people see. He talks to them about this world and they appear to attach words to objects in exactly the same way as he does. Language appears to be a pellucid medium of communication, which enables him to see inaccessible tracts of the world through other people's eyes. For everyday affairs this is almost true, but he makes the mistake of using words like 'power', 'good', 'system', 'the town', 'productivity' as though they were in no way different from the ones which refer to commonplace, tangible things like 'table' and 'chair', or which are readily demonstrated like 'red', 'walking'. As Ogden and Richards have said, he is 'guided merely by his linguistic habits and a simple faith in the widespread possession of those habits'. Unfortunately this faith is not always justified. To counteract the tendency of language to mislead, we can learn to apply a canon of critical tests which are mainly the product of philosophical enquiry. Wittgenstein, as the quotation at the head of this chapter indicates, has singled out the refinement of these critical tools as the main purpose of philosophy. Other philosophers may disagree with his order of priority, but the practical importance of this type of analysis is difficult to deny in this age, when far-reaching decisions are taken on the basis of supposedly accurate descriptions of alternatives which are quite beyond the scope of a single person's first-hand knowledge. Information used by vast corporations or government departments needs to be subjected to a degree of criticism which would normally be inappropriate in small organisations.

Semantic errors and organisational performance

The further two people are moved away from the tangible objects of their conversation, whether the distance be measured in space, time or degree of abstraction, the further apart will be the meanings of their words. This will be true even though they come from the same cultural background, but the discrepancies will be more marked if they come from different ones. The result may be a bland lack of mutual understanding, which could remain quite unnoticed by either party, if no practical consequences were expected to flow from their discussion. Their lack of mutual understanding may be revealed by consequences at a verbal level. Very often, for fear perhaps of wasting time over what is thought to be 'mere semantics', a verbal inconsistency will be allowed to stand. In a casual conversation there may be no harm in simply dropping the subject but in a business discussion, which must be followed by actions, a failure to resolve semantic problems while they are still at a verbal level will expose itself, perhaps many months later, in practical consequences that may be disastrous. People working in close proximity to one another can more readily discover their verbal confusions as they translate words into action, early enough to avert serious trouble. But, in large organisations, and in carrying out large projects, people may be separated by time or space to an extent that makes it wasteful to rely upon informal methods to resolve their misunderstandings. This difficulty arises in its most acute form when we are faced with a complex design problem to which many people are expected to contribute, such as the design of a large, computer-based information system. Systems analysis, much of the time, is concerned with resolving semantic problems in the relationships between an actual system and its description, or between a design and some future system or between computer files and what they represent.

The evolution of our modern, science-based, economy is not only dependent upon our discovery of techniques, but also upon our growing ability to use information in a strictly factual way, which ensures that messages, regardless of the time, place and circumstances, will always be interpreted in the same way.

When commerce evolved from the barter system to the use of money a major step forward was taken by the economy. By substituting a symbol, money, for one of the goods or services involved in any transaction, exchange was made simpler and a great deal of needless movements of goods was avoided. By using accurate and detailed descriptions of goods, as we do today, we are able to reduce even further the transport of goods and people by permitting buyers and sellers to act purely on the basis of information. This trend has a long way to go before it is complete, but it will rank with the acquisition of a monetary system as a fundamental advance in the evolution of the economy. However, a more important commercial use of factual information than for describing existing goods and services is for describing artefacts that are not yet in existence and are too expensive to make until the need arises. These artefacts can be designed and evaluated while still on the drawing board, then, when required, they can be created with confidence that they will perform as designed – provided that the design is an accurate and adequate representation of something which can really be produced.

Producing designs is by no means a new concept – presumably designs and drawings were made of the pyramids – but on the scale at which it is now becoming possible it will be new. Formerly it was possible to introduce into a design only minor variations upon a well-known theme: we were unable to predict the consequences of larger innovations upon the behaviour of whatever was to be constructed, a vehicle perhaps or a building. The growth of systems engineering, especially the mathematical tools of analysis associated with it, is removing this obstacle. It is becoming possible to predict more accurately the performance of new and complex artefacts when they are still on the drawing board; this reduces the risk of producing an unsatisfactory aeroplane, bridge or chemical plant. We can innovate much more quickly. It is even possible to predict gross performance of a product whilst only the outlines of its design have been specified, with a consequent saving in design effort. We may be able to apply similar methods to the design of administrative and organisational systems. Systems analysis is extending our ability to create information systems which fulfil given organisational objectives in the new ways made possible by information technology. Nevertheless, we must exercise caution when trying to extend a design process appropriate for the development of machinery into the sphere of organisational design. It is impossible to attain the degree of objective knowledge of organisations which is attainable in engineering; therefore, a description (design) of a hypothetical organisation can never have quite the same standing as a description of a hypothetical machine. The need to recognise how his work is affected by the limitation upon his knowledge supplies another reason why the information specialist should have an understanding of semantics.

Ways of signifying things

One could easily devote a lifetime to the task of making an exhaustive classification of signs, according to the ways in which they signify things. Making these distinctions and testing them is an important part of the philosopher's work. Our task is quite limited, however, because we only require a classification that is sufficiently detailed to help us solve a practical problem.

The practical problem is this: how do we managers, administrators and information specialists justify labouring among records, reports, forecasts, plans, policies, instead of getting down to the reality of actions, goods, services and human satisfactions at first hand? We can only justify ourselves by showing that we are busy at our desks and computers manipulating signs that reliably signify what either is real, or might be. We must be able to defend our information against strong criticism whenever its relationship to the world of reality is challenged.

Relationships between signs and things cannot all be established in the same manner. This is easily shown by a rough and ready classification scheme. Table 1 makes use of the distinction drawn in Part Two, between denotative and affective modes of language, that is between signs which refer to objects or actions, and those which refer to human feelings. The table also uses a distinction, which is appropriate in a

Table 1 Classification of information according to its signification

Signification	Mode of	
Intention of	Denotative	Affective
Descriptive	designations, facts, evidence, forecasts	appraisals, value judgements
Prescriptive	instructions, plans, policies, orders	inducements, coercion, threats, rewards

(Notice that the *ritual* and *formal* modes of language are not entered because they are ways of using language without reference.)

decision-making context, between information that describes states of affairs, past, present and future, (the input to the decision) and information in which the decision-maker prescribes what shall be done (the output). The four resulting categories of information have quite different kinds of signification which must be justified in quite different ways as indicated below.*

* This classification resembles those given by Charles Morris in his books of 1946 and 1964. Compare them with the classification of signs in chapter 2 of volume II of C. S. Peirce's collected works.

Denotative descriptions

Designative signs must be justified by showing their relationships with things which can be observed by anyone. This is easy when one is dealing with an ordinary physical object, which you can exhibit for anyone to inspect, using his senses directly to do so. It is far more difficult to justify the designative signification of a statement about a past event or a name for an historical person. Predictions, designs, descriptions of courses of action are designative signs which 'refer' to what might happen or what can be made to happen. Science has always faced problems of trying to justify designative terms, e.g. 'gravity', 'phlogiston', 'aether', 'neutrino'. At least science can subject its designative terms to criticism through experiment, but in business and administration the language of the decision-maker must be full of descriptions of mere possibilities or, as in law, it must deal with unique unrepeatable events upon which a judgement must be made. The kind of *factual* information that must be employed in business systems can be difficult to justify. Most of the rest of this chapter and the next three will deal with this problem.

The other modes of signifying will not be referred to very much, but before pushing them to one side (for lack of space and not for any imputed lack of importance), let us note how they require signs to be justified.

Affective descriptions

Information which flows in an organisation frequently embodies value-judgements: reports on staff, reports on the fitness of a dwelling, estimates of the relative difficulties of jobs. It is pertinent to enquire *whose* value judgements are embodied in this information. The answer to this question can make a vast difference to the decisions that are based on the information; for example, in the appraisal of staff, it is essential to appraise also the appraiser. As another example, note that the acceptability of a decision, such as fixing rates of pay according to some job appraisal scheme, will depend upon whose judgements are embodied in the job analysis.

The key, distinguishing, characteristic of appraisive information which must always be kept in mind is that, ultimately, it must refer to individual human feelings. When an individual person appraises a steak as he actually eats it, or a film when he has just seen it, he can make an appraisive judgement that is very firmly based. Unfortunately the appraisals that matter much of the time are aggregates of many personal judgements, concerning events or circumstances that have never been experienced. Town plans must be discussed in appraisive terms without there being any opportunity for people actually to experience the different environments they are being offered. In these conditions, the only satisfactory appraisals are those based upon plans which are well understood and whose consequences are fully appreciated. One cannot begin to appraise what one cannot imagine experiencing.

The businessman may have even greater difficulty in obtaining adequate appraisive information, because he may be compelled by the nature of his work to guess what other people's appraisive judgements will be. For example, he may be deciding upon mounting some new entertainment or selecting some designs for ready-to-wear dresses or patterns for fabrics. Judgements of the responses of the potential consumers may be almost impossible to obtain. The only appraisive information which can be acted upon is at second hand, an anticipation of consumer reaction.

Very often appraisive information represents the combined judgements of many people. The manner in which individual judgements are combined can be very important. Sometimes the abstracting and generalising process takes place informally. One person (say a politician) will respond to the views that are brought to his notice (by the press, pressure groups, personal acquaintances); his judgement may not represent his own personal view but rather an amalgam of the opinions pressed upon him. A man who cannot be influenced in this way will make a poor leader in any kind of democratic organisation. (The politician who refrains from committing himself according to some abstract principle on a practical issue should not be regarded automatically as 'shifty' if it means he is open to the influence of the opinion of others.) Sometimes this aggregating of judgements can take place through a formal mechanism, such as a voting procedure. In both cases, informal and formal, the result will depend upon what degrees of influence are wielded by different groups.

It is interesting to note that appraisive judgements are fundamental to the designation of 'things'. Consider how a human organism singles out regular patterns impinging upon its senses, as worthy of being labelled as 'things' or 'properties'. It will be more likely to recognise those patterns which enable it to achieve some desirable end or avoid an unpleasant experience. All problems of recognising patterns in data must ultimately appeal to a criterion of their value in human terms. Abstract criteria for identifying patterns can be suggestive, but they do not prevent the identification of useless patterns, or guarantee the discovery of all the useful ones; given *any* miscellaneous jumble of data there is *some* abstract test that will identify it as a single pattern. Only by reference to the human organism and its power of appraisal can we justify designating a supposed pattern of data as a 'thing'. Statistical analysis which uses abstract criteria of significance can lead one into the error of drawing attention to useless relationships whilst neglecting important ones.*

Prescriptive information

Information that says what must or ought to be done is very different from information which conveys facts, or information which passes judgements, but it relies on both these other kinds of information. Typical prescriptive information includes orders and instructions, rules and regulations, recommendations and advice. To justify prescriptive information one must appeal to the consequences of acting upon it or failing to act upon it.

An order, a rule or a recommendation will denote the objects to which the prescribed action must be related, and the conditions when the action is appropriate. From an objective, denotative viewpoint, a prescription is justified if it can be shown to be feasible. The feasibility test is necessary to justify an order but not sufficient; we must also examine its consequences in human terms. The consequences may be natural ('Don't drink that, it will poison you') but more often than not they depend heavily upon the sanctions that can be imposed, or the rewards that can be granted, by a person or group, or by society as a whole. These sanctions range from the directly physical, in love and war, to the subtle, unspoken devices for conferring respect or withdrawing notice which we employ in social intercourse.

Any critical appraisal of prescriptive information must attempt to identify the sanctions and rewards that lend it force. Words may have the superficial appearance of a command or law but their prescriptive standing is only justifiable in so far as they arouse expectations about the consequences of obeying or disobeying them. For people who do not fall within the scope of the reward and punishment system, the command or law loses its prescriptive signification. This is also true when a person (e.g. a psychopath) is not capable of appreciating the consequences, even though he lies within the jurisdiction of the system. What sanctions can be applied very largely depends upon the consent of those to whom they are supposed to apply; this is a subtly drawn line which shifts with the changing attitudes of those who are governed or managed. Orders which would have been obeyed twenty years ago might be coolly ignored today.

* There is a vast difference here between the scientific use of statistics and the decision-maker's use of them. In science there is always the possibility of collecting more data to clarify the picture. In business there is normally a time limit, and a very limited amount of data. Abstract criteria may serve the scientist but, for the decision-maker, a relationship which is hardly significant statistically may be much more important than one which is overwhelming in the statistical sense.

The most important prescriptive information used in an organisation is financial information. Money serves to regulate behaviour. Social custom, supported by a framework of financial law and backed by legal sanctions, determines the way in which money sets bounds upon an individual's or a company's freedom of action. A budgetary system and notional cash flows are used to extend the prescriptive machinery of the external monetary system to the interior of the organisation.

There is yet another important aspect to the justifying of prescriptive information. We have said that a prescription must derive its force from the imposition of sanctions or the granting of rewards. We have also indicated that the admissibility of the reward and punishment system very largely depends upon the consent of those under its sway. If it is not to be imposed through the barrel of a gun, the problem arises of how to justify a prescriptive system so that people will regard it as admissible. One way of doing this is to appeal to very abstract, normative principles of fairness or reason or consistency. It is then possible to judge the effects of proposed rules and regulations, for example, by using these abstract principles. The formulation of normative principles is slow and difficult. In our society it is a major concern of certain academic disciplines. Jurisprudence, the philosophy of law, is concerned with identifying principles which should govern the formulation and administration of law. The philosophy of science is concerned with principles governing the formulation and testing of scientific hypotheses. There are also principles which should govern the acceptability of information which purports to be factual, and upon which business decisions are taken; *these* abstract principles are exactly what the next few chapters are about. We must ask: what conditions must be satisfied if we claim that a word refers to some 'thing'? How can statements be tested so that we may confidently use them as a basis for action? When is a number a genuine measurement? An abstract, normative principle must derive its prescriptive force from the need to avoid confusion and misunderstanding in law, science and other practical affairs. It can be justified by demonstrating the undesirable consequences of ignoring it, or the benefits of conforming to its normative direction. (One extensive example of this appears in this book in the chapters dealing with probability; we shall see that, as normative rules are invoked, the resulting measure of probability becomes gradually more objective but gradually less widely applicable.)

The classification of messages

For the successful functioning of an organisation it is vital to ensure that the different kinds of information which regulate its behaviour can be adequately justified. Decisions are made using words and numbers; instructions are given using language; policy is a linguistic regulator; files and data-banks purport to reveal the state of a company and its business. All this organisational information can serve its supposed purposes, of describing and appraising the real state of affairs and of influencing real events, only in so far as the words and numbers are genuinely related to real objects, judgements of actual people and the performance of feasible tasks. There is no foolproof way of ensuring this relationship between signs and reality. Only a constant awareness of the problem and the continual exercise of critical analysis can prevent the messages from degenerating towards fantasy.

The critical analysis of information is made easier if one is habitually accustomed to distinguishing between the different kinds of messages which call for justification in different ways. We have noted, above, that signs can be classified by their denotative or affective mode, or their descriptive or prescriptive intention. To these we can add many other refinements. There are, for example, various dimensions of abstraction. An aggregate of many numbers is more abstract than a single observation. A buyer's judgement of how customers will favour fashion goods is highly abstract, being a judgement of a judgement, and the manufacturer who must judge how the buyers will react must work at an even greater order of abstraction! Time also compels us to deal with what are essentially abstractions: statements about what *did* happen, what *will* happen or what *might* happen. Signs, which are highly abstract in any of these ways, are more difficult to justify than simple, direct, concrete terms or statements. Their 'semantic standing' is bound to be shakier. Nevertheless, it is the highly abstract information which most seriously concerns the organisational decision-maker: it is his job to discuss what *might* be done and what it *might* be worth.

We shall now embark upon an examination of some critical techniques which can be employed by the information specialist to check the quality of information. It would be a task out of proportion in a book of this kind to look at all classes of message: emphasis is therefore given to designative or factual information. The question that must be answered is: how can we test information, which supposedly describes the state of a business and its environment, to discover whether it forms a sound basis for action? The answer lies in finding a generalisation of the auditing procedure. The following three chapters examine some of the relevant underlying principles.

7 Giving Names to Things

The myth of physical objects . . . has proved more efficacious than other myths as a device for working a manageable structure into the flux of experience.

Quine, *From a Logical Point of View*

We use vocal sounds and marks on paper to serve as signs for things. Language used in this way enables us to influence events beyond our reach in time or space through other people – or, today, through the use of computers: machines which can respond to language. When we use a word to point 'to a thing', we are dependent upon being able to perceive that thing, and upon the belief that other people will perceive it, and relate that perception to the same word, in much the same way as we do ourselves. In addition to the problem of communicating with other people, there is the problem of how we, ourselves, preserve in our own minds a verbal record of some 'thing' which will occur again in our experience and which is worth thinking about. To ensure that we are using language correctly for this purpose, we must be careful to understand the links between things, perceptions and words, and how to submit them to tests that ensure they are forged correctly. In this chapter we ask what happens when *naming* those things which we can perceive directly with our senses, and we also examine the process of *abstraction* by which we attach words to 'entities' further and further removed from the possibility of immediate perception. This problem is approached by asking how we can ensure that abstract terms are well defined. In the next chapter we shall examine general and particular *statements* and how the limits of their justifiable use may be determined.

Perception

A manager, to control his company or department, must perceive the way it operates, and the goals he is trying to attain. He cannot do this without words or other symbols.

In chapter 5, experiments were cited to show how a person, primed verbally to perceive something in an ambiguous set of signals, would indeed tend to see or hear whatever he had been led to expect. In chapter 4 experimental evidence was cited to show that even perception of a quite unequivocal visual kind could be distorted if social pressures could lend enough support to any mental predisposition caused by words. How exposed, then, is a manager or administrator to the tyranny of words, as he tries to understand the company or department he runs, sitting at the centre of his web of communications, receiving rather unreliable signals, and forced to think about his problems in somewhat abstract terms!

To visualise the perceptual process, think of yourself as a tiny infant, aware only of the signals which reach you through the windows of your senses. Things and words do not exist, only unrelated sensations. Given sufficient data, your brain is able to isolate relatively stable patterns which are consistently associated with sensations of pain and pleasure. This process is refined until, gradually, a 'picture' of the 'world' begins to emerge. This stage is almost entirely a personal process. The 'things' that the world contains depend upon how our brains analyse the stimuli received by our senses, not the other way round. The physical objects which we see are, as Quine says, a myth, but one that puts 'a manageable structure into the flux of experience'. Wherever this structure touches experience, it may be in conflict with the messages received by our senses; we may dismiss the messages as hallucinations, or we may be forced to adjust the structure of our knowledge. We do this at a trivial level when we realise that the 'umbrella' we picked up in the dark cloak-room was really a walking-stick, and at a serious level with each of those conceptual leaps forward that occur during our education.

Words and perception

At some stage we begin to include words as a part of our 'world picture'. Their use interacts with our perceptual processes; we learn about the patterns other people consider important; the names of these patterns enable us to share experiences with other people and so obtain indirectly more data against which to test the structure of our knowledge; they serve also as agents of thought. In relation to our perception of the world, a word, as Dewey has suggested, is three things: a fence, a label and a vehicle.

Perceiving that one thing is separate from another is accomplished more easily if we have distinct names for them. Our own English language imposes upon our perception a structure which depends upon the way its vocabulary fences off certain patterns rather than others. It may be difficult to accept this idea, because we are accustomed to finding that the other languages with which we are familiar, normally European ones derived from the same Indo-European root language, incorporate almost the same assumptions about the world. But other families of languages, far removed in ancestry from our own, are based upon entirely different assumptions about the structure of the world.

Benjamin Lee Whorf has written many fascinating essays revealing just such contrasts between our own and the American Indian family of languages.* Whereas our language assumes that the world is composed of objects (nouns) which have properties (adjectives) and perform actions (verbs) at some time, past, present or future (tense) and stand in spatio-temporal relationships with one another (prepositions – 'under', 'before'), such distinctions are not necessarily found in American Indian languages. Some make no use of the sentence structure:

subject + predicate

which is obligatory if we wish to make a meaningful sentence in English. Others have verbs which do not use tenses to indicate time, but employ grammatical forms of verbs to convey the *degree of validity* of the sentence; this useful distinction we can convey only crudely in our own language. The contrast that we draw between form and substance ('a block of ice' and 'ice' or 'a lake' and 'water') cannot be made in one of the American Indian languages which, instead, makes other distinctions quite unfamiliar to us; for example, it contains a large grammatical category of words expressing types of intensity, duration and manner of change, having no equivalent in any European language.

Admittedly we cannot escape from the harness that language places upon our minds, but we must be careful not to presume that the familiar harness is the only one for pulling ideas along. Commonsense notions are largely verbally determined. They depend upon patterns which evolved before the dawn of history to meet needs that are far removed from those of modern society. It would be surprising if our commonsense use of language were equal to all the demands we place upon it today, especially in business and administration, not to mention science and technology.

Words as labels

Words, when they act as labels, facilitate the recall of clusters of ideas and sensations. We can use the label to help us find something in our own memory, or we can pass it on to someone else to induce him to rummage round in his own store. What the label happens to be fastened to will greatly affect our response to the word and, indirectly, to the world it describes. Much of our thought is verbalised. Consequently our behaviour is likely to be influenced by how we verbalise a situation, not purely by what we see. Again Whorf provides† some apt examples.

---

* Collected under the title *Language, Thought and Reality*.

† In the essay 'The Relation of Habitual Thought and Behaviour to Language'.

Before he turned to the study of linguistics, he was a chemical engineer and, in that capacity, was called upon to report on accidents. He noticed often that people had behaved quite correctly in relation to the customary verbal framework of the situation, but that unfortunately they had been misled by words, which labelled too small a part of the picture, or implied relationships that were inappropriate. For example, he noticed that people who behaved carefully enough in the vicinity of 'gasoline drums', when near 'empty gasoline drums' were dangerously disarmed by the word 'empty', with its connotation of 'null and void, negative, inert'. In another case, he describes a design error that probably originated verbally. There had been a fire in a room for drying hides. Sparks from an overheated bearing on the blower had been carried by the current of air into the room and had started a fire. The designer or installer of the fan probably verbalised its function as one of 'blowing air over the hides to dry them'. These verbal labels did not serve to remind him that such a device can blow not only air but sparks; the word 'blow' also implies very strongly that the fan should be situated at the inlet vent, where he had, in fact, placed it, instead of at the outlet where it would have drawn air safely through the drying room.

A similar kind of myopia can affect the conduct of a business. There is the well-known case of the shoe company which valued its assets on the assumption that it was in the shoe trade, until profitably taken over by someone who saw that it was also in real estate, and had been sitting on a gold mine in every small-town high street. Then there are the railways which seem to perceive their task as being one of running trains. Perhaps this is not surprising; all small boys, and many grown men, have a passion for railway engines; but, when one has spent longer trying to discover (by telephone) how to make a journey than one would have spent on the journey itself, one begins to wish that the railway authorities saw themselves as providing a means by which people, not knowing the time-tables by heart, can take themselves and their goods from one point (not necessarily a station) to another point (not necessarily a station). Not only the railways but many businesses and nearly all bureaucratic organisations suffer from having no word to label the whole bundle of goods, services and information which constitutes their 'product', and which is needed by their customers, or the people they serve, as a complete package. In the study of marketing, this is perhaps one of the major conceptual hurdles to be crossed. The labels we have for goods and services fail to tie up the whole of the 'product' bundle and, like the phrase 'empty gasoline drums', they let fall from the mind some vital part of the picture, like the explosive vapour inside the drum.

Words as vehicles

As vehicles, words permit us to re-arrange our perceived patterns in order to picture how things might be. Planning, designing and making decisions all depend upon this. We shall return to this topic in the next chapter when we examine statements. Meanwhile, we can enquire how we might diagnose perceptual errors induced by words, and help ourselves and others to avoid them.

Devices to help clarify the relationship between words and what we perceive

To help us avoid being ensnared by the naive assumption that our language supplies a clear, accurate and detailed picture of the world around, Korzybski (in *The Role of Language in the Perceptual Process*) has suggested that we employ a number of practical analytical devices. These force us to be consciously aware of the mental processes that intervene between our receiving an impression of something through our senses, and our attaching words to what we perceive. It can be most instructive to use Korzybski's method to annotate a document in which you suspect that words are being misused.

One technique that he recommends is to employ a variety of 'extensional devices' which remind us that a word does not refer to some single 'thing', but that it is a label attached to a vast conglomeration of particulars, e.g. members of the class embraced by a common noun. So, if the discussion is about a 'lorry', it is as well to remember that this word covers 'lorry$_1$', 'lorry$_2$', 'lorry$_3$' . . . which may differ very markedly in characteristics of size and performance. Even when we think of a particular lorry, it is as well to remember that lorry$_1$ (1960) is not the same as lorry$_1$ (1970), or say that driver$_2$ (start of journey) is different from driver$_2$ (end of journey). I was reminded the other day of the force of this particular cautionary device when a well-known hymn book was referred to as 'Hymns Ancient and Late Victorian'. A superscript could be used to emphasise that we do not perceive things in isolation, nor can their behaviour be understood in isolation from the environment. Lorry$_1$ (M), on the motorway, should be distinguished from Lorry$_1$ (T), in town traffic, etc. Anyone who is devising a policy, planning or designing anything, should pay heed to the way he uses words. The various subscripts can be used to help explore the ranges of particular circumstances in which his proposals are valid.

Korzybski also suggests extensional devices that make clear the way in which words lead us to fence off only limited portions of the world and then in an arbitrary way separate *verbally* what cannot be separated *empirically*. One device is simply to conclude a description with 'etc.' to betoken the parts of the picture omitted. Another is to hyphenate words that represent entities which should be considered in conjunction with one another. This is a fruitful device when one is faced with complex behavioural problems; examples encountered in business studies are 'socio–technical' systems, 'man–machine' systems, which, respectively, have yielded valuable insights into organisational behaviour and into the design of working situations. The recent craze for a 'systems approach' to almost everything shows that we recognize a need to correct our linguistic tendency to dissect the world, and instead give greater emphasis to the study of the connectedness of things.

Mathematical extensions of ordinary language

The devices described above help to uncover the tendency of language to lead us into oversimplifying complex problems, and into finding solutions more by verbal habit than by reference to the facts. However, they do not enhance our language sufficiently to enable us to find new ways of describing problems and of solving them. Mathematics can fulfil this role; one reason why it has a valuable place in business and administration is that it takes over where everyday English loses its powers of description and reasoning.

The extensional devices of Korzybski are to be found as normal features of mathematical nomenclature. The use of subscripts and functional notation is commonplace. $L_1(j,t)$ could represent, say, the conditions of $lorry_1$ at place j and time t. In mathematics, functions and sets of equations serve the same purpose as Korzybski's hyphen, but more fully because they specify the nature of the connection instead of merely suggesting that one exists. Relationships do not have to be exact in the familiar numerical sense to be compassed by mathematics. Modern mathematics is much concerned with the characterisation of loose, non-numerical structures that are very widely encountered, even in biological and social applications.

European languages have a tendency to force everything into one of two verbal categories: good/evil, black/white, right/wrong and so on. We have a wealth of prefixes, such as un-, dis-, in-, which convert words into others with an opposite meaning. Statements are easily converted into their negations by inserting 'not'. This linguistic emphasis on dichotomies can be seen in *Roget's Thesaurus* where it is used as a major principle for the classification of words by their meanings; if you look in that book for words that help us to talk about intermediate values you will see that they are less common than words that help us to exaggerate a distinction. If you attempt always to indicate subtle gradations of value, you will have to insert so many additional words and use so many uncommon expressions that your listeners will find you tedious. You will have difficulty avoiding the use of simple dichotomies if you speak in any European language.*

Mathematics can help us overcome these deficiencies in our ordinary language. We can replace the two-valued property by a measurement; instead of two values (good/bad), and a simple comparative relationship (better/worse), a measurement can convey a continuum of possibilities, and far more complex relationships than are expressible in words.† The very idea of constructing a measurement can be a powerful aid to criticism. When a person makes judgements in two-valued terms, one may ask him to indicate more clearly the scale he is using by showing how specific examples would be evaluated on the scale. For example, a teacher in a highly selective school should use this critical technique to remind himself where the children his colleagues call 'dull' would be placed on a scale which includes the full range of abilities.

The two values, 'true' and 'false', which are used to categorise statements, are extended into a full scale by the mathematical concept of probability. It is a concept of the greatest utility for discussing business problems. Whereas ordinary physical objects are clearly defined (you can see where an object is, what colour it is, etc.), the 'objects' of interest to a businessman commonly do not possess clear outlines and un ambiguous properties. To ask 'Where is our market and how big is it?' cannot yield a reply like the answer you would expect to 'Where is our factory and how big is it?' The best we can expect is some reply on the lines of: 'Here is a map which is divided into areas in each of which I have drawn a graph, showing the chances of selling in that area given amounts in a week.' This concept is of a 'thing' very different from an ordinary physical object; the description says not what you will find it to be if you go and look at it, but what its propensity is to behave in various ways if put to the test. For the description of inherently variable phenomena, this is the best we can hope to achieve. Notice that the probability distribution does not indicate an inaccuracy in our knowledge of something exact, but it gives an accurate description of something inherently variable.

Sharing our perceptions of the world

Having examined the difficulties inherent in attaching labels to the

* Not all languages have this in-built two-valued logic. See Whorf's essay: 'Some verbal categories of Hopi'. See also Hayakawa.

† See also pp. 106–108.

'things' we can perceive directly with our senses, we must examine a more difficult problem. How can we ensure that other people are using a label just as we do, even when the label is for an abstract notion that does not correspond to a simple, demonstrable object, property or event.

The simplest form of abstraction is a process of using terms which describe larger and larger classes of things, thus:

John→person→family→tribe→ethnic group→race→mankind.

At a certain level, probably 'tribe', it ceases to be feasible to show anyone an example of the whole 'thing' to which the word refers. Problems of definition increase with the degree of abstraction. To formulate business and administrative problems, we use terms of a fairly high degree of abstraction, for the simple reason that the magnitude of these problems demands the verbal shorthand of abstract words. Therefore, the definition of terms can be an important practical matter for a manager who wants to be sure he is referring to the same things as his colleagues, his customers or people with whom he is negotiating.

Ostensive definition

The most reliable way of ensuring that people use a word in the same way at different times and places is by showing them the object, property, action or relationship being named, preferably using a wide variety of examples. In business, when we need to be absolutely sure of the practical consequences that will flow from our use of terms, this must be the preferred method. Samples of goods, exhibitions, displays, visits, are all parts of the apparatus needed to provide a common framework of direct experience, which is the only sure basis for reliable communication. Likewise, zoos, botanical gardens, nature reserves, museums, demonstrations and replicated experiments provide the solid foundation of *ostensive definition* upon which the empirical sciences are based. Ostensive definition is slow and expensive, but it is the ultimate assurance that we are all using the same words to refer to the same things.

Strictly speaking, ostensive definition does not require the use of words and therefore achieves a degree of independence of language which places it in a category apart. All other forms of definition must indirectly be founded upon an appeal to direct experience, or to the use of ostensively definable terms, if they are to give us equal reassurance that our discourse is factual, rational or objective.

Operational definitions

Other valid definitions are operational. That is, they indicate with

appropriate precision a practical way of obtaining an ostensive definition, or of testing whether or not the word being defined can be said to
refer to something or other. An operational definition is implied if,
for example, I ask what 'majolica' is, and you say that it is 'a kind of
ornamental Italian ceramic with an opaque tin glaze, rather like the
better-known faience or Delft pottery'. Given such a definition, there
should be little difficulty in finding a specimen of the ware in an
appropriate place, such as the Victoria and Albert Museum in London.
The detail and precision of the definition should depend upon the
purpose it is to serve.

Operational definition can be taken to include the other standard
methods of constructing definitions. *Genus and differentia* is the technique of naming first a class which contains the objects being defined,
and then listing characteristics which differentiate such objects from
the larger class or genus; e.g. a ruminant=a mammal (genus) that is
vegetarian, grazes and chews its cud (differentia).

Definition by *extension* is simply a process of listing the members of a
class of things called by the word being defined, e.g. 'Member of E.E.C.
in 1970'=France or Germany or Italy or Belgium or Holland or
Luxembourg. The method of *defining by intension* uses a list of
properties which must be exhibited by the object whose name is being
defined, e.g. 'a soft, blue-grey metallic substance of specific gravity
between 11·34 and 11·37 at 4°C, coefficient of expansion $3·7 \times 10^{-5}$,
specific heat 0·0303 at 0°C, melting point 325°C, boiling point 1,150°C,
not attacked by weak acids=lead'.

It should be noticed that, although operational definition has its
roots in ostensive definition, it can be used to define things which are
only *in principle* capable of ostensive definition. Classes of objects may
be described operationally even though they are too vast ever to be
displayed. Processes can be set down in operational form that are too
expensive, too unpleasant or dangerous to realise just for the sake of
making a definition clear, but which require discussion (e.g. the motorway box in London, bacteriological warfare . . .). Such matters may be
far removed from our concrete experience, but they are carefully linked
to it in being realisable in principle.

Our present-day ability to use operational definition so widely and
reliably is a consequence of the growth of science, which furnishes us
with a vocabulary for describing operational procedures, a wealth of
techniques for measurement, commonly available instruments that have
been calibrated to some standard, and also a large number of people
who understand and can apply these techniques. This evolution in our
use of scientific language as a normal part of our culture is very
important in the organisational and commercial revolution which we

are currently experiencing. Increasingly, elaborate artefacts are being procured when they exist only at the design stage. To the piecemeal solution of complex social and administrative problems is being added a 'systems approach', whereby comprehensive solutions to vast problems are planned and 'tested' theoretically before any action is taken. In these circumstances, when we wish to commit vast resources on the basis of a design or a systems proposal, we must be especially sure of the link between the drawings, the formulas and the language used and the supposed 'real' artefact or system we wish to procure or construct. One aspect of this is the problem of definition.

Definition by context

Many abstract words, however, cannot be given an ostensive definition. Many objects, operations and properties that we refer to in our discussion of the world can never be directly sensed, even in principle or in part. Neither ostensive definition nor operational definition will serve these theoretical words. They can only be defined within the context of other words or symbols.

The language of the businessman, as much as the language of the scientist, abounds with theoretical terms such as 'potential demand', 'depreciation', 'mobility of labour', 'bargaining power', 'price trend'. These are 'entities' which cannot be observed directly; we understand them because they are used in the logical context of statements with other, more directly meaningful words. They may be names given to numbers which are mathematically related to directly measurable quantities. Obvious examples are furnished by the physical sciences: 'momentum', 'energy', 'absolute zero' are not capable of ostensive definition; they are defined by their use within the framework of the laws of mechanics and thermodynamics. In some cases it is possible to use the laws to derive methods for calculating approximations to the theoretical 'entities' in particular circumstances. These approximations are operationally definable, but they can be very clumsy to use. For example, in economics, elasticity of demand may be defined as

$$\frac{\text{(the fractional change in demand)}}{\text{(the fractional change in price)}}$$

This can be defined operationally by using four observable variables:

old demand,   old price
new demand,   new price

and it makes sense only to talk of the elasticity over a *range of prices*.

Economic theory which uses this concept can be formulated much more simply by assuming a 'mythical' elasticity of demand which exists at every *exact price*.

The virtue of theoretical terms is that they enable us to describe complex phenomena with much greater economy, by enunciating simple, general laws about how events occur.

In the natural sciences, these very general, abstract, theoretical terms present relatively few problems, compared with those used in the social sciences. The possibility of using empirical techniques makes it comparatively easy to define most of the vocabulary used in physics, chemistry, biology, etc., by ostensive or operational methods. The theoretical terms used in these sciences are embodied in laws which can be used to predict events capable of observation. The validity of the laws is then open to test by an objective, empirical process. In the social sciences, this formulation of empirically testable hypotheses is difficult to achieve. Consequently, it is difficult to impart to the theoretical terms used in the social sciences the same kind of *semantic standing* as to those used in the physical sciences.

Technical decisions can be discussed in language derived from the natural sciences, but managerial decisions call for language more appropriate to the social sciences. However, it is seldom that managers use language even with the kind of precision that is attainable in the social sciences. They may use the same abstract theoretical terms, but they often employ them with more affective than denotative signification. Decision-making would be more objective if the critical analysis appropriate to the social sciences were more often used. The information specialist should employ the same critical methods when making design decisions.

Testing the precision of language

There is no harm in using language or mathematical symbols with the utmost lack of rigour, for example as an aid to the imagination, provided that we are critically aware of what we are doing. There are some simple, practical aids to remind us when critical tests must be applied. For example, Korzybski suggests the device of putting quotation marks round what he calls 'elementalistic and metaphysical terms [that are] not to be trusted'. A slight enlargement of scope of the rule can be made by suggesting that quotation marks should enclose any word which is not clearly defined, until the definition is provided. This should readily draw attention to a host of problems which need to be tackled.

If we are anxious to have facts to work with, then only the admissible methods of definition discussed above can be used. Ostensive definition might be invoked if you can go and see whatever is being discussed (the 'hazard', or the 'site' in, say, a discussion about safety in a factory), but the less costly operational definition will be more likely to serve your purpose. Definition through a logical or mathematical context is less likely to be found in business or administrative discussions because, at the present time, we possess few extensive, deductive theories which could harbour sound theoretical terms. As you succeed in tracing a definition for each term, remove the quotation marks, and mark it thus: profit$_{OST}$ (if ostensively it rattles in your pocket), profit$_{OP}$ (if operationally it can be derived by a fairly explicit sequence of calculations), or profit$_{LOG}$ (if logically it is defined, say, as a residue from some theoretical income and some theoretical expenditure).

Care must also be taken to recognise when different occurrences of a term refer to different things. In conversation, this semantic shift is readily accomplished. As a precaution, denote the different referents by attaching distinguishing letters to the otherwise deceptively identical words: profit$_A$ (retail margin), profit$_B$ (gross trading profit), profit$_C$ (allowing for depreciation, using assumption x), profit$_D$ (same but using assumption y), profit$_E$ (allowing for notional interest paid to shareholders at market rates). It is surprising how many people in business are thrown by the possibility of multiple definitions for terms such as 'profit', which they employ frequently with the confidence that accompanies any well-established verbal habit.*

It is useful to work in the opposite direction also, and equate those terms which are synonymous but have been introduced to relieve monotony of expression, or, less excusably, for their emotive weight. Words with powerful emotive connotations are a major hazard. A simple device is to underline them and substitute a neutral synonym. A related problem, and one that is particularly difficult to recognise, is the tendency we have to treat problems in an either/or two-valued manner. The corrective, as suggested earlier, is to assign a scale of measurements linking the extremes.†

Finally, words without an objective referent must be sought out and nailed to the wall where they can be seen for what they are: mere vocalisations or marks on paper, or vehicles for emotive messages purporting to be a statement of fact or clear instructions. Some managerial tasks (examples are setting objectives and negotiating) demand great care in using language. It is no good asking for 'no demarcation disputes' as a condition in a productivity deal, without being prepared to give this vague and inherently emotive phrase an

---

* For an interesting discussion of the problems of defining 'profit', see Joel Dean, *Managerial Economics*.

† See Hayakawa, *Language in Thought and Action*.

exact, *operational definition.* Until this has been done, one may charitably assume that the parties in the dispute know what they, themselves, are talking about when they use this phrase, although their meanings differ; less charitably one may guess that the phrase is being used as an emotional token. Similarly, if you cannot be sure of a general agreement about objectives, it can be risky to commission a manager or an organisation to perform a task unless you are prepared to give an operationally testable standard of performance.

Language for a purpose

Language which can meet the tests prescribed above for deciding whether its terms are properly defined has a special standing. The tests provide us with a kind of linguistic filter, permeable only to a limited type of information, which experience has proved appropriate for the accurate description of the physical world, in a manner that enables us to predict its behaviour and to control or coordinate widely separated events. Not all the information we employ can satisfy these stringent tests. The historian or the critic must use language that is intrinsically incapable of passing the stricter scientific tests; the manager faced with a problem, such as who embezzled the funds, can only test the information submitted as evidence in the same way as a historian, whilst any discussions with his colleagues about degrees of guilt, or the justice of one course of action compared with another, must be couched in the evaluative language of the critic. The problem is to ensure that, in our business communications, we employ information that satisfies criteria of validity that fit our purpose. Failure to do this is sometimes deliberate and is intended to deceive other people but, more often than not, it is unintentional, unnoticed and deceives the user also.

Lest there be a misunderstanding, let it be re-emphasised that information which cannot pass various rigorous tests for designative significance should not be dismissed as nonsense, but recognised as perhaps serving a different purpose: an appraisive or prescriptive function. An organisation must be as permeable to expressions of human values as it is to facts; this chapter has tried to emphasise the need to distinguish between them so that information can indeed inform, and not just obscure and mislead.

8 The General and the Particular

*Thus science must begin with myths, and with the criticism of myths;
neither with the collection of observations, nor with the invention of
experiments, but with the critical discussion of myths and of magical
techniques and practices. The scientific tradition is distinguished
from the pre-scientific tradition in having two layers. Like the latter,
it passes on its theories; but it also passes on a critical attitude
towards them.*

Popper, *Conjectures and Refutations*

The formation of general concepts seems to be a necessary part of man's
nature. On a behavioural level it seems also to be true of other animals.
Rats, cats and people, we all develop reflexes which are generalised so
that, if we are shown a number of square objects and subjected simultaneously to electric shocks, we begin to exhibit a distaste for anything
in which 'squareness' can be discerned, not just for the original stimuli.
Only by being able to form generalised behaviour patterns are we able
to learn how to cope with experiences that are not exact replicas of
earlier events. Experience in a particular business will enable a man to
acquire a set of responses appropriate to the typical problems of that
business. Fortunately we are not restricted to acquiring such knowledge
through experience; using language we can formulate generalisations
about the world and how it functions, and about people and what they
should do in various circumstances. By means of theoretical descriptions, and through the use of general principles of behaviour,
we can share the experiences of other members of society. But to
avoid being led astray by general statements we must subject them to
severe scrutiny.

As we saw in the previous chapter, words can be used as verbal
gestures to point to things, but to say anything with our verbal gestures
we must perform one of those little verbal pantomimes that we call
'statements', 'propositions', 'hypotheses', or, on a grander scale, 'theories'.
The interpretations of words must be stable; they are stereotyped
gestures, rooted in the social process of communication, uniform for a
particular society, and determining the way its members perceive objects
in the world around them. Given these reliable components of language,
we are able to construct a limitless variety of descriptions of real or

imaginary worlds. The reliable, factual use of the verbal components can only be guaranteed by subjecting them to the kind of test described in the previous chapter; now, in this chapter we shall examine the construction and testing of statements.

Conjectures

All verbal knowledge depends upon our conjecturing statements. This linking of perceptions to symbols Peirce calls 'abduction', a creative stage of reasoning which must precede all inductive and deductive argument. In the growth of scientific knowledge, abduction is the process of describing the world in new ways that summarise our knowledge more succinctly than before, and simultaneously point to new ways of observing things, new activities to pursue, new ways of discriminating among our experiences.

It is customary to think of information reaching us through our senses from some external 'real world'. It is as well to remember that our picture of the external world can be overturned by the mental process of restructuring the patterns imposed upon the data collected by our senses. This is often illustrated by those well-known ambiguous pictures such as fig. 6.

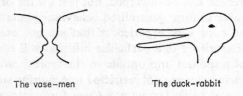

The vase–men   The duck–rabbit

Fig. 6. Ambiguous pictures.

A history of ideas reveals the same human ability to impose quite different patterns upon data. The history of science is rich in accounts of conceptual leaps from one pattern to another more comprehensive and more satisfying than the first; science even provides a well-known example of the ambiguous picture: the corpuscular and the wave theories of light, both of which are supported by experiment – if you look for corpuscles you will find corpuscles, and if you look for waves you will find waves – just like looking at one of the pictures in the figure. We should be prepared to discover that problems in business and administration are open to varied and radically different formulations, and we should be careful not to demand only one correct explanation. It may be possible to find ways of discriminating between rival explanations, and this will be a subject examined at length in this chapter, but it is equally important to have a choice of explanations.

New ideas as an input to a business system

In order to make a decision, we must choose from the courses of action we can conceive; to design a complex business or administrative system, or to establish a plan for urban development, are tasks calling for complex sequences of decisions, choosing from among the envisaged systems or plans. Given a set of alternatives, there are often ways of making this choice rationally, bringing accounting, economics and operational research to bear upon the problem. People are very happy once they are on such well-trodden ground, but they are often surprisingly reluctant to devote themselves to conjecturing a wide range of alternative courses of action, although this is the necessary, imaginative preliminary to any rational decision-making. New ideas constitute a necessary input to any decision process, and we may think of them as a type of information radically different from the usual kind of business information derived from recorded data by some rational process.

Innovation gone mad is harmful to any organisation and to society at large. Nevertheless the suppression of a person's creative ability diminishes the chance of his solving the problems, or of performing effectively the tasks entrusted to him. We need better means of employing human inventiveness in a controlled manner. At present we seem to have the worst of both worlds.

On the one hand, innovations in routine work are suppressed or not encouraged. How many shop-floor workers would exert themselves to find better ways of doing a job? How many graduates recruited by business and administration discover that 'thinking' tends to be regarded as synonymous with 'sleeping', whilst any activity is preferable provided that it is reasonably conspicuous? People recruited for their creative abilities – designers, copy-writers, consultants in various fields of management science – tend to be organised in groups that can be isolated and readily ignored. How many managers, civil servants or local government officers are appointed for their creative abilities? Creativeness is difficult to measure or to test in examinations, unlike conformity; perhaps that is why it is not given its due weight.

On the other hand, we seem capable of initiating technological innovations which are capable of overwhelming the machinery by which society should be controlling them. Organisations lack the means of discussing plans in their early stages. In administrative affairs this results in technological juggernauts being foisted upon us all, we are then invited to comment on details of the colours in which they are painted before we immolate ourselves beneath their wheels; we need to open out the creative phases of planning; instead we are forced to await the promulgation of detailed plans linked to political commitments which ensure their rigidity.

As it becomes cheaper to calculate the feasibility of any new proposal and to communicate with those who may be affected, information technology will enable us to meet the growing demand for a wider involvement in decision-making, but in consequence organisations will have to change their style. On the lowest level judicious job enlargement will replace the division of labour to the limits of sterility. On the grand scale, major public investment will not progress from secret planning through massive propaganda but through a cycle of well-defined phases in which, in their turn, creative contributions and critical appraisals will be welcomed. Although rigid adherence to plan or rule may be imperative at times, new ideas need not be suppressed if appropriate times, places and channels of communication are organised. Politics and business will change as the community becomes less willing to acquiesce in plans flowing from superior fountains; they will change too as electronic communications and computing power remove the excuses for restricting consultations and ignoring alternatives.

Alternatives, conjectures, hypotheses, theories – call them what you will – these are the raw materials from which decisions are made and new worlds constructed. As 'objects' they are constructed from words, numbers and other signs, so we may criticise them by enquiring into their validity as descriptions; this is another semantic problem. But, before continuing to review the critical apparatus which can be used to judge statements, we should examine some of the effects that words and other signs can have upon the creative process itself.

Language in decision-making

Planning, designing systems and making decisions, are activities based on symbols. In the first place, they require the construction of hypothetical artefacts or conjectured courses of action. Only when this abductive process is complete can the deductive and inductive procedures of the 'scientific' decision-maker be employed. There is no point in talking about 'utilities', 'costs', 'probabilities', 'optimisation' or 'expected returns' until the descriptive framework has been drawn. In our eagerness to get on to the familiar ground of rational decision-making, where we can enjoy the routines of the accountant, or the operational researcher, we often fail to examine the mechanics of the essential phase of abductive reasoning that must come first.

From a linguistic point of view, decision-making and design call for the manipulation of abstract terms, and the gradual descent of a ladder of abstraction, as the plan or design is specified in more and more detail until, finally, the words, numbers and drawings are realised in actions or manufactured into a physical form. The processes of abstraction and the tests applied to definitions of abstract terms, which were described in the previous chapter, must function in reverse. For example, designing a commercial information system may entail considering a series of functions at different levels of abstraction, see fig. 7. A function at one level must be analysed into a group of interrelated functions at a lower, more concrete, level until, after several iterations, the functions define unambiguous tasks which can be given to people, or processes which can be performed by machines. At any stage, the analysis may reveal inconsistency or infeasibility, and so force the designer back to a higher level of analysis.

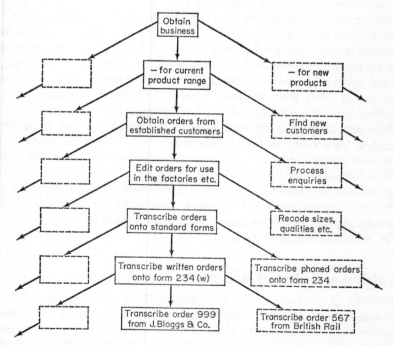

Fig. 7. Descending a ladder of abstraction in the 'top-down' design of an information system.

The kind of problem that is being examined at any stage is clearly closely related to the degree of abstraction in the language used to discuss it. The solving of management problems, or the designing of organisational information systems, calls for skill in choosing the appropriate level of abstraction, and being able to think in a sustained way at that level.

Sometimes problems cannot be solved effectively at one level without reformulating them in terms of the next higher level. Always a change contemplated at one level implies that there is an opportunity to find a more effective solution by treating it in the context of a problem formulated at the next higher level. Obviously one must avoid turning every minor change into an excuse for a review of everything at the highest level, but we may also err in the other direction by being blind to the wider implications of changes being made. The second kind of error too often accompanies the introduction of computers; managers and administrators often regard them as merely improved office machines, when, in fact, they make possible entirely different ways of conducting business.

We often try to solve a problem that needs to be tackled in fairly abstract terms by analysis at too detailed a level. For example, in fig. 7 on the 4th level up, the problem of how to edit orders needs to be examined in terms of why the editing is done, without any reference being made to the physical means of doing so – whether by clerk using hand-written documents or by computer using magnetic tapes. As soon as one descends from the more abstract to the more concrete, either deliberately or by default, one has made part of the decision. To be deliberate about this decision process, the problem solver must first analyse his problem at the more abstract level: within this framework he must conjecture a variety of possible solutions; only after this stage of abductive reasoning can he enter the more concrete level of analysis by making a rational choice among the alternatives. His opportunity to choose is pre-empted if he is unable to think about or discuss the problem in abstract terms, because he will force himself to examine only a few specific concrete proposals.

Critical appraisal of statements

In order to use the powerful abstractions of words and mathematics, it is necessary constantly to assess one's statements to be sure that they can be translated into more concrete terms. A decision may be discussed in very abstract terms, or a design problem may be stated in terms of some high-level objective. For an effective decision to be taken or a feasible design to be produced, we must be able to find a route from the high peak of abstraction down to the firm ground where our ideas can be finally translated into actions. Only factual statements that can withstand a number of tests can serve as footholds along the route.

There will be many descents to choose from, and we shall use value judgements and prescriptive information to guide our choice of route. Even the illogical, vague or ambiguous statements which we reject on the way may serve a purpose in turning our step in a new direction. In the process of innovation or abductive reasoning it is difficult to dismiss even the most insecure and speculative statement as worthless.

A great deal of management and organisation theory can only be regarded as speculation. Some of the attempts to unify science through 'general systems theory' and 'cybernetics' seem to constitute metaphysical systems rather than genuine bodies of science. Nevertheless, by causing him to look at problems in quite new ways, these speculative ideas can assist the decision-maker and designer. It is important to recognise that new ideas are not all derived by logic from what we learn in the laboratory, but often come from excursions into cloud-cuckoo land; as long as you can return with a hypothesis that will not evaporate under the glare of critical appraisal, you will have what you need – new insight into your problem.

We need some canon of critical principles to enable us to appraise the hypotheses, conjectures, supposed statements of fact, the platitudes, the dogma and all the other kinds of statements which go to form a discussion about a business problem. The scientist is fortunate because philosophers have explored the problem of what constitutes firmly-based scientific knowledge. Their methods may also be applied to business problems, provided there is time to be scientific, and provided that the problem can be resolved by appeal to facts rather than people's values.

Let us now examine some ways of testing supposedly factual statements. This is a problem of scientific philosophy. The manager should also subject his evaluative and prescriptive information to the criticism of ethics and aesthetics. This other side of the problem will not be attempted here.

Logical consistency

The most important test of any theory in science is that it should be consistent within itself and with the stated facts. The same critical rule is clearly valuable to the business decision-maker. Whereas the scientist is mainly concerned with statements describing the world as it is, the decision-maker is also vitally concerned with statements describing actions that have never yet been performed, and artefacts that have never yet been constructed. So, for the decision-maker, the test of logical consistency operates both to ensure that his deliberations are grounded upon a consistent description of the state of affairs with which he is dealing and also that he does not talk about performing sets of actions that are incompatible with one another. Recognising logical inconsistencies in any complex practical problem can be difficult, especially when many different people are contributing towards the description of such a problem, say the design of a new factory.

One of the major functions of mathematical models used in operational research and systems analysis is to reveal logical inconsistencies in complex designs, decisions, rules or policies. This is why such techniques as network planning or critical-path planning have been so widely adopted in the management of complex development or construction projects: by making explicit the logical constraints upon the sequencing of the thousands of individual tasks that contribute towards a project, such as the building of an underground railway, it is possible to reduce the chance of issuing instructions that are infeasible.

The decision-maker usually subjects the logical compatibility of various hypotheses to a purely verbal criticism. For example, he may point out the non-sense of asking for the separate optimisation of each of several interdependent factors, so that (a) shorter time to repair machines, (b) reduced capital expenditure on maintenance stores and (c) fewer maintenance staff, may be revealed as the incompatible local aims of, respectively, works manager, chief accountant and chief engineer. Logical incompatibilities among policies such as these are obvious when expressed in a unified statement, but business problems are found not on one person's desk but diffused throughout an organisation. One of the most important tasks of operational research or systems analysis in a company or other organisation should be the construction of models which display the relationships between a company's policies, and make explicit the constraints placed upon their execution by the nature and limitations of the company's resources. This will expose inconsistencies so that they may more readily be resolved.

The recognition of illogicalities in a framework of decision-making and their resolution can be very difficult if purely verbal analysis is employed. Mathematical formulations or the use of schematic diagrams with a mathematical foundation are especially valuable for revealing complex interrelationships which are either obscure or impossible to express in prose.*

The *logical test* is valuable because it rules out some, but not all, kinds of inadequacy in the descriptive framework adopted in decision-making. It is a serious but common error to assume that logical consistency is not only necessary but sufficient. A great deal of what passes today for management science consists of models that bear some superficial resemblance to organisational problems; in themselves they may be

---

* For an example see the chapter on Logic and Organisation.

logically perfect and, hence, constitute satisfactory examples of applied mathematics, but, in a practical situation, they must pass far more tests than their own logical self-consistency before they attain a status exceeding that of a well-constructed parlour game. The deficiency of the logical test is that it is concerned only with the words and other symbols used in stating the facts and the hypotheses, and has nothing to do with the semantic problems of ensuring a reliable connection between those symbols and the events or objects which they purport to describe.

Occam's Razor

A critical principle of a different, almost of an aesthetic kind, is known as Occam's Razor. Occam was a Franciscan scholastic who lived between 1290 and 1350. He enunciated the maxim: 'It is vain to do with more what can be done with fewer.' In other words, given two explanations or descriptions of equal generality, the simpler is preferable, that is, the one which introduces fewer hypothetical abstractions or assumptions. Why should such a rule be valuable? The maxim that advises us to trim our conjectures or hypotheses into the most economical shape is probably worth following for several reasons.

Firstly, economy and simplicity enhance the informative power of a description or theory, because we may hold only a limited number of ideas in our mind at one time. General hypotheses serve to codify our knowledge of the world, and the more compact that code is, the more clearly in focus is our intellectual view of a problem.

Secondly, simplicity in a theory normally carries with it simplicity of application. A classical example is the Copernican model of the universe: it is simpler to understand the earth orbiting the sun, and to explain the diurnal motion of the sun as the rotation of the earth about a N–S axis, than to make sense of the earlier theory that the sun travels round the earth each day; consequently, the Copernican model provides a far simpler basis for astronomical calculations. On a more humdrum level, one may compare the present-day use of a simple algebraic formula for tax calculations replacing acres of tables. If, in a business, a pricing schedule is studied closely, perhaps with a view to using a computer to make price quotations more quickly, it is normal to find a system of elaborate tables and lists of special cases, a large part of which can usually be replaced by a relatively simple mathematical formula. Also, to change the pricing schedule based upon a formula is easy and tables, if required, can be obtained automatically from the formula.

Thirdly, Occam's Razor ensures that the test of logical consistency is fairly stringent. Without such a requirement of simplicity and economy, it is possible to stretch any theory or description, explaining any awkward facts by making endless ad hoc extensions to the original logical framework in order to do so. Thus to preserve the theory that fire is one of the elements, phlogiston had to be postulated, and then, to account for the products of combustion being heavier than the original material, phlogiston had to be given not weight but the opposite, 'levity', and so on. A similar accretion of ad hoc ways of accounting for exceptions is typical in any body of rules and regulations or laws; eventually the procedure becomes too elaborate for clear decisions to be arrived at, and a sweeping reorganisation becomes imperative. This may involve employing new basic principles.

Fourthly, it is possible to subject the validity of a simpler description to more stringent tests. The more hypothetical entities that are introduced into an explanation, or the more parameters that may be adjusted in a model, the easier it is to make them fit *any* actual observations. But this brings us to our next criterion for judging hypotheses.

Testability

The touchstone of scientific statements is that they can be tested empirically. The two criteria mentioned above, logical self-consistency and economy of formulation, do not help us to determine under what conditions statements can be subjected to empirical tests. General statements, which make an assertion about every event or object of a certain kind, are not capable of being tested empirically. Only particular instances of them can be tested. To test a general statement it must be possible to deduce from it particular statements which can be tested, and not every particular statement is testable.

First, a practical requirement must be established. Statements, to be capable of being tested by observation, have to fulfil some very stringent conditions. *They must refer unambiguously to particular events and objects which are large enough in scale and duration to activate our senses, directly or through instruments, at a location in time and space sufficiently well-defined for us to be sure that we have a clear positive or negative result to our enquiry.* Testable statements are, therefore, particular statements in a very strong sense.

Secondly, the logical principle of *falsifiability* must be noted. Evidence may reveal a general statement to be false but it can never prove it is true. This is so because it is possible, by correct logical reasoning, to deduce from a true statement only true conclusions, but from a false premise conclusions may be deduced that are both false and true (e.g. $3 > 4$ is a false statement but given also the statement $4 > 2$, we may conclude that $3 > 2$, which is true enough). This means that, if we are able to demonstrate that a conclusion is false, there can be no doubt that at least one of our premises is false, but that, if our conclusion is true, we are still unable to decide whether our premises are true or false.

Now, theories are general statements which cannot themselves be tested directly according to the first practical requirement laid down above. But generalisations taken together with accepted facts enable us to deduce particular, testable statements. Only if this can be done, can the generalisations be granted scientific status.

These are the requirements of testability.* They do not enable a theory to be proved true, but only expose it to the risk of being proved false. To illustrate this, take a theory that would not pass this test: astrology. The astrological rules and tables may be formulated in a logically consistent and an economical manner (so that they pass the earlier tests for hypotheses) but their predictions, the horoscopes, fail to satisfy the conditions given above, because they are ambiguous and because they fail to specify, precisely enough, a time and place for making an observation which will in any way serve as a test. Any hypothesis which, by such devices, can avoid being falsified does not qualify to be called scientific or factual. Of course, events do occur in conformity with horoscopes, and people take these events as empirical support for astrology, and, because of these successes, they fail to abandon the theory when its predictions are falsified by experience. But, by the logical principle enunciated above, it does not matter how many observations you can fit into the theoretical framework; only a false prediction gives a clear decision. It is not only astrology that survives by such means, but also a great deal of folklore and pseudo-science current among men of finance, business and politics, especially where the harder facts go counter to the prejudices they cherish.

So, being unable to *prove* generalities, we must conclude that the only way of convincing ourselves of their worthiness is to subject them to the risk of being revealed as false. The most compelling theories are those which, on account of their boldness, expose themselves most fully to these risks and yet survive. If a theory can predict an event which, in the absence of the theory, would seem to be very unlikely, then it exposes itself to a severe test indeed. If it passes the test, then it commends itself to our approval more strongly than a relatively platitudinous generalisation which is unable to predict with confidence anything that would be regarded as surprising. In the physical sciences, there are many instances of theories which have led to predictions of remarkable events which have nevertheless been supported by observation: Newton's mechanics united under one descriptive generality both terrestrial and celestial motions: Einstein's Theory of Relativity predicted a larger deflection of

* For a thorough discussion see Sir K. R. Popper, *The Logic of Scientific Discovery* and *Conjectures and Refutations*.

light by a heavy body than otherwise expected, and this was confirmed by observations of stars which were near to the sun during a solar eclipse; the same theory also predicted that particles of matter would increase in weight with increasing speed – a strange idea but one confirmed by observation. Organisational decision-makers can apply tests of logical consistency and economy of formulation to their hypotheses but stringent empirical testing of the kind used in the natural sciences is often impossible.

Objectivity of tests

A further criterion which we might impose upon general statements is that, when they are subjected to empirical testing, the test procedures and the criteria for judging the evidence should be as objective as possible. Objectivity is increased by making the evidence more independent of human judgement, although, of course, we can never, ultimately, exclude judgement by someone. Perhaps the most objective tests are those which employ well-constructed thoroughly tested instruments for making the observations, and a mechanical procedure for judging the acceptability of the evidence. This is common enough in the physical sciences. Measurement itself is a process open to critical appraisal and it will be considered in chapter 9.

In management, administration and the social sciences, it is seldom possible to thrust the subjective aspects of evidence into the background by employing instruments, but it is possible to achieve a degree of independence of individual human judgement by combining the judgements of a group of people; this may be achieved by requiring them to vote or by getting them to reach a consensus in an informal way. An interesting problem arises when we enquire if a group of people can be induced to agree in the face of enough evidence. It is quite possible that any amount of evidence will fail to bring about a reconciliation of opinions, because different people may interpret the evidence in such diverse ways that it serves only to make their differences of opinion greater! (See chapter 12.) On the other hand, they may reach agreement through the mechanism of group norm-formation (chapter 4).

Testing the admissibility of evidence becomes even more difficult when, in addition to judging the facts, it involves judging also the people who report them. But this is the normal state of affairs; we like to see our informant face to face because of the greater opportunity this gives us to estimate his veracity. With historical and legal evidence we must always look for indications of the reliability of the source or witness; this is also true of much information used in business and in the social sciences. Because of the cost and time required to replicate observations in a manner like that which is normal in physical sciences, the manager is forced to act upon hypotheses about which serious doubts must remain. This, however, should never be made an excuse for not subjecting information and assumptions to the most severe tests available in the circumstances.

Universality

The physical sciences are normally able to adopt, as a basis to all theories, the principle of the uniformity of nature. That is to say, a generalisation that forms a part of a theory is hypothesised as true not for one locality but for everywhere and for all time. Naturally, this exposes the general statement to a much wider range of empirical tests than would otherwise be possible. The social sciences may aim to produce theories of a universal kind, but mostly they deal with models that are dependent upon specific local properties of the societies and individuals which they describe. However, nothing is lost by testing social theories in communities outside the limits to which their formulation is expected to apply. It is useful to preserve a distinction between a model and a theory. Local models describe how particular things work, whereas theories are universally general laws which must be combined with particular facts before they can describe any particular observable thing. Managers are usually much more concerned with models than with theories.

In the foregoing sections I have outlined a series of tests that enable statements with special properties to be isolated. Scientific generalisations are those which pass the crucial test, that they permit themselves to be falsified by observation or experiment; factual statements of all kinds are akin to scientific generalisations, but they need not be universal, and they may be open to empirical testing only by forms of evidence that cannot themselves claim the highest degree of objectivity. For example, an auditor who conjectures that a certain former employee of the company has been dishonest cannot normally adduce experimental evidence; he must rely upon reports of transactions, the veracity of which must be judged as an integral part of judging the evidence. Historical, legal or scientific facts all acquire their status because they can pass tests which enable us to say that physical events, directly perceived or reported by other reliable sources, can be used to attest to their truth. It is natural that statements of this kind normally prove to be the most satisfactory basis for dealing with the world of physical happenings.

Analogy – an application

One of the most powerful linguistic devices that the mind can employ is analogy: a verbal model developed for one purpose may be used to represent something quite different, by suggesting a different assignment of terms. Analogy is most useful for conveying ideas about structure. Analogies are built into the language itself; for example, we treat time as an analogue of space, talking of 'length' of time, 'at' an instant, 'through' the night, the 'end' of an hour, an 'interval', 'point' of time, of events 'behind' us and those 'in front of' us, etc. These analogies are so much a matter of 'common sense' that we fail to recognise that we are employing an analogy, and, consequently, unless we are careful, they can reduce the clarity of our thought. A typical example of this is our attempting, in a commonsense way, to look for 'meanings' of words in a manner suggested by their grammatical categories. One can say 'I have changed my mind' just as one says 'I have changed my shirt'. Therefore, arguing by analogy, we say that as I can readily answer the question 'What is a shirt?', I should also be able to answer the question 'What is a mind?' This problem has been treated, at least partially, by the analysis of the problem of definition undertaken in the previous chapter. 'Mind' is not a term used in any testable scientific theory, therefore it fails to attain definition within a rigorously justifiable context on the lines described earlier, but it names a concept which is very useful in everyday conversation. The error is to fail to recognise that everyday discourse often lacks the rigour which is necessary for objective decision-making. We are misled by the use of identical verbal structures; as the syntax is the same, we expect to be able to understand the sentences in the same way. These grammatically imposed analogies are one of the treacherous pitfalls in commonsense language.

Today we are accustomed to using symbols within the rigorous syntax of mathematics. The danger of being misled by mathematics is no less than by words. Modern mathematics has much to do with the study of rigorous analogies – 'isomorphism', 'homomorphism' and other 'mappings' that in special ways preserve structural properties. For example, certain differential equations can be used equally well to describe the vibration of a bridge or the oscillation of an electrical circuit. Powerful analogies like this provide a means of summarising our understanding of many diverse phenomena, a way of codifying our knowledge in a very compact form. In management literature today, there are current some key analogies *apparently* of this kind; one of them is the notion of negative-feedback, and the control cycle in a homeostatic system. No doubt the idea is valuable in guiding our intuition about many organisational problems, but we should be careful to recognise the difference between two kinds of analogy: a *scientific* one between a thermostat and a mathematical description (see fig. 8, which is based on exact assignments of symbols), and a *literary* one between a business control-system

Equations of the system:

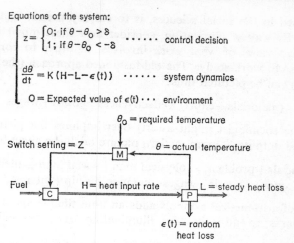

$$z = \begin{cases} 0; & \text{if } \theta - \theta_0 > \delta \\ 1; & \text{if } \theta - \theta_0 < -\delta \end{cases} \quad \cdots \cdots \quad \text{control decision}$$

$$\frac{d\theta}{dt} = K(H - L - \epsilon(t)) \quad \cdots \cdots \quad \text{system dynamics}$$

$$0 = \text{Expected value of } \epsilon(t) \quad \cdots \quad \text{environment}$$

θ_0 = required temperature

Switch setting = Z

θ = actual temperature

Fuel

C — H = heat input rate — P — L = steady heat loss

$\epsilon(t)$ = random heat loss

Fig. 8. A thermostatic control system.

and a thermostat, as in fig. 9. This is suggestive and useful, but it falls far short of passing the test that enables it to qualify as a scientific description. Sometimes an author will go so far as to quote the equations like those for the thermostat as an extension of his literary analogy to make it look more scientific.

With the present fashion for the 'systems approach', we find organisations pictured in flow diagrams like the one in fig. 9, and others used

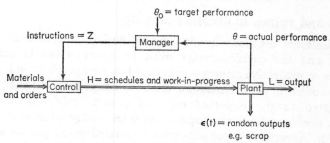

θ_0 = target performance

Instructions = Z

Manager

θ = actual performance

Materials and orders

Control — H = schedules and work-in-progress — Plant — L = output

$\epsilon(t)$ = random outputs e.g. scrap

Fig. 9. The popular analogy between a business and a control system.

in this book. This illustrative device is valuable, but it easily suggests that it represents a kind of technical analysis of organisational behaviour akin to that obtained by an engineer through his use of flow diagrams. This is dangerous because it tempts one to assume that the basic question of assigning referents to the terms used – the problem of definition – has been answered. As a cautionary exercise, take a list of theological and metaphysical terms (good, evil, hope, the infinite . . .), and picture their relationships in a 'systems' diagram! Another device, widely used in the social sciences, is to employ pseudo-mathematical symbols. By way of illustration, consider how these might be used to picture two views of what work involves, in order to contrast two approaches to work-study. 'The old-fashioned approach (the argument might go) can be pictured thus:

$$(\text{materials}+\text{effort})\times\text{effectiveness}=\text{goods}+\text{wages}$$

which (the sociologist might assert) oversimplifies the picture of the inputs and outputs; a more modern picture might be given by:

$$(\text{materials}+\text{problem})\times(\text{physical man}+\text{social man}+\text{intellectual man})=\text{goods}+\text{wages}+\text{companionship}+\text{interest.'}$$

The use of arithmetical symbols adds an unjustifiable air of analytical thoroughness to an otherwise illuminating but essentially literary analogy.

It is not my intention to condemn the use of these descriptive techniques. They are very helpful when one is groping towards solutions to very complex problems, and they help to fill a gap in our language by emphasising the interrelatedness of things. But there is a widespread uncritical acceptance of ideas expressed in this pseudo-scientific way, and an apparent contentment with this level of description too often to be found among people interested in a scientific study of business information systems.

Facts and values in decision-making

Organisational decisions involve the resolution of conflicting judgements, and the decision-maker must be open to the influence of appraisive, evaluative messages. He should also know whose judgements are embodied in those messages. Whereas designative statements may be related to the impartial logic of events, only human beings (unless one introduces the supernatural) can judge what is or is not desirable. Appraisive statements must be related to the goals and satisfactions of human beings. When a decision is being taken affecting individuals or communities of people, and not merely machines, then it is just as important to identify the evaluative information that is relevant to the decision as it is to know the objective facts. This is always so in administration and management, as opposed to theoretical engineering or pure science.

It is often forgotten that, today, technology is concerned with decisions of such a scale that consideration of appraisive information is essential; people who endeavour to force technology forward with a scientific imperative are open to charges of either cupidity or stupidity.

The goal of science is to extend our understanding; science aims to describe the world, not change it. Technology has an entirely different goal; it aims to employ science in remoulding the world. Too often technology is treated as a form of science and, either deliberately or accidentally, technological decision-makers fail to pay enough regard to human value-judgements, although they are just as important as any facts. The design of computer-based information systems too frequently suffers from this error.

It is very common, especially in the creed of *management science*, to fail to recognise the evaluative ingredients in what purports to be an objective and wholly rational aid to decision-making.* The way in which a descriptive framework for a decision is formulated can easily embody unseen evaluative judgements; they may be just as important as any of the explicit criteria used for selecting a desired course of action. In the design of an information system this is also likely to happen. For example, if the Department of Education and Science keeps records of school teachers, employing some limited set of descriptors for the computer record, the choice of those descriptors and their possible values establishes what can be said about those teachers. The selection of this very limited 'language' embodies a judgement of what is important and what is not; it may allow you to describe the unfavourable but not the favourable characteristics of someone; if that is so, he will present a very poor image to anyone reading his record! It is difficult to catalogue books so that their descriptors retain their relevance in a changing environment – how much more difficult must it be to describe people in a rapidly changing profession! A medium-sized business may be permitted such evaluative distortion of the semantic basis for making decisions about its staff; its members can normally hope to influence decisions, because the computer record will be supplemented, in most cases, by their being known directly to the decision-makers, and in the last resort, they can go elsewhere; but in a very large organisation, a system can embody semantic errors that may be difficult to detect and, in a national system, they may be inescapable.

The human sciences face very similar problems. Their theories and models may embody hidden value-judgements. Often the logical complexity of the theoretical edifice may obscure the fact that it is built upon premises of an essentially ethical kind. Economic analysis presents just such a problem.† It assumes a model of human behaviour, inspired by cupidity and hedonism, justifiable when applied to an auction or a stock exchange; it assumes that all values may be reduced to a single variable,

---

* See I. Hoos, *Systems Analysis and Social Policy.*

† I. M. D. Little, *Critique of Welfare Economics.*

money, with the imprecise proviso that this may only be realisable 'in the long term'; other assumptions of a more or less explicitly ethical nature are employed. The resulting theory, closely reasoned and largely mathematical, hides the judgements upon which it is based. This is no criticism of economics. A professional should be aware of the ethical basis of the theory. The danger is not that a theory in economics, or an operational research model, or an accounting scheme, cannot be related to observable events, just as well as a hypothesis in physics, or molecular biology, but that, in the socially descriptive sciences, factual statements can have an evaluative force also, if only because they emphasise some facts and not others. Serious dangers to an organisation or to society can be the consequences of forgetting this dual function. Many people feel that the apparent rationality and objectivity of the methods employed is sufficient to justify solutions to organisational and social problems arrived at by extensions of engineering analysis, management science or systems design. The apparent rationality may only be superficial. It is often supplied by the use of mathematics, which is much in vogue today. Mathematics does make possible the discussion of many complex problems which are quite beyond the compass of our ordinary language, so the vogue for its methods should be encouraged; what must be discouraged, however, is the unwillingness to question the meaning of the mathematics, simply because symbols and numbers are used instead of words. A statement in mathematics, no less than a statement in words, has no semantic standing until it has undergone the kind of critical testing described in this part. Perhaps, as children, we were so bludgeoned into doing our sums as we were told, without asking what the numbers meant, that we are still afraid to ask. The next chapter has the effrontery to do so.

Coda

This book is not suggesting that a manager should go about his tasks applying critical methods to whatever he is told as though he were engaged in a philosophical disputation. He will have to apply his critical acumen without the luxury of much time for reflection. The information specialist, on the other hand, may have to diagnose organisational failures, and he may find it necessary to use the philosopher's methods to expose the misuse of information which has caused them. As organisations and their tasks grow larger, and the people running them are less exposed to the immediate criticism of their decisions by events or by the reaction of a market, then more and more we shall have to rely upon the auditing of the organisation, not only by the methods of accountants but by the critical analysis of information.

Part Four

Semantics of Numerical Information

In business and administration, much of the information that we employ is numerical. We use numbers to refine and extend our purely verbal language by making it more exact and also easier to process. Part Four does for numbers what Part Three did for words.

The numbers used by a manager or an administrator are not the abstract numbers used by the mathematician. They must either be measurements, serving to *describe* aspects of the organisation's resources or environment, or they must be included in policy or instructions, serving to *prescribe* the actions someone should perform. A manager is unwise if he bases any decision upon a numerical value without knowing how its use can be justified. This problem is examined in chapter 9, with the emphasis being given to descriptive numbers or measurements. The following chapter discusses some methods of discovering patterns in aggregates of numerical information.

It is possible to measure items of information. The most important numerical property of a statement is its probability. From measurements of probability we can derive measurements that correspond to various intuitive notions of *amounts of information*. There are several ways of assigning a probability to a statement, and correspondingly many different information measurements. These problems are discussed in two chapters called 'Judging Statements' and 'Reaching Agreement'. The final chapter of this part shows how a number of principles can be invoked in order to demonstrate the objectivity of some kinds of evidence and the statements derived from it.

9 Measurement

Measure all that is measurable and attempt to make measurable that which is not yet so.

Galileo

To many it will always seem better to have measurable progress towards the wrong goals than unmeasurable, and hence uncertain progress towards the right ones.

J. K. Galbraith, *The New Industrial State*

When a theory or a general description has been evolved verbally as a framework within which to account for the properties and behaviour of things, it then becomes possible to introduce refinements by incorporating numerical forms of expression. Nevertheless, Galileo's optimism should be tempered by Galbraith's warning that measurements can over-emphasise what they refer to.

The use of numbers enables us to extend the scope of our vocabulary. Words enable us to identify a few degrees of quantity, and to name some differing shades of each quality. Using numbers, we can give precise meaning to infinitesimal gradations of quantity and quality. This vastly enhanced precision is essential in practical matters of management: for example, when discussing the allocation of resources, we are obliged to talk not just of 'more' or 'less' but of exactly how much more or less.

Precision in describing a single variable is not the only benefit from the use of numbers. It also becomes possible to describe relationships among two or more variables that are quite beyond the compass of words alone.

Often we must cast a description into the form of a mathematical model before it is possible to deduce what it implies in terms of practical consequences. It can prove impossibly difficult to use a verbal model deductively.

These are sufficient reasons for using measurements to describe organisational and social phenomena. We must be prepared to justify any numbers we use by clarifying the relationship between a numerical variable and a 'real thing'. This is another process of semantic criticism, and one which helps to emphasise that mathematical descriptions in social sciences are not necessarily objective. It is the subject of this chapter.

To have complex operations performed, on your behalf, by people remote from you in time or place, usually requires measurement. The essence of organisation is our ability to coordinate work done by many people over a wide area and throughout an extended period of time so that all the individual efforts will contribute their precise components to some major enterprise. Cooperation in industry and commerce, on the scale to which we are accustomed today, would be impossible without measurement.

Achieving action at a distance, without the need constantly to refer to the source of instructions to make sure that the correct actions are being performed, requires a kind of measurement that has a special status; such measurements must be related to properties of things by procedures that can be reproduced by the person who is acting for someone else. However, numbers can be assigned with various degrees of rigour, as will be explained below.

Failures of organisational behaviour stem, not infrequently, from a failure to use measurements correctly. Measurements can be used in meaningless ways, as though they represent something, when careful analysis would reveal their misuse.

The fundamental problems of measurement

Obviously there are practical problems in applying any measuring procedure, and technical problems in devising reliable and sensitive instruments. These problems do not concern us here.

Less obviously, there are these questions of a more fundamental kind: What constitutes an adequate measuring procedure? Are there different kinds of measurements? In what ways do they differ? When can measurements be used meaningfully and when not? What guarantees can be found for any claims to objectivity, universality and consistency in a measuring procedure?

These are the semantic problems of assigning numbers to things; they are like the problems of establishing what words refer to, which were discussed in chapter 7.

New problems arise when we assign numbers instead of words. The numbers themselves are not arbitrary signs; unlike words, they are related to one another in their own right as *members of a system* of signs. Measurement consists not so much of assigning numbers as of assigning a structural property which can be expressed numerically. Semantic errors in the use of measurements can stem from the failure to respect the structural properties of different *scales* of measurement.

This rigorous assignment of numbers according to some well-defined structure or scale cannot always be achieved, especially in many psychological, social and business uses of numerical information; hence there are serious difficulties in justifying the use of numbers in these fields.

Fundamental measurements

Let us consider, first of all, measurements that can be constructed with mathematical rigour. These will provide a basis of comparison for other kinds of measurement that are more difficult to justify.

When a fundamental measurement is made, some very rigorous conditions must be satisfied by the process to be performed.

First: we must identify quite clearly what *things* we are measuring;

Second: these things must be capable of being related to one another in terms of the property being measured and an *operation* must be laid down for determining these relationships;

Third: the resulting structure of relationships among the things being measured must be associated with a system of numbers and arithmetical relationships, and, to do this, a procedure for associating a number with each thing must be precisely specified.

An example will make the import of each of these conditions quite clear.

A scale for measuring the hardness of minerals can be constructed as follows. The first step, defining the substances which can be subjected to the measuring procedure, may be quite simple: there may be seven minerals to be measured, A, B, C, D, E, F and G. The second step is to define the operation which can be applied to test whether mineral X is as hard as mineral Y: this test is to see if Y can scratch a polished surface on a sample of X. If it cannot, the result can be recorded briefly as X→Y (i.e. 'X is as hard as Y'); results of all the comparisons may yield a system of relationships among our seven samples which can be depicted thus:

$$D \rightarrow A \rightarrow E \rightarrow C \rightarrow G \rightarrow F \rightarrow B$$

together with the additional information that *any* mineral cannot be scratched by *any other* mineral that is further to the right in this list. In other words, the relationship 'is harder than' is *transitive* or, in symbols,

$$\text{if } X \rightarrow Y \text{ and } Y \rightarrow Z \text{ then } X \rightarrow Z.$$

This is one of the important properties of the relationships established by the scratching test. There is another. Clearly, it is desirable that our measure of hardness should assign the same number to minerals that are equally hard – that is, if two minerals cannot scratch one another, or if X$\overset{\longleftarrow}{\longrightarrow}$Y, we can classify these minerals together. The system of relationships among our seven samples may then look like this:

$$\left\{ \begin{array}{c} D \\ A \end{array} \right\} \rightsquigarrow \left\{ E \right\} \rightsquigarrow \left\{ \begin{array}{c} C \\ G \end{array} \right\} \rightsquigarrow \left\{ \begin{array}{c} F \\ B \end{array} \right\},$$

where the crinkly-shaped arrow is used to make it clear that it represents a new relationship 'is *definitely* harder than', because it is a relationship which cannot apply in the reverse direction.

The third and final stage in making the measurement is to assign numbers which can mirror this structure. Obviously we can simply assign the same number to all the minerals of equal hardness, and larger numbers to the harder minerals. Thus the assignment of numbers given by the table:

A	B	C	D	E	F	G
4	1	2	4	3	1	2

together with the relationship 'greater than' or $>$ maps the system of empirical relationships on to an identical system of arithmetic relationships.

$$\left\{ \begin{array}{c} D \\ A \end{array} \right\} \rightsquigarrow \left\{ E \right\} \rightsquigarrow \left\{ \begin{array}{c} C \\ G \end{array} \right\} \rightsquigarrow \left\{ \begin{array}{c} F \\ B \end{array} \right\} \quad \text{empirical system}$$

$$\begin{array}{ccccccc} 4, & > & 3 & > & 2, & > & 1 \\ 4 & & & & 2 & & 1 \end{array} \quad \text{numerical system}$$

This is called an ordinal scale of measurement. Notice that this assignment is to a great extent arbitrary. *Any* numbers could have been assigned which preserve the necessary equalities and comparisons. So that,

$$\begin{array}{ccccc} 200 & > & 58 & > & 2 & > & -18 \\ 200 & & & & 2 & & -18 \end{array}$$

would have been quite as justifiable, although a trifle eccentric. It preserves the ordering of the specimens, which is the important structural property of an ordinal scale, and accounts for its name.

All fundamental measurements are made in the same way: by finding a system of empirical relationships among the things being measured, and then finding a numerical system with the same structure. (Strictly speaking, it is also necessary to furnish a mathematical proof of the equivalence of the structures.)

Designative and appraisive measurements

You will have noticed, in the above example, that it was assumed that the scratching test would establish a *transitive* relationship between the specimens, so that, if X cannot scratch Y and Y cannot scratch Z, we can be sure that X will also be unable to scratch Z. If this relationship did not hold, we should not be satisfied with the procedure as a way of measuring hardness. The fact that the relationship is transitive is a very important *objective empirical* property of hardness measured in this way.

Now, contrast the ordinal scale of hardness with a different kind of ordinal scale. Suppose a manager has to assess capital projects for the degree of risk that they involve. He might consider that the best he can do is arrange them on an ordinal scale. To do this he could make comparisons between pairs of projects, placing them in the same risk category if he could not satisfy himself that they differed, otherwise recording his belief that X is definitely more risky than Y by writing X⤳Y. As for the hardness test, a set of seven projects *might* be arranged:

$$\left\{ \begin{matrix} D \\ A \end{matrix} \right\} \rightsquigarrow \left\{ E \right\} \rightsquigarrow \left\{ \begin{matrix} C \\ G \end{matrix} \right\} \rightsquigarrow \left\{ \begin{matrix} F \\ B \end{matrix} \right\}$$

However, there is no guarantee that his pair-wise comparisons will not introduce, fortuitously, a cycle of relationships such as:

$$D \rightsquigarrow E$$
$$\searrow \quad \swarrow$$
$$G$$

which would upset the simple ordering of the projects. It is obviously desirable that this should not happen, because, when we talk about risk, we tend to assume that if A is more risky than B and B is more risky than C then A is also more risky than C. This is the transitive rule again. It can only be made to apply by the manager himself. He must treat any failure of the transitive rule as a mistake on his part, and he must revise his judgements until they conform.

These two examples – the measurements of hardness and of comparative risk – illustrate measurements with differing designative and appraisive significations. The hardness test yields the transitive relationship, which is essential to the construction of an ordinal scale, as an *objective empirical* property of the mineral samples. The risk assessment we feel *ought* to display the same transitive property, which would then justify the use of an ordinal scale, so we *prescribe* the transitive relationship as a *normative rule* to be satisfied by any 'reasonable' judgements of comparative risk. In the case of the hardness test, all the structural properties of the measurements reflect objective, empirical relationships. In the case of risk assessment, the structure of relationships among the capital projects is *prescribed*. The hardness measurement is clearly more designative and the risk assessment more appraisive in signification. The distinction is not absolute, because the hardness test requires some human judgement to be made about whether one mineral has actually succeeded in scratching the other, and because the risk assessment of a company's proposed capital projects would hardly be useful if it were entirely an idiosyncratic judgement on the part of a single manager. (That is not to suggest that other appraisive measurements cannot be peculiar to a single individual.)

The social sciences and business information abound in measurements with a high appraisive signification. Many of their useful structural properties are normatively imposed rules which say that the judgements being made must satisfy such-and-such conditions in order to be considered 'reasonable'. A normative rule is prescriptive but no one will feel obliged to obey it unless he is persuaded to do so by the need to avoid confusion, misunderstanding or some other consequences more directly unpleasant – therein lies the justification of a normative rule, the affective underpinning of its denotative prescription. The discussion of probability in later chapters will illustrate further the gradual application of normative rules to judgements to produce a series of different measurements, ranging from the frankly appraisive to the indisputably objective.

Scales of measurement and their characteristics

In order to explain how a fundamental measurement is defined, the ordinal scale was used by way of illustration. The full range of measuring scales includes such familiar ones as the nominal, ordinal, interval, ratio and absolute scales, which are discussed below.

The *nominal scale* most people would probably not classify as a measurement. It is simply the arbitrary assignment of a unique number to each member of a class of things. Thus the towns: Birmingham, London, Glasgow, Edinburgh and Norwich may be numbered respectively, 1, 2, 3, 4 and 5. The only actual relationship between the towns implied by any arithmetical relationship between the numbers is their individuality and uniqueness.

The *ordinal scale* has been illustrated earlier.

The *interval scale* is familiar in the examples of the Fahrenheit or Centigrade scales of temperature and the scales of time; in business, examples are the various indices of manufacturing costs or changes in demand for a product. All these scales are characterised by the arbitrary choice of any convenient origin for the scale: e.g. 0°F is the freezing point of a mixture of 1 part snow and 1 part salt, 0°C is the freezing point of pure water; many notable years are taken as the bases of different calendars, whilst an arbitrary allocation of overheads and an arbitrary choice of base-year determine the origins of the indices of manufacturing costs and changes in demand. The interval scale also permits the arbitrary choice of the unit of measurement: for the examples mentioned the units would be degrees Fahrenheit or Centigrade; years, minutes or seconds; pounds sterling for units of cost and index 'points' which depend on the weighting constants employed.

The *ratio scale* is less arbitrary than the interval scale, because only the unit of measurement is open to choice. A scale of this kind employs a naturally determined origin. Examples are: length or mass in physics, and volume of production or sales in business.

The *absolute scale* is one based upon enumeration, a simple counting procedure which allows no arbitrary choice of zero or unit.

The consequence of the arbitrariness of all but the absolute scale is that one is quite justified in substituting certain other scales for the one being used. The kind of substitution or transformation which is permissible very largely characterises a type of measurement, and determines how its values can meaningfully be used.

From any *ratio scale*, another equivalent scale may be derived by transforming each value, x, into the value ax. This is simply a change of units such as,

$$x \text{ lb} = 0 \cdot 4536 \, x \text{ kilograms}$$

and a is the constant of proportionality. This is called a *similarity transformation*.

Any *interval scale*, such as a temperature scale, can be replaced by an equivalent scale by changing the unit of measurement *and* shifting the origin of the scale, e.g.

$$x°\text{F} = \left(\frac{5x}{9} - \frac{160}{9}\right)°\text{C}$$

This is called a *linear transformation*.

An *ordinal scale* preserves its essential structure under any transformation that either preserves order or totally inverts it. This is called a *monotonic transformation*.

The *nominal scale*, which is just a coding or naming procedure, may be transformed by any *permutation* and still yield a perfectly valid number assignment.

Notice that each of these scales includes its less arbitrary predecessor as a special case. Starting with an absolute scale, exemplified by counting (e.g. the number of persons in a room, which admits no transformation) we have:

	Scale	Transformation	
least arbitrary	absolute	none valid	} quantities
↑	ratio	similarity	} (extensive)
│	interval	linear	}
↓	ordinal	monotonic	} qualities
most arbitrary	nominal	permutation	} (intensive)

Besides these, there are many other scales of measurement. For example, there are what are called the ordered metrics and bounded interval measures (see Fishburn), which occupy a place intermediate between the ordinal and interval scales.

Sometimes a distinction is made between *extensive* and *intensive* properties. The properties which can be measured on the absolute and the ratio scales are called 'extensive', and the measurements themselves are called *quantities*.

Extensive properties, such as length, mass, heat, population or items sold, are additive. That is, if quantities are associated with two things, there is a meaningful way of forming from them a composite entity, which can also be measured in the same way to yield a quantity equal to the arithmetical sum of the quantities of the components. Intensive properties called *qualities* do not have this characteristic. Interval measurements, e.g. temperature, or ordinal measurements, e.g. hardness, or nominal measurements, e.g. colour, cannot meaningfully be added together.

The less arbitrary a scale of measurements is, the more informative are measurements based upon it, in the sense that more conclusions can be deduced from a set of measurements which are constrained by strict rules. The fact that a quantity, such as length, obeys very stringent rules enables one to deduce that two objects placed end to end in a straight line will measure the same as the sum of the measurement of the parts. A number system which mirrors such important structural relationships among things cannot help but serve to predict and explain. *The immense importance of numerical information stems not from its ability to name things, which it shares with ordinary words, but from its ability to represent, within a formal system of signs, a structure of empirical relationships between things, or a structure of normative relationships governing 'reasonable' judgements.*

Meaningful use of measurements

The ways in which numbers can be manipulated meaningfully are related to this question of what rules they obey, in other words, to what kind of scale they belong. Central to the question of deciding what statements involving measurements are meaningful is the problem of discovering what transformations may be applied to a measuring scale.

To illustrate this, consider the statements:

(a) 'This ingot weighs twice as much as that.'
(b) 'The temperature of this ingot is twice the temperature of that.'

In symbols:

(a) $w_1 = 2w_2$
(b) $t_1 = 2t_2$

Now apply a simple test of meaningfulness to these statements: if the statement remains true when any permissible transformation is applied to the scale, then it is meaningful, otherwise it is meaningless. For the weight scale, the general similarity transformation $w = aw'$ gives

$$\text{(a') } aw_1' = 2aw_2'$$

which reduces again to $w_1' = 2w_2'$.

So (a) is always true when (a') is true. Hence (a) may be deemed meaningful in the above sense.

For temperature, a linear transformation is permitted.* The general transformation $t = gt' + h$ gives

$$\text{(b') } gt_1' + h = 2(gt_2' + h)$$

or
$$t_1' = 2t_2' + h/g$$

which implies, if (b) and (b') are both true, that

$$h/g = 0,$$

a statement which is false in general (in particular $h = -\frac{160}{9}$ for the transformation from °F to °C). Hence (b) is a meaningless or inadmissible statement.

It is correct to say that, if we are told that the temperature of the first ingot is 800°C, we may deduce that the temperature of the second is 400°C using the given statement, but this deduction can be made, not because of the property, *temperature*, of the ingots, but on account of a purely fortuitous choice of origin and unit of measurement; it depends upon arithmetical properties of the symbols we happen to be using that are quite unrelated to the objects we are talking about.

This misuse of measurement is common in business, not surprisingly, because of the plethora of data which must be used, in circumstances that do not normally permit the time for close scrutiny of all the

---

* Unless we are using an absolute, thermodynamic scale which only permits a similarity transformation.

assumptions underlying the measuring processes by which they are derived. Arbitrary choice of origin or unit of measurement is quite satisfactory, provided that everyone sticks to the same arbitrary choice. Such standardisation may be achieved in one company; however, in such matters as international comparisons of statistics, or in comparisons of company accounts published in this country, lack of standardisation in measurement makes meaningful statements involving such figures difficult to formulate. For example, it is reported that one company calculated its return on capital employed in nine ways, all different, but all acceptable legally; the results ranged from 8 per cent to 39·8 per cent.*

The commonest causes of such errors are the arbitrary choice of origin on a linear scale (e.g. through allocation of overheads by an arbitrary rule) and the use of an ordinal scale as though it were an interval or even-ratio scale.

Justification for fundamental and 'derived' measurements

The most semantically respectable measurements are those based upon the kind of rigorous procedures outlined above. Their justification is partly ensured by the procedures themselves. The most important feature is that an empirical or a normative structure is imposed upon the class of things being measured, by means of comparisons that are defined *directly* in terms of the property which is being measured, and these comparisons are made by someone who himself observes the property exhibited by the things being measured; that is to say, no instruments are needed. These conditions ensure that the observer has direct control over the measuring procedure.

In addition to the fundamental measurements, we employ many *derived measurements*. These are arrived at from fundamental measurements via some arithmetical operation. For example

$$\text{density} = \frac{\text{mass}}{\text{volume}}$$

In semantic standing, the derived measurements are one stage removed from the direct experience which supports the fundamental measurements. The step is a simple, secure one, requiring only a formal manipulation of the fundamental measurements, so there is no difficulty in justifying derived measurements. Some additional caution, however, must be exerted to make sure that derived measurements are not used meaninglessly, in the sense discussed above, because their legitimate transformations are usually more complicated.

* *Published Accounts – your yardstick of performance*, Centre for Interfirm Comparison, 1969.

Instruments that simulate fundamental measurements

In practice, we do not very often take measurements by making the basic comparisons through which the measuring scale is defined. We use instruments. Some are simple, like the ruler; some, like the flow-meter for measuring volumes, are complicated. They find their ultimate justification in the rigorously defined measuring procedures that they conveniently imitate. But that ultimate justification has to be supplemented by demonstrating their ability to imitate the basic procedure. The instrument has to be calibrated against rigorous measurements directly, or at second-hand, or even at some greater remove. Alternatively, the instrument must behave according to some well-established laws, so that, by accurately measuring the components and carefully constructing the mechanism it is possible to give adequate assurance of the accuracy of the instrument's scale. Normally, though, these are combined: calibration, which is laborious, is used to fix a few values, and reliance upon theoretical calculation acts as a guide to the interpolation of intermediate values on the scale. Notice that the use of a well-corroborated theory is essential to justify any measurements by instruments constructed and calibrated in this manner.

Other instruments that assign numbers: pointer measurements

The use of measuring instruments is so widespread, and the performance of the full measuring procedure according to the rigorous definition is so rare, that we fail to distinguish between the respectable kind of measuring instrument described in the last section, and other instruments that merely assign numbers unsupported by any structural framework. In the absence of a rigorous procedure in the background to justify their use, these other instruments cannot claim to provide measurements in the same semantic category as those discussed above. These less rigorous measurements are sometimes called *pointer measurements*.

Fundamental measurements are derived by the direct observation of the property being measured. Other measurements, derived from fundamental measurements by calculation or by the application of well-corroborated laws (e.g. speed=distance÷time) can claim a similar status. Pointer measurements substitute for the observer some mechanism (e.g. sphygmomanometer for reading 'blood pressure'), or some mechanical procedure (e.g. administering a battery of questions as a basis for assessing 'intelligence'). Direct perception of relationships based on the property being measured and the use of an empirical or normative structure are abandoned. Instead, the mechanism or procedure is made to supersede the intuition, and is used to define the property which it purports to measure. This added arbitrariness of a pointer measurement cannot be ignored. It means that to justify the measurement there is not much use in appealing to direct human intuition, and because there is no empirical mathematical structure behind the resulting scale, it means that comparisons between measurements have no clear empirical interpretation.

Justification for pointer measurements can only be grounded in pragmatic tests such as:

(a) Can the instrument be readily reproduced, and do the various versions of it yield approximately the same results when applied to the same member of the class it is intended to measure?
(b) Can the property, defined by the pointer measurement, help in making useful predictions?*

The property (a) ensures that the instrument will help people to communicate accurately about the property it defines; it may not matter that the definition is initially rather arbitrary or artificial because usage alone will remove that objection. The test (b) more directly ensures the practical value of the procedure. Relationships between pointer measurements can tell us nothing about relationships between things, until these tests have been carried out. With a pointer measurement a numerical structure is defined first and an empirical structure later, whereas the opposite is true of a fundamental measurement.

Accuracy and calibration of a pointer measurement

In the social sciences, and in business and administration, pointer measurements are common. It is important to recognise that their *a priori* basis is rather arbitrary, compared with the fundamental measurements and their derivatives. Problems of standardising them, estimating their accuracy and validating their predictive capabilities need to be examined.

The kind of problem encountered is revealed by an example. In our training-conscious age we do not necessarily recruit people who can do a job, but those who have an aptitude for it, and then we train them. The problem of deciding who has and who has not an aptitude is most important, because training can be costly. Consequently there is a tempting market for purveyors of aptitude tests, and it is quite easy to devise an instrument, a battery of tests, that looks as though it can

---

* If an instrument or measuring procedure can be justified by appealing, directly or indirectly, to some fundamental measurement, then it is an instrument which simulates, more or less accurately, a fundamental or derived measurement; it does not give rise to a 'pointer measurement', in the special sense reserved for that term in this context.

measure a particular aptitude. How many such instruments are subjected to the tests mentioned above, before they are employed by organisations? Until a new aptitude test can prove itself in use by making predictions, there is only one justification for it. It must be proved reliable in so far as the *same tests* applied to the *same people* will yield results that are equal or nearly so. Even this is difficult, because it would not be a fair experiment to require the same questions to be answered in the same way, and in the same amount of time, when administered to the same person on two different occasions. This calls for a test based not upon specific questions (though in a published form the aptitude test may have only one version), but upon stated *ways of constructing* questions. Without such a basis, which enables replication of the test on the same person, an estimate of accuracy cannot be made; with it, there still remains doubt because a person who has taken the test once will have been changed by his experience.

Calibration of the test instrument can be performed in two ways. The first, *by fiat*, is the cheaper. You have only to assert that '0 answers correct give a score of 0, 100 correct scores give 10 and *n* correct scores *n*/10.' and that is the scale fixed. The second is *by normalising the results*. If there are no obvious standard bench-marks against which an instrument may be calibrated, (and we have no standard persons kept by national standards institutions), then a comparison may be made against the whole population to which the measurement is supposed to apply. To do this, the test must be administered to a large enough *random* sample of the accurately defined population. The results then provide a 'natural' origin and unit of measurement, for we can use the mean value of all the observations to locate the origin, and the variability of the population to define a unit of measurement. The frequency distribution of results *may* be very close to the familiar bell-shaped curve of the normal distribution. If so, the procedure can be pictured as in fig. 10.

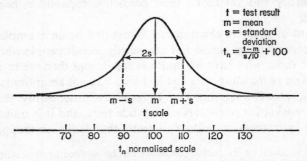

$$t = \text{test result}$$
$$m = \text{mean}$$
$$s = \text{standard deviation}$$
$$t_n = \frac{t-m}{s/10} + 100$$

Fig. 10. Normalising a pointer measurement.

By using the normalising procedure, the results from different batteries of questions can be made comparable. This enables an estimate of accuracy to be obtained, because several of these test batteries, which purport to measure the same thing, ought to yield the same result for the same person. From the spread of results for individuals, an estimate of the accuracy of the pointer measurement can be derived.

Once a pointer measurement has been standardised, calibrated and its accuracy assessed, it can justifiably be employed *to communicate information describing an individual* in relationship to the population used in the standardisation procedure but not for prediction.

Prediction: further justification for a pointer measurement

In practice, pointer measurements are used as predictors, not merely as descriptors. Some, such as a measurement of aptitude, are of little use unless they can supply predictions. It is not satisfactory to assume that prediction is possible because the name given to the number assignment implies it. The name 'aptitude test' is like this but the measurement is valueless if there has been no well-founded demonstration that the numbers can serve as predictors in operational conditions like those in which the measurement is to be used. This demonstration can be laborious and is often expensive. Many so-called aptitude tests currently being hawked around have never been validated.

How can a pointer measurement be justified as a predictor? To illustrate some of the difficulties, consider an aptitude test. To justify a measurement on the grounds that it works demands the experimental testing of a hypothesis stating what it is supposed to do. This type of experiment can only be constructed correctly, therefore, if it is known

(i) why the measurement is being made,
(ii) under what circumstances it will be applied, and
(iii) what other information would be used if not the measurement.

A scheme for validating an aptitude test is shown diagrammatically in fig. 11. In a correctly run experiment, the administration of the tests, the conduct of the training, and subsequent assessment of performance would all be independent of one another. This is very difficult to achieve in practice; this is one reason why aptitude tests are expensive and slow to validate. Because training is expensive, there may be a temptation to admit only those who pass both the aptitude test and also some second test (e.g. interview). If this is done, subsequent results will provide no evidence at all and because this is normal practice, the charlatan has little need to validate his wares. If the less severe rule is adopted, that passing either test admits people to training, then, at least, the results will be able to give an estimate of the tendency of each test to admit failures, but they will do nothing to show how much talent has been wasted because it is going unrecognised by both the tests. Strictly speaking, the tests should be administered to the recruits who should be

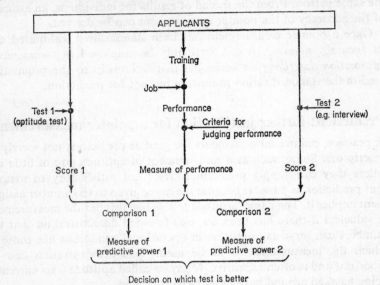

Fig. 11. Testing a prediction based upon a pointer measurement.

admitted to training (at least a proportion of them), regardless of the test results; it is even desirable to keep those responsible for the training ignorant of the test results. Only in this way will it be possible to discover both the chance of rejecting a suitable person, and the chance of training an unsuitable person, as a result of relying on the aptitude test. By not revealing the test results, the instructors will be less likely to turn the test into a self-fulfilling prophecy.*

Meaningful uses of a pointer measurement

Numbers, therefore, do not qualify as pointer measurements merely because they are assigned to things or people by some reproducable procedure or by using an instrument. They must be subjected to a process of standardisation against the population to which they refer, and any use they may have in making predictions must be justified by experiment. Such numbers have a valid *descriptive* signification.

Any number assignment can be made meaningful in a *prescriptive* sense: all you have to do is to specify what actions should be associated with what numbers and persuade or coerce people into behaving

* See chapter 3, p. 39 and Rosenthal, 1966.

accordingly. To qualify as a measurement, a number must refer to some property or value judgement; i.e. it is a number used descriptively. A single number serves no purpose because a measurement is only meaningful within a context of other similar number assignments. Only for fundamental measurements is this context rigorously defined. The various processes of standardisation and testing of predictive power constitute the background against which the meaning of statements incorporating pointer measurements must be judged. It is worth remembering that standardisation is based upon:

(i) a *large* (the actual size depending upon the use of the measurement)
(ii) *random* sample from
(iii) an *accurately defined* population

which, incidentally, should be fairly

(iv) *homogeneous* in all respects (except the property being measured) which might affect the response obtained from the measuring instrument or procedure.

Failure to observe this fourth condition will leave the pointer measurement open to the objection that it reflects not only the property being measured but also the ways in which different sub-populations interact with the measuring instrument. It will not be possible to decide how much these secondary influences contribute towards the pointer measurement, unless the mechanism of interaction between the instrument and the subject being measured can be exposed. For example, a thermocouple, used satisfactorily to measure temperatures in the vicinity of a gas furnace, may be very unreliable when used near an electric induction furnace, because of the possibility of interference from strong electromagnetic fields; in this case it is possible to check the results, if necessary, by using the fundamental measuring procedure for temperature. Less tractable are the procedures for measuring intelligence or aptitudes; these, when administered upon groups that are not culturally or emotionally homogeneous, give results that may be completely obscured by different reactions to the test procedures.

Predictions using a pointer measurement must be based upon

(i) *experimental* justification
(ii) carried out in *operational conditions* very similar to those to which the predictive statement refers;
(iii) there must have been *no feedback* from the measuring procedure to the experiment, otherwise the experiment may have become self-fulfilling, and
(iv) the population supplying the subjects used in the experiment must have have been statistically the *same population* as used for standardisation.

A pointer measurement can be used to make tentative statements about an individual relative to the standard population. For example, given a pointer measurement, it is justifiable to quote the proportions of the population that could be expected to rank 'higher' or 'lower' than that individual, subject to a reservation dependent upon the accuracy of the measurement.

Some statements about pairs of individuals may be also justified, as when one is ranked higher than the other. If the difference in the scores is comparable with the degree of error inherent in the measuring procedure, then this comparison is dubious. The ordinal structure, imposed by the scale upon the things it is supposed to measure, may be difficult to justify. For example, an aptitude test may rank candidate A, with 11 correct answers, higher than B, with 10 correct answers. The assumption that the scale is ordinal is tantamount to the assumption that every set of 10 correct answers indicates a lower aptitude than every set of 11 correct answers. This is almost impossible to check.

If the attribution of an ordinal structure to a pointer measurement rests on wobbly foundations then there is even less reason to believe that a pointer measurement can possess the more elaborate structures associated with the interval or ratio scales. Nevertheless, people are easily persuaded into treating pointer measurements as though they do possess these properties. They can be tempted to regard differences of marks, say between 40 and 45 and 45 and 50 as representing equal differences of aptitude; even less justifiably, they will say that a mark of 80 shows twice the aptitude corresponding to a mark of 40. Statements of these kinds are only meaningful for measurements which have the demonstrable structures, respectively, of the interval and ratio scales.

Minimal structural properties of a pointer measurement

In business and administration it can be very difficult to justify number assignments. We cannot rely upon being able to justify measurements as rigorously fundamental nor as even validated pointer measurements. There are two ways of proceeding. One way is to admit that we are making no attempt to define a measurement, that we are simply laying down a procedure for assigning numbers and rules for responding to those numbers. This is a prescriptive number assignment, not a measuring scheme. Another answer is to attempt to find some minimal justification of the 'measuring' scheme, by referring to the structural properties that the use of the numbers implies.

To illustrate this, consider a measuring procedure and look at the way the 'measurements' are employed. You may well find judgements being based upon the assigned numbers that imply that they belong to an interval or a ratio scale. For example, suppose a management incentive scheme for the managers of a group of banks awards points for:

> average credit balance of all accounts;
> distribution of size of account;
> numbers of new accounts;
> bad debts;
> staff training accomplished;
> level of staff turnover;
> estimated 'standing' of the manager in the local community

and so on. . . . The resulting total score may be described as a 'measure of branch-manager performance' and used in the allocation of bonus payments, fixing of promotion priorities, etc.

Having established this points scheme, perhaps merely as an administrative convenience, it would be surprising if people did not begin to look for some 'meaning' in the numbers it assigns. 'Meaning' is used here in the sense that people would tend to expect common arithmetical relationships between the assigned numbers to parallel an empirical structure in some 'real' property that the numbers are thought to represent. It is likely that they will ask: to what extent does the award of equal numbers of points imply equal 'something else' such as *merit in the managers?* or *benefit to the company* in the past year? or *additions to the earning potential of the company* in future years? The implication is that three managers awarded, say, 200 points, 300 points or 500 points ought to be ranked in that order if assessed in a commonsense way according to the particular 'real' property that the points are supposed to reward. Some people may even assume that the third manager performed in a way equal to the performance of the others combined, thus imputing that the 'measurement' should obey the law of addition.

Within a company, it may never be necessary to answer such questions, but a public body which allocated money to persons or organisations on such a basis might find itself obliged to justify the semantic implications of its points system. In this kind of situation it is usually out of the question to define a rigorous measuring scheme and a pointer measurement is ruled out because the laborious methods of testing it and validating its predictive properties cannot be applied in the available time. There does remain a minimal justification for calling the number assignment scheme a 'measurement'.

First, it is necessary to look at the ways in which the numbers are to be employed in statements, and thereby discover the structural properties which they are presumed to reflect. For example: do equal points imply that the managers are equal in respect of some property to which the points refer? Does the ordering by the points awarded correspond to the ordering of the managers according to the quality referred to? Suppose we are likely to say that the award to a particular manager of twice as many points this year as last indicates that the potential earning power of the branch has doubled. For this to be meaningful, the structure of a ratio scale is implied. What happens if two branches in a small town are amalgamated; would the assessment scheme award the manager of the amalgamated pair a number of points equal to the sum of the awards for the individual branches?

Given this analysis, it should be possible to find a few cases in which actual comparisons of the kind mentioned in the previous paragraph can be assessed. This may be done subjectively by 'experts', or, perhaps, by using other methods of calculation, for example, by referring to records for past years *notional* awards might be calculated and related to *actual* recorded performance. Notional amalgamations of branches might be made and the awards of points compared. By doing this it may be possible, in a limited but objective way, to justify the use of arithmetical operations or relationships that, strictly speaking, are only properties of highly structured fundamental measurements.

Pointer measurements and the prescriptive use of numbers

In business and administrative systems, as indeed in society at large, many numbers are assigned to things by applying some formula, as in the example in the previous section, or by personal *fiat*, as when someone states a price for an article he wishes to sell. *These* number assignments are not measurements unless *either* they can be shown to be a part of a self-consistent system of numerical labels with the same structure as a system of empirical relationships or judgements, *or* they can be given the kind of experimental justification set out in the previous section.

The residue constitute numerical signs or signals that have no power to describe any property, but they may have a prescriptive function if they are used to regulate behaviour according to rules which include such numbers. The numerical information used in business and administration often has some weak claim to be a measurement, whilst still being largely prescriptive. In other words, the numbers lay down what ought to be done, but carry a thin veneer of objectivity which persuades the user that the information is somehow factual or even scientific.

It is very easy to conjure up a procedural rigmarole for assigning numbers, and then persuade people to accept that the numbers refer to some objective property. When decisions are then made using these numbers, it will be imagined that they represent facts. The extent to which this is true depends upon the extent to which the number assignment can claim the status of a measurement.

For example: a hospital authority may devise some points system to decide the priority of admissions and the use of scarce medical resources. This may be done in the belief that the points refer to some important facts about the chances of success of the treatment, and the degree of improvement in the patient's condition. It is incumbent upon a public authority to justify such a use of number; it is much easier to evade such awkward problems in a private business. An education authority may use a pointer measurement, such as an examination taken by eleven-year-olds, to decide who gets the lion's share of educational resources. In the absence of a thorough justification, the results of such tests may masquerade as facts about the children, whereas they are actually numerical re-statements of a political policy.

Information, including numerical information, which is prescriptive, must seek its justification through criticism in ethical terms, or in terms of the practical consequences of the policies and rules which it embodies. Measurements are neutral about what should be done: they describe things. Prescriptive numbers say what should be done: they convey instructions. Numerical information used in business, administration, and the social sciences often simultaneously describes and prescribes.* This is inevitable and a source of dangerous confusion if not recognised.

Conclusions

Numerical information may look as rigorous as mathematics, but its apparent rigour must be subjected to an examination of how the numbers are assigned. One must ask what measuring procedure has been used and in what circumstances the measurements can be related meaningfully to one another. If the numbers have a prescriptive signification, this will be revealed. Anyone who does not ask these questions is exposed to the Great Number Trick.

The Great Number Trick depends upon the fact that numbers, however they are assigned, can be subjected to any amount of *arithmetically rigorous* manipulation. These complicated prestidigitations conceal from the onlooker that the resulting, numerical statements may be incapable of referring meaningfully to anything at all. The conjurer then induces his audience to jump through all kinds of administrative hoops according to the numbers he produces, by persuading them that it is

---

* Money is a very important kind of numerical information. In the market place, it serves to prescribe what the potential purchaser can do; social norms, backed by the law of contract and criminal law supply the affective force behind the denotative prescription implied by setting a price. Away from the market place, money is used, also, to describe how people behave. Financial information presents too complex a mixture of problems to be analysed in the context of this book.

very reasonable to do so on account of the supposed objective and scientific character of the numbers.

Watched by the slow-motion camera of critical appraisal, the conjurer will be seen to do a number of things which are not admissible. He may employ perfectly good fundamental measurements as though they possessed structural properties of a kind which cannot be ascribed to them, e.g. adding together measurements for which no empirical, additive property can be defined. He will do the same with pointer measurements with even less excuse. More likely still, he will not standardise the pointer measurements correctly, nor demonstrate the validity of the predictions he ascribes to them. As a result of this legerdemain his numbers will have little to do with the properties that they supposedly measure.

Once the truth has been exposed, the antics of the conjurer's audience may seem ridiculous. The numbers which they respond to may be almost meaningless, in the sense that they can *refer* to nothing. They may still be meaningful in the sense that they *prescribe* the actions to be performed. If all the audience were to see through his great number trick, the conjurer could still force them to jump through his hoops according to his numbers if he had sufficient power of coercion or persuasion. Numbers which look cool, reasonable and rational may be merely political circumlocutions or policies in disguise.

10 Perceiving Pattern in Numerical Data

Such tricks hath strong imagination,
That, if it would but apprehend some joy,
It comprehends some bringer of that joy;
Or in the night, imagining some fear,
How easy is a bush supposed a bear!

Shakespeare, *A Midsummer Night's Dream*

An organisation is not like a majestic argosy, being steered through a prosperous, well charted archipelago, under the clear Mediterranean sunlight, towards its corporate objectives. It is more like a company of soldiers stumbling its way across an unknown heath, through a turbulent mist which obscures the captain's vision of both the landscape and the disposition of his forces. Often the manager or administrator can only 'see' where he stands in the misty light of the numerical data which reach him both from within his organisation and from its environment. He may not care for the labour of analysing these data, believing that he can tell what is coming 'by the pricking of his thumbs', but he should be cautious lest imagination play tricks with him. So important is this process of analysing the raw data gathered by a business that many writers use it to define information; for example: 'Data (are) first condensed into information, and from this information meaning is distilled' (Keay, 1969). For me, this conjures up the image of a captain of industry, like Macbeth upon the heath, seeking 'strange intelligence' from the accountant, the statistician and the economist whose cauldrons distil fearful apparitions of past misdeeds and tempting visions of the future. The captain of industry has no less need to be careful how he interprets what he is shown than had Macbeth. Although this view of information is incomplete it is useful, especially as the weird sisters are nowadays replacing their old fashioned cauldrons by computers which can distil more amazing revelations from richer infusions of data.

The computer makes it possible to condense and analyse data using statistical methods that were previously unthinkable because of the impossible labour of doing the calculations by hand. Traditional accounting methods are very simple by comparison because all the calculations had to be performed cheaply by clerical staff. The computer removes this constraint. The accountant, manager or administrator of the future will have access to vast computing power at a cost that removes the primary economic obstacle to employing statistical methods. The problem will shift from how to get the elaborate calculations performed to how to understand the significance of the results. This chapter will examine some of the statistical methods of summarising data; chapter 12 will examine a related theme: statistical reasoning. By separating these topics into different chapters their distinction can be emphasised. Here we are concerned, as in the previous chapter, with the ways in which numbers can be related to observations. This time the emphasis is upon numbers which are at a higher level of abstraction. Statistical reasoning is about the assessment of statements rather than numbers.

Business Data

It is possible to think of a business as a kind of organism surviving in a complex environment which it must understand and to which it must respond effectively. An animal uses some of its senses (eyes and ears) to recognise significant features in its environment, and others (balance and kinaesthetic sense) to know the state of its own body. Most of the analysis of the primary sense data for this purpose is performed by the sense organs themselves, or the closely associated parts of the nervous system. Obviously an organisation expects its human members, dealing with customers or operating lathes, to respond directly to the information relevant to their tasks but they also need to respond in another fashion. The employees are also the senses, the eyes and ears of the whole company and, just as the sense organs in an animal convey electrical signals along nerve fibres to the brain, so do the employees, by their reports in words and numbers, convey to the organisation as a whole the raw data about the environment – customers, suppliers, competitors, etc. – and about the state of the organisation's own resources: work done, stock held, machines out of order, etc.

The signals that our brains receive from the environment and from our own bodies are filtered, aggregated and analysed, so that we can respond selectively to major features and events in our environment, and to significant states of our bodies. An organisation must do the same with the verbal and numerical signals that serve as its nerve impulses. Logical and numerical processes must be used by an organisation to filter, aggregate and analyse the data in ways that are analogous to the functions built into the organs of sense and their associated parts of the brain. Logical methods of the kind described later, in Part Five, and the statistical methods, described here, may be thought of as aids to perception by the organisation, which must recognise the state of its own resources and the shape of its environment both in broad outline and in detail. Just as our senses enable us to discriminate one shape or sound from another, so do statistical methods enable us to discriminate between patterns in numerical data. Experience has shown that identifying numerical patterns is something that people do very badly without help from statistical analysis. Often in business, spurious relationships, seemingly apparent in a limited amount of data, are made the basis of important decisions, whilst significant changes, obscured by extraneous random features of the data, go unnoticed.

Selecting the useful patterns in data

Two important aspects of numerical pattern recognition are: the discovery of the stable features which the data display and the selection of the patterns that are useful. At the biological level, some of the machinery for analysing data appears to be built into such brain structures as the visual cortex, but, beyond this basic level of analysis, the brain must recognise which patterns are accompanied directly or indirectly by significant sensations of pleasure or pain. Vital patterns at the biological level include the stable features of the physical world. These are the 'myths of physical objects' which as Quine says, 'work a manageable structure into the flux of experience'.

Above the biological level of pattern recognition, the appraisal of perceived structures is unlikely to be accomplished by reference to immediate sensations of pleasure or pain. In the natural sciences patterns are sought which help to explain universal phenomena; the natural scientist therefore requires his patterns to pass some very stringent tests. This was discussed in chapter 8 in terms of the criticism of statements. In so far as they are concerned with eternal, universal but ethically insignificant hypotheses, the social sciences can emulate the natural sciences and use the same canon of critical tests, but this is not always possible. In administrative and managerial decision-making and in the social sciences we are often concerned with hypotheses that are limited to a particular group of people at a particular time, and that are also ethically, highly significant. In these circumstances, the rational administrator or manager, or the social scientist, may only be able to apply to his data *some* of the tests which are used by the natural scientist. Also, the local significance and possibly crucial nature of his problem will make these tests inadequate. He must, in addition, ask questions about who will benefit or suffer as a result of promulgating one theory rather than another, or applying mathematical model A rather than model B or taking this action instead of that. The importance of selecting patterns, from all those perceived, in accordance with their ability to increase human welfare, i.e. to help us avoid pain and attain satisfaction, is quite obvious (and easier to justify) at a biological level. If a pattern perceived by a creature cannot be associated with some direct consummatory experience (i.e. it cannot reach out and touch it, or eat it or make love to it), then that pattern will be forgotten because it is useless. For an organisation to function effectively it must filter out of the data presented by its environment those patterns that are useful. Therefore, in an organisational context, the judgement of an observed pattern, or a theory or model which known facts can support, must take account of its utility. This opens Pandora's Box full of questions about how the utility is to be estimated, by whom is the judgement to be made, how is he to be appointed and dismissed. But we shall hastily close the lid on these difficult problems and direct attention upon the simpler ones.

In the following pages we shall examine only the limited problem of how to recognise those patterns which *might* be of value to an organisation. The chapter deals only with statistical techniques which are essential for the most basic level of numerical pattern recognition. Above the statistical level is the formulation of models and theories. Above both statistical analysis and model-building lies the stage of critical appraisal which was the subject of chapters 6 to 9.* Above all there lies the final judgement in terms of the resulting pleasure or pain felt by human beings.

Descriptive statistics

Everyone is familiar with the usual methods of summarising a body of data about a large population or assemblage of things. Averages, proportions, simple totals, ranges, and so on, are single numbers, each one called a *statistic* (singular), embodying some important feature of the population. Taken together, a few well-chosen statistics can summarise the nature of the population as a whole, by reducing a large amount of raw data to a few informative figures. In this sense, statistics do convey the nub of the 'information' about a large population. They are abstractions arrived at numerically. All the usual routine accounting and other figures which summarise an organisation's performance fall into the same category. The methods whereby they are derived are straightforward, arithmetical ones in which we all have confidence. Despite the convincingly objective, indeed scientific, look of a mass of figures, their use must be subjected to the kind of critical appraisal described earlier.

---

* Their relevance to this chapter should be appreciated, lest it be thought that the rather automatic analysis techniques of statistics can easily be augmented by similarly automatic procedures of appraisal.

Frequency distributions

All the statistics mentioned above can be related to one key idea: the frequency distribution. Although the idea is commonplace, it must be

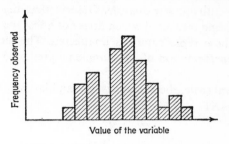

Fig. 12. A frequency distribution.

given a brief examination here because so much else stems from it. Given a population and one measured variable, the information can be presented as a histogram, a number of cells or appropriate divisions of the variable, as in fig. 12.

In each cell is displayed the number of members of the population in that category. The obvious way of summarising the histogram, to produce a yet briefer account of the data, is by indicating two major features:

(i) the centre or location of the typical member of the population and
(ii) the spread of the histogram around that value.

These are the average and measure of dispersion.

The choice of average or measure of dispersion depends upon the type of measuring scale used for the variable (the subject of the previous chapter). For a *nominal* scale which is a number of named classes without any significant order (e.g. nationalities) there is an obvious average: the most popular class, or 'mode' as it is called. There are two measures of dispersion that can accompany the mode, but they are seldom used for that purpose. One is the statistic known as 'chi-squared' whilst the other is called the 'entropy function'. It is not normally used in elementary statistics, but entropy will be a major topic in Part Six, because it is used in the theory of signal transmission as an engineering measure of 'information'. Both chi-squared and the entropy function measure how unevenly the values are spread over the available categories.

For an *ordinal* scale there is an additional measure of central tendency called the *median*, a value which exactly bisects the population: half have larger and half have smaller values than the median. The measure of dispersion is given by the locations of the upper and lower 'quartiles', the values which, with the median, divide the population into quarters. Thus three typical members of the population can be chosen to represent the position and spread of the distribution: for a population of $4h+3$ observations placed in order: the $(h+1)$th=lower quartile; $(2h+2)$th =median; $(3h+3)$th=upper quartile. Observe that any transformation of the variable being measured which does not affect the order will leave the choice of these representatives unaffected. This accords with the ideas on the transformation of measurements presented in the previous chapter.

For the interval scale, the average is the familiar arithmetic mean; for the n values $X_1, X_2 \ldots X_n$

$$m = \frac{(X_1 + X_2 \ldots X_n)}{n}$$

One measure of dispersion is the sum of the squared deviations from the mean:

$$\text{Sum of squares} = (X_1 - m)^2 + (X_2 - m)^2 + \ldots + (X_n - m)^2$$

which increases as the number of observations increases; by taking the average squared deviation, the *variance* is obtained; this is a more useful measure because it depends less upon the number of observations:

$$\text{Variance} = \frac{\text{Sum of squares}}{n}$$

(This should not be confused with the 'variance' used in accounting.) Another measure is the *standard deviation*, s, defined by

$$s = \sqrt{\text{Variance}}$$

If the interval scale is changed by applying a linear transformation, then the same transformation applied to m and s will give their correct values.

It is important to notice that these statistics cannot be defined meaningfully for scales less structured than the ones mentioned. Thus:

Statistics / Scale	Mode, chi-squared entropy function	Median and quartiles	Mean, variance, standard deviation
nominal	defined	meaningless	meaningless
ordinal	defined	defined	meaningless
interval	defined	defined	defined

For the ratio scale, a fourth average is also available, the little-used geometric mean. Special statistics could be developed for other scales but when we employ an unusual scale, we normally make do with the statistics of those scales in the above list whose structure it incorporates.

The three kinds of statistic, based upon the nominal, ordinal and interval scales, seem intuitively to convey different amounts of 'information'. The more 'structured' the scale of measurement, the more 'information' is conveyed by the statistic. Imagine you know accurately, in advance, the mode, the median and the mean for some population, and that you are given data on the population from which you calculate these statistics again. Many inaccuracies in the data could occur without affecting the mode, but the median would be more likely to reflect their presence, whilst the mean would reveal all but an unusual set of compensating errors. This illustrates a very general property of signs, not only of measurements and statistics: the 'informative power' of a sign depends upon the structure to which it is known that the sign must conform; if that structure is very stringent, placing many constraints upon the interpretation of the signs, then their informative power is enhanced. Perhaps for a similar reason, the better theories (as observed in chapter 8) are those that are restrictive in the interpretations that they impose upon facts.

Frequency tables and overlapping information content

We also commonly encounter the kind of statistical table which gives the numbers in a population having various combinations of two (or more) variables. The technical term for this is the bi-variate (or multivariate) frequency table. Now, these tables raise some interesting ideas about information. Take the example shown in Table 2. An engineering

Amount of tube (t)

Amount of plate (p)	1	2	3	4	5	6	7	8	9	10	11	12	13	14	15
1															
2		1	1	1		1									
3	1	2	3	3	2	1	2								
4		1	2	5	6	8	3	1		1					
5		1	2	4	8	10	9	7	2						
6			1	2	5	9	14	10	5	1					
7				1	3	6	9	11	7	4	1				
8		1		1	1	4	6	6	4	2	1				
9						1	1	3	3	2	1				
10								1	1	1	2				
11								1					1		
12															

Table 2. A bi-variate frequency table.

company manufactures special kinds of heat exchangers, on a one-off basis. A major problem is how to make a quick quotation of approximate price and delivery. Suppose that it is possible, using the drawings, to estimate the length of tube and the area of plate required. These are major indicators of cost. Suppose also that engineers seek estimates of cost at a very early stage of design, before adequate drawings have been made. It may be possible to produce quite a firm estimate of the length of tubes required, on the basis of calculations about the necessary rates of flow through the tubes and transfer of heat across them. The table shows an enumeration of over 200 recent orders categorised by the amount of tube (t) and plate (p) which they required. (The actual unit of measurement used is not relevant to the discussion.) Evidently this table can be used to assist in the provision of cost estimates on the basis of an estimate of tubework only. The two variables are *correlated*, so that, given that 9 units of tube will be required, you could offer a 'best guess' that the amount of plate will be near $6\frac{1}{2}$ units and that a 'normal' range of variation would be 2 units greater or less.

When two variables are correlated in this way, there appears to be some overlap between the information given by the two variables. There are several statistics which measure in some sense the information content common to messages about the two variables. For interval scales, the measurement is called the *correlation coefficient*, for the ordinal scales, there is a *rank correlation coefficient* whilst, for nominal scales, chi-squared may be used and also *mutual information* which, as we shall see in Part Six, is used in communications engineering.

Artificial variables which carry distinct information

For anyone interested in trying to 'distil' information from data, this notion of an overlap between the information contents of two or more messages is important. It suggests that it might be possible, by a process of analysis, to identify separate messages that convey quite distinct kinds of information which are confused in the original messages. *Principal component analysis* is just such a technique. It enables data based on, say, 20 measured variables to be described using 20 artificial variables. These artificial variables, unlike the original ones, are uncorrelated with one another. Often it is found that most of the information in the original data can be conveyed by only a few of the artificial variables, in the sense that they account for most of the variations between members of the population.

To illustrate how this method works with two variables, we can use the frequency table given in the previous section. If you look at the area of the table where observations are concentrated, you will notice that it has the shape of a fat cigar. The major axis of the cigar is used to give the best guess at the amount of plate required, given t, the amount of tube, whilst the thickness of the cigar measured slant-wise gives the variation about the norm. As the actual numbers are not important – only the general shape – the frequency table can be replaced by a graph which uses contours to reveal the varying frequencies of observed values of t and p. See fig. 13.

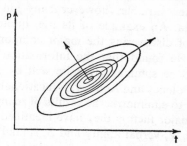

Fig. 13. Correlated variables.

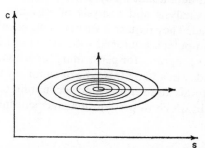

Fig. 14. Uncorrelated variables.

Fig. 14 shows a similar diagram, but, in this case, the axes of the cigar-shape are parallel to the axes of the graph. Now, if the observations had been like this, then there would have been no useful relationship between the variable t and the variable p. Their being uncorrelated would have meant that the two measurements of the heat exchanger gave quite independent information. It is a simple mathematical task to find two formulae which will enable the original pair of measurements t and p to be replaced by two artificial and uncorrelated measurements, S and C. (The formulae will look like this:

$$S=(t-\hat{t}) \cos \phi-(p-\hat{p}) \sin \phi$$
$$C=(t-\hat{t}) \sin \phi+(p-\hat{p}) \cos \phi$$

where ϕ is the angle between the major axis of the cigar and the t axis, and where $\hat{t}$ and $\hat{p}$ are the mean values of t and p.) These two independent components will perhaps correspond to the notions of 'size' of heat exchanger for variations along the major axis, S, and 'complexity' of design, for variations along the axis C.

Principal component analysis, as in the above example, will generate as many independent new variables as there were old ones, but usually only a few of them can account for most of the variability in the original data. Another related method, called *factor analysis*, deliberately identifies the best 3 or 4 new variables (however many you care to specify) for 'explaining' the data. An example of its use, quoted in chapter 5, is Osgood's method of discovering the major components in our judgements of quality. He found that the information from 50 different quality scales could be summarised quite well by 3 factors which he called Evaluation, Potency and Activity. Educational psychologists have used this technique to summarise the results of many tests of academic ability. The three major factors they have identified are now called G, general intelligence, V, verbal ability and S, spatial ability.

There are other statistical techniques for extracting information about a population from data about many of its characteristics (multi-variate data); regression analysis and analysis of variance are two methods that are widely used. They require a vast amount of calculation, an ideal application for computers. Equipped with these machines and the many standard computer programs for performing these analyses, there should be no difficulty today in adding this type of summary information to the usual totals, sub-totals and ratios which accounting tradition regards as the normal form in which to present 'management information'.

Grouping of data

It will be instructive to consider another method of summarising data. It is the problem of selecting coherent groupings of elements: the problem of classification or taxonomy.

The problem of recognising coherent clusters in a population described by a large number of variables may call for a monumental effort. The classical example, of course, is to be found in the work of the biologists (Darwin's *Origin of the Species* is based on this type of analysis and twenty years elapsed between his major data-gathering expedition in H.M.S. *Beagle* and its publication); the work of classification in biology is by no means complete. Numerical methods are now being devised to assist in this problem of taxonomy,* and many potential applications in business and administration seem evident when the computer makes them easy to use.

An analogy can be drawn between our visual discrimination of objects, as apparently coherent clusters of optical signals, and the

---

* See Sokal and Sneath, for example.

numerical discrimination of taxa, as apparently coherent clusters of members in the observed population. We recognise visual signals as coming from the same source because they share similarities of colour, illumination, direction and movement. Discovering coherent clusters of products, customers, machine-failures or jobs for example, is like trying to identify objects visually, but as though through a fog, because the numerical data tend to be too few to indicate more than a hazy outline. When we distinguish objects visually, we do so because we need to behave differently towards them. It would often be profitable to have distinct policies towards different groups (for example groups of products with similar uses, groups of customers who appear to behave the same way, groups of machine-failures which might have a similar cause or jobs that apparently demand the same kinds of skill), but identifying them in the numerical data which describe these populations is very difficult.

It is easy to gain an intuitive idea of how numerical clusters can be identified. Essentially it depends upon measuring the 'distance' between any two members of the population. Almost any formula for distance can be used, provided that it is zero for identical observations, and increases with greater disparity between the pair. Initially a rough clustering of the observations can be made, based upon the distance function. The 'coherence' of the clusters can then gradually be improved by a process of trial and error. For this very laborious process, the computer is indispensable. One by one each observation is moved to some other cluster which might claim it; if the move results in a net increase in coherence, the shift is confirmed. When no further shifting of any observation to any other cluster results in an increase in coherence, the desired clusters have been found. Several of the original trial clusters may have been merged in the process.

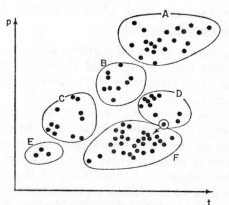

Fig. 15. Cluster analysis.

As an illustration, imagine that the firm which manufactures heat-exchangers had found that the data on recently made products was not as described earlier, but as in fig. 15. This rather blotchy arrangement of data may suggest that the products can be classified in some rough way that may serve as an adequate guide in quoting a tentative price. The diagram shows an intermediate stage in the formation of clusters. One observation, now in cluster D, is about to be tried in cluster F. The distance function for observations (t_1, p_1) and (t_2, p_2) might be defined by:

$$(\text{distance})^2 = (t_1 - t_2)^2 + (p_1 - p_2)^2$$

or, with different weights given to the variables

$$(\text{distance})^2 = W_t(t_1 - t_2)^2 + W_p(p_1 - p_2)^2.$$

These weights may be chosen to reflect the accuracies attainable in measuring t and p, or they may reflect purely subjective judgements of the relative importance of variations in values of t and values of p. The 'coherence' of a cluster is then related to the sum of the distances of all its points from its centre of gravity (found by treating the observations as equal particles). The coherence for D and F can then be compared with the coherence for the two new clusters D' and F' formed by shifting one observation. The new clusters will be preferred if there has been a decrease in the sum of all the distances of observations from the centres of their respective clusters.

For only two variables, the identification of clusters can probably be performed by eye just as well as by computation. Of course the methods are really useful when many variables are employed. Then it is very difficult to organise the data into taxa merely by inspection.

Ideas on the measurement of information suggested by methods of summarising data

There are many other ways of summarising data in addition to those described here. The methods illustrated above have been selected to illustrate ways in which some commonsense notions about information can be made more precise.

We have seen how the 'informative power' of the ordinary statistical measures of average and variability is linked to the structure imposed upon the original measurements from which they are derived. It would be possible, but by no means a simple matter, to attach a measurement to this 'structural information'. Also, some of the measurements of variability in the data, such as variance, chi-squared and entropy, can be treated as measurements of the information content of the whole body of raw data. This coincides with our intuitive notion that very little information would be needed to describe a homogeneous population compared with the information needed to describe a very diverse population.

We have already noted a number of ways of measuring the extent of the overlap between the information supplied by a number of variables. These measurements lead to methods of defining new variables that convey quite distinct information – for example the educational psychologist's factors G, V and S, representing 'general', 'verbal' and 'spatial' abilities, which can be used to summarise a host of results from different psychological tests.

Also, the methods of numerical taxonomy, described in the previous section, suggest some ways of measuring the information conveyed by summary statistics. For instance:

(a) A given taxonomy represents one method of summarising all the descriptive information about a population; it will have associated with it a measure of 'coherence' which can be regarded as a measure of the part of the total information which it takes into account. This, in turn, suggests another measurement.

(b) Ways of choosing the 'most meaningful' classification: going progressively from one extreme taxonomy, which places every element in a class of its own, to the other extreme taxonomy, that recognises only one class for all the data, there will be a gradual decrease in total coherence but a corresponding economy in the description of the population; a really informative taxonomy would display a relatively high coherence in proportion to its number of classes.

(c) Yet another measurement of 'information' might be attached to an incomplete description of an individual member of the population. Relative to a given taxonomy, one could ask how accurately the partial description enables one to determine the class membership of the individual. A measurement could be based on the degree of precision attainable.

These are examples, (a) of information regarded as a structural property, (b) of 'meaningfulness' as a kind of economy of expression and (c) of information conferring the power of decision. Similar ideas recur in differing forms throughout the study of information.

Conclusion

People are easily mesmerised by figures. Managers and administrators often have not taken the trouble to equip themselves with the rudimentary skills of numeracy. Mathematicians, natural scientists and accountants frequently display a bland confidence that the numbers used by organisations are meaningful in much the same way as simple weights and measures; they are only too eager to exercise the computational routines that have been drilled into them in their training.

The information specialist has a responsibility to ensure that numerical information is summarised in the most meaningful ways, using appropriate techniques such as those described in this chapter. He also has a duty to ensure that numerical information is employed critically, being tested in the manner suggested in the previous chapter. He should keep in mind the common causes of the misuse of statistical information:

(a) *Inadequacy of the original measurements*, because the measuring procedures have not been correctly defined or justified.

(b) *Analysis by inappropriate methods*, because statistical procedures have been applied without any regard for the assumptions which underlie them. Here the type of measuring scale and its admissible transformations may be very important.

(c) *Erroneous conception of the problem*, which may result in the failure to collect details of important variables, or may lead to a definition of the population that is inappropriate. The cause of the misconception may be very deep. There is no simple cure. Clear perception, good judgement and insight are needed.

(d) *Misconception of what the statistics refer to*. This is a matter of checking the definitions in order to know exactly what is measured, rather than assuming a 'self-evident' interpretation of the terms employed.

(e) *Misreading of the results*. Poor presentation of statistical information to a busy executive can destroy its value, and it can be just as futile to present statistics well to someone who has never learnt how to read them. It is also worth remembering that bad presentation may be deliberate.

These are usually more important in organisational uses of data than the more obvious ones:

(f) *Erroneous raw data*, caused by difficulties of reporting, observation, recording, transmission and transcribing. Good design of the information system can do something to reduce these errors.

(g) *Incorrect calculations*, which can be minimised by using well-disciplined procedures, or perhaps by using a computer, and always by incorporating checks.

It is more likely that the degree of error will never be made apparent to the user. So we should remind ourselves of:

(h) *The objective error*, caused by the inaccuracy of the raw measurements; this could be expressed by giving a range of accuracy of the statistics, but it is seldom done.

(i) *The subjective error*, caused by incorporating into the computational procedures guess-work and arbitrary assumptions, even of a conventional kind. There are few statistics used in administration and business that completely avoid this fault.

Because of these problems, the computer can often be a great hindrance to the correct use of information. Too readily it encourages the massive manipulation of data without regard for its meaning. Skill in the critical appraisal of information should rank as high as, if not higher than, the mastery of a recipe book full of data-processing techniques.

11 Judging Statements

If a man will begin with certainties, he shall end in doubts; but if he will be content to begin with doubts, he shall end in certainties.

Francis Bacon, 'The Advancement of Learning'

*Note:*Although from now on a little mathematics is unavoidable, the reader may rest assured that any demands made upon his knowledge or patience will be very light. There is no better way of revealing the multi-faceted nature of our everyday concept 'information' than by attempting to measure it. More important than the semantic differential (discussed in chapter 5) and various statistics (chapter 10) are the measurements derived from subjective probability dealt with in this chapter, from logical probability (the subject of chapter 17) and from relative frequency probability (chapter 18).

When we are about to decide what to do, we base our choice of action upon our current mental picture of the world. This picture can be made explicit in the form of statements which may be statements of what we consider to be objective fact, or statements embodying value judgements or ethical principles. Some such statements you may confidently accept as constituting a part of your view of the world, and therefore, serving as a sound basis for action. Such statements you would regard as *true*. The negation of a true statement would be deemed *false*, and vice-versa. This way of defining truth makes it a property of statements relative to one person, at a certain time and place, and in certain circumstances. These personal assessments of the truth about a problem are what determine how an individual will tend to behave; to discover them is to know his attitudes.

From the point of view of anyone trying to understand the nature of information, there are two very interesting problems which can be examined, taking this idea as a starting point. The first is suggested by the observation that signs, signals or messages of all kinds may cause a person to change his attitude or belief, and, in so far as this happens, it would be reasonable to assume that the signs convey information to him. This appears to be the start of a fruitful line of enquiry, which may lead to definitions and measurements of information if the effect of the sign or message can be measured. The second problem is concerned with how we reach agreement about a statement. Much of the information which circulates in an organisation is intended to cause people to reach agreement about factual hypotheses, predictions and value judgements; this is vital in an organisation, because its members must work with an agreed body of facts and expectations about what they are doing, and they must also reconcile their opinions about what should be done.

These problems can be examined from both descriptive and normative view points. That is, we may ask: how *do* individuals actually change their opinions and groups reach agreement? and how *should* a person or group make these adjustments? The emphasis in this chapter is upon the development of normative rules that should govern 'reasonable' judgements about statements. (You will recall that chapter 4 described how people actually do reach agreement through the interplay of social pressures.) An important by-product of the normative approach is that it enables us to develop a variety of measurements of what common sense suggests might be an 'amount of information'.

For the sake of completeness, this chapter begins by mentioning two ways in which the amount of information in messages could be measured in a purely descriptive way. That is, without expecting people to be reasonable (in any sense of that word) about the judgements they make. Then the chapter introduces a series of normative rules which should govern how a reasonable person should adjust his attitudes and beliefs. These simple rules lead to a variety of measurements of probability from which measurements of information can be derived. Unfortunately the simplest normative rules do not guarantee that two 'rational' men can be led to agree with one another. This problem of reaching agreement is examined in chapter 11, while chapter 12 introduces additional rules to ensure that reasonable men do eventually agree, given enough carefully collected objective information. This leads to the relative frequency probability which is discussed in detail in Part Six.

Measurements of information based on behaviour and changes of attitude

In a business situation we give people information in order to affect their behaviour now or some time in the future. One natural way of measuring the information in messages that a person receives is by observing the effect upon his behaviour. Obviously it is no good observing the behaviour of one person on a single occasion because there would be no way of distinguishing the effect of one item of information given to him from all the other information he was receiving through his senses. However, the method can be applied if many people can be placed in the same decision-situation so that the information they receive can be varied systematically. This can be done and their behaviour noted.

For example, to understand how customers respond to the information about a product given on its packaging, it would be possible to prepare an experimental display. For different experimental subjects, various factors believed to influence the purchasing decision could be altered: the location of the package within the display, the colour and the size of the package, even the arrangement of the whole display. A well-designed experiment could yield results from which careful statistical analysis could separate the effects of each of these variables. If the size and colour of the package are shown to affect a customer's choice, then it would be natural to say that these signs carry information relevant to the customer's decision. It may be possible to estimate the effects of different colours and sizes. These estimates might then be employed to construct a pointer measurement of the differences in 'amounts of information' conveyed by different messages.

Sometimes it is quite impossible to observe the effect of information on people's overt behaviour. For example, you might be developing a new style of prefabricated modular house and you might suspect that, because of lack of understanding, people would be ill-disposed towards your new product. You would be interested in measuring the information conveyed by various kinds of propaganda. One way of doing this would be to get a number of people to complete a questionnaire once before and once after they had received various forms of propaganda. Such a questionnaire might be designed by making use of semantic differentials (see p. 56) to reveal changes of attitude. It would then be possible to base a measurement of the information conveyed by the propaganda upon an observed change of attitude.

When it is possible to observe the effects of messages of limited kinds upon behaviour or attitudes, the results may be construed as indicating the amount of information which is conveyed. Unfortunately, these methods are limited in their range of application to sign situations which can often be repeated. They tell us about typical effects of a few standard messages upon typical members of a known population in circumstances that are reproducible. There are plenty of problems about communicating commercial or administrative information to a large population which satisfy these constraints. Nevertheless, it would be desirable to have ways of measuring information that can be applied to a specific message, received by an individual, in a unique situation.

One of the potentially most fruitful ways of investigating the information conveyed by messages is by asking people their opinions, not of packaging or prefabricated buildings, but of *statements*. This is a more abstract approach to our problem: it thrusts the subject matter of the statements into the background. If information is to be studied, rather than packaging or prefabricated buildings, this seems to be a step forward.

The obvious scale on which people might judge statements ranges from 'false' to 'true'. The rest of this chapter is mostly about such measurements. They are fundamental as opposed to pointer measurements, which is an advantage. The structure underlying them can be very loose if the judgements are not expected to be mutually consistent. We shall see, however, that various normative conditions can be imposed upon a 'rational' person's judgements of degrees of truth and falsity. Not all the possible normative structures are considered (ordinal structures are neglected, for example), the emphasis being placed upon measurements which conform to the mathematical structure known as a *probability*.

Two other ways of judging statements

It would be misleading to launch into a discussion of how people judge statements on the basis that there is only one scale ranging from true to false. One additional scale that is obviously important to the decision-maker is the scale ranging from relevant to irrelevant. It has been argued that there is another important scale upon which statements should be judged in relation to making a decision. Shackle has pointed to a scale ranging from 'quite impossible' to 'perfectly possible'.* He points out that the routine, repeatable decisions are relatively unimportant in business and administration. What matter far more are the unique, crucial decisions – decisions affecting large investments, major innovations and relationships with people – they are what management is really about. Such is their complexity and the lack of information about them that these decisions often turn upon knowing what is and what is not within the bounds of possibility rather than upon any finer judgements of what is more or less likely. To make this distinction clearer, consider how a person might respond to a question such as: 'Has your house been flooded this morning?' Even on a very rainy day, the person is likely to reply: 'I suppose it is *perfectly possible* but I think it is *most unlikely.*' The fact that he regards the flooding as perfectly possible means that he is prepared to take that eventuality into his framework of decision-making; he has probably already taken appropriate action by paying an extra premium on his household insurance. However, because he thinks it is a most improbable happening he is unlikely to rush home, just in case. If you asked a similar question about an earthquake instead of a flood, then, living in England, he would probably regard the destruction of his house by an earthquake as so far beyond the realms of possibility that he would never dream of introducing it into the framework of his decision-making.

* G. L. S. Shackle, *Decision, Order and Time in Human Affairs.*

Readers, if they turn to Shackle, may not be convinced by his argument in favour of this very different way of judging statements. It may be especially difficult to accept Shackle's plea that we should abandon probability measures when discussing crucial, unique decisions in favour of what he describes as the scale of 'potential surprise' which assigns zero to any outcome which is 'perfectly possible', such as flooding, and higher values to propositions which can virtually be excluded such as the earthquake. I think there is a valuable way of interpreting this distinction in terms of what has been said earlier about the different stages of reasoning.

Consider the decision-making process. One can imagine it taking place in two stages: the first is the creative stage of formulating a framework for the problem. This will involve imagining what the present state of affairs might be, what possible courses of action can be envisaged and what imaginable consequences there might be. This is a highly creative phase which corresponds to the stage which Pierce has called *abductive reasoning*. Once the decision-maker has settled upon a descriptive framework he can begin mentally to quibble with himself about the probabilities which he should attach to the various statements that his framework admits to be perfectly possible. This second stage corresponds to the process of *inductive reasoning*. The final choice, of course, will also take into account the decision-maker's value judgements.

Most theories of decision-making assume that it is easy to draw up a framework for making a decision and therefore they have placed most emphasis upon the stage of inductive reasoning. Shackle is right to remind us that in making unique and crucial decisions it often happens that the most important stage is the first abductive process of recognising what is remotely possible. The final choice is often quite obvious once the first stage has been completed.

In what follows it will be assumed that the decision-maker has constructed a framework suitable for the analysis of his problem. We can then measure the effects of messages on his judgements of statements within this framework. It is worth remembering that some messages might cause the decision-maker to change his framework altogether. Messages that were able to indicate that previously unimagined things were perfectly possible would convey information of a very special and important kind. No attempt will be made here to take any further an analysis of information based upon Shackle's scale of potential surprise.

Betting odds and probability

Once we have settled upon a framework for analysing a decision-situation we may embark upon the inductive stage of weighing the evidence which has a bearing upon the problem.

There is a natural way of enquiring about the strength of a person's beliefs, and that is by asking him to bet on them. The higher the odds a person is prepared to give in favour of a proposition, the more strongly, one may conclude, does he believe in it. His belief can only be put to the test, however, when it refers to an event or a state of affairs which can be affirmed or denied by observation, either by direct observation or experiment or by reliance upon reports. There is no reason why we should not ask about his feelings of confidence in statements of all kinds, whether of particular factual propositions, general scientific hypotheses, ethical principles or even mystical beliefs; but only on the first of these, particular factual propositions, does it make any sense to place a bet.

Gambling odds may be converted to the more useful scale of probabilities, by the relationship:

$$\text{probability} = \frac{\text{odds}}{1 + \text{odds}}$$

Whilst odds range from zero upwards without limit (being the ratio of the money you would stake on the truth of the proposition to the sum you would expect to have set against your bet), probability ranges from 0 for a proposition you regard as false to 1 for a proposition you regard as definitely true. Probabilities are much more convenient quantities to manipulate than odds, and it is possible to discover some very natural conditions to impose upon probabilities if they are to be mutually consistent.

For example, you might ask someone what odds he would bet on the proposition that the development costs of some project *will* be kept within budget limits. You might also ask him his odds on the converse proposition, that costs *will not* be within budget. These propositions constitute hypotheses which can conveniently be labelled H and not-H. His opinion will be dependent upon his present *state of knowledge* which can be called K. His stated odds can be converted into probabilities using the formula given above. Call them:

$$p(H \mid K) \qquad \text{and} \qquad p(\text{not-}H \mid K)$$

standing for 'the probability of H given the information K', etc.

If your informant agrees that the only possible outcomes are H or not-H (that is to say his model for the problem does not include such eventualities as the changing of budget limits or the cancelling of the project) then

(a) $$p(H \mid K) + p(\text{not-}H \mid K) = 1$$

should be true. If not, you can demonstrate that your informant is inconsistent in his betting. If the probabilities add up to more than one he is envisaging a situation in which both H and not-H are true. On the other hand, if the sum of the probabilities is less than one he is implying that, in some circumstances, neither H not not-H is true.

Other important forms of the addition rule

The above relationship (a) establishes the important additive property of probability. It can be generalised in the following conditions

(i) we have a set of propositions H_1, H_2, ... H_n;
(ii) these propositions are mutually exclusive;
(iii) taken together these propositions exhaust all the possibilities, then:

(b) $$p(H_1|K)+p(H_2|K)+ \ldots +p(H_n|K)=1$$

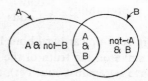

Fig. 16. The proposition 'A or B' represented as three disjoint propositions.

Also, if two propositions, A and B, are not mutually exclusive, then you may ask your subject what odds he would give for each proposition independently and for the two compound propositions.

A & B (i.e. both propositions are true)
A or B (i.e. one proposition or the other, or both, are true).

To test these judgements for consistency, find the associated probabilities and notice that:

$$p(A \text{ or } B|K)=p(A \ \& \ \text{not-}B|K)+p(A \ \& \ B|K)+p(B \ \& \ \text{not-}A|K)$$

as shown by the areas in fig. 16, which show that 'A or B' can be made up of the three mutually exclusive propositions A & not-B, A & B, not-A & B. The relationship above follows from (b). Now, by a similar argument:

$$p(A|K)=p(A \ \& \ \text{not-}B|K)+p(A \ \& \ B|K)$$
$$p(B|K)=p(\text{not-}A \ \& \ B|K)+p(A \ \& \ B|K)$$

Hence, by substituting these in the formula above

(c) $$p(A \text{ or } B|K)=p(A|K)+p(B|K)-p(A \ \& \ B|K)$$

which is another rule which must be satisfied by consistent judgements of probabilities (based on odds).

Before going any further with the examination of the use of a probability, the next three brief sections will focus attention on some important aspects of the meaning of the concept discussed above.

Mathematical and other kinds of probability

In mathematics, the term 'probability' can be used for any measurement which conforms to the rules derived above, plus the implied rule that the values range between 0 and 1. This abstract, mathematical, scale can be applied to many different things. What a probability refers to depends upon the semantic rules and empirical steps that must be obeyed in assigning a probability value to something or other. Different operational procedures will result in semantically quite different kinds of probability. The resulting measurements will all obey the same abstract mathematical rules for probability. This should cause no more confusion than the fact that the very different operational procedures for finding lengths or weights or volumes lead to measurements, all of which obey the abstract mathematical rules for a ratio scale. Unfortunately, such confusion is common.

The above section has shown how a probability-measure can be associated with an individual person's judgement of propositions.

Several other probability-measures will be presented in this book. They are as different from one another as length and weight and volume, although they share the mathematical properties of the same measuring scale. This is important to recognise, because measures of 'information' arise naturally as derivations from probability; a rich variety of probability-measures implies a plurality of information-measures.

Extending subjective probability to propositions on which bets are meaningless

The earlier discussion has shown that, in the case of statements on which bets can be placed, rules (a), (b) and (c) must be adhered to if the judgements of probability are to be mutually consistent. Although it does not make sense to place bets upon many kinds of proposition (statements of ethical principle or metaphysical speculation or factual statements that cannot be tested operationally), there is no reason why we should not ask a person to indicate his feelings about using any statement as a basis for action. The position is summarised in fig. 17.

There is nothing to prevent us from also demanding that the probability rules apply to judgements upon statements of *any* kind. This will

F

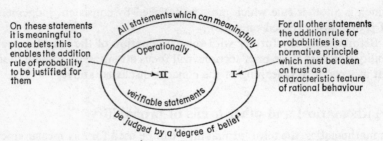

On these statements it is meaningful to place bets; this enables the addition rule of probability to be justified for them

All statements which can meaningfully

Operationally

II

I

verifiable statements

be judged by a 'degree of belief'

For all other statements the addition rule for probabilities is a normative principle which must be taken on trust as a characteristic feature of rational behaviour

Fig. 17. Where the addition rule for subjective probability can be justified.

have the advantage of ensuring that, wherever the propositions can be subjected to empirical test, these estimates will be consistent with one another. These rules impose a normative structure upon subjective estimates of feelings of confidence. The resulting scale of measurement has great practical advantages. The rules we have adopted enable us to deduce the probabilities of many statements from probabilities of only a few fundamental statements. People *may* not behave according to the normative rules much of the time, but in some circumstances (region II of fig. 17) it should be easy to persuade a man who is trying to be rational and deliberate about making up his mind that he *ought* to conform to the rules. It will be simpler for him to conform all the time (region I as well) than to risk the potential inconsistencies that may emerge when he comes to act upon his assumptions.

Measures of information derived from subjective probability

If we give a person some information relating to a decision, he may change his assessment of some proposition H. It will be convenient to refer to his two judgements as

$$p_i = (H \mid K_i) \text{ and } p_j = p(H \mid K_j)$$

before and after receiving the information altering his state of knowledge from K_i to K_j. As noted earlier, this information in a message can be associated with its power to cause a person to alter his judgements; so, by measuring his probability estimates of a set of statements before and after being exposed to a sign or message, the change in the probability he ascribes to an individual statement can be taken as *a measure of information relative to that statement for the person concerned.* This measurement of information, like the earlier one, takes account of any emotional impact in the message, not only of its rational import. If you are interested in giving information to decision-makers, this sort of measure may be more important than one that only takes account of the rational content.

Using differences and ratios of the old and new probabilities, all kinds of information measures may be conjectured. One could, for example, treat the difference between the two probabilities given to a statement before and after receiving a set of messages as a measure of their information content, or

$$I_1(i, j) = p_j - p_i$$

The amount of information will be either positive or negative depending upon whether it tends to affirm or deny the statement, the range of values is from -1 to $+1$ and the measure has a convenient addition property:

$$I_1(i, j) + I_1(j, k) = I_1(i, k)$$

but it ascribes the same value to a message that will augment an opinion of near certainty as to a message that will halve a doubt in someone's mind.

In some respects intuition might demand that the shift, as shown in fig. 18, from p_1 to p_2 should be regarded as showing more response to

Fig. 18. A shift of opinion along a scale of probabilities.

the information than p_3 to p_4. To reflect this notion in a measurement, information could be defined on a scale from minus infinity to plus infinity, as

$$I_2(ij) = \log\frac{p_j}{p_i}$$

which still has the addition property. However, you may argue, on the contrary, that messages contain most information when they result in a shift of opinion to one of the poles of certainty so that the statement can be either clearly affirmed or denied. Another measurement of information can be derived with the desired characteristics. Much innocent mathematical recreation can be obtained from the construction of measures of information, based upon changes in subjective probabilities, displaying a variety of commonsense properties that we associate with information but never capturing all of them. The measures may be based upon changes in probabilities ascribed to a single hypothesis or more ambitious ones could take into account the effect of a message upon many logically independent hypotheses. Without a great deal of analysis that would be out of place here, little can be said about the rival merits of these measures. They do help to reveal, by their plurality, that there is no simple answer to the question: what is an amount of information?

How should a rational individual adjust his opinions?

When we ask this question, we are led to discover yet another rule which should be satisfied by probabilities. It concerns judgements based upon different background knowledge. Suppose, when discussing the proposition H about development costs, you introduce the possibility: J='Mr Smith, leader of the development team, leaves before the project is complete.' You could then ask for odds on H (that development costs will be kept within budget limits) given, not only present knowledge, K, but also the additional knowledge, J; the probability $\bar{p}(H \mid J \& K)$, of H conditional upon J & K, could then be calculated using the formula:

(d) $$\bar{p}(H \mid J \& K) = \frac{\bar{p}(H \& J \mid K)}{\bar{p}(J \mid K)}$$

$\bar{p}$ is used to emphasise that this additional constraint gives rise to a measurement with a different and, indeed, richer structure.

There is no way of justifying this formula, except in relation to a set of statements even more narrowly defined than those to which estimates of odds can meaningfully be attached. If you bet on events that are outcomes of *repeatable* experiments or trials, such as those in games of chance, then experiment will demonstrate the validity of the formula quite well but never perfectly. There is also a mathematical argument in favour of formula (d) based on the exact analogy between probabilities and areas. Suppose all the distinct outcomes of an event, given knowledge 'K' are assigned areas within the rectangle, K, in proportion to their probabilities. Composite outcomes, such as H and J, will correspond to selected parts of K. Given the additional knowledge that the outcome satisfies J, we reduce the total area to J & K to form a new model of the probabilities. Thus:

The following formula, which is easy to check, is the exact analogy of (d).

the proportion (of H/ inside J & K) $= \dfrac{\text{the proportion (of H \& J/ inside K)}}{\text{the proportion (of J/ inside K)}}$

Note how this argument turns on knowing a simple relationship between the probabilities of the outcomes given K and given J & K as prior knowledge. Games of chance can be modelled this way, the world in general cannot.

Rule (d) differs from the other probability rules in a very significant way. It lays down a criterion for judging the mutual consistency of probability judgements which are based on *different evidence*. Unlike rules (a), (b) and (c) which refer to a fixed state of knowledge K, rule (d) can say something about the way in which a 'reasonable' man should adjust his opinion in the light of additional information. By deriving it from an examination of a simple game of chance, rule (d) can be made to look like an incontrovertible mathematical necessity, so be careful to notice the assumptions on which it is based. Rule (d) depends upon our knowing the probabilities of the elementary outcomes of the experiment, and upon our having a model upon which we can confidently base our calculations of the probabilities of composite events and upon which we can base our interpretation of any relevant evidence. Confidence in the model can be obtained via *a priori* arguments about the symmetry of the dice or cards and the precautions to be taken in performing the experiment. Unless a great deal of practical experience suggests that symmetry and fair play can be expected the model will have to be validated by experiment.

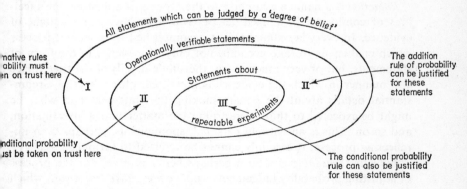

Fig. 19. Where the addition and conditional probability rules can be justified and where they must be taken on trust.

Therefore we must be careful to recognise that rule (d) can only be thoroughly justified for statements about repeatable experiments (see fig. 19). In other circumstances, we can impose rule (d) as a normative condition of reasonable behaviour. For example, it can be applied with reasonable confidence to statements concerning a unique event such as the first throw of a die at Crockford's Club after midnight on 1 April 1980 but it can only be *tested* experimentally for replicable events.* The

* The fact that Crockford's Club was denied a gaming licence after I had written this statement serves to emphasise the importance of the framework within which we conduct any discussion about probabilities!

kind of problem which is most important in business and administration concerns unique and crucial events; these may be analysed in terms of probabilistic models, but there is no possibility of testing these models experimentally (except perhaps for parts of them), hence the use of the conditional probability rule, (d), is much more difficult to justify.

Induction and inductive reasoning

The remainder of this chapter is mostly concerned with ways of making our response to evidence formalised and explicit. This can be done by using rule (d), provided that conditional probabilities can be obtained for the receipt of all the possible items of evidence given each of the rival hypotheses. It can be very difficult to apply these formal rules for the weighing of evidence, simply because the conceivable range of items of evidence can be too vast. For example, imagine the variety of possible statements which might be regarded as evidence if you were trying to decide among the rival hypotheses: $H_1 \equiv$ Mr X is guilty of embezzlement; $H_2 \equiv$ Some other person is guilty; $H_3 \equiv$ There is an innocent explanation.

Induction is a name we can give to the process of adjusting one's feelings of confidence in a fixed set of rival hypotheses, in the light of evidence. In everyday affairs this is accomplished by a mental process which enables us to take account, not only of evidence in the form of statements, but of very much more: the subtle details of the time, place and manner in which the evidence is presented, plus a host of circumstantial details about the person making the statement and what he might be expected to think concerning the matter under investigation, and so on. This is an entirely personal, spontaneous, perhaps even unreflecting process; it certainly cannot be reduced to formulae.

Inductive reasoning is a term perhaps better reserved for the process of adjusting probability judgements *within a normative framework* which gives, to conclusions arrived at inductively, some of the logical force which we associate with strict, deductive reasoning. If the normative framework can be accepted generally, then the process of adjusting opinions about the probable truth of various hypotheses, like those above, can be made as public as adding up a bill, although the judgements remain personal. The above rule, (d), for conditional probabilities can be made the foundation of a normative framework for inductive reasoning.

Limitations of inductive reasoning

Before adopting a logical method for inductive reasoning, let us note carefully what it embraces and what it excludes compared with the everyday, unsophisticated intuitive process of weighing evidence. If you ask a person to estimate a probability of some hypothesis, H, about keeping development costs within budget, conditionally upon some event, J, such as the loss of the project team leader (that is $\bar{p}(H \mid J \& K)$, then you are asking him to make up his mind *in advance* about his response to a message he may receive, such as 'Mr Smith has resigned.' You invite him to commit himself to this potential future change of mind on the basis of a statement only, excluding all the subtle emotive influences surrounding an actual announcement of the fact of Mr Smith's resignation. It may or may not be desirable to exclude these hints. Some could be included in the statement; thus, instead of J, $J' \equiv$ 'Mr Smith leaves the company regretfully before the project is complete.' But, however we extend and refine the statement J, it will not be feasible to capture in words all the subtle information about the circumstances and the manner of its happening, should Mr Smith actually leave. Hence, a normative rule to govern how the manager should change his opinion will be able to provide only a very crude model of how the reasonable man should behave. In contrast to this, the inductive rule does provide an accurate guide to rational behaviour, when the subject of the hypothetical proposition is an event in a game of dice which admits few subtleties, and which, therefore, can be described accurately in a formal verbal or mathematical model. The point I wish to make is that we should take care to acknowledge the inevitable inadequacy, when applied to a complex real-life situation, of a probability rule that appears overwhelmingly exact and justifiable in the context of parlour-games of chance. The rule is, nevertheless, valuable in *some* real-life situations.

Bayes' Rule

If you can persuade a person to commit himself by making a conditional probability judgement on all the evidence which could possibly be presented, then you can hold him to the adjustment of his opinion by invoking the rule presented to the world in 1763 by the Rev. Thomas Bayes. Its derivation is a mathematical consequence of the rules given above for absolute and conditional probabilities. The same formal rule therefore applies not only to subjective probability, but equally well to any other probability function which satisfies the rules (a), (b), (c) and (d) above.

The derivation of Bayes' Rule requires only some algebraic manipulation. Suppose there are only three rival hypotheses: H_1, H_2 and H_3. Call any one of them H_1. A piece of evidence, E, may be forthcoming to help us clarify our judgement on probabilities of the H_1. The conditional probability rule (d) can be re-written:

$$\bar{p}(H_1 \& E \,|\, K) = \bar{p}(H_1 \,|\, K)\, \bar{p}(E \,|\, H_1 \& K)$$
$$= \bar{p}(E \,|\, K)\, \bar{p}(H_1 \,|\, E \& K)$$

The second of these expressions gives:

$$\bar{p}(H_1 \,|\, E \& K) = \frac{\bar{p}(H_1 \& E \,|\, K)}{\bar{p}(E \,|\, K)} \tag{1}$$

for which i $=1$, 2 or 3. The expression on the left, $\bar{p}(H_1 \,|\, E \& K)$ is called the *posterior probability* because it is the value to which a conditional probability judgement commits one, given that E is true. The quantity $\bar{p}(H_1 \,|\, K)$ is the judgement before knowing E and is called the *prior probability*.

It is customary to change the right-hand side into a more convenient form by noting that one of the hypotheses must be true, or:

$$\bar{p}(H_1 \,|\, E \& K) + \bar{p}(H_2 \,|\, E \& K) + \bar{p}(H_3 \,|\, E \& K) = 1$$

so that, using formula (1):

$$\frac{\bar{p}(H_1 \& E \,|\, K)}{\bar{p}(E \,|\, K)} + \frac{\bar{p}(H_2 \& E \,|\, K)}{\bar{p}(E \,|\, K)} + \frac{\bar{p}(H_3 \& E \,|\, K)}{\bar{p}(E \,|\, K)} = 1$$

or $\quad \bar{p}(H_1 \& E \,|\, K) + \bar{p}(H_2 \& E \,|\, K) + \bar{p}(H_3 \& E \,|\, K) = \bar{p}(E \,|\, K)$

hence, substituting for $\bar{p}(E \,|\, K)$ in formula (1)

$$\bar{p}(H_1 \,|\, E \& K) = \frac{\bar{p}(H_1 \& E \,|\, K)}{\bar{p}(H_1 \& E \,|\, K) + \bar{p}(H_2 \& E \,|\, K) + \bar{p}(H_3 \& E \,|\, K)} \tag{2}$$

This formula can be used if you wish to discover how a rational person should respond to a message, E. In advance of his receiving this message you must ask for his estimates of the joint probabilities of the evidence with each of the hypotheses in turn. If he thinks the evidence supports the hypothesis H_1, he will give $\bar{p}(H_1 \& E \,|\, K)$ a high value and vice versa.

More measurements of information

Already, in this chapter, several measurements have been adduced to show what varied, exact interpretations can be given to the vague term 'information'. These were all based upon the actual effect of the signs or messages conveying the information upon an individual person's judgement of some statement. Now, using the concept of conditional probability, we can define a measure of information based upon an individual's direct judgement of the information-bearing statement.

The foundation for this new measurement is the above formula:

$$\bar{p}(E \,|\, K) = \bar{p}(H_1 \& E \,|\, K) + \bar{p}(H_2 \& E \,|\, K) + \bar{p}(H_3 \& E \,|\, K)$$

which combines the three separate judgements of the possible evidence E occurring jointly with each of the three disjoint hypotheses H_1, H_2, H_3; these hypotheses must exhaust the possibilities but of course they need not be limited to three. This probability is still relative to one individual but it takes account of all his relevant current knowledge.

Measures which reflect commonsense notions about information might be derived by formulae such as:

$$\text{Info}_1(E) = 1 - \bar{p}(E \mid K)$$

and

$$\text{Info}_2(E) = \log \left\{ \frac{1}{\bar{p}(E \mid K)} \right\}$$

i.e.

$$\text{Info}_2(E) = -\log \bar{p}(E \mid K)$$

Note that $\bar{p}(E \mid K) = 1$ for a piece of evidence we are certain of receiving. This information will obviously tell us nothing and, appropriately enough, both $\text{Info}_1 = 0$ and $\text{Info}_2 = 0$, in this case. When we do not believe that E could possibly be true $\bar{p}(E \mid K) = 0$ and $\text{Info}_1 = 1$ but Info_2 = *infinity*.

The superiority of Info_2 over Info_1 may be argued as follows. Consider the apparent meaning of the formula:

$$\bar{p}(E_2 \mid E_1 \ \& \ K) = \bar{p}(E_2 \mid K) \tag{1}$$

This says that, even when your knowledge includes E_1, your judgement about E_2 is exactly as it would be given K alone. This is a way of saying, in some precise sense, that E_1 and E_2 supply *independent information*. When this condition applies it can be shown that

$$\text{Info}_2 (E_1 \ \& \ E_2) = \text{Info}_2(E_1) + \text{Info}_2(E_2) \tag{2}$$

– the precious addition law, a boon to anyone who would try to make deductions on the basis of measurement. Info_1 does not have this virtue. To prove the addition law, take the conditional probability rule (d) in the form:

$$\bar{p}(E_1 \ \& \ E_2 \mid K) = \bar{p}(E_1 \mid K) . \bar{p}(E_2 \mid E_1 \ \& \ K).$$

Independence of information in E_1 and E_2, expressed by formula (1), gives by substitution:

$$\bar{p}(E_1 \ \& \ E_2 \mid K) = \bar{p}(E_1 \mid K) . \bar{p}(E_2 \mid K)$$

taking logarithms of the reciprocals we get:

$$\log \left\{ \frac{1}{\bar{p}(E_1 \ \& \ E_2 \mid K)} \right\} = \log \left\{ \frac{1}{\bar{p}(E_1 \mid K)} \right\} + \log \left\{ \frac{1}{\bar{p}(E_2 \mid K)} \right\}$$

from which the addition rule, (2), follows immediately.

From the point of view of practical application, the difficulty lies in assessing every possible piece of evidence against every basic hypothesis. This is quite feasible and normal practice in statistical work, which relies upon a detailed model for purposes of analysis. Unfortunately, statistical methods will not serve in a court of law or in many business situations where, for want of a sufficient model to show how evidence is to be interpreted, we cannot apply the conditional probability rule (d) and are forced to rely upon intuitive induction.

I have attempted, in this chapter, to show how the methods employed in the critical analysis of the meaning of measurements, described in chapter 9, can be used to identify two different, fundamental measurements of statements p and p̄. Both these measurements obey the rules of probability, which provide the number system with its structure. This mathematical structure can be shown to have an empirical counterpart for those statements upon which betting can take place. The second probability measurement, p̄, incorporates the first (just as an interval scale incorporates an ordinal scale) but it adds the conditional probability rule to the structure. It was shown that this rule has an empirical counterpart for statements about repeatable events.

Measurements of information were then derived from p and p̄. Those based upon p can only be used to estimate the information in messages received between two occasions when p had been measured. The measurements based on p̄ enable the information in a statement of potential evidence to be estimated with respect to a person's present knowledge.

12 Reaching Agreement

In all negotiations of difficulty, a man may not look to sow and reap at once; but must prepare business and ripen it by degrees.

Francis Bacon, 'Of Negotiating'

In choice of committees for ripening business for counsel, it is better to choose indifferent persons, than to make an indifferency by putting in those that are strong on both sides.

Francis Bacon, 'Of Counsel'

It has been shown in the previous chapter how we might persuade a person to judge statements about a problem on a scale of 'degree of belief' in a way that conforms to certain rules. The rules reflect a number of assumptions. These assumptions are simple and so natural in certain circumstances that any rational person would be prepared to accept them. The rules have the effect of imposing upon his judgements of 'degree of belief' a structure of relationships which, in mathematical terms, qualifies the scale to be referred to as a probability-measure. There are many probability-measures, but this one is a personal and subjective measure which reflects only the opinions of one person.

The rules enumerated so far are the following three. The first might conveniently be given the title: *The Principle of Prescribed Possibilities.* It is the assumption that, before a problem can be assessed, it must be decided what is relevant and possible. The result is a model, embodying only those possibilities considered to be of interest throughout the weighing of the evidence. Any retreat from this position automatically throws the problem back into the melting pot of abductive reasoning. The second rule is the *Additivity Principle.* This is the assumption that, given any set of mutually exclusive propositions: H_1, H_2 ... H_n, one of which must be true, then their probabilities add up to unity:

$$p(H_1 | K) + p(H_2 | K) + \ldots + p(H_n | K) = 1$$

The additivity principle can be demonstrated in a practical way in the case of propositions which are also capable of being tested operationally, that is, if it makes sense to bet on these propositions. The third rule is *Bayes' Rule* which is a form of the conditional probability formula but more convenient for studying the problem of how a 'rational' person should adjust his opinion in the light of new information. It depends upon the severe assumption that a person can assess evidence, in advance of receiving it, without regard for the precise manner of its presentation.

The need to impose these constraints upon an individual's judgements can be demonstrated in some circumstances. The same constraints can be imposed, in wider circumstances, as normative rules which define a kind of 'rational' behaviour. Whilst they ensure that *one* person is self-consistent, they do nothing to ensure that two or more people hold the same opinions nor, even, do they guarantee that they would reach closer agreement in the light of evidence. This deficiency of subjective probability is the next problem to be examined.

Assessing the evidence*

In an organisation, or in society at large, it is usually intended that evidence should lead to a consensus. The subjective probability measure, which has been evolved in the previous chapter, will not guarantee that people starting with different opinions will interpret the same information in the same way. If people are to be sure eventually to reach agreement, then a further normative rule must be invoked. Such a rule must demand from the protagonists some slight measure of prior agreement about the interpretation of evidence. This assertion is illustrated below, using a few graphs.

Suppose there is a problem concerning the cost of developing a supersonic jumbo airliner which would be capable of circumnavigating the globe in 5 hours, at 5,000 m.p.h. One faction, the aerospace lobby, is backed by the Ministry responsible for aviation, who regard this as the ultimate in air transport. Their estimate of the cost is fairly modest compared with the estimate considered more likely by the Treasury. The tourist industry is almost queuing to offer round-the-world packages to the humblest traveller, but the typical, tax-paying potential traveller remains doubtful about the project.

Both sides in the dispute have sharply defined opinions, the ranges of predicted costs which they think at all likely are concentrated in two narrowly defined regions, as shown in fig. 20. The optimists expect it to

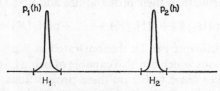

Fig. 20. Two sharply divided opinions about the development cost for a new aircraft.

* This section and the next may be skimmed by anyone not accustomed to a mathematical style of argument.

be in the range H_1 and the pessimists in the range H_2. You may read p(h)* as 'the probability that the ultimate cost will be £h'.

A committee of experts is appointed to review the project in the hope of narrowing the difference of opinion in the light of its report. The only soundly-based evidence available will be the considered view of the experts. The extent to which agreement can be reached will depend both upon the evidence itself and how persuasively it is presented, but let us suppose that the only significant part of the experts' judgement will be their figure for the estimated cost.

In advance of the experts' report, suppose that, by gathering data from two representatives, we have been able to discover how the two factions are likely to react. From these data it has been possible to construct graphs showing how the two factions would assess all the different estimates which the experts might favour, from the most optimistic to the most pessimistic. Suppose, also, that we have just been shown the draft report and know that the figure of projected costs that will actually be quoted is £e.

The reliance placed upon the expert opinion by each side can be represented by a series of graphs of conditional probabilities like those in fig. 21. This one is the graph for the value, e, which we have selected

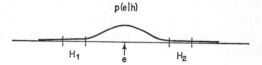

Fig. 21. Conditional probability that the committee will favour e, given that the final value will actually be h.

because we already know what the report will say. The graph specifies for each value of h (the *true* ultimate cost) what probability the individual attaches, in advance, to the suggestion that the committee will quote the value e. The shape of the graph reveals the individual's opinion of the accuracy of the expert committee. A poor opinion of the experts' ability to forecast costs with any precision is reflected in the flatness of the graph shown in the figure.

Although the two sides *may* agree on how to interpret the evidence, and accept the *same* graph of p(e|h), as in fig. 21, it is more likely that they suspect the committee of being loaded with members holding the opposing view from their own, and make due allowance for this. By way of illustration, if e is midway between H_1 and H_2, the two sets of conditional probabilities might be as shown in fig. 22.

---

* This probability-measure is the one designated by $\bar{p}$ in the previous chapter. For brevity $\bar{p}(h|k)$ is written p(h).

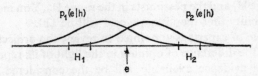

Fig. 22. Two different and rather suspicious views of the expert opinion.

If they were *extremely* suspicious of each other, they might even give these graphs so much compensation for expected bias that they were disposed as in fig. 23. There would be graphs like those in figs 21, 22 or 23 for all the other values of e which *we* know the committee has rejected.

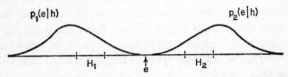

Fig. 23. Two very suspicious opinions about the expert evidence.

The effects upon opinions

What will be the effect of the evidence, e, upon the two opinions?

The new opinion, or posterior probabilities $p(h|e)$ held by one side or the other, can be derived from the formula for a 'rational' man's change of opinion:

$$p(h|e) = p(h).p(e|h)/p(e)$$

so it will depend not only upon the two graphs given above, but also upon the value of $p(e)$. Now, $p(e)$ will be a constant and its value will be roughly the same as the value given to the flat curve of $p(e|h)$ in the narrow region H because most of the contribution towards $p(e)$ will come from the values of $p(e|h)$ in the only cost bracket, H, that the individual regards as at all likely to contain the true final figure.* This means that, if $p(e|h)$ is very flat in the region of H, then the result will be either a slight fall or rise in the confidence placed in his predictions of h. This is shown in fig. 24(a), when the flat region is the 'tail' of $p(e|h)$ and in 24(b), when it is the high plateau of the curve $p(e|h)$. Where values of $p(h)$ are low, so also will be values of $p(h|e)$ and the region H will not alter very much.

---

* $p(e) = \int p(e\&h)dh = \int_{H} p(e|h)p(h)dh + \int_{\text{not-H}} p(e|h)p(h)dh \cong p(e|h)\big|_{\text{heH}} + 0$ because the value of $p(e|h)$ in the region of H is almost a constant and $\int_{H} p(h)dh \cong 1$ whilst $p(h) \cong 0$ over the region not-H.

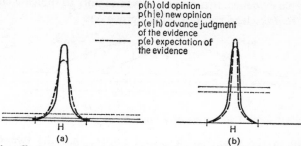

Fig. 24. The effect on opinion of a rather undifferentiated view of the evidence; confidence changes but opinion does not shift (note: different ordinal scales are used for p(h), p(h|e) and for p(e|h), p(e)).

What is important is that these flat graphs of p(e|h) in the zone H cause no *shift* of opinion to one side or the other. This only happens when the values of p(e|h) vary across the region H. This is illustrated in fig. 25.

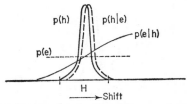

Fig. 25. The effect of a strongly differentiated view of the evidence: the opinion shifts (see note on ordinal scales to fig. 24).

The results of this analysis are rather interesting. If the committee of experts is thought unbiassed and not very accurate, as in fig. 21, the estimate, e, may have little effect, because the value of p(e|h) is almost constant over the regions H_1 and H_2. Also, because e is well outside these regions, both parties will think e very unlikely ($p_1(e)$ and $p_2(e)$ both very small), they will dismiss the report as unreliable and so their opinions will hardly be affected.

However, in the second case (fig. 22), where both parties are rather suspicious of the committee, they may succeed in bringing the sloping part of p(e|h) over the favoured region. If this is true of both sides, the result will be to shift the favoured regions H_1 and H_2 towards each other! In the third case (fig. 23), because of excessive suspicion of a loaded committee, the effect will be to move H_1 and H_2 even further apart.

Conditions that will definitely lead to closer agreement

Having demonstrated that two self-consistent but sharply divided opinions will not necessarily be brought into closer accord by supplying the best available evidence, it is possible more readily to indicate conditions that will *definitely* lead to quite close agreement.

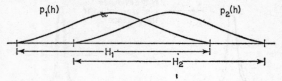

Fig. 26. Two cautiously open-minded prior opinions.

Suppose, in the situation described above, that the two opposing factions were prepared to admit that their own estimates of the final cost of the proposed aircraft were rather hazy, then their prior probability graphs would be like the flattened shapes in fig. 26, instead of the tall towers of opposing bigotries in fig. 20. They may even overlap, as shown. If, in addition, both sides had confidence in the accuracy *and* lack of

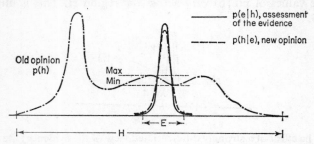

Fig. 27. The overwhelming effect of accurate evidence on a vague prior opinion. (Note: ordinal scale for p(h) different from that for p(e|h) and p(h|e).)

bias of the findings of the committee of experts, then this opinion would be represented by a graph of p(e |h) that has a narrow base and a high peak (accuracy) centred over the point where h=e (lack of bias). This is shown in fig. 27. The graph also includes the fragment of one of the graphs of old opinion, p(h), and the new opinion which takes account of the evidence.*

The new opinion, in these circumstances, will be almost entirely determined by the evidence. This susceptibility to evidence depends on the following specified conditions:

(a) the value of p(h), the prior opinion, must be greater than zero in the narrow zone, E, which the evidence strongly favours;

(b) the actual shape of the graph of p(h) does not matter very much, provided that its fluctuations are modest over the zone E;

---

* This graph of p(h) is not intended to be related to the other graphs of p(h) in earlier figures. All they have in common is that p(h) always designates a prior opinion of one kind or another.

(c) elsewhere the shape of p(h) is almost irrelevant provided that it is nowhere very sharply peaked.*

The rule which states these conditions as a basis for reaching agreement is called the Principle of Stable Estimation.

Another possibility would arise if neither side doubted the accuracy

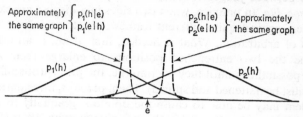

Fig. 28. When bias is ascribed to presumably accurate evidence.

of the expert view but both sides expected it to be biassed (in opposite directions, of course). Then the result would be new opinions largely determined by the evidence, provided that the zone E lay within both the zones, H_1 and H_2, originally favoured. The difference of opinion may have been narrowed, but the common ground may also have been reduced. See fig. 28.

Yet another interesting case arises when the experts, regarded as reliable in both accuracy *and* lack of bias, give, as their opinion of e, a value which is regarded by both factions as almost impossible. That is, the zone E is well outside both of the zones H_1 and H_2. This is as shown in fig. 29. This picture, on closer inspection, highlights some instructive

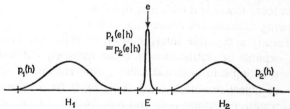

Fig. 29. An accurate unbiassed estimate that is not thought credible.

problems. Evidently, beforehand, neither of the factions would have judged the committee as reliable or unbiassed if they had contemplated such a value of e being proposed.

The only way of imagining that this kind of picture could arise would be by assuming that it had been agreed that the experts would be regarded as unbiassed and reasonably accurate over the whole range of possibilities, without first establishing where the two sides placed the limits

* For mathematical details see Edwards, Lindman and Savage, 1963.

of the credible range. This kind of situation arises often enough in practice when it is hoped to resolve a dispute by some type of arbitration, only to find that the expert opinion is rejected by both sides. The two sides are operating with different models, which admit different ranges of possibilities. This observation helps to emphasise again the essential difference between judgements of what is *possible* and judgements of what is *probable*. In practice, when two sides in a dispute are examining the problem against quite different frameworks, there is little virtue in a process of arbitration. What is needed, first of all, is an attempt to undermine the two entrenched positions to enlarge their zones of admitted possibilities until they overlap (i.e. the prior probability distributions must be flattened and spread). Then, perhaps, information about the problem may be able to cause the opinions gradually to coalesce. In the early stages, as we noted in the case shown in fig. 18, it would not matter if the information were regarded as biassed by both sides.

The social mechanism in group decision-making

The analysis which has been sketched above reveals that differences in the individual personal assessments of a problem are not necessarily resolved, even when all concerned are informed by a common fund of evidence. This need not be a result of some people being obstinately inconsistent (although this is common in life) whilst others are paragons of rationality (scarcely possible in practice). It is simply a consequence of the fact that each individual can be self-consistent according to the rules for 'reasonable' subjective judgements which do not include any rule that conduces towards a common opinion.

The following sections are concerned with the kind of rule that ensures a uniformly acceptable interpretation of evidence. This type of rule is only capable of justification in some narrowly defined circumstances. Often enough, in practical affairs, even matters of fact which are capable of objective study, given time, must be resolved without objective information because time and resources do not allow it to be obtained. Too often, unwise decisions are made on a subjective basis, when objective methods would have been available and appropriate. The information specialist in an organisation should have an important role to play in advising where the line should be drawn. Today, information technology is rapidly changing the limits to what is feasible in time and resources. It cannot, however, affect the boundary between what is capable, *in principle*, of objective assessment and what is not.

Many facts are accessible to us only through words or other signs; they can never be demonstrated. Criminal and historical evidence is of this kind. Statements about unique historic events cannot be checked by having them re-enacted while a jury watches! Business or administrative decisions are frequently concerned with statements about an imagined future, a future that must be created by the process of decision-making and action, not a future that can be passively observed by the curious. These unrepeatable decisions, like the decision to invest in developing a new aircraft, depend upon judgements that must be made on the basis of very limited evidence.

In these circumstances, we can attain only a diluted kind of objectivity by seeking a consensus among the people involved. There are many commonly employed means of achieving this end: the business committee, the Royal Commission, the jury, the learned symposium. All of them, in differing measure, rely upon evidence in the form of statements, preferably accompanied by an account of their source and how they were arrived at. In their appraisals the members of these groups take account of how the evidence is presented and how it is received by other members; their judgements also reflect the influence of the 'standing', 'authority', 'probity' and similar qualities thought to be possessed by the advisers or witnesses or whoever is supplying the evidence. This process is best explained in behavioural terms by the social mechanism of norm-formation (which was the subject of chapter 4) rather than by some kind of normative theory of 'rational' judgement.

In group decision-making the demeanour of people providing evidence and the reactions of the other members of the group receiving it may provide non-verbal information which is at least as important as the logical content of the statements exchanged. This is not necessarily a bad thing. When a group of people are sufficiently well acquainted with one another to be able to read the idiosyncratic, non-verbal signals that other members use to register degrees of doubt or certainty, they can probably reach a sensible agreement on complex matters more swiftly than a group of more erudite strangers. If the erudite strangers fail to learn to interact on a personal level and try to weigh all the evidence according to the lights of their own independent powers of judgement they may never reach agreement. This is because opinions about some kinds of statements can only be brought into line with one another by the interplay of social pressures. This is the essential role of political process in organisations.

The structure of an organisation, the physical juxtaposition of its departments and the overlapping membership of its working groups will affect an organisation's capacity to attain a consensus of opinion. Organisational design must take this into account, at least as much as it does the flow of formal messages.

One incidental lesson to be learnt from this by designers of business information systems is that the information they present to managers has its effect, not only by virtue of its actual contents, but also by virtue of the authority and standing of those responsible for producing it. The designer, if he is convinced of the objectivity, reliability and value of the reports his system is to supply to management, should ensure that they are not discounted because they are less convincing than other information given to decision-makers. A computer print-out has a singular lack of persuasiveness to anyone who does not believe in the infallibility of the machine. The general level of integrity and reliability imputed to the people who design and run the system may be as important a part of the information as its logical content. In this respect a management information system differs sharply from a clerical or routine information system, in which a message (e.g. notification of a despatch) is followed automatically by an action (e.g. sending an invoice); decision-making, when it is not merely the interpretation of rules, involves not only logic but what someone feels about the matter.

13 Objective Information

He is no wise man who will quit a certainty for an uncertainty.

Dr Johnson, *The Idler*

In the previous chapter, which dealt with subjective probabilities, it was shown that self-consistent individuals need never agree with one another, even in the face of any amount of relevant information, if they choose to place differing interpretations upon the evidence. Therefore we must discover principles, which any 'reasonable' man should adopt, to ensure the emergence of a consensus.

It has already been shown that agreement about subjective judgements *can* be reached if prior judgements of the evidence satisfy certain conditions. Most of the previous chapter was about this problem. If these conditions could be characterised precisely, they would provide the most general normative rules which could possibly serve to draw differing opinions into closer agreement. However, the mathematical problem of characterising these conditions is too complicated to deal with in this book.

Instead, much more stringent normative rules will be examined: the ones that are invoked as the basis of statistical reasoning.

Repeatable observations

One of the fundamental problems facing the ministers making the decision about the supersonic jumbo airliner is that they cannot appoint one expert commission after another, to produce a series of estimates of the development costs. This is the normal situation in which a businessman or administrator finds himself when taking a crucial decision; he cannot gather evidence repeatedly to check its validity in an objective way.

There are plenty of other routine decisions for which evidence can be gathered repeatedly, at a cost. There is a chance that agreement can be reached about these in an objective manner.

Suppose you have a problem of deciding whether a particular batch of metal castings will be strong enough. Suppose, also, that the only possible test of their strength is a destructive test. Obviously, if any usable components are to be left after inspection, only a sample from a batch can be tested, while the strength of the others must be arrived at by inductive reasoning. If only one casting is tested and its breaking strain is $x=50$ units, you are no better off than the minister with the airliner decision. It can be argued that the observation is compounded of two values:

$$x = S + E$$

where S is the true average strength of the castings and E is an error made by the testing machine. Hence, one person may argue that

$$S = 48 \text{ and } E = 2 \qquad \text{(Mr A)}$$

and another person with equal justification might assert that

$$S = 34 \text{ and } E = 16 \qquad \text{(Mr B)}$$

What arguments can be adduced to oblige these two reasonable men to agree?

Before you begin smashing any more castings, you could try to persuade Mr B that he is exaggerating the likely error of the testing machine, or, on the other hand, Mr A may be prepared to acknowledge that such errors are not at all rare. You need another argument because you may have to admit that the test is not very accurate.

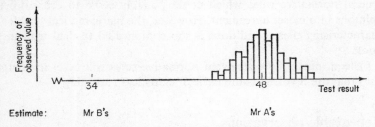

Fig. 30. The results of destructively testing a sample.

So, on the next round, you begin a discussion on the possible bias of the testing machine. You check that it has recently been back to the makers and has a certificate to say that it has been standardised. You inspect the machine, yourselves, and you agree that it is unbiassed, albeit not very accurate. Quite confidently, you remove a few dozen castings from the 500 in the batch, smash them in the machine, and record the test results as a frequency distribution. See fig. 30. Triumphantly you take the average of these results and discover it is 48. You are about to congratulate Mr A on his estimate and give instructions to despatch the remaining castings when Mr B, who is the technical representative of the customer, refuses to accept them, saying that the result is biassed. He persuades you that he really did not intend to suggest you had cheated by selecting only very strong-looking specimens, by indicating that the bias may have been caused by selecting all the castings from the top of the bin; these, being the last ones made, are likely to be the strongest. This you do not believe but you cannot get him to change his mind. You cannot test any more from that batch without having too few to meet the order. You resolve not to be caught on sampling the next batch, so you seek the advice of a statistician and his first words are 'random sampling'. He explains.

Random sampling and avoiding bias

Mr A and Mr B can be forced, by the accumulation of evidence, to agree if they are both prepared to admit that the measuring device is un-biassed, that it behaves in a uniform way and that *the sampling proced-ure makes it equally likely that any one casting will be selected, as any other.*

If we are to claim the observed, relative frequencies of errors as a sound *objective* basis for judging probabilities, then we must secure agreement, from those whose judgement is involved, that the processes giving rise to observations (e.g. the selection of a sample of castings from a batch and the sequence in which they are tested) do not introduce bias. We need a method of sampling which, like the shuffling and cutting of cards or the shaking and throwing of dice, strikes people as 'fair'.

Random sampling and bias

All too often, when data are gathered in the course of administrative or business decision-making, no steps are taken to ensure that the method of observation does not introduce bias. Unless this is done, the facts may be highly coloured by the method of gathering them. The principle of random sampling or of randomising experimental designs is the statistician's method of avoiding bias in routine or repeated observations.

The idea is *not* that you ask someone to make a *haphazard* choice of members from a population to form your sample (of castings, say) or subject them to some experimental procedure (destructive testing, say) in a haphazard manner. Reliance upon this method is dangerous, as can easily be demonstrated. Ask someone, or try yourself, to write down quickly 100 haphazardly chosen numbers with 5 digits each; then make a frequency table for the ten different digits; this will almost certainly reveal strong predilections for some digits rather than others. You can see the same effect in the choice of final digit in measurements that people make; the even numbers and 5 do much better than others as a rule. A case I once encountered was in the demand for blood for trans-fusions; one might expect this to be a random variable, determined biologically. In fact, there was a clear indication that even numbers of bottles were given disproportionately often and, wherever possible, doctors gave 6 bottles, a full crate! This human tendency to superimpose systematic effects upon a haphazard process can easily lead to a consistent bias being introduced.

If you would like to try an experiment along these lines, assemble a tray of 100 stones of varying sizes; weigh them to find their average weight and then ask people to take a number of samples of, say, 20, to be used to find the average weight of the stones; weigh the samples and divide by 20. Even when your subjects are trying to be fair they will almost invariably introduce a consistent bias, usually towards the heavy side.

Genuinely random processes

It is extremely difficult to sample members of a population quite randomly without making use of some uniform, physical process that can generate random numbers *in a manner that can be demonstrated to be consistently free from regular patterns*. Suitable simple processes are throwing a die or tossing a coin. In practice, methods include the automatic counting of radio-active emissions or random, thermal movements of electrons.

It is usually most convenient to use recorded tables of random numbers, which have been generated by some electronic device, and have already been subjected to rigorous tests to ensure that they are free from any discoverable regularities of behaviour. With tables of random digits, you can be confident that the numbers generated from them by any simple routine (such as taking every 7th digit) will be as fairly 'shuffled' as is possible. Any 'rational' person would ascribe a probability of 0.1 to the proposition that some given digit, say 2, will be the next one selected.

A fixed frame of reference is necessary when using these tables, so that a random number can be associated unambiguously with a member of the population. Thus, if everyone in a company has a unique number associated with him, say a clock number, then a string of random digits which, together, constitute a clock number in current use, corresponds directly to a choice of employee. There can be no better way of making demonstrably sure that any one employee is as likely to be chosen as any other. If these chances are *equal* you have a *simple* random sample, but they need not be. Quite often it is desirable to give a larger chance of inclusion to the more significant members of the population. For example, a sample of farms in the U.K. could be chosen by using random numbers to give fictitious map references; those covering the U.K. would be extracted; each valid one would identify the farm which included the map reference and the chance of selection would be proportionate to the size of the farm. Thus, the farms at the large end of the size 'spectrum' would be chosen more often. This would be desirable if you were interested in estimating, say, the use of artificial fertilisers which would be greater for the larger farms.

In the case of the testing of the metal castings, it may be desirable to use random numbers to control the choice of the sample taken from a batch, and to decide the order in which chosen castings are subjected to the test. This would eliminate possible risks of systematic bias.

Fundamental role of randomising procedures

There is an apt analogy between what we 'see' in statistical data and what we see visually. If we look at an object illuminated by a blue light, we shall have a mistaken impression of its colour unless we are aware of, and can take account of, the blueness of the light. That is why we try to look at things in white light which includes all the colours equally in its spectrum. This property of whiteness is like the property of a simple random sample. In fact, we can think of the photons of light as sampling the surface for us; if the illumination includes too few photons of a given wavelength, then that colour will be under-represented in the image. If, likewise, a sampling technique gives some part of the population too little chance of being selected, the resulting statistics will also be 'coloured' in a misleading way. Some parallel to this can be found in every repetitive process of observation or transmission of information; that is why the idea is so basic (see chapter 20).

Often, in collecting business data, you cannot control either a sampling process or an experimental set-up. If this is the case, it is essential to recognise that one of the props supporting the relative frequency concept of probability is missing. Correspondingly, greater caution is necessary in interpreting the data. It is important to try to notice any regularities or pressures upon observers which might introduce a bias in the process giving rise to the data. For example, data on the observed defects of steel may seem to be good, basic facts on which to judge the performance of the plant and method of manufacture. But it is difficult to judge whether a mark on the surface of a billet of steel is a defect or a mark which will simply disappear during the next manufacturing process. An inspector is quite likely to be influenced, perhaps quite subconsciously, by what he believes to be the stringency of the customers' requirements. Consider another case: samples, taken at regular intervals, from a list of people, *may* produce an unrepresentative sample because of a regularity in the list; such a 'periodic' sample taken from an electoral roll, in which names are listed house by house, street by street, would be less likely to include members of the same family than would a random sample. And again: questionnaires which are not returned cannot be regarded as randomly discarded data; there may be strong correlations between a tendency not to return the questionnaire and the particular answers that those people would give.

Failure to use a satisfactory randomising procedure *always* casts doubt upon the data collected.

Randomising relative frequencies and objectivity

The *randomising principle*, described above, helps people to achieve agreement about how data are to be interpreted. When procedures can be employed to gather data by randomised experiment or observation, we can demonstrate that using *relative frequencies* is a justifiable way of determining probabilities. This enables probabilities to be arrived at by a commonly agreed, public process. This is important in the pursuit of objectivity. Decisions based on data obtained in this manner are more exposed to public criticism or, conversely, it is no longer justifiable to leave the interpretation of such data to the subjective impressions of each individual person.

Inductive criteria: Bayes' Rule and the likelihood principle

Despite the two principles of randomising and using relative frequencies, there still remains a strong personal, subjective influence upon the conclusions reached by inductive reasoning on the basis of objective evidence. This is because of the initial, subjective probability. Bayes' Rule can be written briefly:

$$p(H \mid E) = k.\ p(E \mid H).\ p(H)$$

Now $p(H \mid E)$ is the 'rational' person's judgement of the hypothesis H after receiving the evidence E. The Rule says that this should be proportional to two terms. One is the likelihood of the evidence, given the hypothesis $p(E \mid H)$. The other is $p(H)$, the prior judgement of probability. This rule for adjusting your opinion in a rational manner is an *inductive principle*. As we have noted earlier in this chapter, Bayes' Rule applied to individual subjective probabilities has a serious drawback: it does not ensure that evidence will cause people to reach agreement. The principles of randomising and of relative frequencies help to remove this defect, when data are open to objective appraisal.

The remaining obstacle, the subjective, prior probability $p(H)$, can be eliminated to yield a new and simpler rule which states that

$$p(H \mid E) = k'\ p(E \mid H).$$

In other words, given some evidence, E, the most favoured hypothesis H should be the one which makes the evidence most likely. This is another rule for inductive inference. It is the most widely used rule in statistics today and it is called the *maximum likelihood principle*. Its application in place of Bayes' Rule can be justified in certain circumstances.

When the maximum likelihood principle is justifiable

The correct use of statistical information in business and administration calls for an awareness of when the underlying assumptions can be justified. Fortunately, two mathematical properties of probability conspire to make the maximum likelihood principle appropriate in many commonly-encountered situations. There are two theorems which demonstrate that this simpler inductive principle will serve on many occasions.

One, the Principle of Stable Estimation, has already been discussed on p. 170 and fig. 27 was used to illustrate it. When the evidence is fairly reliable and accurate, (i.e. $p(E|H)$ has a graph which does not spread very far), and the prior probability, $p(H)$, has a fairly uniform non-zero value in the region favoured by evidence, then the posterior probability $p(H|E)$ is overwhelmingly governed by the evidence, rather than by the prior opinion of the probability.

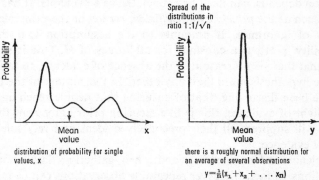

Spread of the distributions in ratio $1:1/\sqrt{n}$

distribution of probability for single values, x

there is a roughly normal distribution for an average of several observations

$$y = \tfrac{1}{n}(x_1 + x_2 + \dots x_n)$$

Fig. 31. How an estimate based on repeated observations achieves accuracy.

The second is the famous Central Limit Theorem. This most remarkable theorem is quite easily illustrated. Look at fig. 31. On the left is the probability distribution of a single value, x, drawn from some population. If repeated observations are drawn from the same population, say n of them, and averaged, then this average can be regarded as a new kind of observation, y. The distribution of y is shown in the graph on the right. This distribution of y will be very compact around the mean value for the population and, in practice, it will tend to be quite sharply peaked when based upon only a dozen observations. What is even more remarkable is that the shape of the graph of y's distribution tends to almost exactly the same shape, called the normal distribution, practically regardless of the distribution of x.* The consequence of this mathematical idea is that you can almost guarantee that the evidence, y, is accurate if it can be based on several observations, and, in such cases the situation is as depicted in fig. 27 and the Principle of Stable Estimation can be confidently invoked.

The above paragraphs are full of words like 'nearly', 'almost', 'about'. A major problem in statistics is to give precise definition to these terms, in specific cases. One thing is certain, however, the use of the simplifying assumption of the maximum likelihood rule is hard to justify, if repeated experiments or observations *cannot* be made.

The principle of insufficient reason

The subjective element in inductive reasoning is eliminated when the maximum likelihood principle can be used. The previous section has shown that this principle amounts to using an approximation to Bayes' Rule. This approximation is a very good one and well justified in the conditions that are common in statistical work.

The approximation, upon which the maximum likelihood rule of induction depends, can itself be enunciated as a principle. It has various names such as the *principle of insufficient reason* or the principle of uniformity of ignorance. It amounts to the assumption that the prior probability, p(H), is a constant for all values of H. One is saying, in effect, that there is no reason, in the absence of evidence, to favour one possible hypothesis more than any other. In the context of the problem we have been discussing, that of ensuring that people reach agreement in the light of evidence, this is like securing prior agreement that both parties will suppress all their preconceived ideas and rely solely upon the new evidence.

In science and engineering, and when gathering data about large populations, in fact, whenever repeatable observations can be made, the principle of insufficient reason is usually justifiable. In business and administrative decision-making, when any reliable evidence is frequently difficult to obtain, it would be folly to suppress the prior judgements of experienced people merely in the interest of a purity of statistical method. In saying this, there is no intention to condone the more common sup-

---

* This statement is not *strictly* true as it is possible to define functions that are 'pathological' in their mathematical behaviour (there is the famous Cauchy distribution for example), but these are not important in practice.

pression of overwhelming evidence in the interest of long-established prejudice.

Hypothetical or logical probabilities

Armed with the last in this series of 'rational' principles, we can turn to the question of how we attach probabilities to the outcomes of parlour games: cards, dice, etc. It is customary to study these games not by actual experiment but by describing the class of possible outcomes, and by invoking the principle of insufficient reason to justify assigning equal probabilities to each member of the class.

Thus, for a tossed coin, there are 2 outcomes H and T, so each has a probability $\frac{1}{2}$. When dealing a pair of cards from a full pack, there are 52 ways of dealing the first card and 51 ways of dealing the second. Altogether there are 52×51 ordered pairs of cards. Similarly there are 4×3 ordered pairs of aces. Hence the probability of being dealt a pair of aces is $(4 \times 3)/(52 \times 51)$. Sometimes arguments like these are expressed in terms of 'relative frequencies', even though a card has never been dealt nor a coin tossed. Such 'relative frequencies' do not refer to any actual events; they are purely hypothetical. The probabilities arrived at by such arguments are *deduced* by purely formal arguments from a model; they call for no operations to be performed either by repeating experiments or by asking people their opinions. Without operational justification, hypothetical probabilities are purely *formal* properties of the signs themselves.

Hypothetical or logical probabilities need not be entirely divorced from reality. In so far as they can claim to be plausible in the light of geometrical symmetry, guaranteed, perhaps, by the known high standards of manufacture, as of playing cards, and in so far as they presume some kind of randomising procedure, as shuffling, hypothetical probabilities can claim *some* semantic standing. Nevertheless we must be careful not to confuse *actual* frequencies discovered by *actual* experiments with *talk about* relative frequencies that *might* be obtained in some *hypothetical* experiments.

In the next part of the book, which deals with the purely formal properties of signs, this kind of probability will be examined in greater detail and its use as a basis for a way of measuring another 'information' property will be discussed.

Models used in inductive reasoning

There are not many occasions when statements about an organisational policy can be related directly to repeatable observations. In order to subject a policy to any objective assessment it becomes necessary to relate it, via a logical or mathematical model, to statements about observations. Whilst greatly enlarging the scope of inductive reasoning, these additional links in the chain make the conclusions dependent upon them more difficult to justify.

To see how models are used, suppose that the Town Council of Leamington Spa is having to decide whether to close the main shopping street to traffic. The kinds of statement which must be examined might say: 'If The Parade is closed to traffic, there will be chaos and hardship.' These statements can be made explicit by defining a series of measures of 'chaos' and 'hardship' such as the probable lengths of various traffic queues and the probability-distributions of journey times. In other words, a number of abstract concepts must be defined within the framework of a model which links them to many individual, concrete observations.* By actually closing The Parade on a few occasions, one might be able to obtain a glimpse of these queues and journey times, but the picture might be very faint. A much better picture could be obtained by using a large amount of objective evidence which can be focused into a clear image of the traffic queues and journey times, using the logical model as a series of lenses and mirrors. The problem of model-building is to find the correct light-source and to ensure that the lenses and mirrors do not distort the image. Take the traffic model as an example:

(a) Traffic flow will be determined by thousands of decisions made by individual drivers. An assumption of how such decisions are made, whether by attempting to minimise time or distance or a mixture, could be postulated and tested objectively by interviewing large numbers of drivers. The assumption may be very crude but it constitutes the light-source for the evidence which the model must focus.

(b) The next stage would be to construct a model showing how to resolve all the individual behaviour patterns into a picture of the total flow of traffic. The experimental closing of the street might help to test the validity of this structural model, under present conditions, but it would have to be taken on trust for future traffic densities and for systems including roads not yet built. Although this stage of the model, being described mathematically, would probably look very 'scientific', it would be very difficult to demonstrate objectively that the resulting picture of traffic flow is free from distortion.

(c) Finally, the consequences of any street closures or the opening of new routes could be 'observed' by analysing their consequences, probably

---

* This is a large-scale, slow-motion version of the relationship between even a simple concept, such as 'house' and the myriad observations which support our confident use of such concrete words. This discussion of models should be related to chapter 7: Giving Names to Things.

by running a simulation based on the model, using a computer. Repeated 'experiments' using the model can give the results an added air of objectivity which can be quite spurious. No amount of relative frequency data, alone, can justify acting on the results drawn from a model. Any claim to respectable semantic standing for the results of the simulation must rest upon the empirical tests in stage (a) combined with attempts in stage (b) to demonstrate that the mathematical rules of the structural model correspond to empirical relationships in the real world between drivers and traffic queues.

In practice, there is an unfortunate tendency, when using decision-models of this kind, to devote massive ingenuity to the mathematical formulation of stage (b) and similar skill to the writing of efficient programs for computers in stage (c). Often the kind of basic behavioural model in stage (a) will be taken for granted because it is expensive and, above all, boring to spend all the time necessary for gathering and analysing empirical data. Similarly, explaining the assumptions about the world embodied in the mathematics of stage (b) to experienced people who can knowledgeably criticise them, seems too tedious a task for busy model-builders. So the model-builders retire to a pure sign-world above the clouds, and then, Moses-like, descend from time to time with computer print-out.

A great deal of economic theory and operational research is open to this kind of criticism. The stage (a) behavioural model of 'economic man' still serves to underpin much economic theory, for want of a simple alternative that does not try to equate both the modern consumer and the modern industrialist with the eighteenth-century mill-owner. Operational research and economic models often exist at so high a level of abstraction, and scatter their practical consequences over the ground of reality so thinly, that these models can evade criticism based upon real events which unequivocally stem from their use.

At a quite different level in the scale of abstraction are the models devised by systems analysts to form components of working information systems; these are used to process live data (orders and payments) and generate hard results (goods and invoices) which can give rise to instant criticism from the people affected. Such models may be at least as complicated as those used in economics and O.R., but the systems analyst cannot afford to take risks with their semantic standing. Perhaps one may say that his task of establishing relationships between the world of reality and the world of symbolic representations is the most important characteristic of the role of the systems analyst.

The *principle of model-building*, described above, is an indispensable part of the framework of inductive reasoning. Without it, objective data can only serve as evidence about trivial problems; using models we can form abstractions that permit us to formulate the large problems faced in business and administration in such a way that they can be resolved in the light of objective information.

There are severe difficulties about reaching this goal of rational decision-making. The appeal to objective data must not be shirked, or the whole exercise will turn into a meaningless parlour game of symbol shuffling. There is no escape from the testing of the model through the intuition and judgement of people who have direct experience of the world it refers to. The model must be understood by those who are responsible *politically* for judging both the assumptions it contains and the results it produces; otherwise, this political responsibility will automatically devolve upon the model-builders. Their political naiveté and innocence is no guarantee of political wisdom.

Quest for rational and objective information – a résumé

We have now completed, in this chapter and the two previous ones, a survey of the assumptions that underlie the use of probability for judging the acceptability of information expressed as statements. This has been done by showing how a series of principles might be invoked to govern 'rational' judgements. Each of these principles is only justifiable in certain circumstances, outside of which they can only be taken on trust. To end this discussion, it may help to recapitulate each of the principles:

A. The principles of prescribed possibilities: Before any problem can be discussed in probability terms, there must be agreement about what should be counted as the only relevant and possible states of affairs. Many business and political decisions do not even admit this simple assumption. To impose a closed model upon an open-ended problem can be dangerous because it says that the stage of abductive, creative reasoning is closed. In many practical situations time is too precious to waste it on any other stage of reasoning.

B. Additivity principle: When A applies, this principle states that a rational person should be able to judge statements on a scale ranging from 0 (=false) to 1 (=true) and that the values for a set of mutually exclusive yet exhaustive possibilities should add up to 1. This rule, together with the logic of propositions, is the foundation of all the mathematical properties of a probability measure. People may not behave this way most of the time, but would probably acknowledge themselves as irrational in not doing so.

C. Conditional probability principle: This embodies the assumption that a person can decide how he would assess some possible evidence in advance of receiving it. If he can do this, then the rule of induction called

Bayes' Rule is a mathematical consequence. This states how a 'rational' man should adjust his opinion in the light of evidence which he has judged beforehand.

D. *Randomising principle:* This enables observations or experiments to be made repeatedly in a way that people can regard as 'fair'. When it is applied, the results will be an unbiassed guide to any results expected in the future. In these circumstances, *relative frequencies* of the different outcomes can justifiably be claimed to be sound bases for judging the probabilities of future outcomes. Without the possibility of repeated observation, this principle and the use of relative frequencies afford no assistance in assessing data objectively. The only ways of reaching agreement about evidence, when repeated observation is impossible, are through the interplay of social forces and the critical appraisal of stated positions. Organisational information is often characterised by its uniqueness, whereas scientific evidence is characterised by its reproducibility.

E. *Maximum likelihood principle:* This is a simpler and more objective inductive principle than Bayes' Rule and it is quite justifiable when the evidence is precise, compared with any prior opinion. It takes account only of the new information and discounts all preconceived notions. It is the generally accepted principle when observations can be repeated.

F. *Principle of insufficient reason:* This principle, if adopted, makes the maximum likelihood principle exact and banishes Bayes' Rule altogether. It is sometimes invoked in model-building to avoid the labour of gathering relative frequency data. Unless its use can be justified by an appeal to the *practical* experience of someone who can vouch for assumptions, such as symmetry and lack of bias in a random process, the resulting hypothetical probabilities will tell us nothing about the real world.

G. *Model-building principle:* Enables the scope of objective evidence to be enlarged, by using a mathematical or logical framework of consistent and simple assumptions to relate statements of a highly abstract character to simple, repeatable observations. The abstractions and the logical framework, which constitute the model, must be subjected to the kind of critical analysis outlined in chapters 7 and 8.

So we come full circle. By applying the methods of semantic analysis, we can stabilise a part of our picture of the world, but we can do so for only a small and privileged area bounded by a series of normative rules of 'reasonable' judgement.

Conclusion – the quality of information

The last seven chapters have explored some problems concerning the quality of information. Words, numbers, statements and other inform-

G

ative signs must not be taken always at their face value. The presumption that these signs refer to things and events and, therefore, inform us about the 'real' world should be subject to critical appraisal.

Normally we behave in response to verbal and numerical signs as though there were no problem, as though words and numbers mean what they say they mean, in a commonsense way. To do otherwise would result in a kind of paralysis, a loss of the ability to respond to messages in an uncomplicated way. However, in an organisation, whilst most people can be expected to treat the communications they receive without the agonies of semantic analysis, it is essential that some few people periodically check the quality of information being circulated. A good manager will naturally question what he is told and not take it at its face value, unless he has already satisfied himself about its justification. As organisations grow in size, managers must act on information which is derived from remote sources, based on vast amounts of observational data, and processed in very complex ways. As a result, it becomes a specialist task to audit the information which is used, not merely to see that it satisfies accountancy standards, but to ensure that the semantic standing of the information is known and taken into account by those who use it. It is a job for the professional information specialist.

The 'semantic standing' of a statement is a shorthand referring to the degree to which it constitutes a reliable guide to action. Tested statements are the weapons we use in 'the battle against the bewitchment of our intelligence by means of language'. The information specialist should see himself at the front line in this battle: organisational behaviour too readily succumbs to the magic of misleading language.

Part Five

Syntactics

If, by using the critical tools of semantics, we can be sure that the signs carrying information through our organisation are firmly rooted in the realities of the world, then we can process our information, with reasonable confidence that the results will be accurate and meaningful.

In order to understand the processing of information, we can dismiss from our minds altogether the difficult semantic problems and think of the information-bearing signs (words, numbers or mathematical symbols) as small, easily reproducible objects which can be arranged and rearranged, gathered, stored and disseminated according to formal mechanical rules. This will be the point of view adopted in the next four chapters.

Chapter 14 is about formal languages and chapter 15 shows how these can be operated upon quite mechanically according to the rules of logic. The problems of storing signs, retrieving them and recombining them to answer questions are examined in chapter 16.

The measurement of information is taken further in chapter 17. This shows how logical probabilities can be defined in relation to a formal language and used to derive another class of information measurements.

14 Formal Systems of Signs

*Formalism . . . means the ideal of exactitude that each deductive
system tries to attain. We say that a deductive system is formalised when
the correctness of the deductions in the system can be verified without
having to refer back to the meaning of the expressions and symbols used
in the deductions. They may be verified, that is, by anyone who
understands the rules of inference of the system.*

Jan Lukasiewicz, *On the History of the Logic of Propositions*

The next four chapters depend upon a point of view quite different from
any we have so far adopted in the discussion of information in this book.
Our concern is still with the understanding of signs and their properties,
but, this time, signs will be treated in their own right, as objects which
can be selected, reproduced, stored, retrieved, transformed and assembled into groups. This approach characterises the branch of semiotics
called syntactics (from syntax). It excludes all concern for the people who
use the signs and it also excludes all concern for the signification of the
signs. Syntactics is only concerned with the formal relationships among
the signs and the operations to which they may be subjected.

This may seem a very arid approach to the nature of information but
it is of immense practical importance. A purely syntactical study of
information is important in business today, largely because of the growing use of computers. These machines can process *any* formal system of
signs. Conversely, if computers are to be used for data-processing, their
tasks *must* be described as purely formal manipulations of signs. It is
becoming possible to reduce many complex intellectual tasks to formal
procedures and so automate them. Consequently, seemingly diverse
problems are found to be identical at the syntactic level, once the
behavioural and semantic complications are stripped away. This is the key
to the vast productive potential of computers: solve one abstract problem and you have solved a vast array of concrete, practical problems.

There is another reason why syntactics is a subject of practical importance in administration: the very nature of many organisational tasks
calls for a formal coordinating mechanism. It may be a body of complex
instructions, like a legal system, or a model which displays the logical
and necessary relationships between some of an organisation's activities,
as does a budget or a critical path plan. These coordinating devices may
be regarded as formal systems of signs; therefore the mechanistic aspects
of organisations can be studied in terms of formal information systems.

The economy of thought obtained by focussing on the syntactic aspects of information depends upon our being able to conceive signs as objects. So accustomed are we to looking for the 'meaning' of a sign, in the senses discussed earlier in the book, that it can be difficult to stop doing so. Systems of signs in their own right can be a rewarding and fascinating object of study, as mathematics has repeatedly demonstrated. Systems which are explored in their abstract, symbolic form can often be used to depict 'real' systems which have similar properties. This enables us to achieve a remarkable degree of increased productivity by solving at one go what were once thought of as many unique problems.

Using a computer, we can design a data-processing system in the abstract as a symbol-manipulating procedure, and then apply it to many different practical cases. Systems can be designed to perform payroll calculations or to schedule production in many different businesses, provided that the analysis of the underlying structures shows that they are of the same type.

Three of the next four chapters introduce some of these formal structures and indicate their relevance to business problems.

Formal languages

It is essential to start by examining the structures called 'formal languages'.

There is a useful analogy between a language and a constructional toy. The construction kit is made up of a large number of components: rods, metal strips and plates with holes cut in them, some flat, and some angled; there are also nuts, bolts, wheels and so on. These components are like the individual symbols which appear in a language. We refer to them as 'tokens'; for the toy we would use the word 'component'. In principle, there is no limit to the number of tokens or components we may employ in constructing utterances in a language or in the modelling kit, but, just as there are a limited number of *types* of components, so in a language there are a limited number of types of *token*. If we want to define a formal language, the first thing we must do is to set down the types of symbol (or vocabulary) that we intend to employ. Next we have to set down the rules by which the symbol tokens can be strung together. With the toy there is no need to do this explicitly, because the shapes of the components themselves physically determine how the components may be joined to one another. In a language, however, explicit rules are required, called the 'syntax' of the language. The language itself is defined as the collection of all the *possible* objects that can be constructed according to the syntax. Languages are not the only structures which can be formed from signs; other, more complex kinds of structure are described later.

The principle of object and meta-languages

When constructing models in a symbolic form, there is a tendency to confuse symbols in the language being used for talking about the model, and symbols belonging to the formal language itself. This arsies because we can use a symbol both as *itself* (within a model) and as the *name* for that symbol (to talk about a component). If you make a model from the construction kit you are not in danger of confusion, because you will employ the words 'nut', 'bolt', 'strut', 'bar', to designate the components and you will use the physical components themselves for building the model. When discussing languages, it is essential to preserve the same kind of distinction. This is done by recognising that two languages are being used; the language which is the object of discussion is normally called the *object language*, whilst the language in which the discussion is conducted is called the *meta-language*.

The failure to recognise this distinction has been the cause of a number of paradoxes, the most ancient of which is the Epimenides. It is this:

Epimenides, himself a Cretan, said that Cretans always lie.

What are we to believe? If Epimenides is right he is certainly wrong, but only if he is wrong can he possibly be right! The paradox vanishes if the object language of *all utterances made by Cretans* and the meta-language of *statements about what Cretans say* (even when they are made by Cretans themselves), are rigidly separated. Subtle confusions of this kind are a common danger to people coming new to computer programming and some parts of mathematics or logic. It is as well to learn to keep a clear distinction in the mind between different languages. Watch out for this problem throughout these chapters!

Anyone who is not accustomed to mathematical or logical notation (which cannot be avoided here) can protect himself from confusion by remembering that the symbols are components in a construction kit, to be manipulated according to the rules laid down. Any attempt to find a meaning in the symbols, beyond the explicitly stated rules, is a mistake and a departure from the syntactic level of analysis. The formal manipulation of signs is the level at which the computer programmer must work on information. The job of establishing the semantic relationships between the signs and 'real' things is the work of the systems analyst or information analyst.

In programming terms, the paradox of Epimenides would be recognised as a closed loop of operations: if you try to resolve its meaning you must mentally switch endlessly from belief to disbelief in Cretans. It is a pathological form of language – a breakdown in the mechanics of words. Logic is about the mechanics of language and hence of computers, which must employ logically rigorous forms of language. For this reason the information specialist must be acquainted with logic and have a thorough awareness of its limitations.

Grammars and machines

As mentioned above, to define a language it is necessary to list the symbols it employs and state the rules for combining them into 'sentences'. This description is called a grammar. Another way of defining a formal language is by describing a machine which can produce all the sentences in the language, or which can recognise when a string of symbols is a correctly-formed sentence. By keeping this duality in mind, it is possible to recognise more easily how computers can be employed for processing information. The computer is another construction kit, from which many language-processing machines can be built. To do this we need a formal description of the language. The job of a systems analyst includes the specification of the languages needed to perform a given data-processing task. (Few analysts today think of their work in these terms, but only by doing so are they going to be able to exploit a valuable body of theoretical knowledge which provides general solutions to many of their problems.)

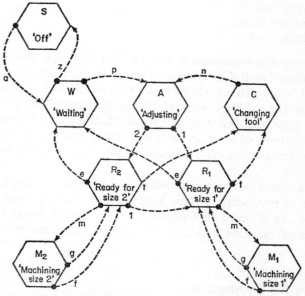

Fig. 32. State transition diagram for a machine tool.

Any machine gives rise to a formal language. Consider a machine capable of producing two different sizes of article; suppose that from producing the larger size it can go on to producing the smaller size without any re-setting of the tools, but that to increase the size of product will call for a new tool. We can imagine the machine reporting its work automatically, using a language in which the 'words' name the items it produces and indicate special events such as 'tool broken', 'size 2 selected', 'end of run'. From a viewpoint of production control this is probably as complete a method of communicating from the machine to ourselves as we require. For reporting purposes, therefore, we need only bother with these messages; a production run could be counted as starting and ending with 'machine off'. It may be depicted as in fig. 32.

The messages transmitted as the machine tool changes state are as follows:

a   machine switched on
p   production run initiated
1   set for size 1
2   set for size 2
m   machining selected size
g   good item made
f   faulty item made
e   end of production run
t   end of tool life
n   new tool fitted
z   switched off

They report the transitions of the machine from one state to another. The machine 'speaks' in 'sentences', which describe periods of operation. They all begin with 'a', when the machine is switched on, and end with 'z', when the machine is switched off. The symbols 'a' and 'z' are like the capital letter and full-stop of English. Between these symbols, only limited patterns of other symbols will occur. Production cycles are the 'phrases' from which the 'sentence' is built; these all begin with 'p' and end with 'e'.

The language has been represented in the form of a machine which is capable of producing it. This is sometimes called a 'state transition diagram'. In the case we have been considering, it would be called a 'finite-state' machine because it has only a finite number of possible states.

Generative Grammars

There is another and rather more convenient way of representing a language. That is by using a 'grammar'. Taking the above example, and using letters to designate the states of the machine, the rules of a grammar can be written thus:

$$S \rightarrow aW$$
$$W \rightarrow pA \text{ or } zS$$
$$A \rightarrow 1R_1 \text{ or } 2R_2$$
$$R_1 \rightarrow mM_1 \text{ or } tC \text{ or } eW$$
$$R_2 \rightarrow mM_2 \text{ or } tC \text{ or } eW \text{ or } 1R_1$$
$$M_1 \rightarrow gR_1 \text{ or } fR_1$$
$$M_2 \rightarrow gR_2 \text{ or } fR_2$$
$$C \rightarrow nA$$

where, for example, $C \rightarrow nA$ says that the machine *can* go from state C to state A, emitting the signal 'n' as it does so.

This tells us no more than the transition diagram, so there appears to be no gain. However, what we are interested in is languages rather than machines. It is natural, therefore, to think of the grammar as furnishing a set of rules or *productions* for generating strings of symbols. That being the case, this language has a very special and limited structure, because its productions permit strings of symbols to grow only at one end.

To obtain more general grammars, consider two kinds of symbol.

Terminal symbols: a, b, c, etc., which appear in completed 'sentences', like the messages above, and

Non-terminal symbols: S, T, U, which only appear in 'sentences' whilst in the course of construction; these are like the states of the machine.

A simple set of productions might be the following:

1. $S \rightarrow UUz$	5. $T \rightarrow c$
2. $S \rightarrow UTUz$	6. $U \rightarrow aU$
3. $T \rightarrow TT$	7. $U \rightarrow d$
4. $T \rightarrow b$	8. $U \rightarrow e$

To grasp the kind of structure which is implied by this grammar, take a scrap of paper and generate a few 'sentences' for yourself. Write down the special, non-terminal symbol, S, and apply the productions in any order you choose until all the non-terminal symbols disappear and you end with a sentence in the language generated by the grammar. For example:

$$S \rightarrow UTUz \rightarrow dTTaUz \rightarrow dbbadz$$
$$2 \quad 736 \quad 44\,7$$

where the numbers under the non-terminals refer to the productions applied to them in order to generate the expanded string. Other examples are:

$$S \rightarrow UTUz \rightarrow aUTTez \rightarrow aeTTTTez \rightarrow aebccbez$$
$$2 \quad 638 \quad 833 \quad 4554$$
$$S \rightarrow UUz \rightarrow edz$$
$$1 \quad 87$$
$$S \rightarrow UTUz \rightarrow aUbaUz \rightarrow aebaaUz \rightarrow baaaUz \rightarrow \ldots \text{ etc.}$$
$$2 \quad 646 \quad 8 \quad 6 \quad 6 \quad 6$$

Unlike the grammar corresponding to the finite-state machine, you will notice that this kind of grammar permits a string of symbols to grow in the middle, not just at the right-hand end. This more elaborate type of grammar generates a language that is beyond the scope of the kind of machine examined earlier. It has a structure typical of some kinds of language used by computers. Despite its much greater generality, it is still limited in a very significant way. To see this, notice that all the productions have only an isolated non-terminal symbol on the left of the arrow. This means that the production can be applied *wherever* the non-terminal appears in an incomplete string of symbols, regardless of the context. For this reason, languages generated by such grammars are called *context free*. This property ensures a certain simplicity but can make the language 'long-winded' in certain applications.

Context-sensitive languages are the most general. Their unrestricted productions greatly enrich the generating procedures by adding functions such as these:

(a) aUz $\rightarrow$ aTz $\left.\right\}$ substitute for 'U' either 'T' or
    bUz $\rightarrow$ bUUz $\left.\right.$ 'UU' depending on the context
(b) abz $\rightarrow$ bza permute symbol string
(c) UUU $\rightarrow$ T condense symbol string

Theoretically, context-sensitive languages are very complicated but they can be subdivided according to the types of productions they employ. They are rich enough to enable any mechanical operations on strings of symbols to be defined formally. In practice, they are important because they enable symbols to carry more interpretations which can be resolved by reference to their context; this way of abbreviating messages is often favoured by people although it complicates the handling of the messages by machinery.

These three major classes of language are associated with classes of machines or *automata* which can operate upon them and generate them. In order of increasing complexity these are:

        finite-state language – finite state automaton
        context-free language – push-down automaton
        context-sensitive language – Turing machine.

Much of the theoretical study of programming and data-processing is concerned with the discovery of the properties of these machines, their related languages, and the tasks they are capable of performing.

Natural languages

More directly on our line of enquiry is the question: of what use are formal grammars for describing our natural languages? This is a question of practical moment for anyone interested in business information systems. Only in so far as our everyday language can be characterised by a formal grammar will it be possible to program the computer to recognise and respond to enquiries in natural language. There is a view, too widely-held today, that computers can communicate in something like a natural language. This is not likely to be true, probably for several decades, although there is no difficulty in programming a computer to handle *very limited* subsets of English, as we show below.

In the late nineteen-fifties, there was a great flood of research into using the computer to translate documents automatically from one natural language to another. Hopes of finding a solution soon foundered under a burden of complexities that had not previously been imagined. Among the difficulties was the inadequacy of the existing descriptive, 'school' grammars for natural languages. Much of the interest in formal languages dates from that discovery. We are now a great deal nearer

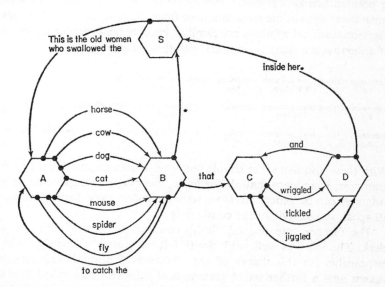

Fig. 33. State transition diagram for a machine to recite variations on a jingle.

having a formal grammar capable of generating a high proportion of those strings of words that are English sentences. But we are still far enough away from the complete answer to make a genuine 'English-speaking' computer a remote prospect.

It is easy enough to make a computer generate some English sentences. A modest number of sentences would present a trivial problem of storage and regurgitation. An infinite number of sentences can be generated even by a finite-state automaton simulated by a computer. An amusing example is shown in fig. 33, which gives an unlimited number of variants on a well-known jingle. (Notice that the words and phrases accompanying the arrows are regarded as single symbols; from B to S is an arrow with a full-stop which terminates sentences without the subordinate clause, e.g. 'This is the old woman who swallowed the horse to catch the fly.')

It is only a small step from this silly example to the writing of serious programs that will enable a computer to hold a simple conversation with a person to help him solve a problem. (See chapters 15 and 16.) It is easy to see how very remote such forms of English are from a true natural language.

To obtain a better approximation to English than with a finite-state grammar, we can employ a context-free grammar. It has been shown that probably only a few types of sentence structure underlie all utterances in English. Three examples are given below. (It is conventional to enclose in pointed brackets non-terminal symbols such as <noun> to distinguish these signs in the meta-language from those in the object language. The non-terminal symbols are familiar grammatical categories. Instead of an arrow the sign ::= is used with this notation.)

<sentence> ::= <noun phrase> <auxiliary> <intransitive verb> <adverbial phrase>
e.g.　　　　　　The time　　　had　　　passed　　　quickly.

<sentence> ::= <noun phrase> <auxiliary> <transitive verb> <noun phrase> <adverbial phrase>
e.g.　　　　　　The boy　　　has　　　caught　　　many fish　　with patient skill.

<sentence> ::= <noun phrase> <auxiliary> <to be> <adjectival phrase> <adverbial phrase>
e.g.　　　　　　This man　　　will　　　be　　　angry　　　too.

With these and five other simple sentence structures, and a context-free grammar, it appears that all the basic, meaningful components of our language can be generated. If we were limited to these forms we should all speak in the style of the comic strip.

'The factory gate opened. Smith counted the men. Smith was the clerk. The job was well paid. Smith felt contented.' Chomsky, who is responsible for this theory of the structure of natural language, has shown how a further set of grammatical rules can be applied to these sentences to give the more elaborate and elegant structures to which we are accustomed.* These rules are context-sensitive and are called the *transformational* part of the grammar. Under them, the above example might become:

'As the factory gate opened, the men were counted by Smith, the clerk. The job was well paid but did he feel contented?' The transformations enable us to use passives, interrogatives, negations, etc. They modify but they add little to the meaningful content of the elementary sentences, or *kernel* sentences, generated by the context-free grammar.

The full grammar proposed by Chomsky has three stages:

(a) generation of kernel sentences by a context-free grammar;
(b) transformations applied to the structure of these sentences;
(c) morpho-phonemic transformations which simply turn the sentence into a string of pronounceable sounds by making the correct selections of parts of verbs, etc., as in:

$$<\text{to take}> \ <\text{past tense}> ::= \text{took}$$

The third stage has been omitted in the example discussed above.

Interpretation of messages

There is little point in having machines or people producing strings of signs unless they are interpreted in some way. Strictly speaking, the 'objects' produced do not rank as 'signs' unless they are capable of interpretation.

When a machine interprets a message, it can decompose the sequence of signs into its constituent parts. This is the familiar process of *parsing* which can be pictured thus:

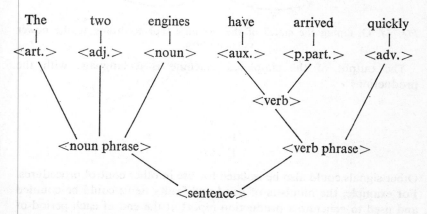

* See Chomsky 1957 and 1965.

This analysis is a necessary preliminary to any response to the message as a whole rather than sign by sign.

The case of the machine tool, described in fig. 32 and on p. 194, presents no problems, because a computer receiving a message reporting a production run can parse it sign by sign, that is, the current state of the machine tool can be deduced immediately. Consider, for example, the following run which produces 3 items of size 2 and 2 items of size 1:

Message: a p 2 m g m g m f m g l m f m f t n l m g m g e z
States: S W A R₂ M₂ R₂ M₂ R₂ M₂ R₂ M₂ R₂ R₁ M₁ R₁ M₁ R₁ C A R₁ M₁ R₁ M₁ R₁ W S

There are numerous transformations of this stream of messages which the computer could obtain for the purposes of higher levels of control. To control the power supply to the factory the computer could report on changes in power consumption by signalling transitions between groups of states, as shown in fig. 34.

Condensed version of fig. 32

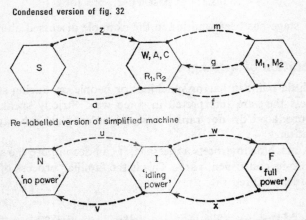

Re-labelled version of simplified machine

Fig. 34. Grouping the states of the machine tool according to the power consumption.

The output of the simplified machine is a language with the productions:

$$N \rightarrow uI$$
$$I \rightarrow wF$$
$$I \rightarrow vN$$
$$F \rightarrow xI$$

Other signals could also be isolated for use in other control procedures. For example, the numbers of good and faulty items could be counted and used to generate a production report at the end of each period of operation.

Languages within languages

The very simple language which reports the basic activities of the machine tool can readily be extended by a procedure called *substitution*. The grammar of that language was:

$$S \to aW$$
$$W \to pA \mid zS$$
$$A \to 1R \mid 2R_2 \qquad \text{where } \mid \text{is the usual}$$
$$R_1 \to mM_1 \mid tC \mid eW \qquad \text{abbreviation for 'or'}$$
$$R_2 \to mM_2 \mid tC \mid eW \mid 1R_1 \qquad \text{in such formulae}$$
$$M_1 \to gR_1 \mid fR_1$$
$$M_2 \to gR_2 \mid fR_2$$
$$C \to nA$$

It would be quite simple to extend the language by treating any of the terminal symbols a, p, 1, 2, m, g, f, t, n, e, z, as the starting symbol for generating another kind of message. For example, when switching on the machine, instead of sending a one-symbol message 'a', we could send a message giving the time, the date and the works number of the operator or operators. This enables us to introduce another little language. Using the other notation it could be:

$$a \equiv \text{<switch on>} \quad ::= \text{<time>} \quad \text{<operator list>}$$
$$\text{<time>} \qquad ::= \text{<date>} \quad \text{<hour>} \quad \text{<minute>}$$
$$\text{<operator list>} ::= \text{<person>} \mid \text{<person>} \quad \text{<operator list>}$$

Notice how this third pair of rules works. It enables <operator list> to be replaced by a string, <operator> ... <operator>, of any length, by a process of successive substitution called *recursion*. The 'switching-off' message, z, could also include the time, thus making possible the automatic logging of work done by staff whose wages could then be derived automatically on the basis of such data.

The message 'm' could be shorthand for a language describing many different items all made on one size-setting. Faults in production could be given in detail, by extending 'f'. In this manner, starting with a simple language which represents the major features of a system, substitution enables an increasingly detailed description of the system's language to be built up.

Notice that the original language-structure remains intact as a gross structure of the more detailed language. It is sometimes possible, when a complicated formal language is difficult to understand, to discover one or more of these cruder structures from which the full language could be re-generated by substitutions. Such a relationship, the reverse of that implied by a substitution, is called a *homomorphism*. The mental process of trying to understand any complex structure is closely allied to the search for homomorphic structures embedded within a complex structure. (This idea is a very general one and does not apply only to understanding language structures.)

Ambiguity

The parsing of messages is not without complications. It is possible for a message to be ambiguous in its structure. An example often quoted is:

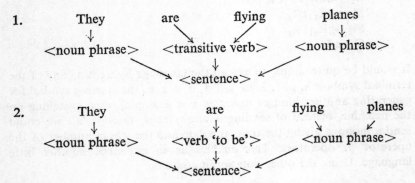

Two different ways of generating the same string of words are thus revealed, corresponding to quite different derivations. This is one respect in which our vague term 'meaning' can be shown to be related to questions about grammatical structure.* In practice, the context or the inflexion of the speaker's voice would resolve the ambiguity; for a machine, the solution is not so simple. It may be possible to find another grammar which does not lead to ambiguous parsing but some languages do not have any unambiguous grammar. The practical solution is to extend the language by introducing markers which remove ambiguity. There still remains a difficulty: there is still no way of making sure that the resulting language really is unambiguous! And, even with an un-ambiguous language, there is not always a straightforward parsing routine that may be applied to analyse its messages.†

In the specimen language for reporting the production of a machine tool it was noted that the signals could be interpreted *immediately* in terms of the new state of the machine. A language for which this is possible is sometimes called an 'instantaneous code'. It is a very useful type of language for operating machinery, because it does not require signals to be stored before they are decoded.

* Other aspects of this problem are discussed in Chomsky, 1965.

† See Ginsburg, 1966.

Contrast the instantaneous code with the language produced by the simple automaton shown in fig. 35. It is not possible to decide how the

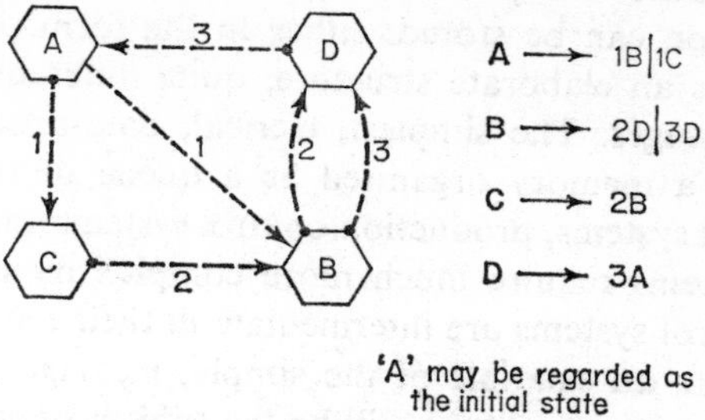

A ⟶ 1B|1C

B ⟶ 2D|3D

C ⟶ 2B

D ⟶ 3A

'A' may be regarded as
the initial state

Fig. 35. A machine which generates a language which cannot be passed instantaneously.

string '123' was generated until a fourth symbol is received:

$$A \to 1C \to 12B \to 123D \to 1233A$$

$$A \to 1B \to 12D \to 123A \to 1231B$$

$$\underbrace{}_{ambiguous} \searrow 1231C$$

ambiguity resolved.

Faced with a language with this characteristic, a machine cannot be made to respond to each signal as it is received; it must have a *memory* which stores as much of the message as is necessary to enable a correct interpretation to be made.

Language and memory

Memory is usually required by any machine which responds to messages in one language, L_1, by responding in another language, L_2:

$$L_1 \to Machine \to L_2$$

An exception to this rule is the simple computer process for translating production data into power-requirement data, as in the example described earlier. Most processes of interest to the manager or administrator require a *very* large amount of memory.

At the level of routine operations in business, information may give rise to an immediate response, for example when it is used to control a piece of plant, say, by signalling when the next item is to move into position. Above the level of process control or very simple routine clerical operations, the information is more likely to be used, in the first place, to build up a picture of the current 'state of affairs'. This will require an extensive memory. The information held in the memory is used to produce very diverse outputs as the need for them arises, normally in response to a question.

The information can be stored, either in the form of the messages themselves, or as an elaborate structure, quite different in form from the original messages. The simplest, clerical, data-processing systems are able to use a memory organised as a queue of messages. More elaborate clerical systems, production-control systems and management-information systems require much more complex memory-structures; production-control systems are intermediate in their requirements. This chapter ends with an example of the simple, message-queue memory. The complex memory-structures will be the subject of chapter 16.

A simple sales-ledger system requires only a series of processes of merging messages in different languages to form more complicated messages which are then translated into the required output. It is sufficient to illustrate the procedure for one customer only:

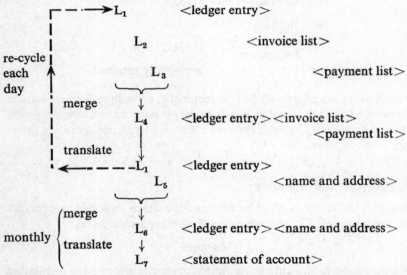

Obviously, it is convenient to process one customer after another in a single computer operation, but, as there is no interaction between one customer and another, there are no additional complications to the data-processing operations shown in the diagram. The information which is stored by the computer, or by the clerical system, comprises *two* bodies of messages: one of the form <ledger entry> and the other of the form <name and address>.

For a simple clerical system of this kind, the whole structure of procedures and messages can be represented using only the formal-language structure described in this chapter. The technique of formal-language definition is a very powerful method of exposing business information systems to searching analysis. Even with a 'simple' clerical system, the translation from an input language to an output language can be a very elaborate procedure. (Consider what operations would be required in going from L_4 to L_1 and from L_6 to L_7, above!) It is one of the major tasks of the systems analyst to discover and specify, in a rigorous, logical manner, all the very complex rules which govern these translations. Some of these methods will be examined in the next chapter.

15 Logic and Organisation

*(3) Without prejudice to subsection (4) and subject to subsection (5)
of this section, where a man is entitled to injury benefit or a
disablement pension there shall be treated as included in the beneficiary's
family for the purposes of this section any child who, on the day for
which the increase provided for by this section is claimed, though not
so included, could have been treated under paragraph 3 of the Schedule
to the Family Allowances Act as so included, or could have been
treated under that paragraph as so included but for the fact that the
beneficiary is contributing to the cost of providing for the child at a
weekly rate which, though not less than the prescribed rate, is less than
the minimum rate for the time being required for the purposes of
section 3 (2) of that Act.*

From Section 17 of the National Insurance (Industrial Injuries) Act 1965

The above slab of opaque prose is typical of the material in which our
laws must be formulated but it often seems, to many an ordinary citizen,
that, instead of paving the quiet legal route to his rights, this language is
used by the servants of bureaucracy to erect barricades of obfuscation
between him and his just goal. Laws which are sensitive to a great variety
of personal situations and special circumstances, and which do not
permit the passage of the proverbial coach and horses driven by even
the most ingenious villain, cannot be set down in simple prose. So we
enact good and inevitably complicated laws, resolving to interest ourselves in their details when special circumstances demand, only to find,
having been summoned for erecting a washing line in the wrong place
or consigning some unsolicited goods to the fire, that these demands can
arise sooner than expected. Pleading ignorance of legal refinements does
not help at all. Flung in our faces will be the maxim: *ignorantia juris
neminem excusat*, which asserts that the application of the law assumes
we have read, understood and remembered it all.

Bureaucracy is a linguistic phenomenon, in some degree at least, and
from that direction it could be attacked with a confident hope of soften-
ing its defences. The law probably represents the largest accretion of
complex interlocking regulations and instructions, but the organisations
which employ us, sell us goods and services, also have their own bureaucratic machinery to confound us. In an increasingly complex society,
greater use will be made of information which embodies complex
directions, rules and instructions: they are the stuff of organisation. If

we are to enjoy the benefits of organisations, we must learn to minimise their unpleasant side effects which their progenitors ignore, in the expectation that we have time and skill to unravel endless conundrums in small print on the backs of forms, or coyly displayed on discoloured paper in dark corners of obscure offices.

Management, as pointed out earlier, is getting things done through information, especially by using language. At one end of the scale is the information which motivates people to work effectively, or endeavours so to do. At the other end is the information of a precise, logical kind which instructs people to perform individual tasks in a specific manner to ensure the dovetailing of their contributions towards some social endeavour, say the manufacture of an aircraft or the running of a social security system. Complex sets of instructions are necessary, not only for administration and law, but also for directing the construction and maintenance of elaborate machinery, and for planning and controlling production. Now, we examine some logical uses of information encountered in organisations, and attempt to show how we can improve their effectiveness. The discussion of formal languages in the previous chapter will be used and extended.

Deciphering statements

When a person hears or reads a statement, it is likely that, in order to understand it, he thinks in stages that correspond roughly to the following.*

(a) First, he parses the sentence in order to discover the functions being served by the words or groups of words. This is normally quite subconscious but the presence of an ambiguity which must be resolved can raise the process to the conscious level of the mind. For example, you may pause to decide whether a sentence should be parsed by grouping the words thus:

'They (use skilfully) woven materials'

or thus:

'They use (skilfully woven) materials'

(b) Next, he will assign 'meanings' to the individual entities referred to, in the sense of conjuring up appropriate mental images (or sounds or sensations). The images so chosen will depend upon the context

*This description of our mental process is speculation. Research on what actually happens is growing; for example, see G. A. Miller, 1968, and the more technical papers in Jakobovits and Miron (eds), 1967.

(e.g., 'wood' has different referents when talking about a landscape, discussing furniture, playing bowls or playing badminton) but the parsing of the sentence will determine whether the word denotes an object, a quality, an action, a relationship or anything else (e.g. consider uses of the word 'last').

(c) The 'images' of the entities referred to will be filled out by attaching to them the simple properties predicated of those individuals by the sentence. This is normally done subconsciously, unless you try to do it for certain kinds of nonsense, such as the Lay of the Jabberwock by Lewis Carroll:

> 'Twas brillig, and the slithy toves,
> Did gyre and gimble in the wabe;
> All mimsy were the borogoves,
> And the mome raths outgrabe.

(d) To finish reproducing the picture embodied in the statement, the mind places the suitably qualified images in meaningful relationships to one another. These relationships are either implied by common knowledge of the things which are spoken about, or made explicit in the sentence by certain kinds of words, for example prepositions ('in', 'on', 'between', etc.) or some kinds of verbs ('give', 'enter', 'support', etc.) This is another prcoess which can be brought to our consciousness by some kinds of nonsense which make it difficult to accomplish this stage of interpretation:

> You boil it in sawdust: you salt it in glue:
> You condense it with locusts and tape:
> Still keeping one principal object in view –
> To preserve its symmetrical shape.

This stanza from 'The Hunting of the Snark' is about as reasonable as any insurance policy seems on a first reading, and for similar reasons.

Statements that convey complex relationships with precision

This process of interpreting individual sentences is normally accomplished without effort, provided that the sentences are well constructed, provided that they do not attempt to convey matters of great complexity and provided that they do not have to avoid all possible ambiguities. It is very difficult to give (in English) a clear yet exact account of anything very complex without supplementing it with such devices as diagrams, tables or mathematical symbols. The problem becomes even more acute when the description cannot be embodied in a simple sentence, but requires compound sentences and groups of sentences. The rules that govern structures that extend beyond the confines of single sentences are those of logic. Our minds are not able to perform logical analyses with the unconscious ease with which we can disentangle an individual sentence. To communicate these more complex patterns of relationships we require languages with different powers of expression from natural ones. For science we have evolved mathematics, which is a collection of highly-structured languages enabling very elaborate inter-relationships to be described with amazing clarity. Although the mathematical methods used in science are sometimes appropriate for administrative, legal and business purposes, the techniques of logic are perhaps more useful.

Logic may be thought of as the study of the inter-relationships between statements. It is therefore exactly what we require to supplement the powers of expression of ordinary English. Knowledge of logic remained fairly static for more than 2,000 years from its virtual founding by Aristotle until the nineteenth century. Since then the subject has increased in scope and richness a thousand-fold, and is one of the greatest intellectual achievements of modern times. Logic is exactly the right tool for solving many of our current problems of organisational communication. It should command the attention of people devising computer-based information systems and those engaged in administration of a legal or quasi-legal type. There is scope in this chapter only to touch upon the subject, but in doing so I hope to indicate some practical applications and also show how it can contribute towards our understanding of what is meant by 'information'. We start by returning to the theme which opened this chapter.

An example

Consider the following (see Lewis, Horabin and Gane, 1967). Recently a leaflet was sent to about 20,000,000 people with their income-tax forms, giving them 'general guidance' on the new capital gains tax. A part of it read:

If the asset consists of stocks or shares which have values quoted on a Stock Exchange (see also paragraph G below), or unit trust units whose values are regularly quoted, the gain or loss (subject to expenses) accruing after 6th April 1965, is the difference between the amount you received on disposal and the market value on 6th April 1965, except that in the case of a gain where the actual cost of the asset was higher than the value at 6th April 1965, the chargeable gain is the excess of the amount you received on disposal over the original cost or acquisition price; and in the case of a loss, where the actual cost of the asset was lower than the value at 6th April 1965, the allowable loss is the excess of the original cost or acquisition price over the amount received on disposal.

If the substitution of original cost for the value at 6th April 1965, turns a gain into a loss, or a loss into a gain, there is, for the purpose of tax, no chargeable gain or allowable loss.

If, indeed, it has any message for the average taxpayer, such prose conveys only the quintessence of bureaucracy.

There are two points which are made by this example. The first, incidental to the main argument of this chapter, is that people understand complex instructions with difficulty unless the purpose of those instructions is made clear at the outset. The above passage might be formulated perhaps a little less obscurely, as follows:

For tax purposes, the calculation of the capital gain (or loss) accruing on stocks, shares or unit trusts after 6th April 1965, will be based upon the difference between the net amount received when they were sold and either:

1. the actual cost price;
2. the quoted market value 6th April 1965.

Only if *both* calculations indicate a gain or *both* indicate a loss will a gain or a loss be taken into account. In such a case, the value used will be the smaller given by the two methods of calculation.

People who draft regulations must surely start by having a purpose in mind, and must employ some general strategy for devising the rules. If the reader is not made aware of the purpose and the strategy, the regulations will be gobbledygook. The same may be said about the presentation of other complex bodies of information, whether in scientific or mathematical papers, business reports or engineering manuals. (However, in English law no judge is obliged to refer to Ministerial statements about the purpose of a statute to help him decide how it is to be applied.)

The second point is germane to this chapter. Often complicated rules can be exhibited in a tabular form based upon the various statements which appear in them. In the example quoted, three different conditions are used to determine how the tax or allowance will be calculated. Thus:

Amount received is greater than or equal to market value on 6.4.65.
Market value is greater than or equal to cost price.
Amount received is greater than or equal to cost price.

Dependent upon these conditions are the additional tax or the allowance and the method of calculating. All the relationships can be given in a table such as:

Conditions				Rules 1	2	3	4	5	6
p	Amount received ≥ M. value			Yes	Yes	Yes	No	No	No
q	M. value ≥ C. price			Yes	No	No	Yes	Yes	No
r	Amount received ≥ C. price			Yes	Yes	No	Yes	No	No
Actions									
a		Tax {	charged	Yes	Yes	No	No	No	No
b			allowed	No	No	No	No	Yes	Yes
c	Calculated as difference between amount received and	{	M. value	Yes	No	irrelevant	irrelevant	No	Yes
d			C. price	No	Yes	irrelevant	irrelevant	Yes	No

This method of setting down rules is widely used in systems design and is referred to as the decision-table method. The rigour of the method is valuable. In the example, it forces one to recognise that the reference to expenses given in parenthesis in the third line of the original is ambiguous, being associated in the text with the reference to the gain or loss. Presumably the expenses must be allowed against the selling price to give the amount received before the net gain or loss is computed.

The logic of propositions

The decision-table is a neat way of formulating a complex set of conditions. It is based upon the logic of propositions, which can be used as the starting point for constructing more general methods to formulate sets of complicated rules. It is also a natural starting point for the exploration of other kinds of logic.

The units of language which are dealt with by propositional logic are *whole statements*. It has nothing to say about smaller items, such as the internal structure of the statements. It can be thought of as a language in its own right, which represents some gross features of our natural language. (That is, it is a homomorphism of English. See chapter 14, p. 201.) It corresponds to the very part of our language which we find difficult: those relationships which require most mental effort to understand.

In the first place, propositional logic, regarded as a formal language system, lays down rules (productions) for constructing compound statements from simple propositions using some logical operators. The operators are:

Negation   (not)   p ≡ Brown is a customer
                        −p ≡ Brown is *not* a customer
Conjunction (and)   q ≡ Brown owes money
                  p & q ≡ Brown is a customer *and* Brown owes money
Disjunction (or)   p or q ≡ Brown is a customer *or* Brown owes money.

There are other operators which we shall use in chapter 17, such as p *implies* q; p is *equivalent to* q; p is *implied by* q; they can all be defined in terms of 'not' and 'and', which, incidentally, is also true of 'or' because (p or q) is equivalent to −(−p & −q).

This formal language can be defined, as others were in chapter 14, by giving the basic symbols:

− & or ( )   the operators and brackets
and
a,b,c . . . p,q,r . . .   any number of elementary propositions

Rules for constructing compound propositions can be written as productions for a formal language in the manner described in the previous chapter, thus:

		Rule
<sentence>::=(− <sentence>)		P1
::=(<sentence> & <sentence>)		P2
::=(<sentence> or <sentence>)		P3
::= <elementary proposition>		P4
<elementary proposition>::=a |b |c |d | . . . |p |q |r | . . .		P5

Using these rules, valid sentences can be generated as before:

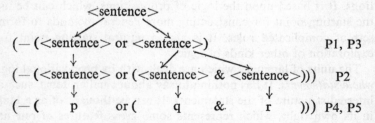

In the context of the capital gains decision table, this logical expression can be used to answer the question 'Am I entitled to an allowance?' because it is true only when the answer is 'yes'.

Evaluating the truth of complex propositions

So far, this logical language of propositions is not very interesting or useful, but consider just how valuable it would be if the truth or falsity of a complex proposition could be *calculated* from the truth or falsity of its constituent, elementary propositions. Then it would be possible to take thousands of individual cases which are subject to a complex decision-procedure embodied in elaborate rules (e.g., about capital gains tax) and, given the facts, make the decisions accurately and automatically. This is a common administrative task and the computer is the natural tool to use for the purpose.

It is quite simple to extend the language of propositional logic to do this. Suppose for a particular capital transaction that the facts satisfy the conditions for rule 4 in the decision table, thus:

Sale price is less than market value.   i.e. p is false.
Market value exceeds cost price.   i.e. q is true.
Sale price exceeds cost price.   i.e. r is true.

We could then substitute, in the logical expression above, the truth values of these elementary propositions, using T=true and F=false: so that (—(p or (q & r))) becomes (—(F or (T & T))).

By using a commonsense interpretation of 'not', 'and' and 'or' we can specify rules for progressively reducing such an expression, to a single truth value.

To find these rules, note that a compound expression such as:

The cup is blue & the tea is hot.

which has the form (p&q), is only true when *both* p is true and q is true. So (T & T) can be reduced to T. In our example this reduces (—(F or (T & T))) to the expression (—(F or T))). An expression such as:

The cup is blue *or* the tea is hot.

is true whenever either one of the elementary propositions it contains is true, or when both are true. So, (—(F or T)) now reduces to (—T).

It is obvious that an expression of the form (—p) will be false when p is true and vice versa. Hence the logical expression (—T) reduces to F. Similarly, (—(p or (q & r))) will also be false for rules 1, 2 and 3 (no allowance) but true for rules 5 and 6 (allowance can be claimed). Thus it is possible to answer the question 'Am I entitled to an allowance?' according to the value of this logical expression.

Incidentally, we have also found the rules for evaluating any similar logical expression; as follows:

		Rule
Substitution:	<elementary proposition>::=T|F	S1
Reductions:	(T or F)|(F or T)|(T or T)::=T	R1
	(F or F)::=F	R2

	Rule
(T & F)|(F & T)|(F & F)::=F	R3
(T & T)::=T	R4
(−T)::=F	R5
(−F)::=T	R6

There is no difficulty at all about performing these operations using a computer, no matter how complicated the logical formulae to be evaluated.

Using a computer for making decisions

It is now worth looking at how these methods can be applied. There are two quite different ways of setting about this, and it is instructive to compare them. Perhaps the obvious way is to use the decision-table for a particular decision, and convert it into a computer program which will make the necessary comparisons and print out a statement of the appropriate actions. The essential features of such a program can be set down in the kind of diagram used in the previous chapter for depicting a finite-state machine, as in fig. 36. The machine begins in a particular, initial

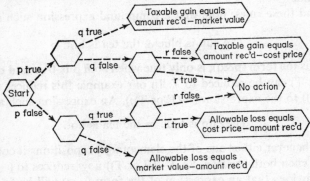

Fig. 36. A 'machine' or program to answer queries about capital gains tax.

condition and, as it is given the facts about the truth or falsity of p,q,r, it changes state two or three times, and, finally, causes the appropriate action to be printed or indicated in some way.

Incidentally, it is interesting to note that this programme would fail to deal correctly with values of p,q and r that are logically inconsistent with one another. You cannot have:

Amount received	⩾ Market value	i.e.	p true
Market value	⩾ Cost price		q true
Amount received	< Cost price		r false

or . . .

$$\left. \begin{array}{l} \text{Amount received} < \text{Market value} \\ \text{Market value} < \text{Cost price} \\ \text{Amount received} \geqslant \text{Cost price} \end{array} \right\} \text{ i.e. } \begin{array}{l} \text{p false} \\ \text{q false} \\ \text{r true} \end{array}$$

for obvious, arithmetical reasons, but the machine would treat the first as a capital gain and the second as a capital loss. The program could be amended to take account of these exceptions and could be written so that the computer, on encountering them, would print some message such as 'inconsistent data'.

Notice that this amendment, to enable inconsistent data to be rejected, or any other amendment made necessary by changes in the regulations being administered, would entail re-writing the program. This kind of problem can be avoided by a more general approach.

A more general method

There is another way of using the computer to make use of the logic of propositions. Any such formal language can be manipulated quite mechanically and this virtue can be exploited by the machine. Instead of writing a program that embodies the decision-making rules directly, as in the method explained above, rather more complicated programs can be written to read logical formulae, check them, substitute given truth values for the elementary propositions, and then compute the truth values of the compound propositions. If these programs are used for decision-making, then the appropriate action can be indicated whenever the compound proposition, embodying a decision criterion, is found to be true. The advantage of this method is that a change in the decision-rules necessitates no change in the programs; this is because rules and actions are simply treated as other forms of data. The same programs would handle any set of rules. Provided that the administrator could furnish a set of logical criteria for making the decision, it would not matter whether he wanted to deal with capital gains tax or decide upon a person's eligibility for a passport.

In the capital gains example, one might imagine the computer indicating on a display what action should be taken in response to an enquiry about a particular case. The computer might display on a screen or print any of the following:

(a) 'Charge tax'
(b) 'Allow tax'
(c) 'based on market value on 6th April 1965'
(d) 'based on cost'
(e) 'No tax or allowance'
(f) 'Error: data are inconsistent'

The logical conditions which govern the relevance of these outputs can be expressed as the propositional formulas which the reader may check by comparing them with the decision-table given earlier (p. 211).

(a) p & r
(b) −p & −r
(c) (p & q & r) or (−p & −q & −r)
(d) (p & −q & r) or (−p & q & −r)
(e) (p & −q & −r) or (−p & q & r)
(f) (p & q & −r) or (−p & −q & r)

The processing is illustrated below. The input data, L_1, on one case would be a string of three truth values for p, q and r; these would be substituted into L_2, the formulae for the decision rules (a) to (f), given above. The reduction rules, R1–R6 (p. 213), would evaluate the truth formulae, L_3, selecting the codes for the required outputs, L_5, which would then be displayed or printed in English, L_6. In practice the input would be the Amount received, Market value and Cost price; extra programs, not included in this description, would use these figures to compute the truth values of p, q and r and, finally, the sums taxable or allowable.

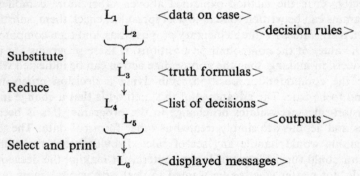

L_1 <data on case>
L_2 <decision rules>

Substitute   ↓
L_3 <truth formulas>

Reduce   ↓
L_4 <list of decisions>
L_5 <outputs>

Select and print   ↓
L_6 <displayed messages>

If the input (T F T) were supplied, the truth formulas would be:

(a) T&T   → T → 'Charge tax'
(b) −T&—T   → F
(c) (T&F&T) or (—T&—F&—T)   → F
(d) (T&—F&T) or (—T&F&—T)   → T → 'based on cost'
(e) (T&F&—T) or (—T&F&T)   → F
(f) (T&F&—T) or (—T&—F&T)   → F

which reduce to the truth values on the right, thereby identifying (a) and (d) as the outputs which should be displayed. These signals can then be used to select the actual words, L_6, to be transmitted to a printer.

The operations of substitution, reduction and selection are quite general and could be used for other sets of regulations.* Despite the simplicity of this example, it should have demonstrated that, by using formal language analysis, programs can be written at a far higher level of generality than is otherwise possible. This is achieved by forgetting what the symbols refer to, and asking, instead, what abstract rules govern their manipulation as objects in their own right. This *syntactic* approach is well justified because it enables computer systems to be designed for one purpose and then applied to other work superficially bearing no resemblance to the original task. This can only be achieved if the designer conceives the original problem in terms of its formal linguistic structure.

There is nothing surprising about this. We are all familiar with the idea of a general mathematical solution; we do not have two different ways of doing sums when dealing with numbers of oranges and numbers of people. The same notion applied to other forms of language may seem remarkable when it is first encountered.

Even among systems analysts, it is not yet common to think in terms of the formal properties of the languages employed in an organisational system. Consequently many systems are being designed that are needlessly rigid. Only by adopting a generalised solution, in the manner suggested above, can a mechanised information system be given the flexibility essential in an evolving organisation operating in a changing environment. The manager or administrator, asked to judge a proposal for a computer-based information system, must understand the two approaches, and he should always enquire how a system can adapt to new circumstances. The general solution will only require some parameters to be changed, but the rigid solution will demand extensive amendments to its programs. Although the general approach reduces the productivity of analysts and programmers in the short term, in the long term it increases productivity. Moreover, its flexibility, so important for a viable business, will force the general approach to be more widely adopted in the long run.

The advantages of generality and flexibility are not obtained without cost. The price is paid in longer processing times. This matters very little in business or administrative data-processing, because elaborate logical operations can be performed by one part of the computer, whilst another part is performing the comparatively slow tasks of reading input, transferring data to and from the store and printing the output. These slow tasks limit the speed of the whole operation. Providing that *they* are not

---

* A general print program is vastly complicated however, because a formal language syntax cannot describe the format of more than a very limited class of printed documents.

increased by the generality of the programs, the processing will take roughly the same time.

Factual truth and logical truth

Now we must look at a problem that is raised by the brief discussion of logic given above. It is one that has an important bearing upon our understanding of some aspects of 'information'; it is the question of formal 'truth'.

Propositional logic lays down rules for constructing complex statements from elementary propositions. Given the truth or falsity of all the constituent elementary propositions, the reduction rules permit the truth or falsity of a compound statement to be determined. It is important to distinguish between the truth of the elementary propositions and the truth of the complex statement. As far as the rules of propositional logic go, the truth or falsity of an elementary proposition is a matter of arbitrary choice, whereas the truth value of a complex proposition is a necessary logical consequence of the arbitrary values of its constituent propositions.

This *formal concept* of truth is in sharp contrast with the *semantic* concepts discussed in the earlier parts of the book. Formal logic by itself cannot establish the semantic truth of a statement, for it is concerned only with relationships among the signs themselves. Concern with relationships between signs and what they refer to, and with the acceptability of a statement as a valid basis for action, are all problems in the province of semantics. When the truth of a statement is considered from a semantic viewpoint, the matter cannot be settled by the manipulation of signs, but only by reference to the world that the statement refers to; this necessitates human judgement and possibly some observational procedure. Truth at the semantic level may be determined subjectively by reference to one person's judgement or by procedures that are, in various degrees, objective (the degree of objectivity being dependent upon the procedures and the extent to which they are exposed to critical scrutiny by other people). Among the critical methods which can be applied to statements are the tests of logical consistency, but these logical tests are not adequate by themselves. Their main application is to the appraisal of very abstract statements which can be related to more directly verifiable statements via a chain of logical argument. One must demand the testing of the abstract statements in terms of operationally testable statements related to them. The test of logical consistency, by itself, only ensures that abstractions belong to a harmonious system of their own; it does nothing to guarantee that the abstractions are connected with what we call the 'real' world. This is a perennial danger especially when plausible mathematical models are applied to social and business problems in the belief that their logical perfection is their warranty.

When we come to the logical concepts of 'truth' we must remember that they are merely *formal* properties of sets of signs. As far as the logical system is concerned, 'T' and 'F' are merely two empty symbols which can be substituted for other empty symbols. If you ask a person to equate his high measure of confidence in a statement, represented by the symbol p, with the logical truth value T, you must remember that this can only be an approximation. Scientific methods are often applied to business problems by people totally oblivious of the assumption which is made when semantic 'truth' is equated to formal 'truth'. Often, in the natural sciences, degrees of confidence can be so high that there is no reason to hesitate about making this equation but, in social science and in the applications of management science to practical problems, one should always carry a mental reservation about the justification for using the formal concept of 'truth'.

Within logic itself it is useful to distinguish two further kinds of 'truth': 'F-truth' or factual* truth, which is dependent upon the assignment of truth values to elementary propositions, and 'L-truth', logical or necessary truth, which is exhibited by some compound propositions regardless of the truth-values of their constituent propositions. This distinction only applies to the truth of compound propositions. It can be illustrated by drawing up a table giving all the possible combinations of truth-values for, say, three propositions, P, Q and R, and then entering the corresponding truth values of various composite statements. One can build up complex, logical formulae, some of which are always true, others always false, and others which are sometimes true and sometimes false.

0=F   1=T

(1)	P	01	01	01	01	
(2)	Q	00	11	00	11	
(3)	R	00	00	11	11	
(4)	−P	10	10	10	10	
(5)	P & (−P)	00	00	00	00	L-false, contradiction
(6)	P or (−P)	11	11	11	11	L-true, tautology
(7)	(−P) or Q	10	11	10	11	factual
(8)	Q & R	00	00	00	11	factual
(9)	−(Q & R)	11	11	11	00	factual
(10)	(−(Q & R)) or ((−P) or Q)	11	11	11	11	L-true, tautology

* This is the kind of usage which, because of our verbal habits, suggests to people, on first encountering formal logic, that it has something to do with reality. Luckily it has, but formal logic itself has nothing to say on the matter.

H

Formulae which are either true or false, depending upon the data, are called *factual*, and if they are true they are *F-true*. Lines 1, 2 and 3 may be regarded as the possible sets of data. Line 5 shows that P & (−P) is a logical *contradiction*: it is *always false* regardless of the data. Line 6 shows that P or (−P) is a *tautology*: it is *always true* regardless of the data. Statements such as

$$P \& (-P)$$
or
$$P \text{ or } (-P)$$

which are totally insensitive to the data are sometimes called 'analytic' statements; they are automatic consequences of the definition of the logical language, and appear to convey no information, at least in the sense that their truth or falsity does not depend on what their constituent statements are about. This can be seen more clearly by imagining that these formulae were incorporated as decision rules in the administrative computer program described earlier; such rules would cause the computer to react with exactly the same output regardless of the input about the taxpayer.

In another sense, tautologies *do* convey information, as can be seen by constructing a more complex one. Using lines 7, 8 and 9 we can construct:

$$(-(Q \& R)) \text{ or } ((-P) \text{ or } Q)$$

which line 10 reveals as a tautology. Unlike the contradiction of line 5 and the tautology of line 6, this is not a matter of common sense, obvious at a glance. Although it conveys no factual information, it does reveal something about the structure of this particular logical language. (To emphasise this, it should be pointed out that the seemingly 'obvious' tautology (P or (−P)) is *not* applicable in all other logical systems, it is a special property of those known as categorical logics.)

This illustrates again the two complementary aspects of information: variety and structure. The idea has appeared already in previous chapters, in many disguises. Perception is the quest for invariant or, at least, stable structures in the variable flux of experience. Measurement is the use of number to display variety within the context of an exactly defined structure. Objectivity is obtained by imposing structural restraints upon the variety of opinions which can be held by 'rational' people. Later, when we look at the transmission of information, we shall see again two similar, complementary properties in measuring signal transmission.

Conclusions

This chapter has illustrated the practical usefulness of one form of logic. The propositional calculus can supplement our natural language in some circumstances for which it was never evolved: the manipulation of complex rules, regulations and instructions both by people and by machines. As this logic is another formal language, the reader should more readily appreciate the scope of the formal-language concept and see its relevance to performing organisational tasks on computers. But let him not imagine that the practical problem is as simple as the examples described suggest. He need only inspect the legal quotation at the head of the chapter to realise that rules and regulations are often too complex to be readily formulated in propositional logic. However, more elaborate logical languages are probably equal to the task (see the author's 'LEGOL' project).

In the next chapter, building on the foundations of this one, we shall explore a more detailed logical system. We shall use it to examine how information can be stored in a way that provides a picture of an organisation's resources and environment, and how this picture can be used to answer questions. This next step examines how a machine can behave with a rudimentary degree of 'intelligence'.

16 Storing Information and Answering Questions

Knowledge is of two kinds. We know a subject ourselves, or we know where we can find information upon it.

Dr Johnson

Organisations which grow above a modest size must overcome the formidable obstacle that their activities, their resources and their environment cannot be perceived, understood or remembered by any one person, except in terms of very crude abstractions. The efficient use of resources is limited by the inability of the unaided human mind to think on a scale, and at a level of detail, commensurate with the needs of many practical problems. The computer is capable of augmenting human intelligence so that larger organisations can evolve successfully; they need not become the sterile, lumbering dinosaurs of society, crushing individuals and lesser organisations wherever they lurch their insensitive bureaucratic weight. The simulation of intelligent behaviour by machines is one of the major aims of computing science, and it raises issues that have much in common with those raised by trying to use the computer to 'sense' and 'perceive' a business scene, and react intelligently to it or answer questions about it.

Analogy between human and organisational data-processing

When we receive information directly, through our senses, or indirectly, in words describing what others have seen, we can sometimes remember the actual picture presented to our eyes, or the actual words that were spoken. This is analogous to the kind of literal storage needed for a simple clerical routine. More often, the exact form of the original message is lost and, instead, we remember its import, because we have incorporated what it says into some kind of mental 'model', the complex structure of related images that constitutes our picture of the world. This 'memory-structure' is what we search or manipulate in order to answer questions, make judgements, solve problems, take decisions and generally behave in an intelligent fashion.

Similar mechanisms are to be found, at least in a very rudimentary form, in organisations. Movements of goods and payments of money and other transactions are 'sensed' or recorded as they happen, and messages describing them are communicated to various ledgers which are parts of the accounting 'memory-structure'. There the transactions are posted. That is, they are deciphered and entered on the appropriate pages of the books of account, or in the correct records of a computer's files. As the transaction is posted, running totals are sometimes changed to keep the picture of where the company stands up-to-date in some important respect or other. This continuous up-dating of the summaries of accounts is subsidiary to the periodic striking of balances, by which transactions in the various books of account are totalled, reconciled with one another, and entered into consolidated accounts containing more abstract summaries of the company's affairs. (It is just a fanciful idea but perhaps dreaming is the mental equivalent of the balancing and consolidating of accounts, and the opening of new pages in the ledgers!)

The information stored in books of account can furnish answers to many questions posed by the running of the business. Sometimes a question can be answered by copying an appropriate ledger entry or a summary of accounts; if so, the question poses no difficulty. Often, however, it is necessary to translate the question into a procedure for analysing the detailed accounts in an unusual way. All too frequently the questions trespass beyond the restricted range of the information originally recorded for accounting purposes, or they require a kind of analysis that is made impossible by the structure of the books of account. Unfortunately, a book-keeping scheme that incorporated all the detailed information that might be needed for running a business and did so without losing track of any actual relationship between transactions far exceeds the capacity of any clerical system. The computer has lessened these constraints, and the problems of what information to retain and how to organise it are wide open to new investigation.

The computer makes it possible to organise and process vast amounts of detailed information in a manner that simulates a kind of intelligent behaviour. Machine intelligence is rudimentary, compared with the full capabilities of even the dullest human being, but, being able to store billions of names and numbers with perfect literal accuracy, the computer can display a formidable kind of intelligence which is quite different from, yet complementary to, the intelligence of man.

Intelligent machines and responsive organisations

This developing field of research into the storage and retrieval of information by machines is beginning to throw new light on notions such as 'meaning' and 'understanding'. At least there appear to be strong parallels between what the human mind does when it understands a message, and what a computer system does when it assimilates a statement of fact or responds to an enquiry. It is still purely a matter of speculation whether the mental processes of memory and recall bear more than a superficial resemblance to the mechanical processes of information storage and retrieval. Perhaps the superficial level is the most important. At the level of overt behaviour machines can be made to seem intelligent, at least in responding to limited ranges of problems and stimuli. There is an intimate relationship between the problems of developing intelligent machines and those of storing and retrieving information.

Machine intelligence is a new field of study which is stimulated by both academic and practical problems. Using the computer to reproduce seemingly intelligent behaviour, some academics are attempting to gain a deeper insight into the nature of the human brain. On the practical side there are obvious applications for machines with a modest degree of intelligence. They could be used to explore regions inaccessible to man: other planets, the interiors of furnaces or atomic reactors, or the ocean bed. They could also be made to perform the complex and skilled but repetitive tasks that are the backbone of our industrial work: numerically controlled machine tools, automatic pilots and traffic control by computers are well established; it is now becoming possible to add to these systems a capacity to learn by experience. One other practical problem should be mentioned again: the automatic translation of languages. In the early days of computers it was felt that this seemingly mechanical, although complex, task could be performed by machines, and large sums of money were spent on efforts to attain that end. In a practical sense they have failed but they have served to crystallise many important academic questions about machines, intelligence and verbal behaviour.

The study of information storage and retrieval has been stimulated, also, by the practical problems faced by the librarian and archivist in an age when the growth in volume of technical information is outstripping the capacity of research workers, engineers and entrepreneurs to know about it and use it. A system for classifying and indexing technical documents for research workers is like a system for filing business information for managers. Both kinds of systems sift the incoming data and notify individuals of current information of specific interest to them. Both kinds of system should be capable of yielding whatever information they contain, current or historical, that is relevant to any new problem.

A worthy objective for the business information specialist would be to make the formal, bureaucratic machine respond intelligently. It is not enough to automate the clerical work of an organisation. This is a very different aim, which can have quite the opposite effect and make an organisation seem even more stupid in its reactions to an individual or in its response to unusual events. As the development of business information systems extends beyond the stage of automating clerical work into the design of management information systems, it will begin to encounter many of the problems now being encountered by people doing academic research into machine intelligence.

Fundamental problems

The storage and retrieval of information, whether by the human mind or by an accounting system or any other kind of data-processing system, usually involves the following steps:

(a) When the input messages are received, they must be analysed into the fragments of the 'scene' which they represent.
(b) These new fragments, as they stand or in some modified form, must be incorporated into the existing memory-structure or mental image.
(c) As this is done, any contradictions between the input data and the existing picture must be resolved.
(d) To allow this stored information to be used selectively, the system must also be capable of accepting questions in a suitable enquiry language.
(e) The questions must be translated into a sequence of procedures for finding an answer.
(f) Some procedures must locate the relevant information.
(g) Other procedures must operate upon the data, analyse them and arrange them in a suitable form for the questioner.

The rest of this chapter will be devoted to examining some of these aspects of the storage and retrieval problem. There is not space to do more than introduce a few elementary ideas. In order to do this we shall exploit, and develop further, the ideas about formal languages and logic that have been developed in the two preceding chapters.

This discussion will contribute towards a deeper understanding of information, which is the main objective of this book. It will illustrate some of the more interesting ways of analysing signs in the narrow framework of syntactics. Some of the mechanical properties of the vast bodies of stored information, which constitute one of the major resources of a large organisation, will be explored. It is the computer's power to store information, far more than its computational power, that will make it so significant in the evolution of our organisations. In the management of information (one of the foremost concerns of the information specialist) the central problem is how to structure the data required by the organisation. As a by-product of this chapter there is a group of concepts which throw further light upon how to measure information. This topic will be reserved for the following chapter.

Predicate logic

The storage of information was mentioned at the end of chapter 14, in an illustration of a simple sales-ledger system. The stored information included the ledger, giving the details of the indebtedness of each customer, and a file giving details of each customer's name and address. From these a statement of account could be prepared. From the data-storage point of view this kind of system is not very interesting, because the records for different customers are quite independent of one another and are just like delayed messages. The two files – the ledger and the customer details – become more interesting when they are regarded as interrelated parts of a picture of the current state of the company and its environment, rather than as queues of messages waiting to be fed back into the data-processing operation.

The simple languages discussed earlier are not adequate for describing a company's resources and environment. We shall need to develop a language better suited to this purpose before we can examine the problems of storing data.

One language which can be used is known as *predicate logic*. It will now be introduced in its most rudimentary form as an elaboration upon the propositional logic which was developed in the previous chapter. Propositional logic, you will recall, treats a whole elementary proposition as the most basic of its components. We need to be able to extend its capability by including the internal structure of propositions. This can be done in a simple way by substituting for an elementary proposition a form which corresponds to the typical *subject–predicate* structure of a simple sentence. The customary notation in logic is:

$$<\text{elementary proposition}> ::= <\text{predicate}> <\text{individual}>$$

thus reversing the order we use in English, but this is immaterial. It will be convenient to use capital letters for predicates and small letters for individuals in what follows; or

$$<\text{predicate}> ::= A|B|C|...$$
$$<\text{individual}> ::= a|b|c|...$$

So, if 'customer a' ≡ a, 'customer b' ≡ b, etc., are a number of individuals and there are predicates such as:

'has a good credit-rating'	≡	G
'is a wholesaler'	≡	W
'is in the home market'	≡	H

We can represent* the propositions:

---

* Letting −G ≡ 'has a poor credit-rating'; −W ≡ 'is a retailer'; −H ≡ 'is in the export market'.

p ≡ 'Customer a has a good credit rating' by Ga

q ≡ 'Customer b is not a wholesaler'   by —Wb

and

r ≡ 'Customer z is in the home market' by Hz

Sentences such as p, q and r which assign or deny *one* property to *one* individual are called *basic sentences*.

As in propositional logic, compound sentences can be constructed such as:

$$((-Ga) \& (-Gb)) \text{ or } (Wa \& Wb)$$

which in English would be 'Customers a and b have poor credit-ratings or both are wholesalers'. It is also possible to imagine very long compound sentences which state *every* property for *all* customers. Such a sentence describes fully an exact state of affairs and is called a *state-description*. It could be written as one long compound sentence:

$$Z \equiv Ga \& (-Wa) \& (-Ha) \& Gb \& Wb \& \dots \& (-Wz) \& Hz$$

but it would be more likely, in practice, to appear as a table which lists the individuals and against their names shows whether or not they possess each characteristic:

<table>
<tr><td>a</td><td>G</td><td>—W</td><td>—H</td><td rowspan="5">or even
as</td><td></td><td>G</td><td>W</td><td>H</td></tr>
<tr><td>b</td><td>G</td><td>W</td><td>H</td><td>a</td><td>1</td><td>0</td><td>0</td></tr>
<tr><td>c</td><td>—G</td><td>W</td><td>H</td><td>b</td><td>1</td><td>1</td><td>1</td></tr>
<tr><td>⋮</td><td></td><td></td><td></td><td>c</td><td>0</td><td>1</td><td>1</td></tr>
<tr><td>z</td><td>G</td><td>—W</td><td>H</td><td>⋮</td><td></td><td></td><td></td></tr>
<tr><td></td><td></td><td></td><td></td><td>z</td><td>1</td><td>0</td><td>1</td></tr>
</table>

where each column designates a predicate, and a 1 or 0 signifies whether the individual has or has not that characteristic.

Using this very simple predicate 'calculus' it would be possible to store a vast amount of information in a readily usable form. A name, or a suitable code number, could be given to each individual of interest, and a record could then be constructed by listing, after each name, the relevant characteristics (a term more commonly used than 'predicate' when talking about business records). This is, indeed, the normal logical structure of the vast majority of records kept by commercial and administrative organisations, so, rudimentary as the predicate logic described above may be, it has a wide range of application in the sphere we are interested in.

Simple operations on stored information

In order to exhibit some of the techniques that underlie the storage and retrieval of information, as normally performed in business information systems which use computers, we shall gradually elaborate a system based upon the simple predicate logic introduced above. By adding one complexity after another it will be possible to reveal what can be accomplished, more or less readily, by various formal methods of data

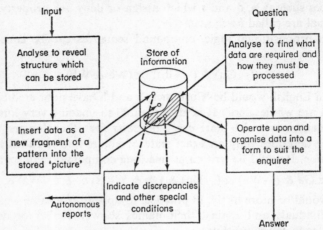

Fig. 37. Major functions in the storage and retrieval of business data.

manipulation. The discussion should also help those not familiar with computers to comprehend the nature of the very formal, rigid and precise languages that are associated with the use of these machines.

The major functions that must be performed in any system to store and retrieve business information are shown in fig. 37. Neither in a computer system, nor in a clerical system, need the functions be separated exactly in this manner, but as systems grow in size there is a tendency to divide the work between specialist computer programs or groups of clerical staff. The separation of functions helps to explain what goes on.

For the time being we shall assume that data are found by scanning the whole store and, when the appropriate part of the store is located, either inserting or extracting data. The data themselves would be held as a state-description in our simple logical language, that is, as a long string of basic sentences, thus:

$$Z = Ga \ \& \ (-Wa) \ \& \ (-Ha) \ \& \ Gb \ \& \ Wb \ \& \ \ldots \ \& \ (-Wz) \ \& \ Hz.$$

Simple inputs

First, consider the input language. The normal input message might consist of a string of basic sentences:

$$Wb \ \& \ Hd \ \& \ (-Gd) \ \& \ \ldots$$

The message could be analysed by a computer program, using a parsing procedure to reveal its component basic sentences. These could then be passed to the next program for insertion into the file or store of information. There would be little difficulty in extending the range of input messages to include a *list* of characteristics associated with a single name, perhaps in the form

$$WH(-G)d,$$

or a list of names associated with one predicate:

$$Wfhgj.$$

These are easily broken down into conjunctions of basic sentences

$$Wd \ \& \ Hd \ \& \ (-Gd)$$
$$Wf \ \& \ Wh \ \& \ Wg \ \& \ Wj$$

ready for storing, as before.

This kind of input language is incredibly simple, but it is all that is necessary for handling the kind of simple, routine facts which are gathered by a business system. Simple observations or reports tend to require only the rudimentary logical structure of the basic sentence, but, in practice, business data tend to be gathered as lists of properties for single individuals or as lists of individuals with a given property. These are catered for by the forms shown above. In some applications one improvement might be to permit the statement of facts in a form approximating to English, instead of in an artificial kind of logical code. With the expense of some ingenuity in writing the program, sentences such as

'Schmidt and Meirs are both wholesale dealers in the export market'

could be parsed and then translated into expressions like:

$$Ws \ \& \ (-Hs) \ \& \ Wm \ \& \ (-Hm).$$

Such elaborations would be mere gimmickry.

Inserting the data

When an input message has been reduced to a conjunction of basic sentences, the information is easily added to the store. As the store is scanned, each basic sentence it contains can be compared with similar fragments of information obtained by the analysis of the input message. If a match is obtained, then the input information can be discarded, as it is already 'known'. If the input *contradicts* a 'known' basic sentence, then there may be several ways of responding to the input. Simplest would be to accept the new information as correct and 'update' the store; this is what you would normally do if the message indicated, for example, that a customer had paid a certain invoice whilst the record said he had not. Another possibility would be to reject the input as wrong; for example, a customer would not be expected to move from the home market to an overseas location overnight; such a change to the record would not be made without careful scrutiny, because it would probably have major effects upon discounts and other procedures. Once the whole file had been scanned, the information which neither affirmed nor contradicted its existing contents could be added as a continuation of the list of basic sentences, at the end of the store. This insertion of new data may be accompanied by producing some report; for example, a list of new customers added, and an indication of any changes to the file, might enable fraudulent transactions to be traced.

It is interesting to notice that most functions in this system are quite standard, and can be performed in exactly the same mechanical way whatever the data are about. The way in which the incoming message must be analysed is a consequence of the syntactic structure of the input language; it does not depend upon the meaningful 'content' of the symbols. Also, the scanning of the file and the insertion of data depend upon the structural arrangement of the data in the store; the same structure will serve any number of applications which are totally distinct in subject matter. This is another example of how a syntactic approach to information can provide common solutions to many diverse problems.

The exceptional function is the program which responds to discrepancies and special conditions in the data. This function is closely dependent upon the nature of the data-processing application. It is normal practice in systems analysis work to devote most of one's energies to the functions which deal with exceptional and special conditions. The main functions can which deal with exceptional and special conditions. The main functions can often be dealt with by standard programs or well-known techniques.

There is no difficulty in extending the functions described above to accumulating totals or making reports on certain data, if the user so requires. This only calls for the inclusion of simple arithmetical operations in the updating function; it does not introduce any new concepts. The totals produced may be used to trigger autonomous responses from the system: for example, it would be quite simple to generate a report on any customer who passes a given credit limit.

It is important to recognise that the system so far evolved can accommodate only very rudimentary descriptions of states of affairs. Its store contains only a string of basic sentences, each one predicating a *single property* of a *single individual* and in any order:

$$Gb \ \& \ (-Hz) \ \& \ Wm \ \& \ ... \ \& \ (-Ga) \ \& \ Wx.$$

The input is a sequence of similar conjunctions of basic sentences that may augment, contradict or replace basic sentences in the store. There is no way of accommodating information which is logically more complicated, such as a message which includes an *or*:

$$(-Gc) \text{ or } (Hb \& Wy).$$

Although simple commercial and administrative systems would be unlikely to generate such data, there are industrial applications in which logical disjunctions could be expected.

Enquiry languages

Far more versatility of expression can be accommodated in an enquiry language than in an input language. This is because the enquiry procedure calls for the scanning of the memory without any need to change it. For practical purposes this suits our needs, because the original data normally become available only in the form of very simple statements, whereas our enquiries may call for quite complex analyses of files. By examining the simple memory-structures mentioned earlier it is possible to gain some idea of what is feasible and what presents serious difficulty in the design of an enquiry language.

If questions are to be answered automatically, using information held by a computer, a means must be devised whereby the computer can translate each question into what may be a very complex series of operations for retrieving the relevant data and transforming it into the answer being sought. One way of seeing how this may be done is to construct a number of typical questions which require progressively more elaborate processing.

To answer a question such as: 'Is customer, a, a good credit risk?' which might be submitted in English as it stands, or more simply, from the programmer's point of view, as a formula ?Ga, all that need be done is to scan the file, looking for a basic sentence 'Ga' or its negation '—Ga'. If one of these is found, the answer is 'Yes' or 'No', but if neither is found the answer is 'Don't know'.

Obvious extensions would enable you to ask:

'What is customer x like?' or '?x'.

This could be translated into an operation to scan the file and extract all the basic sentences which refer to x, and then compose an answer listing the characteristics of x, WHGx, thus:

'x is a wholesale customer in the home market and a good credit risk'.

If you were to ask:

'Who is a poor credit risk?'

the machine would scan the file and submit a list of the customers marked '−G'. A more complex question would be:

'Who, in the export market, is a poor credit risk?'

To answer this would require scanning the file and building up two lists (one list only would be required if the basic sentences were in customer-number sequence, but this cannot be assumed), one of customers marked −H ('not home market', i.e. 'export') and another of those marked −G. These two lists would have to be compared, to find just those customers whose names appeared on both lists. The amount of processing, to answer this question, is greater than for the simpler questions, even such questions as

'How many wholesale customers are there?'

This calls for only a single scanning of the file to locate the wholesale customers while the expression 'How many' invokes a counting procedure. Similar questions asking for simple arithmetical functions of the data such as:

'What is the percentage of poor credit risk customers?'

would be easy to answer; in this instance by scanning the file once, and accumulating two totals, one of all customers and one of those marked '−G', from which the percentage is derived.

Even a question such as:

'What percentage of customers is there in each possible category?'

can be answered by scanning the file once only, *provided that there is room, inside the machine, to accumulate all the totals.* For the three predicates we have used in the example, these would be totals of

G W H	G−W H	−G W H	−G−W H	Grand
G W−H	G−W−H	−G W−H	−G−W−H	Total

For three properties, each with two values, there are $2 \times 2 \times 2 = 2^3$ sub-totals to accumulate. That is easy, but if 100 properties are ascribed to each customer there are 2^{100} or approximately 10^{30} possible sub-totals. Obviously one would not attempt to accumulate a whole table of this kind. Although a partial table could be constructed, including only those totals that were non-zero, the normal solution would be to sort the file into groups of customers with the same characteristics and then count them. Sorting requires repeated scanning of the file and, even at a computer's speed of operation, it is a time-consuming task.

Sorting requires the examination of most pairs of records. The number of these is $\frac{1}{2}n(n-1)$, if there are n records. As one attempts to ask questions that require comparisons of all triples, quadruples, and so on, the amount of processing required soon becomes astronomically large. As an example of an innocuous-looking question of this kind, consider what happens when a customer pays a sum of money for some of the goods you have sent him; you will need to know which invoices he is paying of those outstanding. One method would be to search for a set of invoices totalling the exact sum paid. You would try all pairs of invoices, then all triples, then all quadruples, but you would be advised to write to your customer and ask him to state exactly which items he intended to pay for. A customer with only a few dozen outstanding invoices will be laborious to deal with when there are:

$$\tfrac{1}{2}\cdot\tfrac{1}{3}\cdot n(n-1)(n-2) \text{ triples and}$$
$$\tfrac{1}{2}\cdot\tfrac{1}{3}\cdot\tfrac{1}{4}\cdot n(n-1)(n-2)(n-3) \text{ quadruples}$$

and so on. Questions which imply so much data manipulation in practice cannot be answered exactly, although in principle the answers can be found. What happens is that approximate answers must be discovered by an effective guess-work program. Typical problems of this kind are found in industrial scheduling.

Storage of data

From the above discussion, although the storage and scanning mechanisms were not mentioned explicitly, it soon becomes apparent that limitations upon what questions might be answered by a machine are imposed by the size and speed of the available machinery, even when we know how to find the answer in principle. Let us examine this machinery.

As a clerk might have a single sheet of paper for his rough calculations and a filing cabinet full of detailed information, so the computer has a relatively small volume of storage for data it is working on, and a relatively large volume of backing store where records normally reside. The working-store can be read at a speed in the order of 1,000,000 characters per second, whilst the backing-store can be read at a relatively sedate speed in the order of 100,000 characters per second.

The amount of storage can vary widely but a working-store of 100,000 characters gives a rough idea of the magnitude of a modern medium-sized machine. The backing-store size cannot be described without first mentioning that there are two quite different kinds of store in common use. One is the magnetic tape which, like the ordinary domestic tape recorder, can be read only by scanning it serially in one direction or the other. A reel of tape holding, perhaps, 20,000,000 characters could be scanned in about 10 minutes. If you want to find, within one reel of tape, a particular item of data chosen at random, then the tape must be scanned until it is encountered; this takes an average of about 5 minutes and is called the 'random-access' time for the storage medium.

The other common, but more expensive, form of computer backing-storage is the magnetic disc device. This is like a juke-box on which it is possible to select, not only the disc of your choice and the side you want, but also the exact part of that disc. This very precise selection is achieved by the computer's using a number which, in effect, gives the spatial co-ordinates of the chosen storage location. You can imagine the disc store as comprising a million or so numbered pigeon-holes, each large enough to store a few hundred characters. The pigeon-hole numbers are called the 'addresses' of the storage locations, and they enable any item of data, chosen at random, to be found in about a tenth of a second, provided that its address is known. This is a very much faster random-access time than for magnetic tape, but still much slower than for working-storage in which the random-access time is about one millionth of a second.

Characteristics of Computer Storage				
Type	Working store	Fixed disc store	Exchangeable disc store	Magnetic tape store
Library use	None	None	Limited by expense	Cheap and virtually unlimited
Capacity on-line to the computer	100,000 characters	200,000,000 characters	20,000,000 characters on several modules	100,000,000 characters on several tapes
Transfer-rate to and from on-line storage	1,000,000 char/sec	200,000 char/sec	200,000 char/sec	50,000 char/sec
Random-access time, on-line	1 millionth sec	1 tenth sec	1 tenth sec	5 minutes
Mode of access	Addressable	Addressable	Addressable	By serial scan only

The figures in this table are only crudely approximate because computers are not like cars, all roughly the same size, but more like marine vessels ranging from the cabin cruiser to the ocean liner; the figures given correspond roughly to the computer equivalent of the modern tramp steamer.

There is another level of storage. The backing store which a computer can read is usually supported by a library which may contain hundreds or even thousands of magnetic tapes. The data on a tape from the library could be processed using the tape itself as backing store, or they could be transferred to a disc for processing. It is also possible, with some kinds of disc devices, to remove the discs and keep them in a library, but these modules of disc-storage, holding 1–10 million characters, are 10–20 times as expensive as the equivalent storage on magnetic tape.

These characteristics of computer storage are summarised in the table. The figures are true in 1971 but they will probably be out-of-date in five years' time, so fast is computer technology improving.

Memory structures or file structures

The previous discussion of how information could be stored and used to answer questions presumed that there would be little difficulty in gaining access to any of the data. At a computer's speed of operation, this is quite an acceptable approximation when only a few hundred basic sentences are stored, but it will not do when many millions of basic items of information must be stored. This is the case in business data-processing. A company may have to keep track of several million individual entities – customers, suppliers, employees, machines and their parts, products and their components, items in production, items in the stores, orders received, goods awaiting payment and so on. Each individual may need a hundred predicates to describe it. In this kind of normal, practical situation, it is no good examining the problem of storage as an abstract logical problem, except as a first approximation. The manner in which the data are organised within the physical storage devices is of paramount importance.

It is useful to identify the patterns of *logical* relationships between items of data, which exist regardless of the method of storage, by calling them the *data-structure*. The physical storage devices, discussed above, also have a structure which determines how quickly it is possible to move from examining one data-item to examining another. This may be called the *storage-structure*. There is a central problem in the design of any large-scale business information system; that is how to match the data-structure to the storage-structure to obtain a convenient physical arrangement. This physical arrangement of data is sometimes called a *file-structure* or a *memory-structure*.* The study of memory-structures is becoming one of the major tasks in systems analysis and design. Already,

* See Stamper, 1971.

large computer installations, with a major investment in data stored on magnetic tapes and discs, are having to face the problem of how to adapt the structures of their files to the changing demands placed upon them by their environment. The choice of a memory-structure is made, partly in order to achieve economy of storage space, but also to accommodate the input data easily, and to facilitate the necessary retrieval operations. The nature of the input data and of the outputs which are required depend upon the way in which the organisation is run. If management decide to run the organisation in new ways, the structure of files will need to be changed if economy in the data-processing operation is to be maintained. A system of files which cannot be modified easily must either be expensively re-structured, or it must force the management to defer the changes they had envisaged. This is one source of the dangerous rigidity which computer systems can introduce into organisations.*

Some memory structures

To illustrate problems of memory-structures, consider the simple data-structure implied by the elementary, logical system described above. How can it be represented in storage devices with different structures?

Because the storage structure of magnetic tape compels the computer to look at everything on the tape in one serial scan, there may be no advantage in arranging the sets of data concerning individual customers in any particular order; this very loose arrangement is called a *random structure*. An improvement on this can be made if you need to answer batches of enquiries concerning, say, many different customers whose code numbers are given. One obvious thing to do is to hold the file in sequence by customer-number; by doing this, and by putting *all* the enquiries, also, into sequence by customer-number, the processing of all translations can be done economically, in a *single* scanning of the file. This would be called a *sequential structure*. In the case of the customer file, the code numbers have no significance, so the sequence of the file has no significance outside the computer system; it is imposed upon the memory-structure to suit the storage-structure. In other cases, e.g. a file of requests for shares in a new company or a local government waiting-list for houses, the sequence given to records may be an essential part of the data-structure, because it embodies an order of priority or some other significant sequence. The priority could also be expressed by adding a priority code to the record, but, if the data are processed in order of priority, then it may be most economical to embody the priority sequence in the storage-structure.

* For a survey of these problems of data management see British Computer Society: 'Proceedings of the Conference on Data Management 1970'.

If the storage medium were disc instead of magnetic tape, the random and sequential structures could still be employed, because the store could be scanned serially as though it were a magnetic tape. There are, however, other, more powerful methods of structuring a file on disc, methods which make use of the fact that its pigeon-holes, or storage locations, all have addresses and can be reached directly.

One way of organising our customer file on disc would be by assigning all the data about one customer to one location. The computer would find the address of the data from the customer's code, by looking it up in an index table (just as you use a telephone directory), or by calculating it from a formula (as you might find a map reference when navigating). This *indexed structure* saves the computer from scanning *all* the data to find one record. It is very convenient if you are looking for the details of one customer and you know his code number.

If, instead of most of the enquiries or requests for data being directed towards known individuals, they are directed towards known characteristics, the indexed structure described above would not help. You would have to treat the file as randomly structured and scan it from end to end. Suppose most of the enquiries concern, say, all those customers possessing certain characteristics, e.g. 'export customers in the wholesale trade who are bad credit risks'. Another memory structure that is useful for answering enquiries of this kind is called the *inverted file*. It is so named because, instead of storing all the data for one customer in one location, which is the normal arrangement, the file brings together the code numbers of all customers possessing each given characteristic. So, if there are 50 different affirmative predicates, there will be 50 lists of customers and one customer's number will appear on the lists of all the properties which are predicated of that customer. To find customers having two properties in common, the computer locates and then compares the lists for the two properties and selects the members they have in common.

The contrast between the normal arrangement of a file and its inverted form suggests how a change in the pattern of work to be performed by the data-processing system influences the choice of file-structure. When a system is first created it will probably be expected to perform only routine clerical work: indicating the credit-standing of a given customer, keeping track of his debts and payments. These are all tasks for which the identification of the customer is known. As the organisation searches for more effective ways of operating, management will soon recognise that the data-processing system is capable of answering questions about the nature and behaviour of the market as a whole. The volume of requests for information about the properties of all customers, rather than about individuals, will grow. The tendency will be to make the normal structure less efficient and the inverted structure more so. The optimum file structure will probably be intermediate between these extremes. It may prove valuable to divide the customer file into several smaller files, on the basis of properties that are frequently used for identifying those classes which are of special interest:

Customers: Home Sales: Product range A
                               Product range B
       Export Sales: Product range A
                               Product range B.

These four smaller files give a partial inversion of the original customer file. This type of structure is only a generalisation of the usual one of holding data about major categories of individuals in distinct files, e.g. Customers, Employees, Suppliers, or Raw materials, Work in Progress, Finished Goods.*

More elaborate memory structures

Using a storage device that is made up of myriad addressable pigeon-holes, it is possible to represent many other sets of relationships between individuals by including, in each record, cross references to related records. By doing this, the information about the relationship is stored

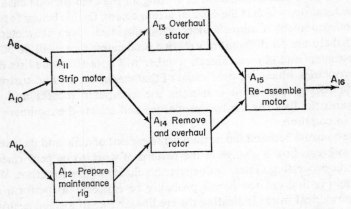

Fig. 38. Fragment of a network for planning a complex task.

implicitly in the cross references; it need not be made explicit in the records. As an example, consider a complex engineering project described as a network of inter-connected jobs which can be performed independently of one another, subject to the constraint that some jobs

* See Lefkovitz, 1969. Waters, 1971 and Stamper, 1971.

have to be finished before others begin. A part of one of these networks (often called a PERT or Critical Path Network) might appear as in fig. 38.

The network could be stored by placing the record for each activity in its own storage location and adding cross-references to the activities immediately preceding and succeeding it. The fragment of network in fig. 38 could be stored in the records:

$$A_{11}: \quad 8, 10: \quad 13, 14$$
$$A_{12}: \quad 10: \quad 14$$
$$A_{13}: \quad 11: \quad 15$$
$$A_{14}: \quad 11, 12: \quad 15$$
$$A_{15}: \quad 13, 14: \quad 16, \qquad\qquad \text{etc.}$$

The cross references to other storage address are called 'pointers' and a whole file of this kind is called a *list-structure*.*

Employing list-structures removes many of the severe restrictions imposed upon the choice of memory-structure by the physical structure of the storage device. Without the use of lists storage devices can accommodate only formal-language structures in the serial stores, such as magnetic tape, plus simple tabular arrangements of data in addressable storage. An effective memory for holding any kind of complex picture of the world must be able to assimilate very diverse and arbitrary relationships. Formal language structures are ideal for describing serial arrangements of signs and are, therefore, perfect for representing structures of messages in which the signs are transmitted one at a time. A list structure, however, is a multi-dimensional arrangement which does not restrict the signs to a straight line. A map has the form of a list-structure, whereas an itinerary has a language-structure. If you imagine yourself trying to transmit to someone else, over the telephone, the information which is stored in the complex structure of a map, then you will appreciate the difference between the two kinds of structure. The only way of transmitting the map is to scan it in some way so that the person you are speaking to can reproduce, on another piece of paper, exactly what is on yours. (Similarly, a television system works by scanning an image in the camera at exactly the same rate as the electron beam scans the screen on your set at home.) You could do it in other ways; for example, by giving him the coordinates and names of the objects in the map, in order of decreasing importance, until he had enough detail, or by giving him a number of itineraries from which he might construct a route map.

* The pointers may be represented either by giving the *addresses* of the other records or by giving their *serial numbers*. The list-structure based on addresses is most economical for processing, but any re-organisation of the file necessitates changing all the records. In some circumstances, therefore, the use of serial numbers may be preferred.

Whatever method you use, it should be clear that the person you are speaking to will have difficulty in understanding the terrain, or in answering questions about it, until he has converted your messages in a simple language-structure into the more elaborate memory-structure which can reveal the rich network of associations. The same must be done by an organisation which receives streams of messages from its resources (machines, work in progress, employees) or from the populations it deals with (customers, suppliers). For the management of the company it is necessary to construct a model of the interrelationships between all these elements. Normally this has been done by the manager in his own mind with the aid of some simple, visible charts, but as organisations become more complicated, the need increases for a detailed, externalised map of the organisation and its environment which can be shared by all those engaged in running the enterprise.

Meaning and memory

Computers are beginning to give us, for the first time, the opportunity to assimilate vast amounts of data into a single, meaningful structure that is 'publicly' accessible. In other words, they are providing a very powerful extension to human intelligence, one which supplements our natural capabilities just where they are weakest: the exact, literal memory for vast amounts of interrelated facts. This is achieved even using the simplest techniques. However, the ability of simple memory-structures to assimilate information is severely restricted to conjunctions of basic sentences. More complex statements indicating multiple relationships between several individuals cannot readily be incorporated into a serial file.

By employing a list-structured memory, a very great advance can be made in giving the computer the power to assimilate a wide range of input messages into a single, coherent picture of the organisation and its world. For example, using lists, a pointer can record a property which is predicated of two individuals; this was done in the network example:

$$A_{12} \text{ immediately precedes } A_{14}$$

is a statement with a two-variable predicate 'immediately precedes'. This is a considerable advance upon the simple predicate logic used earlier. It becomes possible to translate many more propositions into a form conveniently stored by a computer for example:

x is upon y	Uxy
x is inside y	Ixy
x dislikes y	Dxy
x is later than y	Lxy

These are predicates represented in ordinary speech by such grammatical forms as prepositions, adverbs, and transitive verbs, not only by adjectives which are single–variable predicates.

Using list-structured memory it is possible to make the computer behave in a more intelligent way than is economical with simpler structures. One may even think in terms of getting it to form concepts. Concept-formation by machine may be regarded as the task of discovering, and incorporating into the memory-structure, patterns that are used so often for generating outputs that they could be used to organise the data in a more economical fashion. For example, a file might have been constructed employing only the relationships of 'father' and 'mother' among a population of interest; if a large number of enquiries were made about people with the same mother and father, then a concept-forming machine would recognise this repetition as important and be able to propose naming the implied relationships; you would, of course, suggest 'sibling' or 'brother' and 'sister'; having defined the new relationships, the machine could then include them directly in its memory-structure by adding cross-references between brothers and sisters. Given the new concepts, future enquiries could be answered more easily.*

There seem to be many analogies between the ways in which human beings and computers operate on information. We can distil the essential features from a body of data, remember the results, and then scour our minds for items of information having a pattern which matches a question we are asked. It appears that the manner in which signs *inform* is closely connected with the nature of the memory-structure or file-structure into which the signs are assimilated. The next chapter will discuss some methods of measuring information by relating messages to a data-structure.

Before ending this chapter, let it be said that, at the present time, only simple file-structures are normally employed to organise business data. If data vital to an organisation are stored in an elaborate structure, the complexities facing the programmers are much increased; the risks of losing the data are enlarged; and there is a greater chance of a temporary inability to use important records. These obstacles are gradually being overcome. When they are, we shall have an instrument for organisational and social control, potent for good or evil.

* See E. F. Codd, 1970.

17 Measurement of Information in a Formal System

We shall talk about the information carried by a sentence, both by itself and relative to some other sentence or set of sentences, but not about the information which the sender intended to convey by transmitting a certain message nor about the information a receiver obtained from this message.

Bar-Hillel, *An Outline of the Theory of Semantic Information*

Note: Although this chapter is technically more detailed than many readers will require, the most technical part has been reserved for an appendix to the chapter.

In the previous three chapters, some aspects of the mechanics of data-processing have been explored. It is now possible to show how these ideas can be used to derive yet more measurements of information, to add to those which have been presented in chapters 5, 11 and 13. All the other ways of measuring information presented so far have used human reactions to signs to reveal the 'information' which the signs convey. In this chapter, the measurements involve no direct reference to the human recipient of the information. Instead, they are based upon the properties of signs regarded merely as parts of a formal, mechanical system. All the information measurements arrived at in this way belong to the syntactic aspect of information. They may be relevant, in practice, to problems of designing computer-based information systems.

Measuring the 'mechanical' properties of signs

The simplest and commonest way of measuring information in terms of its mechanical or syntactic properties is by counting the numbers of signs employed to convey the information. Many problems in the transmission, reproduction and storage of information call for no measurement more subtle than that. We use measures such as: numbers of documents to indicate the size of a library, numbers of words to indicate how large a book is, numbers of characters for the size of a computer file. No one imagines that these measure precisely what we mean when we talk of an amount of information, because they do not indicate the ability of the signs to 'inform' (whatever that means!). As was explained earlier, by using a person who is capable of being 'informed' when presented with signs, it is possible to measure how much they inform *him*. However, if one wishes to treat signs on a mechanical, syntactic or logical level, one cannot employ the response of an individual as a measuring instrument.

This chapter will show how the logical analysis of a message can be used to identify the elements of information it conveys. These elements are used to construct syntactic measurements of information.

A logical language for a very simple measurement

In the previous chapter we defined a simple kind of predicate logic which could be used as a language for capturing and storing basic elements of data. It made use of basic sentences, each of which makes a statement about *one* property of *one* individual, e.g.

$B_1 = Wa = $ Customer a is a wholesaler
$B_2 = Hb = $ Customer b is in the home market
$B_3 = -Ga = $ Customer a is a poor credit risk
$B_4 = -Hb = $ Customer b is in the export market.

The logical language which was used to illustrate the storage of information also included conjunctions of basic sentences such as:

$$B_1 \ \& \ B_2 \ \& \ B_3 \ \& \ B_4$$

Although this language, which permits only the use of basic sentences and their conjunctions, is very limited, it is adequate to describe much of the data normally gathered by a commercial organisation and stored on its files. There is one obvious way of measuring the information in a statement given in this simple language.

Using 'Information (S)' to mean the amount of information in statement 'S', we could assign a value of *one* unit of information to each basic sentence so that

$$\text{Information } (B_1) = 1.$$

Then, add up the number of basic sentences in a complex statement, first eliminating all the repetitions of basic sentences. For example:

$$\text{Information } (B_1 \ \& \ B_2 \ \& \ B_1 \ \& \ B_3 \ \& \ B_4 \ \& \ B_4)$$
$$\equiv \text{Information } (B_1 \ \& \ B_2 \ \& \ B_3 \ \& \ B_4) = 4,$$

where B_1, B_2, B_3 and B_4 are the distinct basic sentences listed above. This is a great advance on merely counting the numbers of characters which appear in a file, and it would be adequate for the simple kind of data-structure discussed early in the previous chapter.

This approach can be extended to measure the information in an input message *with respect to the information already in store*. If the stored information were:

$$S \equiv B_1 \ \& \ B_2 \ \& \ B_3 \ \& \ B_4 \ \& \ B_5$$

and an input message M such as

$$M \equiv B_2 \ \& \ B_6 \ \& \ B_7$$

were received, then it would be natural to reckon

$$\text{Information } (M \,|\, S) = 2$$

as the content of the message given in the file, i.e. the Information in the two new, basic sentences. (How to measure the information in a message which contradicts the contents of a file is not a problem which the syntactic measures of this chapter can solve except in an entirely trivial way.)

A more general logical language

The simple method of measuring information described above, using basic sentences as the smallest units of information, is difficult to extend in an intuitively satisfactory way to the more general predicate language which, you will remember, admitted not only:

$$\begin{array}{ll} \text{basic sentences:} & B_1 \quad B_2 \quad B_3 \quad B_4 \\ \text{and conjunctions:} & B_1 \ \& \ B_2 \ \& \ B_3 \ \& \ B_4 \\ \text{but } also \text{ disjunctions} & B_1 \text{ or } B_2 \text{ or } B_3 \text{ or } B_4. \end{array}$$

When sentences can be joined by ' or ', the basic sentence can no longer define the smallest unit of information. The single basic sentence:

$$B_1 = \text{Customer a is a wholesaler}$$

seems intuitively to convey more information than the vaguer, disjunction:

$$B_1 \text{ or } B_3 = \text{Customer a is a wholesaler } or \text{ a poor credit risk}$$

because this only tells you that the customer might be any of the three possibilities:

1. a wholesaler and a good credit risk;
2. not a wholesaler yet a poor credit risk;
3. both a wholesaler and a poor credit risk.

The only definite thing it tells you is that:

4. the customer is *not*, simultaneously, a good credit risk and a retailer.

The more basic sentences that are linked by 'or' in a lengthy disjunction, the vaguer becomes the resulting statement.

If the function Information (S) is to be extended to serve the more general predicate language which includes 'or', then an interpretation must be given to

$$\text{Information } (B_1 \text{ or } B_2)$$

in a manner that accords with our intuition about the information content of B_1 or B_2 compared with the single units of information in B_1 and in B_2. It is not immediately obvious how to do this, if the basic sentence is retained as the standard unit of information.

State descriptions and Content elements

The problem can be solved, however, by using another kind of statement as the smallest unit of information.

As pointed out above, the more basic sentences are joined together in a disjunction, the weaker is the resulting statement. So, imagine that the subject-matter you are dealing with includes n individuals (customers), each of which can be credited with p predicates (characteristics); the weakest possible statement you can make would be a disjunction of np basic statements, each one affirming or denying one characteristic of one individual. For example, if n=2, the individual customers, a and b, and if p=3, the characteristics G, W, H, then the weakest possible statement in the language is one such as:

$$E = \text{Ga or} - \text{Wa or} - \text{Ha or} - \text{Gb or Wb or} - \text{Hb}.$$

All that such a statement tells you is that exactly one possible state of affairs (state-description) is ruled out. It says that:

$$Z = -\text{Ga \& Wa \& Ha \& Gb \& } -\text{Wb \& Hb}$$

is impossible. A state-description like Z is one of the strongest possible statements in the language: given Z there is nothing more to know within the permitted field of discourse. It is the negation of one of the weakest statements E

$$Z = -E$$

if $\qquad E = B_1 \text{ or } B_2 \text{ or } B_3 \text{ or } \dots \text{ or } B_n$

then $\qquad Z = -B_1 \text{ \& } -B_2 \text{ \& } -B_3 \text{ \& } \dots \text{ \& } -B_n.$

The state-descriptions, Z, as they were called by Carnap, were used by him to define probability-measures which he has called 'logical probabilities'. The negations of the state-descriptions, E, or the '*content elements*', as they have been called, have been used by Bar-Hillel to define some measures of information. The arguments used by Carnap and Bar-Hillel are set out in an appendix to this chapter. The appendix does not require any more knowledge of logic than is introduced in this book. The logical and mathematical formalism is quite indispensable to the accurate presentation of even the bones of the ideas about logical probability and the related measures of information. The reader who does not wish to dwell upon the details of the argument in the appendix is, nevertheless, recommended to skim through it in order to see its general direction.

Logical probability and the measurement of information

The key ideas which the reader should notice when he skims through the appendix are the following ones.

First, a strict logical definition is given to what is meant by saying that one statement S_1 implies another, S_2 or, in symbolic form:

$$S_1 \supset S_2.$$

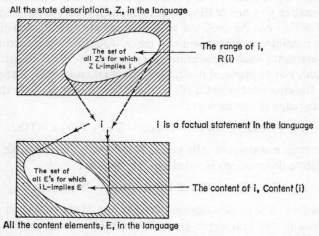

Fig. 39. How a factual statement is related to two sets of standard statements.

Second, when one complex statement *always* implies another, regardless of the truth or falsity of the basic sentences upon which S_1 and S_2 are built, then it is said that the one *logically* implies the other or

$$S_1 \text{ L-implies } S_2.$$

Third, an especially important assumption is that, when we are given a message, we can deduce all that it logically implies in the language we are using. This means that, given a message, the information it conveys includes all its logical consequences.

Fourth, is the crux of the argument. The notion of logical implication can be used to relate any statement to the two sets of *standardised statements*: the state-descriptions (the Z's) and the content elements (the E's) of the language. These relationships are exhibited in fig. 39. If the factual statement were

$$i \equiv Wa \ \& \ -Hb$$

then it would be L-implied by any Z which includes *both* the two basic sentences, 'Wa' and '—Hb', such as

$$Z_1 \equiv -Ga \ \& \ \overset{\downarrow}{Wa} \ \& \ \ Ha \ \& \ Gb \ \& \ -Wb \ \& \ \overset{\downarrow}{-Hb}$$
$$Z_2 \equiv \ \ Ga \ \& \ \underset{\uparrow}{Wa} \ \& \ -Ha \ \& \ Gb \ \& \ \ Wb \ \& \ \underset{\uparrow}{-Hb} \qquad etc.$$

An i would L-imply any E which contains one or both of the basic sentences 'Wa' and '—Hb' such as

$$E_1 \equiv -Ga \ or \ \overset{\downarrow}{Wa} \ or \ Ha \ or \ Gb \ or \ -Wb \ or \ Hb$$
$$E_2 \equiv Ga \ or \ -Wa \ or \ Ha \ or \ -Gb \ or \ -WB \ or \ \underset{\uparrow}{-Hb} \qquad etc.$$

These two sets of standardised statements are called the Range of i, R(i), and the Content of i, Content(i).

Fifth, is the idea of using the size of these sets to measure respectively the 'logical' probability of i and the information content of i. As a statement is made more and more specific, the Content (i) will increase in step with its increasing 'power to inform'; simultaneously, as the statement, i, is made more specific, the value of R(i) will decrease in step with the decreasing probability one would assign to it.

Sixth, the actual measurements are defined using the expression

$$m(i) = m(Z_1) + m(Z_2) + \ldots + m(Z_j) + \ldots$$

for the logical probability of i. The values of m range from 0 to 1, and the right-hand side includes a term for every Z in R(i), the range of i. Then by definition;

$$cont(i) = 1 - m(i)$$

for the content information of i.

Seventh, cont(i) is extended to form a measurement of the 'content information' in a statement, j, relative to what is already known or on the file, i, using the definition

$$cont(j|i) = cont(j \ \& \ i) - cont(i).$$

This measurement is shown to satisfy some of our intuitive notions about information but not others.

Eighth, is a method of overcoming the major deficiency of cont$(j|i)$ – its lack of a simple addition law – by defining yet other measures of information:

$$\inf(i) = -\log_2 m(i)$$

and

$$\inf(j|i) = \inf(i \& j) - \inf(i).$$

These are shown to embody some of our intuitive notions about information but still not all of them.

The deficiencies of information measurements based on logical probability

There is one major deficiency in the measurements of information based on logical probability: they all depend upon the assumption that the recipient of an item of information knows its entire logical consequences. This assumption is essential if the amount of information in a message is to be measured with respect to the logical language employed, that is, with respect only to the data-structure, quite ignoring the processing required to assimilate the data into a memory-structure.

This is another example of the ambivalent way we use the word 'information'; this simplifying assumption often fits our commonsense notions quite well. For example, if I am told that a stick is exactly 2 feet long, I do not reckon that I have been given any more information if I am told that it is exactly 24 inches long. However, no one, knowing some set of mathematical axioms (say for probability) would regard their logical consequences (such as statistical formulae and tables and the whole of probability theory) as devoid of information. Similarly, no managing director would accept a crate full of vouchers, recording all the individual transactions for the year, plus a handbook on accounting, in lieu of the annual statement of accounts.

It follows, for many practical purposes, that other measurements of information are needed to take account of the labour of assimilating raw data into a memory-structure and then generating the useful outputs. The information that you receive in reply to an enquiry could be measured as a function of the amount of processing necessary to arrive at the answer. (In human terms, perhaps, the amount of information given in reply to a question depends upon the thought which is needed to produce it.) It is a formidable task to measure the amount of processing necessary to up-date files, and to retrieve and process information taken from them, whether by a computer or by more conventional clerical means. It might be done by measuring the numbers of elementary operations that have to be performed to yield the desired result. All processing of data can be reduced to a few kinds of elementary steps which include: reading one character, writing one character, shifting a character from one storage location to another, and performing basic logical and arithmetic operations. The numbers of these elementary steps would depend upon the question to be answered, upon the memory-structure, and upon what other data, irrelevant to the given question, are also held in store. These numbers would measure the structure of the logical steps in the procedure without referring to the physical devices used for carrying it out. From computer systems to clerical systems, and from one kind of file structure to another, (random, sequential, indexed or inverted), the costs of the elementary operations of reading, writing and shifting information will differ greatly.

It ought to be regarded as one of the major tasks in the field of programming theory to discover techniques which would estimate the magnitude of the data-processing operations needed for up-dating files and retrieving information.

Conclusion

Except for the technical appendix to this chapter, this very brief survey of the formal properties of signs is now concluded. This group of four chapters has dealt with three major ideas.

The first of these ideas is that there exists a close relationship between the problems of organisation that require a mechanistic solution and the design of formal information systems. One of the most significant features of our age is the ubiquitous bureaucratic machine. In the right circumstances and provided that it is working properly, the bureaucracy can ensure efficient organisation on a vast scale, combined with impartial administration of bodies of regulations which are elaborate enough to deal justly with complex situations; but in the wrong circumstances and badly run, such mechanistic forms of organisation cause frustrated incomprehension and time-wasting confusion. Routine bureaucracy is characterised by its rigidly logical use of language which both underpins its impartial efficiency and undermines its acceptability. Many of the troubles of bureaucracy arise because it requires a strict formality in the treatment of messages and the application of rules which, for human beings, is a most unnatural way of handling information. Fortunately, the formal manipulation of signs is a task ideally suited to the computer – indeed, it cannot be applied to administrative tasks unless they are first cast into a bureaucratic mould. This involves identifying some activities which can be carried out using strictly formal languages instead of natural language and using data structures stored in a computer instead of concepts retained in the human memory; it also involves matching these formally defined activities to the other, less precisely structured parts of the organisation. Regrettably, systems analysts, wedded to the computer, too seldom understand formal systems from an organisational point of view; consequently, they are liable to design efficient computer systems that are *organisationally* ineffectual if not catastrophic.

The second main idea is that it is important to look for general methods and widely-encountered structures in the analysis of systems. It has only been possible to cite rather trivial examples, but the real applications which a systems analyst must tackle are exceedingly complex. Unless he can acquire a style of analytical and descriptive method which exploits relatively few, easily recognisable, general principles, he will only succeed in writing a description, which is a tangled skein of shapeless intricacies, and as difficult to comprehend as the system being described. When dealing with the mechanics of data-processing, one way of cutting through the complications is by thinking in terms of the manipulation of signs at the syntactic level, quite without regard for their semantics, which can be treated quite separately. The other important simplification is to think in terms of formal languages and logical structures. These abstractions are essential intellectual tools for any systems analyst.

The third main idea in this Part has been the extension of the rigorous definition of information by showing how it can be measured relative to a formal language. We examined in Part Four measurements of information derived from shifts in human judgments caused by the information being measured. In the next Part we shall examine the statistical theory of signal transmission and the measurements which arise from it. Deliberately, this engineering approach to information has been postponed until the next part of the book. It employs a measurement of 'information' which has much in common with other measures of information dealt with so far, but only at a formal mathematical level. Formal similarities between information measures do not make them equivalent to one another, any more than do the mathematical similarities between measurements of 'size': mass, volume or height. I hope the reader will be hardened against these misconceptions when he reads Part Six. Armed with a substantial analysis of information in terms quite distinct from those of the statistical theory, the reader should be less inclined than many of its devotees to believe that the statistical theory of signal transmission holds the key to 'information theory' in general and, in particular, solves the problem of measuring information.

Technical Appendix to Chapter 17: Logical Probability and Information

The following pages fill out the ideas briefly sketched in the middle of chapter 17. They are entirely drawn from the work of Rudolf Carnap, especially his 'Logical Foundations of Probability' and of Yehoshua Bar-Hillel, especially his paper 'An outline of a theory of semantic information'. Although these authors use the term 'semantic' to describe their measures of information, this would not be correct in the context of this book. Here 'semantics' is reserved for the analysis and critical appraisal of signs in terms of the actual procedures by which they are supposed to be related to 'reality'. The measurements of information which are described in this appendix involve only formal properties of signs with respect to a simple logical language. It would be more appropriate, in the context of the usage established in this book, to call these measures of information *'syntactic'*. The measurements of information developed in chapter 11, based upon subjective probabilities, would more aptly be called 'semantic' measures, in the sense given to the term here, because they do involve asking real people their judgements about statements concerning what we are pleased to call the 'real' world.

Résumé of definitions of logical language employed

The measures of information to be developed here apply only to statements in a limited kind of logical language which has been developed in previous chapters. The essentials of the language are now reviewed.

A statement in the language can be constructed from other statements by joining them together by '&', as conjunctions:

$$<statement> ::= <statement> \ \& \ <statement>$$

or by 'or', as disjunctions:

$$<statement> ::= <statement> \ or \ <statement>$$

The elementary statements, from which the ordinary statements are built, are called basic sentences. These can be constructed from the name of an individual object or person, linked to a relevant characteristic called a predicate.

$$\langle \text{basic sentence} \rangle ::= \langle \text{predicate} \rangle \ \langle \text{individual} \rangle$$
$$\langle \text{predicate} \rangle \quad ::= \quad G|W|H|...$$
$$\langle \text{individual} \rangle \quad ::= \quad a \mid b \mid c \mid ...$$

So, typical basic sentences would be:

$$Ga, Wb, Hb.$$

Also, the negation of a basic sentence is another basic sentence:

$$\langle \text{basic sentence} \rangle ::= -\langle \text{basic sentence} \rangle$$

Hence, using the examples above,

$$-Ga, -Wb, -Hb$$

would also be examples of basic sentences.

A file giving a complete description of *all* the individuals (your customers, say) from the point of view of *all* the properties included in your language is called a *state-description*. It could be written as one long compound sentence:

$$Z = Ga \ \& \ (-Wa) \ \& \ (-Ha) \ \& \ Gb \ \& \ Wb ... \& \ (-Wz) \ \& \ Hz.$$

Using 'Z' to designate a typical state-description will be quite convenient in what follows.

So we see that defining this language makes possible the picturing of many different states of affairs. In fact, if there are n individuals (customers) and p predicates, there will be n records in the file. Each record will have each of the p predicates fixed in one of two ways – it applies to that individual or it does not – hence there are 2^p possible forms of every record. Therefore, there are

$$(2^p)^n = 2^{np} = z$$

possible state-descriptions.

This is a good starting-point for trying to find an exact interpretation of the notion 'information'. Each message received concerning our customers enables us to rule out some of these possible state-descriptions as inconsistent with the facts. The more 'information' we receive, the more possibilities can be ruled out until, eventually, we have gathered enough 'information' to restrict us to only one state-description. If we presume that the information received was correct, this constitutes a true and complete description of the real state of affairs. Surely, the vague idea 'information' can be related to this very precise idea of using messages, progressively, to narrow down the range of possibilities. We shall see that this kind of analysis can lead to many different measurements of information.

Implication

We need to add two more logical ideas to our repertoire: the ideas of 'implication' and 'equivalence'. If one statement, S_1, *implies* another, S_2, or if S_1 and S_2 are *equivalent* to one another, we write, respectively:

$$S_1 \supset S_2 \quad \text{and} \quad S_1 \equiv S_2.$$

These give us yet other ways of linking statements to form more elaborate statements. They may be written into the grammar of the logic as:

$$<\text{statement}> ::= <\text{statement}> \supset <\text{statement}>$$
$$<\text{statement}> ::= <\text{statement}> \equiv <\text{statement}>$$

We have already used '&' and 'or' for combining statements. Their meanings were embodied in formal rules enabling the truth or falsity of S_1 & S_2 and S_1 or S_2 to be determined from the truth values of S_1 and S_2. Similar *reduction rules* are needed for $S_1 \supset S_2$ and $S_1 \equiv S_2$ if the signs $\supset$ and $\equiv$ are to acquire a meaning within the formal logical system.

Equivalence can be defined as an abbreviation for

$$(S_1 \supset S_2) \ \& \ (S_2 \supset S_1)$$

that is, the two statements imply one another. So we need only be concerned with implication.

As a matter of common sense, an implication is made when, starting from given premises, S_1, we transform them, by valid reasoning, into some conclusion, S_2. What relationship should there be between the truth of the premises, S_1, and the truth of the conclusion, S_2? Evidently it would be disastrous if correct reasoning, applied to true premises, led to a false conclusion; hence, if S_1 is true and $S_1 \supset S_2$ is true, so must S_2 be true. False premises, as we all know to our cost, may lead us, even with correct reasoning, to either true or false conclusions; so, if S_1 is false and $S_1 \supset S_2$ is true, S_2 may be either true or false. Common sense also requires reasoning to be called 'false' when false conclusions are reached on the basis of true premises, and, when S_1 is true and S_2 is false common sense requires $S_1 \supset S_2$ to be labelled 'false'. All these relations between truth values are summarised in the table below, which includes, as a reminder, the reductions for '&' and 'or'.

S_1	S_2	$S_1 \,\&\, S_2$	S_1 or S_2	$S_1 \supset S_2$	$S_1 \equiv S_2$
T	T	T	T	T	T
T	F	F	T	F	F
F	T	F	T	T	F
F	F	F	F	T	T

This definition of implication, in the context of a simple logic, comes quite close to the common-sense notions listed above. Its deficiency, from a common-sense point of view, is that it makes nothing of the idea of S_2 actually being derived from S_1. Consequently,

$$\text{'Mount Etna is in England'} \supset \text{'}2=1\text{'}$$

is a true implication if you regard the two statements it links as false. It is clear that $\supset$, the logical symbol for 'material implication', as it is sometimes called, is able to reflect only some of the character of our everyday word 'implies'. The missing idea of *derivation* (S_2 being derived from S_1) is a very complex notion which is not needed for the following argument.

What we do need is the idea of an implication which is true regardless of the truth or falsity of the basic sentences which constitute S_1 and S_2. Thus the truth of

$$\text{Ga} \,\&\, (-\text{Wa}) \supset \text{Ga or Wb}$$

regardless of the truth of the basic sentences Ga, $-$Wa, Wb. This can be demonstrated using a truth table (0 is used for F and 1 for T to make the table easier to read):

Ga	01	01	01	01
$-$Wa	00	11	00	11
Wb	00	00	11	11
S_1, Ga $\&$ $-$Wa	00	01	00	01
S_2, Ga or Wb	01	11	01	11
$S_1 \supset S_2$	11	11	11	11

This is found by using the definitions of '&', 'or' and $\supset$, given above. As you see, the implication is true for all 8 possible combinations of the truth values of Ga, $-$Wa, Wb. Such a statement is called a 'tautology' or an L-true statement, in which case we say S_1 L-implies S_2. A statement which is not a tautology will be called a *factual* statement.

This idea of logical or necessary implication, and the related one of L-equivalence, can be used to give a precise meaning to the notion that the information in a message is everything that it tells us. We can define *the information in a message as the class of all those sentences in the language that are L-implied by it.* Given the facts in the message, all these L-implied sentences could be derived by mere mechanical processing. This idea can usefully be refined by relating a message, not to *all* that it L-implies but just to those statements which are the smallest (*not* the shortest!) meaningful statements in the language.

The range and the content of a sentence

We are now going to develop two closely related complementary sets of ideas. One will lead us to a definition of logical probability, whilst the other will give us a definition of a quantity of information.

First of all, notice that a state-description, Z, is the strongest factual statement you can make in the language. If you are given any additional information, it will either be found already in the state-description itself (i.e. the complete file) or it will contradict that description. Right at the other end of the scale is a negation of a state-description, $-Z_1$; this says that all the other Z's except the one negated, Z_1, *could* be true. This is the weakest possible factual statement that can be made in the language, and it is called one of the *content-elements*, E.

E.g., for a very simple language which can refer to only two individuals, a and b, and two predicates, P and Q, a typical Z is:

$$Pa \ \& \ (-Qa) \ \& \ (-Pb) \ \& \ Qb;$$

the related E can be expressed as:

$$(-Pa) \text{ or } Qa \text{ or } Pb \text{ or } (-Qb).$$

Given a message, i, we can define
the Range of i R(i) as all the Z's which L-imply i and
the Content of i or Content (i) as the set of all the E's which i L-implies. The more information in i, the smaller is R(i) and the larger is Content(i).

Properties of the range and content of a sentence

The next obvious step is to find some ways of measuring the Range and Content of a sentence. But first let us ask: What are such measurements likely to tell us?

The measurements, because they are associated with the numbers of elements in the sets, R(i) and Content(i), are like measurements of two areas. Some of their properties can be seen, in fig. 40, by taking a series of sentences:

i_1, which is L-true;

i_2, which is factual but true for most states of the world;

i_3, which is also factual but mostly false;

i_4, which is L-false.

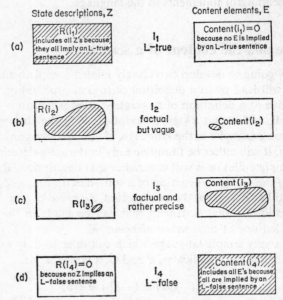

Fig. 40. The Range and Content sets for different statements.

The 'areas' of state-descriptions and content elements which they enclose are shown in fig. 40, which should be studied carefully.

Now consider *two* factual sentences, i and j, when we know that i L-implies j: how are their Contents and Ranges related? As you would expect, j has at least the Range of i and i has at least the Content of j. This is shown in fig. 41(a). There are several situations which can usefully be distinguished, besides the one where i L-implies j. These are also pictured in fig. 41. You will notice that the figure contains the definitions of L-exclusive and L-disjunct pairs of sentences. Study this diagram carefully.

The most interesting case is the last one in the illustration: the general case. If the overlap of the *Content* sets is large, it suggests that i and j convey roughly the same *information*. If there is a large overlap of the *Ranges* of i and j, there seems intuitively to be a suggestion that when i is true there is a good '*chance*' that j is also true. These intuitive notions, which relate the Content to information and the Range to probability, are given further pictorial support by fig. 42 which shows what happens when 3 messages are received.

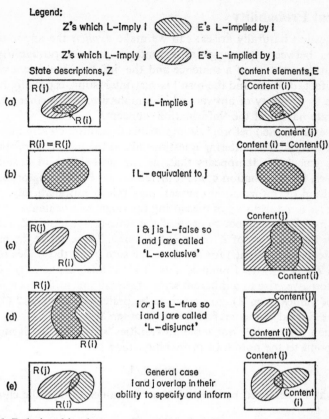

Fig. 41. Relationships between Ranges and Contents of pairs of statements.

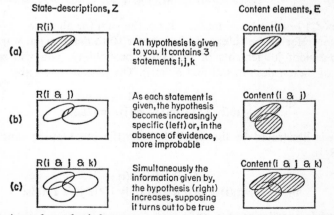

Fig. 42. As an hypothesis becomes more specific it becomes less probable but potentially more informative.

Logical Probability

The question naturally arises: can we make *explicit* the apparent connections between the range of a sentence and its probability, and between the content of a sentence and the 'information' it conveys? It can, in fact, be done and the result is very interesting, especially because it leads to a variety of answers which emphasise, still further, the conglomerate nature of the 'information' concept.

As we have noted before, it is impossible to enquire closely into information without encountering questions about the nature of probability. This is true here. It appears that, as the probability of a statement decreases, its information content increases, so, by defining probability, a definition of 'information content' may follow automatically.

There is a natural way of measuring the range of a sentence, i: simply attach a positive number to each of the state-descriptions, Z, (call this number the 'measure of Z' or m(Z) for short). Then, define the measure of the sentence i, or m(i) for short, as the sum of all the values of m(Z) for the Z's in R(i) the Range of i, or, if i is L-false, make m(i)=0. This definition gives rise to a different scale of measurement for every assignment of values to m(Z). Are some to be preferred to others? Can one scale be singled out as preferable to all others?

We can begin ruling out some possibilities by noting that if m(i) is to correspond to the notion of probability, then

$$0 \leqslant m(i) \leqslant 1.$$

This may be achieved by insisting that the values of m(Z) be chosen so that

$$0 \leqslant m(Z) \leqslant 1$$

and $m(Z_1)+m(Z_2)+...+m(Z_n)=1$, i.e. the sum for all Z's.

If you refer to the rules used in chapter 10 to define what was meant by consistent judgements of subjective probability, you will see that some of these rules are satisfied by m(i). The parallel cases are:

I $0 \leqslant m(i) \leqslant 1$
II $m(i \text{ or } j)=m(i)+m(j)-m(i\&j)$

which is illustrated by fig. 41(e) showing the overlapping ranges R(i) and R(j).

II' $m(-i)=1-m(i)$
II'' $m(i \text{ or } j)=m(i)+m(j)$ if and only if (i&j) is L-false

are simple corollaries.

This is enough to show that any m(i) will serve as a consistent measure of logical probability, in an absolute sense, but not as a measure of conditional probability, because there is no equivalent of the rule:

III
$$P(A\&B)=P(A) \cdot P(B/A)$$
$$=P(B) \cdot P(A/B).$$

This deficiency can be overcome by defining what Carnap, in his 'Logical Foundations of Probability', calls 'the degree of confirmation of a hypothesis h on evidence e':

$$c(h, e)=\frac{m(h\&e)}{m(e)}$$

(The evidence, e, must not be L-false or self contradictory!)
If the only evidence available is a tautology, t, then

$$c(h, t)=m(h)$$

because $h\&t \equiv h$ and $m(t)=1$, as the range of a tautology includes all Z's. This means that, for the purposes of defining logical probability, nothing is lost by using c which retains all the properties of the m-function employed to define it. The c-functions fulfil the necessary rules for a consistent measure of probability:

I $0 \leqslant c(h, e) \leqslant 1$
II $c(h\,ori, e)=c(h, e)+c(i, e)-c(h\&i, e)$
III $c(h\&i, e)=c(h, e) \times c(i, e\&h)$
           $=c(i, e) \times c(h, e\&i)$
also
II′   if $h\&i$ is L-false
           $c(h\,ori, e)=c(h, e)+c(i, e)$
II″ $c(-h, e) =1-c(h, e).$

There are as many of these logical-probability functions as ways of assigning values of $m(Z)$. In the next section we shall look at some of the restrictions which might be imposed upon this choice, and the possible effects upon inductive reasoning of the values assigned to $m(Z)$.

The logical analysis does not suggest how the values of m should be assigned. Logical probability is a purely formal property of a system of signs. It has, in the sense used in Part Three, no signification unless you equate the m-values either to probabilities arrived at subjectively so that

$$m(Z)=subj.prob.(Z),$$

or to probabilities reached by making repeated experiments when

$$m(Z)=rel.freq.(Z).$$

It is still possible to avoid both these denotative significations by laying down a normative *principle* that a 'rational' man *must* employ some m-value assignment that has neat and tidy logical properties like one of those reached in the next section. This kind of probability is a pure, logical probability and, if used as a basis for guiding your actions, its signification is *prescriptive*, because it says what you should believe, without making operational reference to any actual or supposed state of affairs.

Restrictions on Logical Probability

A natural way of selecting the most appropriate single measure of logical probability would be by trying to find one which, as far as possible, is independent of any particular formal language.

One step is to insist that the m-function values are chosen so that the value of m(i), for any sentence, i, is unaffected by the particular individuals or properties it mentions.

So that $$i_1 \equiv (Ga \ \& \ Wb) \text{ or } (-Ha)$$

has the same m-value as

$$i_2 \equiv (Gx \ \& \ Wy) \text{ or } (-Hx)$$

which talks about customers x and y instead of a and b.
Similarly

$$i_3 \equiv (Ha \ \& \ -Wb) \text{ or } Ga$$

has the same value as i_1 although the properties H, $-W$ and G have been substituted for G, W and $-H$.

A further restriction to be placed on m is that, for a given sentence, i, about some customers already included in the file, m(i) will remain unaltered as more customers are added to the file. The m(Z) values will change, of course, because the number of state-descriptions is multiplied by 2^p for every new addition to the file. The sentence, i, will still be valid in the enlarged formal-language (or file) and, therefore, it should retain its original m-value.

One of the most important and interesting restrictions is based upon an analogy with the multiplication rule:

III′ $$P(A \ \& \ B) = P(A) \times P(B)$$

which is used to *define* inductive independence between A and B. When this rule is applied to subjective probabilities it means that information relevant to A has no influence on our views about B, and vice-versa. A similar rule can be imposed upon m-functions so that, in circumstances when we expect two sentences i and j to convey quite independent information, for example when i and j have no predicates in common, e.g.

$$i \equiv -Wb \ \& \ Ga$$
$$j \equiv Hb \ or \ -Hc$$

then the values chosen for m must satisfy:

$$m \ (i\&j) = m(i) \times m(j),$$

the rule for inductive independence.

The above restrictions narrow the choice to what are called 'proper' m-functions. One function consistent with all these constraints is the simplest m-function of all, where, for every state-description:

$$m(Z) = \frac{1}{z}$$

Z being the total number of state-descriptions. This particular choice of m, which Carnap calls m†, leads to a c-function c† which has the following property which leads Carnap to reject it. Suppose you have a file with details about 101 customers, the last being a new one. If you know that *all* the rest are in the home market, i.e. the evidence is

$$e \equiv Ha_1 \ \& \ Ha_2 \ \& \ldots \& Ha_{100}$$

then it would be natural to make the inductive inference that customer 101 is very likely also to be a home customer. However this hypothesis:

$$h \equiv Ha_{101}$$

is not given any confirmation by the overwhelming evidence e. In order to demonstrate this simply, assume that H is the only predicate in the language, in other words we are only interested in whether a customer in the home market or not. Then, e&h is a state-description and $m(e\&h)$ $= \frac{1}{101}$; e is a sentence that is implied by exactly two state-descriptions e&h and e&$-$h, so $m(e) = \frac{2}{101}$. Hence the degree of confirmation of h on e

$$c†(h, \ e) = \frac{m(h\&e)}{m(e)} = \tfrac{1}{2}.$$

Now if e were to be replaced by other evidence, even diametrically opposite evidence, e, where

$$e \equiv (-Ha_1) \ \& \ (-Ha_2) \ \& \ldots \& \ (-Ha_{100})$$

you would get just the same value:

$$c†(h, \ e) = \tfrac{1}{2}.$$

Hence m† and c† cannot lead us to adjust our judgements of hypotheses on a purely logical basis, that is, they do not provide a principle of inductive reasoning, if we wish to draw general conclusions from limited evidence.

Carnap favours another m-function which he calls m*; there is a related confirmation function c*. This he would define for the file of customers as follows. Lump together all the state-descriptions which correspond to identical market structures, the market structure being given by the numbers of customers displaying each possible combination of properties, regardless of who they are. If there are s structures, then all the m(Z)'s added together for *one* structure, S, will equal $\frac{1}{s}$ and if there are t state-descriptions with the same structure, each Z has an m-value

$$m(Z) = \frac{1}{st}$$

Take a very simple example (as in Bar-Hillel, 1952) of a language with 1 predicate A and 3 individuals, a, b, c. All the state-descriptions, Z, the structures S, and the corresponding values of m*(Z) and m*(S) are shown in the table below. There are eight possible state-descriptions which have been grouped according to the four structures they represent. The values of m† (Z) are found by giving equal values to the Zs whilst the values of m* (Z) are found by assigning equal values to m* (S) for the four structures and then dividing these among the Zs within a structure.

i	Z_i	m† (Z)	m* (S)	m* (Z)
1	Aa&Ab&Ac	$\frac{1}{8}$	$\frac{1}{4}$	$\frac{1}{4}$
2	Aa&Ab& —Ac	$\frac{1}{8}$		$\frac{1}{12}$
3	Aa&Ac& —Ab	$\frac{1}{8}$	$\left.\right\} \frac{1}{4}$	$\frac{1}{12}$
4	Ab&Ac& —Aa	$\frac{1}{8}$		$\frac{1}{12}$
5	Aa& —Ab&—Ac	$\frac{1}{8}$		$\frac{1}{12}$
6	Ab& —Aa&—Ac	$\frac{1}{8}$	$\left.\right\} \frac{1}{4}$	$\frac{1}{12}$
7	Ac& —Aa&—Ab	$\frac{1}{8}$		$\frac{1}{12}$
8	—Aa&—Ab&—Ac	$\frac{1}{8}$	$\frac{1}{4}$	$\frac{1}{4}$

Suppose we wish to know whether Ac is true or —Ac and our evidence is

$$e \equiv Aa\&Ab$$

then, noting that two state descriptions, Z_1 and Z_2, are the only ones which L-imply e, we compute for hypothesis $\quad$ $h \equiv Ac$

$$m^*(e\&h) = m^*(Z_1) = \tfrac{1}{4}$$

and $\qquad$ $m^*(e) = m^*(Z_1) + m^*(Z_2) = \tfrac{1}{4} + \tfrac{1}{12} = \tfrac{1}{3}$

so $\qquad$ $c^*(h, e) = \tfrac{1}{4} \div \tfrac{1}{3} = \tfrac{3}{4}$

whereas for the hypothesis

$$-h = -Ac$$

$$m^*(e\&-h) = m^*(Z_2) = \tfrac{1}{12}$$

$$m^*(e) = m^*(Z_1) + m^*(Z_2) = \tfrac{1}{3}$$

and $\qquad$ $c^*(-h, e) = \tfrac{1}{12} \div \tfrac{1}{3} = \tfrac{1}{4}.$

Thus, by using m^* as a basis for logical probability, the evidence, e, leads us to favour h rather than $-h$. This result accords with our intuitive ideas about inductive reasoning in those circumstances when we can presume that one observation of a property has potential relevance to the next observation.

The two special cases $m\dagger$ and m^* represent extreme choices of m-function. They represent sign-posts among the range of possible functions that can be chosen. Each probability function would lead to a different set of information measures, of the kind that will be discussed in the next sections. The choice of an m-function is discussed by Carnap in his monograph *The Continuum of Inductive Methods*.

The 'content' measurements of 'information'

Probability and information, as we have seen before, appear to be the converse of one another in some respects. In normal usage, both are rather vague concepts, but we have seen how 'probability' can be given three distinct interpretations. In Part Four some suggestions were made about measuring 'information' using subjective probability. In Part Six we shall examine information-measures based upon relative-frequency probability, whilst in the next few paragraphs we develop information-measures based upon the logical concept of probability. From the one definition of logical probability, they show that two different information measures can be derived; both of them are justifiable.

The first of these measures is the obvious counterpart of m(i) which measures the Range of the sentence i. Instead, by measuring the Content of i, a quantity, cont(i), can be defined. For every m-function there is a corresponding cont-function so we can use all the previous results for m by defining:

$$cont(i)=1-m(i)$$

or

$$cont(i)=m(-i).$$

This measurement has many of the properties that we would intuitively consider appropriate to the notion 'amount of information'. Looking at figs. 40 and 41 (pp. 256–7) for example, we notice the following:

(a) If i L-implies j, then you would presume that it contains at least the amount of information contained in j, and indeed $cont(i) \geqslant cont(j)$ in these circumstances.   (fig. 41(b))

(b) A tautology, t, does not really say anything so

$$cont(t)=0.$$ (fig. 40(a))

(c) For a factual sentence, i, $cont(i)>0$.   (fig. 40(b) or (c))

These are all natural properties of 'amount of information'. There is one strange feature of 'cont': only for a contradiction, $-t$, does 'cont' reach its maximum value $cont(-t)=1$. See fig. 40(d). The most information that you can have in a sentence is conveyed by a single state-description, e.g. Z, which L-implies every content-element except the one that is $-Z$. Hence, if m† is the logical probability upon which cont† is based, cont† $(Z)=\frac{z-1}{z}$, but for cont*(Z), based upon m* there is a more complex formula taking account of the state-structures. The special feature of 'cont', which is fairly obvious from the right hand diagram of fig. 41(e), is its additivity law.

(d) $cont(i\&j)=cont(i)+cont(j)-cont(i$ or $j)$

However, it is only true to say:

(e) $cont(i\&j)=cont(i)+cont(j)$,

if and only if (i or j) is L-true, in other words that i and j must L-imply quite distinct sets of content-elements (see fig. 41(d)). The notion, which is sometimes appropriate, that the information in two statements taken together cannot exceed the information they convey separately, is conveyed by the relationship:

(f) $cont(i\&j) \leqslant cont(i)+cont(j)$

It appears that the function 'cont' provides one satisfactory way of measuring the information in a sentence, relative to the language in which it is couched. Another information measure would tell us the amount of information in j relative to the 'knowledge', i, that we already have on our file. Such a function can be defined as:

$$cont(j/i)=cont(j\&i)-cont(i)$$
$$=m(i)-m(i\&j).$$

These 'content' measures have some properties that accord very well with our intuitive notion of 'an amount of information' yet, in some circumstances, they display rather weird properties which lead us to seek other ways of measuring information!

Deficiencies in the 'content' measure of information

Both the absolute measure, cont(i), and the relative measure, cont(j/i), appear to be at variance in some respect with our intuitive concept of information. Take the relationship (e) above

$$\text{cont}(i\&j) = \text{cont}(i) + \text{cont}(j)$$
if and only if (i or j) is L-true.

This is far too strong a condition, because in most situations we should say that the two statements:

and

$$i \equiv Wa \equiv \text{'Customer a is a wholesaler'}$$
$$j \equiv Hb \equiv \text{'Customer b is in the home market'}$$

convey quite separate 'information', whose quantities we should expect to be additive. But 'Wa or Hb' is *not* L-true, so that the additivity condition for 'cont' does not apply. The reason for this can be seen by observing that both i and j L-imply some of the *same* content-elements. Such as

or

$$\text{Ga or } \overset{\downarrow}{W}\text{a or } (-Ha) \text{ or Gb or Wb or } \overset{\downarrow}{H}\text{b or...}$$

$$(-Ga) \text{ or Wa or } (-Ha) \text{ or Gb or } (-Wb) \text{ or Hb or...}$$

or any other in which Wa and Hb both appear! Hence the sets Content(i) and Content(j) overlap, and their measures cannot simply be added to find the measure of Content (i&j).

This has an odd consequence for cont(j/i). If you are told j when you already have knowledge of i, the relative information cont(j/i) is less than the absolute measure cont(j) *even though i seems to have nothing whatsoever to do with j*! But for the two quite unconnected sentences i and j given above

and

$$\text{cont}(i\&j) < \text{cont}(i) + \text{cont}(j)$$

hence

$$\text{cont}(j/i) = \text{cont}(i\&j) - \text{cont}(i)$$

so that

$$< \text{cont}(i) + \text{cont}(j) - \text{cont}(i)$$

$$\text{cont}(j/i) < \text{cont}(j)$$

which may be a desirable property of information if j seems less informative when i is known than when otherwise totally ignorant.

The above argument applies to *all* the different 'cont' functions, but, if only the very well-behaved ones are considered, those based upon the more restricted or 'proper' m-functions such as m† and m*, then it is possible to make the anomaly more explicit, as illustrated in the next section.

Detailed illustrations of the deficiency of 'cont' as an information measure

A sentence such as 'i or j' given above, which states *one* simple property of *one* individual, is called a 'basic' sentence. A basic sentence, B, rules out exactly half the possible state-descriptions, hence, for all *proper* m-functions (which give equal weight to all individuals and all predicates, positive or negative),

$$m_p(B) = \tfrac{1}{2}.$$

Also, for a pair of basic sentences which mention distinct predicates, the multiplication rule for inductively independent statement holds:

$$m_p(B_1 \ \& \ B_2) = m_p(B_1) \times m_p(B_2) = \tfrac{1}{4}.$$

As we have noted before, this rule is just an exact way of stating the intuitive idea that two sentences convey separate 'information'. For a string of r, mutually independent, basic sentences $B_1, B_2, B_3 \ldots B_r$,

$$m_p(B_1 \ \& \ B_2 \ \& \ B_3 \ldots) = m_p(B_1) \times m_p(B_2) \ldots \times m_p(B_r)$$
$$= (\tfrac{1}{2})^r$$

Hence

$$\mathrm{cont}_p(B) = 1 - m_p(B) = \tfrac{1}{2}$$

for an isolated basic sentence, B, whilst

$$\mathrm{cont}_p(B_1 \ \& \ B_2 \ \& \ldots \& \ B_r) = 1 - m_p(B_1) \times m_p(B_2) \times \ldots \times m_p(B_r)$$
$$= 1 - (\tfrac{1}{2})^r$$

for a conjunction of r, mutually independent, basic sentences.

If you have prior knowledge of all but one of these basic sentences the relative content of the last one can be expressed thus:

$$\mathrm{cont}(B_r \,|\, B_1 \ \& \ B_2 \ \& \ldots \& \ B_{r\text{-}1})$$
$$= \mathrm{cont}(B_1 \ \& \ B_2 \ \& \ldots \& \ B_r)$$
$$- \mathrm{cont}(B_1 \ \& \ B_2 \ \& \ldots \& \ B_{r\text{-}1})$$
$$= 1 - (\tfrac{1}{2})^r - (1 - (\tfrac{1}{2})^{r-1})$$
$$= (\tfrac{1}{2})^{r-1} - (\tfrac{1}{2})^r = \frac{2-1}{2^r}$$
$$= (\tfrac{1}{2})^r$$

If you are told, therefore,

$B_1 \equiv Ga$ (Customer a is a good credit risk)
$B_2 \equiv Wb$ (Customer b is a wholesaler)
$B_3 \equiv -Ha$ (Customer a is not in the home market)

in succession, each message conveys half as much 'information' as the previous one as measured by the 'content' function.

Although these properties of cont(i) and cont(j/i) have deficiencies from the point of view adopted above, they are appropriate in some circumstances. For example, if you are interested in information as a means of decision-making, you will be looking for facts that help to rule out certain courses of action. You can formulate your problem by regarding all the imaginable courses of action as the state-descriptions, Z, which must be whittled down by your knowledge of the facts to the few feasible Z's. A message in the form of a basic sentence will eliminate half the Z's, and another inductively independent basic sentence will eliminate half of those that remain, and so on. Hence, in this context, the properties of 'cont', which seem so unsatisfactory in some respects, are able to reflect our intuitive notion of the diminishing marginal return on information used for decision-making.

The conclusion that must be drawn is that our vague intuitions harbour not only the 'cont' measure of amount of information but another which obeys a different addition law.

Another measure of 'information'

The trouble with 'cont' is that it ascribes unequal values to each of a series of basic sentences. Now suppose that we arbitrarily fix the information-value of a single basic sentence as the unit on a new scale. This new scale can be related to the cont-scale because

$$\text{cont}(C_r) = 1 - (\tfrac{1}{2})^r$$

where

$$C_r = B_1 \,\&\, B_2 \,\&\dots\&\, B_r$$

is a conjunction of r mutually inductively independent, basic sentences; hence

$$2^r = \frac{1}{1 - \text{cont}(C_r)}$$

or

$$r = \log_2\left[\frac{1}{1 - \text{cont}(C_r)}\right]$$

but, on our proposed new scale, r is exactly the amount of information in the r basic sentences, so we try the following definition. For any sentence i

$$\mathrm{inf}(i) = \log_2 \left[\frac{1}{1 - \mathrm{cont}(i)} \right]$$

in order that

$$\mathrm{inf}(C_r) = r$$

or, alternatively, the definition can be written:

$$\mathrm{inf}(i) = -\log_2 m(i),$$

making use of the formula

$$\mathrm{cont}(i) = 1 - m(i)$$

where 'inf' is the symbol for the new function. A corresponding relative 'inf' measure can be defined:

$$\mathrm{inf}(j \mid i) = \mathrm{inf}(i \& j) - \mathrm{inf}(i).$$

The properties of 'inf' show that it behaves in a satisfactory way as a measure of an amount of information. In particular:

$$0 \leqslant \mathrm{inf}(i) \leqslant \infty$$

$\mathrm{inf}(i) = 0$	if, and only if, i is L-true
$\mathrm{inf}(i) = \infty$	if, and only if, i is L-false
$0 < \mathrm{inf}(i) < \infty$	if i is a factual sentence
$\mathrm{inf}(i) \geqslant \mathrm{inf}(j)$	if i L-implies j
$\mathrm{inf}(i) = \mathrm{inf}(j)$	if i and j are L-equivalent.

Relationships of this kind,[r] as we saw earlier, are also true for 'cont', and justify its use as a measure of information. The major deficiency of 'cont' as a measure of information is its failure to satisfy an addition law, except under conditions that may offend our intuition. 'Inf' does not have that failing. If it is based on a proper m-function that satisfies the multiplication law:

$$m_p(i \& j) = m_p(i) \times m_p(j)$$

for two mutually independent sentences i and j; then, because

$$\log m_p(i \& j) = \log m_p(i) + \log m_p(j),$$

$$\mathrm{inf}(i \& j) = \mathrm{inf}(i) + \mathrm{inf}(j).$$

Hence, for basic sentences not only does

$$\mathrm{inf}(B) = 1$$

but the relative information of B_r is not affected by knowledge of other basic sentences with different predicates, $B_1, B_2, \ldots B_{r-1}$, or

$$\text{inf}(B_r \,|\, C_{r-1}) = 1$$

where

$$C_{r-1} = B_1 \,\&\, B_2 \,\&\, \ldots \,\&\, B_{r-1}.$$

These properties make 'inf' seem more plausible than 'cont' in some respects.

There is another difference. For 'cont' there was a relation:

$$\text{cont}(i \& j) \leqslant \text{cont}(i) + \text{cont}(j).$$

There is no equivalent for 'inf'. Sometimes we feel intuitively that the amount of information in two sentences taken together cannot exceed the amount they convey separately, a constraint satisfied by 'cont'. At other times, we are prepared to admit that two pieces of vague information, when taken in conjunction, can amount to a very specific statement or at least suggestion: if 20 people had a motive for a crime and 50 had the opportunity, suspicion would fall heavily on a single individual appearing in both lists. In just this way $\text{inf}(i \& j)$ may exceed $\text{inf}(i) + \text{inf}(j)$.

Review

This appendix has indicated the nature of a wealth of different ways of measuring the amount of information in a sentence, both with respect to the *language* being employed using

$$\text{cont}(i) \text{ and } \text{inf}(i),$$

and with respect to any prior knowledge or, in computer terms, with respect to the contents of the files, using

$$\text{cont}(j \,|\, i) \text{ and } \text{inf}(j \,|\, i).$$

The two different kinds of measurement, 'cont' and 'inf' appear to have different spheres of relevance. Whereas 'inf' has properties that make it more apt for describing the amount of information in a single sentence, it may seem that 'cont' gives a better indication of the value of a message, in the context of a decision-making problem.

The wealth of possible measurements stems from the many m-functions which can be used to define them. Reasons for choosing some special functions rather than others have been mentioned.

Part Six

Empirics

This Part deals with the most highly developed branch of the study of information. It owes its development to communications engineering. It is an approach that relies upon the empirical properties of sets of signs or signals used to transmit messages.

Yet another method of measuring information, based upon the relative frequencies of messages, is defined. This method of analysis, developed in the first place for the study of electronic communication equipment, can be used, quite validly, to describe the transmission of information by people performing repetitive tasks.

It is shown how this method of analysis can be applied to business systems and, in particular, to the analysis of control systems. A warning is given that these engineering methods can only be used meaningfully in the context of an organisation when talking about routine information-processing.

18 Signal Transmission

The fundamental problem of communication is that of reproducing at one point either exactly or approximately a message selected at another point. Frequently the messages have meaning. . . . *These semantic aspects are irrelevant to the engineering problem.*

Shannon, *The Mathematical Theory of Communication*

In the days when messages had to be carried by a courier, on foot or on horseback, and given to the recipient in a written document or reported to him by word of mouth, the problem of transmitting information was a trivial adjunct of the ordinary problem of physical mobility.

The use of telegraphy, radio and other means of transmitting information which are quite separate from the ordinary means of transport, raises a new set of questions about the capacity, unit costs, reliability and other qualities of these more ethereal communication devices. There is, today, a well-developed branch of engineering concerned with answering these questions. It is best called the *Statistical Theory of Signal Transmission*, although it is often called 'Information Theory'. (There could not be a better example of the unfortunate tendency of words to misdirect the course of the mind than this example of the use of a generic term, 'Information Theory', to describe a very particular and limited part of a large subject area.) The limited part of the subject of interest to the engineer concerns only the physical problem of transmitting messages, and the properties of the communication channels used for the purpose.

In order to measure the capacity of an information channel, the engineer need only understand information in a very narrow way. Such problems as meaning or the nature of language can be forgotten. The engineer designs communication channels for others to use. He has no idea, whilst doing this, what messages in a language will be transmitted, nor is he remotely interested in what they mean. He is only concerned with the kind of signal used to transmit them. Most frequently this will be speech, in which the information is coded in the form of vibrations of various frequencies. For the purpose of showing how to measure the statistical properties of signals, it is easier to consider a much simpler type of signal.

A simple communication channel

Imagine this situation: in Birmingham there is a factory, in London a sales officer, between them runs a simple kind of telegraph line. Once every second, from London to Birmingham, a signal travels down this line. These signals always have exactly the same pattern. What information can we send from London to Birmingham? The answer of course is none at all, if we are unable to change the pattern of the signal – remember that we can neither stop nor start the stream of signals, it just goes on, once a second in exactly the same uninformative way. However, if our transmission system is provided with some modulating device which will enable our 'carrier' signal to be modified so that we can make it into either a 'dot' or 'dash', then we have the power to transmit messages. This is called a *binary* channel and one signal is called a *binit*. (This should not be confused with 'bit' which is probably a more familiar term that will be introduced with its correct meaning in due course.)

We have already touched upon an idea of the greatest importance. The absence of 'variety' in a signal is intuitively equivalent to the absence of 'information'. The blank face of uniformity tells us absolutely nothing. But the simplest display of variety presents us immediately with the possibility that it conveys information. Energy transmitted in a uniform, unchangeable way affords us no means of sending messages, but, given only two different signals, a dot and a dash, we can begin to communicate. Using a code for the alphabet we are able to transmit words; we can use a dot for the presence of a spot on the television screen and a dash for its absence, and hence with our two signals we can code pictures and, similarly, any other kind of information.

This observation is reassuring because it makes it clear that, although we are examining a communication channel which uses only two signals, we are nevertheless looking at a problem that can be related to *all* kinds of communication. It is even used for transmitting the human voice in modern 'pulse code' modulation systems.

The communication channel between London and Birmingham is capable of transmitting, once a second, either a dot or a dash. Let us see how this channel can be used for transmitting a certain set of messages. For example, we may have two major lines of goods. Let us call them a, b, c and d, and w, x, y and z. We will assume that at 9 o'clock every morning a sales clerk sits at the transmitter, reading through a pile of orders for a, b, c and d. Only one item appears on each order form, and as he reads it the clerk sends an appropriate code word of dots and dashes. The question naturally arises: 'What is the best code to use?' (We assume that the clerk has no difficulty in keeping pace with the maximum speed of transmission attainable over the channel.)

The effect of coding

One suitable code would be the following:

Message (Product)	a	b	c	d
Code	− −	− ·	· −	· ·

This means that each message out of the set of four messages, a, b, c, d, requires just two signals, and so we can transmit our messages at the rate of one every two seconds, or 30 a minute on average. The question now arises, can we do any better than this, perhaps by recoding our messages?

If our messages a, b, c, d, occur with *equal frequency*, then the answer is: No, we cannot transmit our information any faster. Obviously, two hundred signals are required for the transmitting of one hundred messages, and you will find that no other code you try will give you a better figure than that.

However, what happens at 10 o'clock each day when the clerk does a similar job transmitting the orders for w, x, y and z? The popularity of these products is far from uniform: $\frac{1}{2}$ of all orders are for w, $\frac{1}{4}$ for x, and $\frac{1}{8}$ for each of y and z.

One way of compressing our messages w, x, y, z, into fewer signals is by using a very short code for the common message w, and longer codes for the others. This, of course, is the principle of the Morse code, which employs shorter codes for the more common letters of the alphabet.* The following arrangement might do:

Message	w	x	y	z
Code	−	− ·	− · ·	− · · ·

With this coding, the average number of signals per message will be: $1 \cdot \frac{1}{2} + 2 \cdot \frac{1}{4} + 3 \cdot \frac{1}{8} + 4 \cdot \frac{1}{8} = 1\frac{7}{8}$ binits per message. Again, we must ask the question, can we do any better? Is it possible, in fact, to improve on this coding? Perhaps you would like to try to find a more efficient code. Before you jump to any too obvious conclusion, check that your code cannot lead to ambiguities when it is decoded.

Many forms of signal

Where does this analysis bring us? We have defined a communication channel by defining the signals that it is able to transmit, and the rate at which the signals can be transmitted. This idea could be extended to any other communication channel, not only ones that transmit just dots and dashes. The telephone line would transmit a range of audible frequencies; a typewriter, considered as a communication channel between the typist and a piece of paper, is able to transmit the range of

---

* Unlike the Morse code, which has an alphabet of *three* symbols, dot, dash and *silence*, the code described in this example has no third symbol which can be used as a terminator for a group of dots and dashes.

characters on the type-face, plus spaces, at a speed that depends upon the person operating the machine.

We could reserve the application of signal transmission for those artefacts which we normally call 'communication channels', but to do so would be to lose the benefits of the generality of the theory. Any machine, or regular kind of behaviour, which is capable of copying or translating a pattern in one medium into a related pattern, perhaps in quite another medium, can be regarded as a communication channel in the general sense. There is one essential condition: it must be possible to discover the statistical properties of the two patterns, the input and output. For example, in this general sense a lathe is a communication channel, transmitting the information on a drawing to emerge at the other end of the process 'coded' in a solid metal shape. The channel capacity of a lathe and its operator depends upon the range of sizes that can be turned, and upon the accuracy with which they can be made.

Whenever, repeatedly, a variety of symbols, shapes, sounds or patterns of any kind are transmitted from one place to another, or transformed from one representation to another, or from one medium to another, there exists a communication channel. All these channels will be more complicated than the simple one between London and Birmingham already described, but they can all be analysed in a similar way. The universality of the idea of a communication channel is exceedingly important. 'Information' in our ordinary discourse tends to be limited to describing signals which are conveyed by books, papers, radios, television sets, telephones, punched cards, forms, computer output and so on. 'Information' needs to be viewed very much more widely than this, as we have seen in the study of social communications (Part Two). It is perhaps preferable to abandon the term 'information' in favour of 'variety', in an engineering context, because the object is only to transmit, to some distant place or time, the variety of behaviour or form exhibited by a stream of messages. This requires the mediation of a physical carrier which itself can adopt, temporarily or permanently, some number of different states, as a piece of writing paper can hold the imprint of words, as air can propagate the vibrations of a voice, or as an electro-magnetic field can carry a radio signal. Problems of message transmission turn upon the question of how best to encode the messages in the different states which can be displayed by the carrier or channel.

'Information' measured by most economical coding

Returning to our simple channel between London and Birmingham, we started to ask the question: how do we measure the capacity of the channel? Obviously, before we can transmit to Birmingham signals about goods ordered in London, there must be a coding scheme agreed at both ends of the line. This can be used to code and decode the messages. It implies that we agree upon a set of messages that we are going to transmit at a particular time. The idea is quite general. For a telephone line this will be a very large set of messages which might be specified as 'any audible signal between certain frequencies'. For a typewriter we should have to specify an alphabet and a set of miscellaneous symbols, whilst for a lathe we would specify a range of sizes and the degree of precision required. In order to find the capacity of our simple London–Birmingham channel, we found that we needed to know the number of different messages to be transmitted, which of course governs the number of codes required; and we also found that, knowing the frequency with which the different messages occurred, we were able to increase efficiency of transmission by giving brief codes to the commoner messages and longer codes to the unusual messages.

One way of arriving at a measure of the channel capacity for a set of messages is by trying to find a better and better code, until it cannot be improved upon. It is a reasonable hypothesis that there is a limit to the efficiency of a code beyond which no further improvement can be found. If this limit can be discovered, it could be the basis of a measurement of the average rate of 'information' transmission, provided that we can in turn define, in a suitable way, the amount of 'information' in a message. So we need yet another interpretation of 'information', and a way of measuring it. The information content of a message is obviously very small if the message tells us little that is new, but a report of an unexpected event should have a comparatively high information content. This is the same commonsense notion about information that we have encountered earlier. Can it be given a suitable interpretation in this context?

'Information' measured using relative-frequency probability

Once again, information can be related to a probability measure; this time the *relative-frequency* probability may be taken as its basis. This measurement may be referred to as the 'statistical information' associated with a given message, call it $I_s(m)$. It measures a property of a message relative to a well-defined source which emits messages, drawn from a specified set, with probabilities that are *statistically stable*. This stability or statistical uniformity must be understood in the following sense: when a person encounters the source of signals for the first time, nothing in the observed pattern would tell him whether the source had been transmitting for a day or a thousand years; he would be able to use his observations to calculate the relative-frequency probabilities to any desired degree of accuracy by taking observations for long enough. A source which is stable in this manner is called 'ergodic' and the 'ergodic' conditions ensure the validity of the relative-frequency measure of probability. The 'information' measurements to be discussed in this Part are meaningful *only* when applied to such repetitive behaviour.

Necessary properties for $I_s(m)$ that intuition demands are:

an inequality rule: $I_s(m) > I_s(n)$; if $p(m) < p(n)$

where $p(m)$ is the probability of the message m being sent by the source. Also, an equality rule:

$$I_s(m) = I_s(n) \quad \text{if and only if} \quad p(m) = p(n).$$

For example, if I were to tell you that I had just thrown an unbiased die, and was about to tell you the result, there would be six messages I could send you, 1, 2, 3, 4, 5 or 6, and each of these messages would have a relative frequency of 1/6. All these messages, being equally frequent, would be regarded as conveying equal amounts of information. In the same way, the messages about products a, b, c and d would be equally informative, whereas the messages about w, x, y and z would not be so. The message w, being the most likely, must provide the least information of the four messages in the set.

Intuition also demands that there be an additivity property for $I_s(m)$. Suppose two messages 'm' and 'n' are received. There is nothing to stop our regarding 'mn', the ordered pair of them, as a single message, it is just a matter of convenience how we choose to group the signals. It is, therefore, desirable that:

$$I_s(mn) = I_s(m) + I_s(n)$$

whenever m and n are inductively independent of each other. That is to say, the relative frequency of 'n' is exactly the same, immediately following an 'm', as it is following immediately upon the receipt of any other character. Without the independence condition, another, more complicated, addition rule would have to apply.

There is a satisfactory function $I_s(m)$ which can be defined in terms of $p(m)$, the probability of the message. It is illustrated by the set of messages 'w', 'x', 'y' and 'z'.

Message, m	w	x	y	z	wx
Probability, $p(m)$	$\frac{1}{2}$	$\frac{1}{4}$	$\frac{1}{8}$	$\frac{1}{8}$	$\frac{1}{2} \times \frac{1}{4}$
$J(m) = \dfrac{1}{p(m)}$	2	4	8	8	8
	$2'$	2^2	2^3	2^3	2^3
$I(m) = \log_2 \dfrac{1}{p(m)}$	1	2	3	3	3

The reciprocal of the probability, call it $J(m)$, satisfies the inequality and equality rules, but not the additivity rule. The chance of the composite message 'wx' being received is $\frac{1}{2} \cdot \frac{1}{4} = \frac{1}{8}$, the product of the separate probabilities of 'w' and 'x'.

Now $\qquad\qquad J(w) + J(x) \neq J(wx)$

because $\qquad\qquad 2 + 4 \neq 8,$

but it is clear that an additive relationship can be obtained by using the logarithm of $J(m)$, so we define

$$I_s(m) = \log J(m)$$
$$= -\log p(m).$$

The choice of base for the logarithm fixes the unit of measurement. Common logarithms, to base 10, give the I_s value in 'Hartleys', named after the engineer who first suggested the logarithmic scale. Natural logarithms are useful for some mathematical purposes, but the most frequently employed scale uses logarithms to base 2, as above; the unit of measurement for I_s is then called a 'bit'.

Notice that 'bit' is the name given to an amount of 'information', in this special engineering sense; it is a *statistical property* of a source of signals, whereas 'binit' is a name given to either one of a pair of characters or states. Put it another way: a pint jug is to a pint as a binit is to a bit. The one refers to the carrier, the other to what is carried. You will always have to carry your pint in a container but it need not always be full.

A source of messages

If you are trying to design efficient communication channels, you will be interested in the whole set of messages to be transmitted, not in individual ones. Hence the function $I_s(m)$ will not be very useful. A more appropriate function is the average amount of statistical information per message. This is known as the *entropy function*, $H(S)$, of the source, S. It may be expressed in bits per message, or bits per second, whichever is the more convenient.

$$H(S) = p(m_1)\log\frac{1}{p(m_1)} + p(m_2)\log\frac{1}{p(m_2)} + \ldots + p(m_r)\log\frac{1}{p(m_r)}$$

or

$$H(S) = -\sum_i p(m_i)\log p(m_i)$$

where $m_1, m_2, \ldots m_i \ldots$ are the messages. For example, the two sources of messages transmitted by the London sales office to the Birmingham factory have entropies as follows

for S_1, the set a, b, c, d.

$$H(S_1) = \tfrac{1}{2}\cdot 1 + \tfrac{1}{2}\cdot 1 + \tfrac{1}{2}\cdot 1 + \tfrac{1}{2}\cdot 1$$
$$= 2 \text{ bits per message}$$

and for S_2, the set w, x, y, z.

$$H(S_2) = \tfrac{1}{2}\cdot 1 + \tfrac{1}{4}\cdot 2 + \tfrac{1}{8}\cdot 3 + \tfrac{1}{8}\cdot 3$$
$$= 1\tfrac{3}{4} \text{ bits per message}$$

The simplest possible source is one which emits only two different messages with relative frequencies p and (1−p) for which

$$H(S) = -p.\ \log p - (1-p).\log (1-p)$$

A graph of this function is displayed in fig. 43; it reaches a maximum

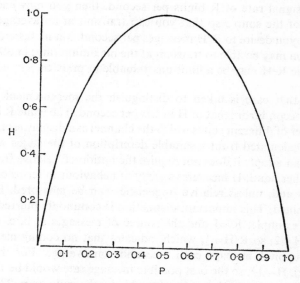

Fig. 43. The entropy for a binary source for different relative frequencies of the two signals.

for a source which emits the two messages equally frequently and is zero for those sources which emit only a single message. This coincides with the intuitive notions discussed earlier.

The fundamental relationship between entropy and coding

The communication channel between London and Birmingham has a capacity of 1 signal per second. The rate at which this channel can transmit messages will depend upon the way they are coded. At the London end of the line is this arrangement:

$$\text{[SOURCE]} \xrightarrow{\text{Messages}} \text{[CODER]} \xrightarrow{\text{Signals}} \text{[CHANNEL]}$$

The entropy of the source can be measured in bits per message, H, and the channel can transmit R binits or binary signals per second. We need to be able to describe the coding process which links them. As we saw earlier, it is possible to use a channel more efficiently by finding a more economical coding for a set of messages. The question arises: what constitutes a 100% efficient code?

The answer is supplied by Shannon's first fundamental theorem. It says this:

If you have a source with entropy H bits per message, and a channel with a signal rate of R binits per second, then you may encode the output of the source so that you can transmit at an average rate as close as you desire to R/H messages per second, but no faster. In some cases you may be able to transmit at the maximum rate; in other cases the value R/H may be a limit unattainable in practice.

Notice that care is taken to distinguish the measurement of R in *binits* per second from that of H in *bits* per second. The value R indicates the number of different states which the channel can display each second; it can be calculated from a suitable description of the states which the channel can adopt; it does not require the notion of 'relative frequency'. On the other hand, H measures variety of behaviour in terms of relative frequency and, unless relative frequencies can be measured, H cannot be determined. This important distinction is commonly blurred.

In our example, R=1 and the source of messages a, b, c, d has an entropy H=2, so R/H=½, which indicates that no coding method can improve upon 1 message each 2 seconds on average. For the source (w, x, y, z), H=1¾, so the best possible message rate would be 1 every 1¾ seconds. The transmission rate attainable by the code on p. 274:

$$
\begin{array}{cccc}
w & x & y & z \\
- & -\cdot & -\cdot\cdot & -\cdot\cdot\cdot
\end{array}
$$

is one message each 1⅞ seconds. It was not unfair, therefore, to suggest that the reader try to find a better code. Shannon's theorem, however, makes it clear that it would be futile to look for a code more efficient than, for example:

w	x	y	z
—	· —	· · —	· · ·

which permits the transmission of one message each $1\frac{3}{4}$ seconds.

(Notice that this code also simplifies the logic needed for decoding messages – a topic discussed earlier on pp. 202–3.) Normally there does not exist such a simple code allowing the maximum transmission rate to be attained.

Efficiency and redundancy

The efficiency of a code can now be measured. If the average length of a code is L binits per message, then the theorem can be interpreted as saying that the *maximum* amount of statistical information or 'variety' which could be transmitted by each L binits is L bits. What is *actually* being transmitted is the entropy of the source, H bits per message. Hence we may define the efficiency of the code by

$$\text{efficiency} = \frac{H}{L}.$$

A channel which can transmit a choice not of 2 characters but 4 has twice the capacity, and one with a choice of 8 characters has 3 times the capacity of a binary channel. In general, each character in a set of n is the equivalent of $\log_2 n$ binits. When the L characters are drawn from an 'alphabet' of n characters, the above formula can be generalised to

$$\text{efficiency} = \frac{H}{L.\log_2 n}$$

A more important quantity than the efficiency of a code is its redundancy (=1−efficiency). This quantity coincides with our commonsense notions of redundancy in language – repetitions, circumlocutions and saying the same thing in a number of ways. Redundancy can be wasteful if the communication channel is reliable, but, in the presence of noise, repetitions of all or a part of a message can help to cut down the amount of error.

Decoding signals

Consider what would happen at Birmingham, if a stream of dots and dashes were received from the communication channel. Given the encoding rules used in London, can the signals always be decoded?

Given the optimum code

any stream of dots and dashes can be decoded; e.g.

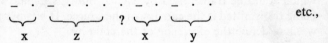

A code that is less than 100% efficient does not permit the decoding of *any* arbitrary string of dots and dashes. For example, using the code with 93·3% efficiency:

on the same string as before,

all is well until a sequence of 4 dots in a row is encountered. There is no way of decoding this, so it is clear that somewhere an error in transmission has occurred. A code which has no redundancy cannot detect any errors. Here we see the practical value of redundancy in communications. It may be desirable to repeat *all* messages with the object of being able to detect most errors and even correct them; this would greatly increase the cost of transmission and may result in a degree of accuracy far beyond what is needed. Evidently, to design effective communication channels, we need to know the relationships between the characteristics of message sources, patterns of error or 'noise' in the channel, and the rates at which accurate transmission can be achieved. To elucidate these matters a noisy channel is examined in the following sections.

Noisy communication channels

Noise is simply unwanted information which distorts the message that *you* are interested in. What is *noise* and what is *message* depends upon your point of view. Someone listening to a B.B.C. broadcast will regard crackling atmospherics as noise, whereas a radio-astronomer studying sunspot behaviour would be more interested in the crackling atmospherics and would regard the B.B.C. broadcast as noise.

To study a noisy channel we must have a look at the effects of the noise on each of the signals that we transmit. Take our simple example once again. We must ask the questions: When we transmit a 'dash', what is the chance of its arriving at the destination undisturbed, and what is its chance of being turned into a 'dot'? Similarly, what happens to a 'dot'? The answers to these questions define the characteristics of the channel. They may be expressed in a tabular form:

Sent	Received dash	dot		Sent	Received dash	dot
dash	1	0		dash	0·9	0·1
dot	0	1		dot	0	1
	Channel 1				Channel 2	

Sent	Received dash	dot		Sent	Received dash	dot
dash	0·5	0·5		dash	0	1
dot	0·5	0·5		dot	1	0
	Channel 3				Channel 4	

Channel 1 is a completely noise-free channel. If we transmit a dash it is certain to arrive as a dash, if we transmit a dot it is certain to arrive as a dot. There is no error. Channel 2 is noisy, because a dash transmitted has a 0·9 chance of arriving correctly, and a 0·1 chance of being distorted into a dot during transmission, whereas a dot is always transmitted correctly. Channel 3 is just as noisy as any channel can be, a dot or a dash has an equal probability of 0·5 of arriving correctly or incorrectly; such a channel is incapable of transmitting any information, because the relative frequencies of the received messages are totally unaffected by the relative frequencies of the messages sent; the channel, therefore, conveys nothing. Contrast this with Channel 4, which has a 100% error rate, so that if a dash is transmitted it certainly arrives as a dot and vice versa. This channel exactly recodes the message that has been transmitted, and, provided that we know that this is happening, we can interpret the message correctly. This phenomenon of *predictable* transformation of the signal is referred to as 'distortion', not 'noise'.

Equivocation

To measure the effect of noise in a communication channel, one must think of the person receiving the message. He must ask himself, 'Although I have just received a dash, what chance is there that I am mistaken in believing that a dash was transmitted?' and a similar question if he has just received a dot. This residual doubt, caused by the noise in the channel, can be measured in terms of entropy. You can imagine the receiver being given the benefit of an auxiliary channel

K

which would flash a red light whenever an error had been made during communication. This red light would be another information source. It would provide just enough information to make up for the information lost because of imperfect transmission. Its entropy is taken as a measure of the equivocation of the transmission, the residual doubt which the receiver cannot escape, unless he has an auxiliary channel to help him.

The equivocation depends not only upon the channel but on how it is being used. Skilful coding of the messages can minimise the effect of noise. This can best be explained by approaching the problem in a slightly different way.

Mutual information

There is another concept which is closely related to, but more general than, the idea of equivocation. Suppose you have two sources of messages, A and B (see fig. 44). Their entropies are H(A) and H(B). Imagine, for the sake of illustration, that they each emit a message once

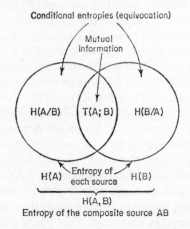

Fig. 44. A composite source and its component entropies.

a second. You can treat the two together as a single composite source, AB, by treating each pair of messages, one from A and one from B, as a single message from AB. The entropy of AB is H(AB).

The question to ask is: what are the relationships among H(A), H(B), and H(AB)? If you turn back to the earlier discussion about the additivity rule: $I_s(mn)=I_s(m)+I_s(n)$, for two statistically independent messages, you will see that this additivity property should apply to the entropies of two sources which are statistically independent. That is:

$$H(AB)=H(A)+H(B), \text{ for mutually independent A and B.}$$

Sources of messages are frequently not independent of one another, because the messages from one source, A, may be correlated with the messages from B, as when, knowing a person's height, you can venture to guess his weight with reasonable accuracy. It is possible to define another entropy function, $H(A|B)$, of A given B, which is the average statistical information in a message from A, assuming that the corresponding message from B is already known. This conditional entropy is related to the others by the law:

$$H(AB)=H(B)+H(A|B)$$

or the equally valid

$$H(AB)=H(A)+H(B|A).$$

The quantity

$$T(A;B)=H(A)-H(A|B)=H(B)-H(B|A)$$

is called the *mutual information* of the two sources. Intuitively interpreted, it measures the amount of statistical information or 'variety' common to A and B. The mutual information of *any* two sources can be measured; there need not be a causal relationship between them. It is like other statistical measurements in that respect.

One way of interpreting T is to take A as the source of messages transmitted along a channel and B as the receiver of the messages. For perfect transmission

$$H(A|B)=H(B|A)=0$$

and

$$H(AB)=H(A)=H(B).$$

For transmission which suffers the perturbations of noise there will be some uncertainty about what message was sent from the transmitter A, although you know which message was received at B. This uncertainty, inherent in a noisy channel, was earlier called the equivocation.

The amount of information which reaches the receiver at B is given by the expression for the mutual information:

$$T(A;B)=H(A)-H(A|B).$$

That is to say: the transmission equals the entropy of the source minus the equivocation.

Capacity of a noisy channel

For perfect transmission, when the signal rate is R the rate of information transmission can attain a maximum of R bits for a binary channel or R $\log_2 n$ for a channel which can transmit n different symbols. For a noisy channel the signal rate is not an adequate guide to the rate at which statistical information can be transmitted.

The channel capacity, C, for noisy transmission can be defined as the maximum value of the mutual information which can be attained by careful selection of the frequencies of the channel's symbols, or

$$C = \max\{H(A) - H(A \mid B)\}$$

The general problem of finding a code for maximising the transmission rate for a given set of messages along a given channel can be very difficult, but there is one simple case which can be used as an illustration. Suppose the channel from London to Birmingham made errors according to this symmetrical pattern:

Received

Sent	dot	dash
dot	1-p	p
dash	p	1-p

$\begin{bmatrix} 1-p & p \\ p & 1-p \end{bmatrix}$ where p=probability of an error

then the chance that any received signal is erroneous will always have the same value, p. To find the equivocation of this channel, suppose that a red light were to flash when an erroneous signal were received. This light would provide exactly the information which had been lost on account of the noise in the channel. Such a light would emit two signals with probabilities p and (1-p); its entropy would be

$$H(p) = -p \log p - (1-p)\log(1-p)$$

which is the function shown in fig. 43 on p. 279. This is the same as the entropy of the channel, hence the capacity of the channel is

$$C(p) = 1 - H(p)$$

which could have been depicted in the same figure by inverting the graph.

Because of the symmetry of the channel the optimum code devised earlier will serve this noisy channel. But in practice messages do not occur with such convenient relative frequencies as in the example nor are channels always symmetrical, so that it is normally much more difficult to devise a code to maximise the transmission on a noisy channel.

Accurate transmission through a noisy channel

In practice accuracy is often more important than speed. Obviously it would be better to make less than maximum use of the channel if we could be reasonably sure that the messages received were correct. Fortunately it is possible to overcome the effects of noise by careful coding and decoding of the messages, provided that the transmission rate does not exceed C, the channel capacity. This important fact is expressed in Shannon's Second Theorem.

Let a source of information have an entropy of H bits per second. Let a channel have a capacity C bits per second.

If $H \leqslant C$

then *there exists a coding system* which will enable the messages to be transmitted with an arbitrarily small equivocation (or frequency of errors).

If $H > C$

then there is a coding that will make the message equivocation arbitrarily close to, but never less than $H - C$.

Notice that there are two kinds of equivocation involved here: the equivocation of the channel carrying the code E_c:

code   code
————————————————→[Channel]————————————————→

and E_m, the equivocation in the messages which are carried by the channel augmented by a coder and decoder:

There will still be errors occurring in the transmission of the code because E_c is a property of the device being used. The construction of a good code can reduce E_m to a value not less than $H - C$. To use the code, however, you must pay the cost of coding and decoding which may be performed by expensive equipment or by time-consuming clerical operations.

The theorem has another important consequence. It tell us that no amount of time or ingenuity will serve to disentangle accurate messages from noisy signals beyond a maximum permitted by the capacity of the channel. Even then, you will need a good code to make best use of the channel. Also, if you have a *series* of channels (say, between the observation of events on the workshop floor and the reporting of them to management), then *the maximum transmission rate will depend upon the capacity of the poorest of those channels.* For anyone interested in processing data in organisations this interpretation of the theorem has an important moral: it is pointless engaging in exaggeratedly precise manipulations of data if you have not checked that it is warranted by the normal performance of every one of the channels which carry the data between the physical event, through the eye of the observer, onto paper and then through a series of transcriptions by clerks to the point when your computations begin.

The cost of accurate transmission

Given some spare capacity in the communication channel, it is *possible* to transmit messages as accurately as you wish, despite the effects of noise. But there is a cost. The cost depends upon the complexities of the coding and de-coding procedures. To see what is involved, consider how noise can be overcome by transmitting additional information to permit errors to be detected and corrected.

Imagine a binary channel, one that transmits only two characters. In a typical case, the error rate, p, would be in the order of 1 in 1 million binits transmitted. With such a small chance of an error, the average chance of finding one error in a block of n signals is $n \times p$. The chance of a multiple error in a relatively small block of signals ($n \leqslant 100$) is very small indeed and may be neglected as a first approximation. Single errors in a block of signals can be detected and corrected by a technique known as 'parity checking'. Before transmitting the block of signals, arrange them in a convenient array of rows and columns:

$$
\begin{array}{ccccc}
o & x & x & o & o \\
o & x & x & x & x \\
x & x & o & x & o \\
x & o & x & o & o \\
\end{array}
$$

Extend this array by adding a column that ensures that each row has an even number of one of the signals (x in this case) and then add a row to give each column an even 'parity', as it is called:

$$
\begin{array}{cccccc}
o & x & x & o & o & o \\
o & x & x & x & x & o \\
x & x & o & x & o & x \\
x & o & x & o & o & o \\
o & x & x & o & x & x \\
\end{array}
$$

You then transmit the whole of this extended array and reconstruct it at the receiving end. An error in the body of the array will show up in both the added row and the added column. An error in one of the parity signals will affect that signal alone. The error is corrected merely by switching the incorrect binary signal to its opposite value.

This is all quite straightforward to describe but to embody such a coding/decoding procedure in a piece of machinery is quite difficult, because it calls for the storage and processing of blocks of signals, in fact it calls for capabilities like those of a computer. In effect, similar methods are employed in clerical systems which use double-entry procedures; failure to strike a balance indicates an error, but normally finding and correcting the error is by no means simple.

Coding and decoding procedures, such as those described above, aim at achieving *optimal* transmission of information through noisy channels with high accuracy at a rate close to the channel's maximum capacity. This always involves three extra costs: imposing a structure on a block of messages before transmission; transmitting some additional messages to describe the structure; and then processing the structure at the receiving end. To get more out of the channel, more elaborate checks, calling for the transmission and storage of larger blocks of signals, subjected to more complex processing, are all necessary.

In designing practical methods of transmitting information in business, it is therefore customary to abandon the pursuit of optimality, and to aim for accuracy at the expense of efficiency. The normal way of doing this is to select a number of signals that are not liable to be confused by noise. A well-known example of this is the use in radio telephony of the names 'Abel', 'Baker', 'Charlie' . . . instead of the normal vocalisations of 'A', 'B', 'C' . . . Thus 'Baker' and 'Charlie' have to be perturbed very severely before they become indistinguishable, whereas 'B' and 'C', (not to mention 'D', 'E', 'G', 'P', 'T' and 'V') have sounds which are much alike*. For the restricted range of signals used, there should be a simple method of deciding, at the receiving end, which message was sent. The use of familiar names makes discrimination of the radio telephone codes very easy for a person. It would not be so for a machine.

For a binary channel, an equivalent method would be to choose a set of codes such as

$$a = 00000$$
$$b = 11100$$
$$c = 00111$$
$$d = 11011$$

which could be distorted by a *single* error without loss of identity. Notice that these all differ from one another in at least 3 places. At the receiving end, a message

$$m = 01011$$

---

* There is a newer radio telephony alphabet: 'Alpha', 'Bravo', etc. which is more proof against distortion.

could be decoded by finding its 'distance' from each of a, b, c and d, by counting in how many places it differed from them:

$$\text{dist}(m, a) = 3 \qquad \text{dist}(m, c) = 2$$
$$\text{dist}(m, b) = 4 \qquad \text{dist}(m, d) = 1$$

and then selecting the 'nearest' code; 'd' in this instance, (cf. cluster analysis in chapter 10).

Conclusion

In this chapter we have seen how a measure of 'statistical information' can be derived from the empirical measurement of probability based upon relative frequency. These measures have nothing at all to do with what the messages refer to, or what any person thinks about them.

Superficially, the engineering measurement of information is very much like the subjective measure, 'Info$_2$', and the logical measure, 'inf', introduced on pp. 163 and 268. This is because they are all measurements derived from a probability using the formula $-\log p$. This purely *formal* similarity must not be permitted to obscure the *semantic* differences each of these derived measurements shares with its associated measurement of probability (see chapter 9). An extensive mathematical theory has been developed for use in communications engineering. In so far as this theory is a formal mathematical consequence of the properties of a probability function, p, and the form of definition, exactly analogous theories exist for the other measures of information. The fact that they are *syntactically* identical should not obscure the *semantic* differences between these theories. Unfortunately the development of a wider information theory is severely hampered by this persistent misapprehension.

Communication channels, to be usable, must be fairly stable in their statistical behaviour, therefore relative frequency measures of their performance are entirely appropriate. It is perhaps a greater assumption to regard the sources of messages themselves as statistically stable, but in most engineering problems (as opposed to problems of human communication), this assumption is acceptable and it is even true at the more basic levels of human communication: thus, the statistical structure of a stream of speech sounds may be regarded as stable enough for purposes of engineering analysis.

In the next chapter, a variety of applications of statistical communication theory will be sketched, especially in the context of business and administrative information systems. This will emphasise that the engineering analysis of signs can be generalised to any situation where the ergodic conditions are met, that is, whenever relative-frequency probabilities can be measured.

19 Human Communication Channels

A human link and a source of random noise are both incorrigible disturbances in a communication system . . . The first step in reducing disturbances caused by noise is to find out the properties of noise and then to take advantage of those properties by some clever method of encoding the message. My plea is simply that we should treat the man with equal respect . . . Only then will we be able to provide channels of communication that are maximally efficient.

G. A. Miller, *The Human Link*

On account of the stimulus it has received from the engineering problems attendant upon the growth of telephone, radio, television and satellite technology, the statistical theory of communication is now one of the most highly developed branches of information studies. The relevance of the theory is not restricted to engineering applications, and the purpose of this chapter and the next is to indicate how it can serve to enhance our understanding of business and administrative uses of information. Unfortunately it is not possible to present a body of theory directly relevant to solving specific problems in the design of business communication-systems.

The engineer is most interested in how to construct codes for his data-transmission circuits; consequently, code design has become the most highly developed part of the theory, but, regrettably, there are few analogous problems in organisational systems to which the engineers can give us ready-made solutions. No doubt another branch of the theory will begin to develop under the stimulus of problems encountered in systems analysis and design.

Our interest is in the qualitative rather than in the exact quantitative results of the theory. The basic notions of channel capacity, entropy, mutual information, noise, equivocation and so on, are helpful for gaining an intuitive insight into some aspects of the functioning of organisations. This is especially true when we face problems of how to match the capabilities of human beings and machines, because they can transmit and process information at vastly different speeds and very different levels of reliability. Systems design is concerned with the construction of socio-technical systems; it is impossible to make the human communication channels behave with mechanical exactness. We shall have to be content with identifying zones of qualitatively similar behaviour, and with discovering rough quantitative measures of the limits of performance.

As most business communications are made via human channels, it is an essential preliminary to recognise that human communicators are subject to exactly the same laws of signal transmission as any telephone circuit. We shall look briefly at some experiments to measure the channel capacity of a human being. Also, in an industrial context, we must remember that *materials* also carry information which is imparted to them by the processes of production and distribution. Therefore, it is important to be aware of the communications aspects of activities which are not normally thought of as having anything to do with communication. We shall examine this topic as a part of the more general problem of modulation: what happens when 'information' is converted from one manifestation to another. Then we shall go on to look at the role played by communications in a control system, and we shall see how entropy can also be used as a measure of the degree of control achieved (or rather its converse: the residual variability, or wobble, in the system, which the control does not eliminate). The qualitative feeling for control obtained from this analysis can be very helpful when thinking about systems design problems. Finally, a few notes at the end of chapter 20 will indicate the limits of the relevance of statistical communication theory to organisational problems.

Statistical aspects of language

Language is the most important vehicle for the messages we use when organising affairs. It is appropriate to start by seeing how estimates may be made of the statistical information carried by ordinary English. We shall confine our attention to the written language, because it is much more precisely defined and is, therefore, limited in a way that makes analysis easier. Spoken language contains many subtleties of tonal inflection that replace punctuation in the written communication, besides carrying even more subtle overtones, with an emotive significance. The written transcription of speech may be regarded as conveying only a part of what is carried by spoken words, but messages skilfully composed in writing can make up for the lack of the auxiliary channels available in face-to-face contact, at least for transmitting factual information.

It would be interesting to know how much statistical information is conveyed, on average, by each letter in written English. If we assume that the available signals are 26 letters of the alphabet plus the 'space', and disregard punctuation marks, then the maximum possible channel capacity is

$$\log_2 27 = 4 \cdot 75 \text{ bits per character}$$

according to Shannon's first theorem. This would only be attained if all letters and the space were used, with equal frequency, and in such a way that the choice of a letter is not affected by the letters that have gone before. This is not so. In the first place, we employ the letters of the alphabet in quite uneven proportions and these proportions vary with the preceding letter; for example, although 'e' is common, it is unlikely to follow immediately after 'q'. In addition to these statistical regularities in a text, we also make use of our knowledge of the context, the author and the form of the document to help us to decipher any written message. How can we allow for this *redundancy* in the text?

A most ingenious way of overcoming these difficulties was described by Shannon himself, in one of his early papers.* He suggested using the services of two imaginary, perfectly identical twins who are identical in every detail, not only by nature but also by nurture, so that they react in absolutely identical ways. In particular, they behave in exactly the same way as each other when asked to guess the next letter in a piece of incomplete text. The skill of the first twin can then be used to code written English, letter by letter, into a numerical form, by using the number of guesses he makes before getting the correct answer. This is shown by the following example (from Shannon). A 'space' is indicated in the code by an italic number, for ease of reading.

THERE IS NO R E V ERSE ON A MOTORCYCLE
1 1 1 5 1*1*21*1* 2 1*1*15 1 17 1 1 1 2*1* 3 2*1* 22 7 1 1 1 1 14 1 1 1 1 1
A FRIEND OF MINE FOUND THIS OUT RATHER
3*1* 8 6 13 1 1*1* 1 1*1* 1 1 1 1*1*6 2 1 1 1*1*1 1 2 1*1* 1 1 1*1*4 1 1 1 1 1*1*
DRAMATICALLY THE OTHER DAY
115 1 1 1 111 1 1 1 1 1*1*6 1 1*1*1‑1 1 1 1*1* 1 1 1

The second twin is then able to decode this numerical sequence by first writing down his guesses for the next letter in order of preference; thus, for the letter after the first three, THE, he would guess:

(1) Space; (2) Y; (3) S; (4) N; (5) R; (6) O; (7) M . . . etc.

and then, using the number 5 he selects the correct letter, R. The second twin is a useful fiction because he shows, at least in principle, that this guessing method provides a satisfactory coding/decoding procedure. In practice there is no need to employ his services; we assume that any person can do the coding. The decoding is quite unnecessary but we have to assume that he has a *doppelgänger*, a mysterious spiritual twin, to justify the procedure.

* See Shannon, 1951.

What is being done in this guessing exercise is to make use of a person's knowledge of the language to eliminate redundancy from the text. The next letter that he guesses must of course conform to rules of spelling, the words must conform to the rules of grammar, and the sense must be appropriate in the context of all the other words and sentences. All these constraints on his choice of the next letter are understood intuitively by a person because of his years of acquaintance with the use of the language. This method of coding a sentence into numbers uses a person's knowledge of all these rules.

The important feature of the resulting numerical code is that it disconnects successive signals from one another, so that it is possible to treat the numbers as statistically independent messages from the same ergodic source, enabling the formula $H = -\Sigma p \log p$ to be applied. To see how this 'uncoupling' is achieved, you can imagine the coding taking place in two stages:

(a) select a list of letters in the sequence of decreasing likelihood, given only the text so far;
(b) look at the next letter and translate it into a number by using its ordinal position in the list already chosen.

By this means, all the information supplied by the preceding text is embodied in the ordering of the letters in stage (a), hence the number resulting from stage (b) conveys only the additional information supplied by the next letter. The structural information is removed by stage (a), but it is available for decoding the string of numbers by virtue of the skills of *both* of the imaginary twins.

By repeatedly carrying out this guessing experiment with long sequences of text, it can be shown that *the average amount of information conveyed by written language is in the order of one bit per character*.

Estimates of human transmission rates

This figure of 1 bit per character gives us the means of estimating the capacity of certain human communication channels. Someone reading aloud from a book at the moderate rate of about 150 words per minute, allowing six-letter words on average, will be transmitting information at the rate of 15 bits per second. A very fast shorthand writer would be able to manage 200 words per minute or 20 bits per second. This is, of course, assuming that no errors are made and that the script can be transcribed by another shorthand writer! A typist working at the rate of sixty words per minute will be transmitting information at a rate of 6 bits per second. Writing quickly by hand it would be possible to achieve about half that bit-rate. For impromptu speaking, estimates have indicated a maximum of about 26 bits per second with an average of about 18 bits per second. Fast speech tends to be cliché-ridden, thus reducing its effective bit-rate.

Peak transmission rates have been investigated (by Quastler and Wulff, reported by Attneave, q.v.) for the use of keyboards. The experimenters used random sequences of 100 letters. In some experiments they used four different letters, in others 8, 16 or 32 alternatives. They found that the rate of transmission increased with the number of symbols, from a value of 5 bits per second with 4 keys on a typewriter, to a maximum of 15 bits per second with 34 keys in use. Similar experiments were carried out on a musical keyboard, using random sequences of notes taken from sets of 3 notes up to sets of 65 different notes (i.e. from 1·3 to 6·0 bits per note). A maximum transmission rate was observed of about 22 bits per second for sets of between 15 and 37 notes.

When a person acts as a communication channel, he must first of all be able to discriminate which one of a set of stimuli he is being asked to transmit. In the above examples, which used words or letters or musical notation, the stimulus is very complex. Further understanding of human

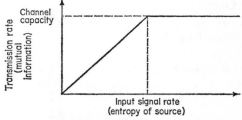

Fig. 45. Transmission rate through a limited channel.

channel-performance has been derived from experiments into our ability to make absolute judgements of simple stimuli, that is, judgements made without the aid of an objective basis of comparison or measuring device. In a number of typical experiments of this kind, a subject is given a stimulus chosen at random from a set of stimuli; as the number of different stimuli in the set increases, so does the information per stimulus increase. The information transmitted by the subject equals the information per stimulus if his discriminations are made accurately; if he makes mistakes, his effective channel capacity can be found by subtracting the appropriate measure of equivocation. If a human being behaves like a telephone circuit, you would expect the information transmission rate to increase until the limit of his channel capacity is attained. The typical graph of results should look like fig. 45 and so it does. The values on the abscissa and ordinate have not been marked, but the shape is always the same, except for a falling off in performance, at higher levels of input, in some cases. The actual channel capacity apparently depends upon two major factors: firstly, the sensory faculty employed in making the discrimination and, secondly, the number of properties which vary from stimulus to stimulus. (More properties employ a greater band width of the full human channel.)

If judgements of only *one variable* are required, such as the pitch of a pure tone or the location of a pointer on a linear scale, the organs of sense permit the accurate discrimination of between 5 and 8 different stimuli. Here is a summary of results of a number of investigations.

Variable	Channel capacity (bits/stimulus)	Number of discriminable categories
1. Pitch of a pure tone (Pollack)	2·5	5·7
(these results are higher for subjects having a sense of absolute pitch)		
2. Loudness (Garner)	2·3	4·9
3. Position on a linear scale (Hake & Garner)	3·25	9·5
4. Saltiness (Beebe-Center, Rogers, O'Connell)	1·9	3·7
5. Appearance of squares (Eriksen)		
size	2·2	4·6
hue	3·1	8·5
brightness	2·3	4·9
6. Skin contact on chest (Geldard)		
intensity	2·0	4·0
duration	2·3	4·9
location	2·8	6·9

(The experimenters are shown in brackets, and they are referred to by Attneave, 1959, and G. Miller, 1968, q.v.)

Of course, we are accustomed to discriminating among the members of sets which have many more than 7 or 8 members: words and faces, for example. This is possible because they are distinguishable by more than one variable feature. Experiments have shown how the channel capacity of a person increases with the number of coordinates needed to describe the stimulus, not proportionately but roughly as the logarithm of the number of coordinates (see fig. 46). The kind of experiment used to indicate this relationship has involved asking people to judge the position of one dot inside a square (2 coordinates), or 2 dots (4 co-ordinates), or to discriminate between liquid solutions that varied both

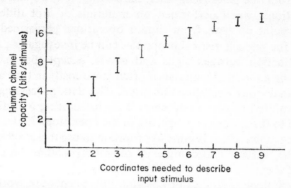

Fig. 46. Increase of human channel-capacity with increasing complexity of stimulus.

in saltiness and sweetness (2 coordinates), or between squares varying in size, hue and brightness (3 coordinates), or to identify aspects of an interrupted tone: frequency, loudness, rate of interruption, percentage time 'on', total duration and direction (6 coordinates).

The improvement in channel capacity obtained by using stimuli having more variable factors seems to be obtained whether these factors are used to reinforce one another (e.g., all large squares are bright and all small ones dim) or combined in more varied ways (some squares being large and bright, others small and bright, large and dim, or small and dim).

Practical applications

These psychological experiments may provide useful pointers for anyone interested in problems of presenting information to people or employing people to process information, especially in conjunction with machines. Even with very crude estimates of human channel capacity it may be possible to obtain a better understanding of the relationship between data-processing work-load and the numbers of staff required. This is especially true when dealing with a situation involving both people, who transmit information at a rate of about 10–20 bits per second, and machines, which normally transmit at rates well above 100 bits per second, up to rates ten million times that. At least the man and the machine can be seen in proportion to each other, and the limits of feasible performance may be discovered before any design work has begun. This is evidently true, for example, when considering a data-transmission system that interfaces with a clerical department.

The same ideas might also help if you are considering a manufacturing process. The transformation of materials by machines and the movement of goods from one place to another, the sorting, re-grouping and assembly operations, when performed on materials do not differ, from a statistical point of view, from similar operations performed on signs. Therefore the same statistical properties can be investigated; there is no sharp distinction between signs and goods, except that moving and transforming goods and materials is often more costly in time and energy than the analogous operations on signs. The data-processing activities that are required to direct and control manufacturing and distribution are related to the statistical properties of the operations for transforming and moving materials. It is quite appropriate to use these statistical tools to study the 'variety' and complexity of activities other than the transmission of signs.

The psychological studies of absolute judgements are worth bearing in mind if you are designing some means of gathering data or making measurements. You may prepare a questionnaire, say, for job assessment, calling for investigators to make judgements about various aspects of a job – how dusty or noisy it is, the maximum muscle-power it demands. The experiments on human channel-capacity indicate that you can probably get all the information which the investigator can give you about a one-dimensional variable by asking him for ratings on a 7-point scale or 2·8 bits per stimulus. If you need more precision then the experiments seem to suggest that it is better to introduce questions about other related factors than to subdivide a scale any further. Similarly, if you are preparing a measuring device, it may be asking too much to require a person to supply the last *decimal* figure by estimating the pointer position. It would be better to mark the mid-point of each interval and expect him to assign the pointer to one of only 5 locations, instead of 10.

Similarly when presenting people with information upon which they must act quickly, you must make allowance for the number of different actions from which they must choose. The signal you present to them must contain enough distinguishable variables to convey the requisite information in the time available This is especially important if the sign is visible for only a short while, e.g. a road sign or a display of operating instructions on a cathode ray tube. The well-known example of this is the use of lower-case letters for road signs, instead of upper-case only, as in fig. 47. This transforms the outline of a word from an uninformative rectangle, in which the ratio of the sides is the only variable, allowing only about 7 types to be distinguished, to a jagged shape, caused by the risers and descenders, which conveys much more information. Allowing for presence or absence of risers or descenders in three recognisable positions, the beginning, middle and end of the word, there is scope for 6 bits per stimulus in this kind of outline, allowing 64 types to be distinguished. Why, then, is computer output nearly always

(i) LEAMINGTON

(ii) Leamington

Fig. 47. The informative outline of lower-case characters.

in upper-case? For legibility it would be far better to have only lower-case letters on a printer. The objection, of course, is that social convention requires people's names to begin with a capital letter.

In an application examined in the next chapter we shall see that human channel-capacity can be an important technical constraint when a person is employed as a part of a control loop. Unfortunately, we are a long way from having adequate psychological measurements to serve in the routine analysis of factory and office work.

Short-term memory and channel capacity

When we transmit information, we do not always do so by perceiving a single stimulus and then responding to it before receiving the next input and so on. In many common tasks, we accept a block of signals and respond to all of them, before dealing with another block. All the simple tasks of transcribing words or numbers are done in this way. These tasks are basic ingredients of most work. The reception of instructions on the shop floor frequently requires the operative to interpret part numbers or job codes. Data-collection often involves an observer in recognising and then recording several variables as a group (e.g. details of a vehicle in a traffic census).

One key question obviously is: how many such items can we hold in our memory when we are performing a simple transcription task? The answer is: normally about 6 or 7; if you try to remember larger groups you will find that your accuracy rapidly falls off. This is not the whole answer because we can enquire: 6 or 7 what? The answer is rather vague: any recognisable 'chunks' of information that you are accustomed to treating, mentally, as single entities; they may be binits, decimal numerals, letters or words for example. This means that according to the code being used, the 6 or 7 chunks which your short-term memory holds can carry very different maximum quantities of 'variety', measured in statistical terms, thus:

1 0 1 1 0 1 0	7 binits	7 bits
8 3 2 1 9 4 6	7 digits	23 bits
N P R S A F L	7 letters	33 bits
Smith, new, steel, lead, page, cut, soap	7 monosyllables from 1,000	70 bits

The performance of our short-term memory for handling one kind of code can be improved if we are able to recode the signs more compactly. For example, we can remember binary numbers quite well if we learn to recode them into 'octal' by grouping trios of binits, thus:

Binary	101	110	001	111	010	100	011
Octal	5	6	1	7	2	4	3

With practice, this transformation is easily made, and long strings of 0s and 1s can be remembered easily. People working close to the computer, which employs binary coded information, normally do this. Recoding is something we tend to do naturally on gaining close familiarity with a code; it gives us so much more mental grasp of the material we are handling. Very often, meaningless codes used regularly in a factory will become familiar enough for those using them to translate them into a briefer, verbal form.

Codes for practical use in business and in such everyday affairs as telephoning are normally designed with little regard for the simple psychological facts about the limitations of short-term memory. These codes will often have to be transcribed or translated into actions. So incorrect actions can easily result from a badly designed code. Longer codes than strictly necessary often have to be used to suit the equipment which must respond to them; e.g. all-digit telephone codes, instead of mixed alphabetic/numeric codes. Equipment that forces the general public to use unwieldy codes will cause a large increase in transcription errors (e.g. reading a number from the directory and dialling it), but we are so used to keeping human and machine operations in quite separate compartments of our minds, that this cost is unlikely to have been set against any engineering advantages at the design stage.*

Other psychological factors

When designing codes, documents, instruments and other displays, many other psychological factors must be taken into account. My object in

---

* However, see Conrad, 1967.

this chapter has been to indicate the appropriateness of treating human beings, in certain circumstances, as components of an 'information machine', subject to just the same physical laws as computers and telephone circuits. This helps to emphasise the underlying unity of the whole socio-technical structure when seen from one important viewpoint. This limited aim has probably been met. However, to avoid painting an over-simplified picture, some other factors that are relevant are mentioned below.

The experiments on human channel-capacity, described earlier, were rather artificial in that stimuli from the available set were chosen and presented to the subject at random and with equal frequencies. In practice it is more likely that some signs will be more common than others. In the case of words, it is well-known that the more familiar ones are more easily identified aurally or visually, even in the presence of noise, and unfamiliar words, if mistaken, are likely to be mistaken for familiar words. This suggests using, in alphabetic codes, groups of letters that are already quite familiar. For example, you may have to construct a code for which it is appropriate to employ, say, 3 alphabetic characters and 3 numeric, of the form:

$$AAA999$$

To keep the error rate down, it would be advisable to build the more frequently used code words so that their three alphabetic characters can be pronounced:

$$AND999$$
$$CUP999 \text{ etc.}$$

Such codes can be treated by the reader as 4 chunks instead of 6 chunks of information in short-term memory. In addition, if you reserve the three-letter words or syllables most frequently encountered in English for the most commonly used codes, then you will increase reliability still further.*

The recognition of words is improved if you know their context. Even a little information about the context can serve to adjust your expectations and enable you to select your response from a very much reduced vocabulary. This has the effect of reducing the information per stimulus and so making recognition easier. If our attention is not directed to a limited perceptual task, our natural inclination will be to respond to a wider range of stimuli than necessary. Drawing attention to a message and indicating the type of message are two ways of improving communication.

Different problems arise when a person has to detect infrequent and

* See Conrad, 1967.

irregular signals, as when monitoring an automatic machine or looking for errors in documents. The difficulty is to keep the human channel 'tuned in' and attentive to the signals it must detect and react to. Such tasks are rather unnatural for a human operator, because he functions best when coping with a fairly consistent and moderate signal rate. Machines are well suited to tasks calling for vigilance; they may replace the human operator or assist him by directing his attention to conditions needing closer scrutiny.

All the problems mentioned above, and many more, should be taken into account when complex systems of displays and controls are designed. The control of an aircraft or power station depends on a circuit which is closed via the pilot or human operator: he is connected to the machine by the signals he receives from the display and he sends back signals through the control levers, knobs and switches. The signal transmission-rate of the operator is the principal limitation upon the attainable degree of control. This signal rate is critically dependent upon how the signals are displayed and how the controls are related to the displays. There is an analogy between this problem and the problem of presenting routine information to a manager or administrator. More will be said about signal-transmission and control in the next chapter.

20 Modulation and Control

The Law of Requisite Variety says that [the] capacity [of a device] as a regulator cannot exceed [its] capacity as a channel of communication.

W. Ross Ashby, *An Introduction to Cybernetics*

This final chapter, on statistical communication theory, will examine briefly the ideas of modulation and control. They are ideas which can help to give us a better intuitive appreciation of some important problems in the use of information in organisations.

Modulation is concerned with the manner in which signals are given some physical representation or have their representation changed – as when a vibrating string causes the air to vibrate and that, in turn, causes a membrane in the ear to vibrate and so on. Modulation underlies all processes of observation, recording and transcription of data. At the routine level, the flow of information in an organisation is dependent upon thousands of these processes, and many organisational ailments can be traced to their inadequate performance: they may be inaccurate or unreliable or simply incapable of transmitting some of the information which they should be transmitting. One use for the modulation concept, therefore, is as a diagnostic aid. The concept is also valuable because it can help us to generalise the idea of a signal and, therefore, enlarge the scope of the engineering theory of signal transmission. Before we can use this theory to study control in an organisation it is necessary to extend the obvious usage of terms, such as 'signal', 'communication channel', 'medium for information', beyond their commonsense limits to include objects and activities which, at first sight, seem to have nothing to do with information.

Control is one of those problems that can be considered in terms of statistical communication theory once one is prepared to 'see' communication channels where, in conventional language, there are none. Goods can convey signals and machines can serve as communication channels. In many senses, goods and machines have nothing to do with information, but, from the point of view of communication engineering, information is simply a statistical property of the forms and behaviour of things. This statistical property is readily generalised beyond the bounds of what we usually call 'information'.

Control is exercised through a 'feed-back' cycle: a signal from the system being controlled reveals a departure from desired performance; this difference causes a controller to take some action to bring the actual performance closer to what is desired. This feed-back loop can be treated as a closed circuit of communication channels. The important idea that will be demonstrated is that the maximum degree of control that can be achieved is absolutely dependent upon the capacity of the communication loop as a whole, and it can be measured using the entropy function. This is true whether the controller is a machine or a person.

What constitutes a sign or a signal?

Let us begin by looking at modulation.

Every message is carried in the form of patterns imposed upon some physical medium, which may be an object (a sheet of paper) or a stream of energy (sound waves). When a message is communicated it usually undergoes frequent translations from one medium to another, the patterns carried by one medium causing correlated patterns to be imposed upon another medium through a process conveniently called 'modulation'. Examples of this are ubiquitous. The temperature of a furnace will regulate the flow of electrons in a thermo-couple attached to it. To know the time by the chiming of a clock, the time-piece must cause a controlled release of energy stored in a spring or suspended weights, via a striking mechanism to the clapper of the bell, and so on. To see the objects on the table in my study, I must irradiate them with electromagnetic radiation in the visible spectrum. For someone's finger-print to be recorded, he must leave an impression of it on some material such as glass or wax or on a special paper. Of course, the sign or signal initially produced in each of these cases may have to undergo a whole series of other translations before it can enter a human nervous system to be *observed*, in an anthropocentric sense. But each such translation follows the same general pattern which is suggested by these illustrations.

The translation process also takes place in the reverse direction, in the sense that not only can a substantial object or a major happening leave a tiny impression of itself or cause a minute perturbation that would normally be called a sign or signal, but, also, tiny signs or minute signals can be translated into physically large forms or the release of large amounts of energy. The larger phenomena can be regarded as signs and signals with as much validity as the smaller ones. A list of the dimensions of material to be cut from steel plate, that is a list of numeric signs, would be called information by anyone, but he would possibly baulk at calling the cut steel plates just another re-coded version of the same information. Why? A numerically controlled machine for cutting metal plate simply translates the numbers on a punched paper tape into the profile of the plate it cuts; the profile is equivalent to the numeric message on paper and there is no difficulty, in principle, in translating the profile back again into numbers using some other machine, like a kind of pantograph.

This point should need little emphasis, but, because they are accustomed to reserving the words such as 'information', 'sign', 'signal', 'symbol', for the contents of documents, spoken words and other forms of transmission employing a very low level of energy or amount of material, some people are unhappy about applying the same words to objects or forms of energy that are very substantial; they sometimes refer to these large objects as the *'real'* things that our information is 'about'. But the signs that convey our messages are no less physical or 'real' than the things they originate from, or the consequences they have. Compared with the 'real' objects a physicist studies and records – individual subatomic events and particles – the notes he makes in the laboratory are vast slabs of graphite laid upon a mountain of paper!

Statistical communication theory is not in the least concerned with kinds of things, large or small; it is about their statistical properties, and there is no point in trying to draw a line between some 'things' which carry statistical information and others that do not. Any attribute of the world which has a number of distinguishable states or values can be regarded as capable of serving as a medium for 'information'. To talk about 'statistical information', 'entropy', 'noise', etc., is merely to declare that you are adopting a particular limited view of the world: you are concerned only with the relative frequencies of certain classes of events. In just the same way one can look at the mechanical or electrical or chemical properties of things.

Some readers will think that I have laboured this point. If they do, they are likely to be as surprised as I am by the numbers of people who can accept statistical communication theory applied to what common sense (=verbal habit) calls 'communication channels', but cannot take seriously the simple generalisations of these ideas. The generalisations are indispensable if the theory is to be applied to organisational and social phenomena.

It is, of course, wise to adopt a cautious attitude towards generalities. One might wish, therefore, that writers who popularise ideas about 'information theory' and 'cybernetics' would lay greater emphasis than they do upon the limitations of these subjects. 'Information theory', as pointed out earlier, is a dangerous misnomer for 'statistical theory of signal transmission', but such is the magic of words that it is frequently believed that this theory, together with cybernetics, which is derived from it, applies to ranges of problems far beyond its field of discourse. That field of discourse has a high fence round it. For example, individual signs and signals are excluded, only the statistical properties of sources, channels and the *sets* of signs are within its domain, and then only in strictly defined circumstances. More will be said about this later.

Modulation

All the communication processes described above can be represented as chains of modulation processes which share a common form (see fig. 48). A well-known example is the transmission of sound by radio using a modulated electromagnetic wave to carry the sound of a voice (see fig. 49).

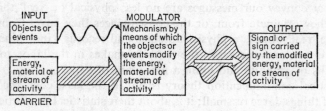

Fig. 48. The general features of a modulation process.

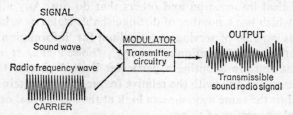

Fig. 49. An example of a modulation process: amplitude modulation for radio transmission.

This analysis can be applied at any desired level of detail, and one must decide upon a level of analysis which serves the practical purpose in hand. Take the example of radio; we can think at a more detailed level as in fig. 50, and so on. Problems of designing a transmitter or of diagnosing faults in one will necessitate this degree of detail. In other cases you will need to think in terms of gross elements of the system. You must choose the detail of analysis to suit your problem, but, whatever the analysis, it will be built from repetitions of the modulator pattern:

$$\begin{array}{c} \text{signal 1} \searrow \\ \text{carrier} \nearrow \end{array} \text{modulation} \rightarrow \text{signal 2.}$$

This may be thought of as an extension of the coding process:

$$\text{signal 1} \rightarrow \text{coding} \rightarrow \text{signal 2,}$$

but with explicit recognition of the role played by the physical medium of communication.

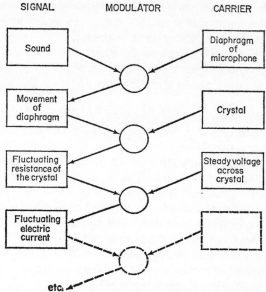

Fig. 50. Very detailed level of analysis of communication processes. The level must suit the problem.

Characteristics of the modulation process

The ability of a modulation process to convert a message from one physical form to another without loss will depend upon the nature of the

	Printing	Camera	Television	Car engine
Input	operations of compositor	light from objects	UHF signal	faults in adjustment
Output	printed page	photograph	fluctuating electron beam	audible signal
Carrier	paper	film	electric current	normal sounds of engine
Modulator	composing and printing process	camera and developing process	TV set	engine in steady motion

carrier, and the performance of the mechanism which effects the translation from the input signal to the output. In order to identify the important parameters, consider some examples.

You will notice that these examples reveal the necessarily arbitrary choice of input and output which mark the boundaries of the system. Two of the examples produce static signs and two produce dynamic signals.

There are a number of characteristics of all modulation processes which govern their effectiveness; we are familiar with all of them in most of the examples given above.

For the input to have any effect at all, it must convey enough energy to activate the modulation process. This is the characteristic of *sensitivity* of the process, familiar enough in the speed of a film and the sensitivity of a TV receiver and aerial. Sensitivity may not be uniform over the whole range of signals, in which case distortion may result.

The process may only be sensitive to a certain *range* of input signals. Signals outside the range are lost altogether. This is the same concept as the 'band-width' of a channel and it relates to the variety of signals which a communication channel can transmit.

The *resolution* which the system can attain is a measure of how precisely the output signal can convey the form of the input signal. This depends, in part, upon the mechanical structure of the carrier (the texture of a paper or the grain of a film) and the mechanical properties of the modulator mechanism (the size of the type-face or the number of lines which compose the TV picture). Resolution also depends upon the unpredictable variations in the carrier or in the operation of the modulator. The smaller the resolution, the greater the equivocation of the modulating process regarded as a communication channel. Lack of resolving power causes total loss of a part of the information. There is not always a clear distinction between range and resolution.

Statistical measures of information take no account of *distortion* caused by unevenness in the operation of the translating mechanism. The camera lens may distort the shape of an object, or the film may make all colours slightly redder than they are to the naked eye. A faulty cathode ray tube may split a TV picture across the middle, or squash it all into one half of the screen. These are examples of distortion which make interpretation of the output difficult but not impossible, because, in principle, further processes could totally remove the distortion.

The example of the car engine, in the table above, differs from the others because it was not designed as a means of translating signals from one medium to another. We should regard it as more like a true, primary source of information, but it exhibits similarities to the other communication devices.

Sources of information

When the capturing or acquisition of information is described as a kind of modulation process, then some caution must be exercised. We must distinguish two important cases.

The first case is concerned with translating a signal which can already be perceived or detected into a form suitable for further transmission or processing. Although most of the data acquired by such a means will never be captured by any other device, there is, in principle, the opportunity to inspect both the input to the modulator and the output. During the use of the device it will be the primary source of certain data but, from a design point of view, the output is the result of a convenient recoding operation, like any other. The designer stands in relationship to his problem as in fig. 51(i). By varying the input, he may learn a great

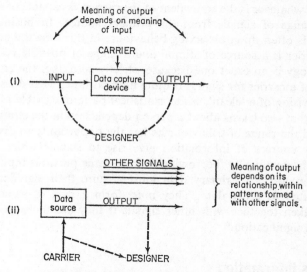

Fig. 51. Data sources: (i) secondary; (ii) primary.

deal about the performance of the device. Very often the mechanism which codes the input into the output is so well understood that the behaviour of the device can be predicted accurately before it is constructed. Instruments of this kind are typified by weighing machines, cameras and counting devices. There is no difficulty about interpreting the data they supply; their meanings can be assigned in the same way as the meanings of the inputs, with suitable allowance made for distortion and equivocation during the modulation. In the sense that the data are available to the designer in their original form these devices are only secondary data sources.

The second case presents difficulties: the primary data source gives rise to output signals which cannot be related to any input, except perhaps in a very hazy way. This is pictured in fig. 51(ii). In these cases, the data are only available to the designer in the form of the output.The data seem to 'describe' the modulator itself. Consider an object which you are looking at; the object, through a process of modulation, imposes information about itself upon the light which it is reflecting into your eyes. When you look at an object, you normally have some control over the illumination which is the carrier of the signals. A uniform white light illuminates best, but if the light is tinted or obscured, you take account of the colour or shadow. Only if light containing all colours is falling on the object can it convey a maximum of information about itself, by selecting the intensity and colour of the reflected light. Similarly, whenever possible, you should make sure that the source of energy, or whatever is the equivalent of the carrier, is capable of exciting the full range of signals from the primary source. In business, the emphasis is often upon observing behaviour; in this case the analogue of the carrier is a source of stimuli and a range of possible responses. (The analogy is an exact one because, strictly speaking, the energy or material of a carrier for signals is quite unimportant; what does matter is the provision of a 'clean', white, statistical pattern, capable of modulation.) What one learns about a person depends upon the stimuli he is given, and the range of behaviour he has the opportunity to display.

Primary sources of information give rise to signals which cannot derive their meaning by 'borrowing' it from some previous input to the modulation process. Primary data must acquire their significance by being related to other data. They must form a part of some useful pattern taken together with other signals if they are to be given any justifiable signification.*

Business information

In business or administration, many information-processing tasks of a routine kind can be examined, quite justifiably, from the point of view of statistical communication theory. One may usefully identify modulation processes and their carriers, and enquire what their characteristics are. Very often one will discover that information is being interpreted at its face value, without any critical scrutiny of how it was obtained. This is a dangerous fault of many business information-systems, and the trouble probably results from habits of mind, acceptable when

---

* This problem has already been examined in chapters 9 and 10 on measurement and perceiving patterns in numerical data; for a discussion of it in the statistical terms of communication theory see Garner, 1962.

dealing with the familiar information open directly to our senses, being transferred to circumstances in which they cannot be justified.

When making everyday observations we do not have to concern ourselves with the sources of energy or material which carry to our sense organs normal information about the world around us. Daylight generously suffuses the objects we wish to see, sounds are derived from the energy of the very actions about which they inform us, smells are molecular samples of their sources, whilst the sensations of touch depend upon sources of energy provided by our own bodies; our observations of people are dependent upon seeing them exposed to the great variety of familiar, miscellaneous stimuli which everyday life affords.

The everyday sources of sense-data are reliable because of their familiarity; we know intuitively the characteristics of the sources of energy and the modulation processes by which familiar messages are imposed upon them – how to discount the loss of illumination caused by a shadow, what gives rise to various rattles in the car, what different materials feel like at different temperatures.

Experimental science enables us to apprehend phenomena beyond the reach of our unaided senses and, to do this, it relies on the use of carefully chosen stimuli or sources of energy. The scientist, who observes things beyond the scope of his unaided senses, must take account of the characteristics of the carrier and the modulation process which he is using, and, quite deliberately, include them in his calculations. He cannot rely upon being able to make allowances intuitively when he comes to interpret the results of his experiment.

Unfortunately it is not yet fashionable to exercise similar caution when collecting and interpreting business information. The manager, unless he is intent on misleading himself, should exercise something of the scientist's caution in the interpretation of the reports he is given, and he should direct the collection of data with a similar kind of rigour.

The things that must be observed by a manager or administrator, such as the behaviour of a market, the movement of a town's population, the attitudes of staff, the efficiency of an office, cannot be observed reliably without careful attention to the process that gives rise to the information he needs. Much management information is misleading, or at best useless, because managers, often fail to appraise their sources of information from this point of view. This is a different problem from the semantic one of defining adequately the rather abstract concepts which management-information and decision-making require; it is assumed that the semantic questions have already been answered before looking at these statistical problems of observation.

The simple lessons are these. Making a process for gathering routine observations reliably requires:

(a) some uniform and predictable source of material, energy or, more commonly in this context, *stimuli* capable of eliciting a response to the full range of the variables to be observed, and

(b) a predictable modulation process which imprints upon the carrier the information we wish to observe, with a suitable degree of accuracy.

Consider these points in relation to the problem of observing how customers behave. Companies sometimes rely upon analyses of their actual sales, without realising how misleading this information can be; the signal they are using is compounded of fluctuations in their own and their competitors' behaviour in addition to the customers' behaviour; it is often quite impossible to analyse such a signal. For some firms it may be too expensive to devote resources to experimental selling and pricing, intended deliberately to vary the stimuli given to different parts of the market. One wonders if the difference between haphazard data and data collected through a controlled procedure is always appreciated. A business-game will reveal that many groups of typical managers do not understand it; haphazard marketing policies are commonly preferred to deliberate probing of market behaviour, using controlled stimuli. Haphazard data are capable of revealing nothing which is not overwhelmingly obvious; even worse is their tendency, through the effects of undetected bias, to reveal an apparent pattern of market behaviour which, when acted upon, turns out to have been a mirage. A deliberate, controlled use of statistically randomised stimuli may be difficult to attain in collecting business data, but the principle must be understood. If you cannot use properly randomised stimuli (white light) you will need to know about the pattern of stimuli giving rise to your data (the colour of the light). An even more serious deficiency in exploring the behaviour of a market is seen in those instances when no variations are made in marketing strategy; this is like switching off the light and expecting to see objects in a room by their own phosphorescence—a practice more likely to fail than to succeed.

The series of questions in a questionnaire, or the behavioural situations in which you place a person in a practical test, are analogous to the signal carrier; through them the respondent or subject conveys some features of his own attitudes or skills by the answers he gives or the performances he exhibits. Similarly, the way in which the questionnaire or test is administered is like the modulation process. In statistical observation this depends very much upon the use of a sampling frame which should ensure that the population being studied is exposed evenly to the carrier. A failure to use an appropriate sampling frame can yield data that are very misleading. For example, it would be difficult to predict the result of an election using a sample drawn from the telephone directory, because of the inevitable bias. This is just like photographing a long, multi-coloured object under a spotlight which illuminates only its blue, right-hand end!

These are examples of fact-finding to which statistical methods could usefully be applied. Perhaps the most important contribution which statistics can make in the education of managers is its contribution towards making people critically aware of the conditions for accurate observation.

Some aspects of this problem have already been dealt with in chapter 13 in the discussion of randomising procedures and their importance in guaranteeing the objectivity of data.

We now turn to the subject of control, armed with the notion that a signal can be translated from a mark on paper to a movement of an arm, to a position of a lever and so on.

Signals and control

If we wish to control any process, we must derive signals from it which tell us how it is behaving; we must also be able to communicate messages to correct its behaviour when necessary. See fig. 52. The complete feedback loop passes through the controller and through the process being

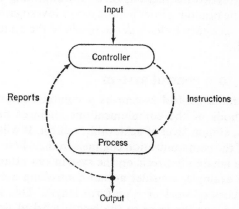

Fig. 52. The basic parts of a control loop.

controlled. Both controller and controlled may be persons or machines; an operator may control a machine for cutting up steel bars; a construction site foreman may control the work of a labourer; or an inspector the work of a whole factory. The output from the controlled process may be lengths of cut steel bar, some aspect of a person's behaviour or some quality of a factory's products. Let us concentrate upon the case of a physical output from a machine. A statistical analysis can be applied to such a problem with reasonable assurance that it is justified. The other cases are amenable to the same kind of analysis only in so far as they display machine-like characteristics.

If the control is perfect, then the lengths of all the bars cut will be exactly as required. Departure from what is required indicates a lack of control. Consistent errors (e.g. all bars are 1″ too long), once detected, can be eliminated, but random departures from the desired performance cannot be escaped entirely, only kept in check by the action of the controller.

One way of looking at the problem is by viewing, S, the whole system of machine and controller, as a communication channel down which you send signals giving the *desired* performance and from which you hope to receive the same signal recoded in the form of *actual* performance:

desired performance⟶ $\boxed{\text{S}}$ ⟶actual performance

Consistent errors of performance are seen to be the same as distortion by the channel, whereas the random errors are caused by noise and can be measured as equivocation in the same statistical terms as used for ordinary signal transmission. The systematic errors can easily be eliminated by giving revised instructions or by re-calibrating the controls on the machine. The random errors require closer investigation. To see how they arise it is necessary to look at the inside of the system, at the feedback loop itself.

An example of a control system

By thinking of the control system as a communication channel, the statistical methods of the communications engineer may be used to measure the maximum level of achievable control. It will be shown that the capacity of the communication channels in the whole feed-back loop determines the maximum precision the system can attain.

As a simple example, consider a man controlling a cutting machine producing batches of steel of a uniform length. This is illustrated in fig. 53. The man sets the lever to the length marked on the scale; the material is fed in automatically and cut lengths emerge from the machine. They move past a measuring device which is connected to a display in front of the operator, and this shows him the actual length of the material. The operator receives a printed 'cutting list' of the lengths ordered; this is the input to the system. The outputs from this system are the *lengths* of the cut material, not the material itself; we are interested in the information flow, not the material flow.

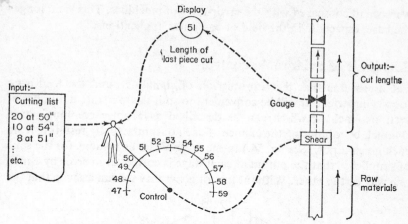

Fig. 53. A control system for a metal-cutting shear.

Signals flow round the loop: from the lever to the mechanism, from the cutting blade to the material, then, carried by the material, to a measuring device; from the gauge an electrical signal goes to the display which shows the last length cut; finally, the loop is closed by the operator who reads the display and adjusts the lever if necessary.

If the signals are transmitted accurately round this loop control will be perfect, but if at any stage there is an error the wrong lengths will be cut. From the point of view of the performance of the sub-system as a whole, it does not matter where this error arises. Of course, in order to do something about the fault, we should have to locate the source of errors. We might deal with mis-reading of the dial by re-positioning the display, or improving the illumination. A malfunctioning of the measuring device or the display or the link between them would need the attention of an instrument engineer; failure of the shear would require a mechanical fitter, whilst distraction of the operator by his environment would call for some re-design of the operator's working situation. The way in which the operator reacts to the error is also important. If he makes the wrong adjustment, because of an inadequate mental 'model' of the shearing machine and how it functions, then once again we shall find the shearing sub-system has garbled its message. Every single stage of the feed-back loop must be considered. It is extremely important to notice that control is lost to the *same* extent whether the operator misreads a length which is correctly displayed, or whether the display gives the wrong figure. The traditional engineering approach has tended to shrug off the first kind of malfunctioning as human error, and concentrate attention on the electrical and mechanical devices. This was quite justified in the days when human error rates

L

were small compared with the error-rates of machines. This is no longer the case, especially in the field of computer applications.

The limit of achievable control

Let us assume that the transmission of signals around the feed-back loop is imperfect. It will be convenient to split the loop into a number of sections, each of which can be described as a noisy communication channel, by tabulating the chance of each output actually resulting from each given input. (See fig. 54.) In the example let us assume, for the sake of simplicity, that the output at each stage is correct or in error by 1 inch one way or the other. Without loss of generality we can assume that the

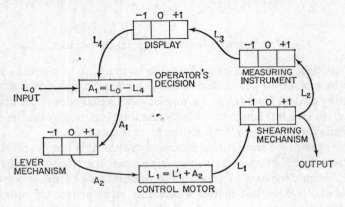

LEGEND

L_0 = Input length (read from the cutting list).
A_1 = Adjustment the operator applies to the lever.
A_2 = Adjustment actually signalled to the motor to re-set the shear.
$\left. \begin{array}{c} L'_1 \\ L_1 \end{array} \right\} = \begin{array}{l} \text{Old} \\ \text{New} \end{array}$ settings of the shear
L_2 = Actual length cut.
L_3 = Measured length as displayed.
L_4 = Length read and used by the operator

Fig. 54. Control of the shear as a communication loop.

operator always applies correctly the decision rule (a simple subtraction gives the necessary lever adjustment) and that the motor then correctly adjusts the setting of the shear before the next length is cut. The process can be depicted by a series of linked tables giving input/output relationships for each stage. Errors can be made at four stages: in the shearing mechanism itself; in the measuring device; in the display; and in the control-lever mechanism. In the figure, these sources of error are depicted as tables, each with 3 boxes in which the error probabilities can be written. These devices are noisy communication channels which can cause errors of only $+1$ or -1 inch. The decision, the control motor and all other stages of the loop are assumed to have perfect transmission.

Control applied on every cycle

Suppose that the whole system is working perfectly except that the shearing machine is misbehaving. Suppose, also, that there is an 80% chance that the correct length is cut and a 10% chance of a 1-inch error in each direction. (These probabilities are high, but this only serves to simplify the example.) Unless the machine is watched very closely, and the lever adjusted after each length is cut, the performance of the machine will drift rapidly away from its intended performance. The following table shows what will happen if no control is applied.

Size of error	% chance of error on cycle				
	0	1	2	3	4
+4					0·01
+3				0·1	0·3
+2			1	2·4	3·9
+1		10	16	19·5	21·4
0	100	80	66	56·0	48·7
−1		10	16	19·5	21·4
−2			1	2·4	3·9
−3				0·1	0·3
−4					0·01

On the fourth cycle of operations without control being applied, there is only a 48·7% chance of its cutting the correct length. There is an even smaller chance that it cuts correctly on all four cycles given by $\cdot8 \times \cdot8 \times \cdot8 \times \cdot8 \times 100 = 41\%$. The operator is there to prevent the machine's performance from drifting, and, by applying control to *every* cycle, he can make the system function as well as the faulty shearing machine will permit. But what if the fault should be somewhere else in the system?

Suppose that nothing is wrong with the functioning of the shearing machine; instead, suppose that one stage of the communication loop is malfunctioning. Let there be an error, say, in the reading of the dial which displays the measured length. If the setting is given correctly for the first bar, it will be cut correctly, but the operator may have difficulty in reading the dial and, from time to time, he may mistakenly believe that an error has been made. The error he makes in reading the dial will then be transmitted to the next bar by the unnecessary adjustment he will make. From that stage onwards, the mixture of bars – too long, too short and of the correct length – will be just as though the shearing machine itself were malfunctioning and the operator were correcting its setting each time. In fact, it does not matter where the fault lies in the control loop; the effect is the same. This is true, not only for simple systems, like the one we have been examining in detail, but, also, for the very complicated feed-back loops which link a manager with the resources that he controls. You may have a perfect plant and a completely acquiescent labour force, but perfect control will depend upon also having perfect communication channels. If management reports are prepared by a person not very interested in the job, with a blunt pencil on a badly-designed form, then sophisticated decision-making techniques will be of little value.

The probability-distribution of the numbers of pieces which are in error by -1, 0, or $+1$ inches can be used to calculate the *equivocation* of the control system. If errors occur at several places in the control loop, the range of material cut will vary more widely, perhaps from -4 to $+4$ inches from the desired size, but the equivocation can be calculated in the same way. It will be found that the equivocation for the system as a whole will be equal to the equivocation for the whole feed-back loop which transmits signals used in control.

Control with delayed or incomplete information

From the example we may also learn the effect of a delay in the feed-back loop. What happens can be deduced fairly readily from the above table of errors, showing how the system would drift if no control were applied. If, instead of being told the length of the material that he has just cut, the operator is told the length of the piece before that one, then the output from the system will be one of the five lengths $L+2$, $L+1$, L, $L-1$, $L-2$, with percentage probabilities 1, 16, 66, 16, and 1. The best that he can do by applying control is to bring the setting of the machine to one of the three possible states of the earlier cycle, $L+1$, L, $L-1$, so that 80% of the time he resets the machine correctly. The rest of the time he can do no better than set the machine to produce a length either 1 inch over or 1 inch under what is required. He would have less control if there were a delay of four cycles in measuring the output from the machine, then the lengths cut would vary between $L+4$ and $L-4$ inches with the probabilities given in the last column of the diagram. Exactly the same result would be obtained whatever caused the delay – measuring the output, displaying the measurement, applying control or resetting the shear.

By way of contrast, consider a system which has no delay in its feed-back loop, but which reports the measurements on only a proportion of the pieces produced. Suppose that every fourth piece can be measured but that we can apply control immediately. The measurements we make will vary between L−4 and L+4 with the probabilities as before. By applying control immediately, the error probabilities on the next cycle will be as for cycle 1 in the table, and, until control can be applied again, the outputs of the next three cycles will continue to drift out of control, exactly as shown in the table. However, *the average performance of this system, with sampled data but no delay, will be better than the performance of the other system, with measurements every cycle, but with a delay in transmitting the information.*

There is a very important lesson here for anyone who is designing business information systems, and among those I would of course include the accountants. The degree of control that can be exercised by a manager is very heavily dependent upon the speed of signal-transmission around the feed-back loop. Any delays compound the errors in the system and cause a rapid decline in the tightness of control. Incomplete information about the process being controlled will also lead to a deterioration in performance, but the loss may not be as serious as that caused by a delay even when the information is complete. This is especially true when the system drifts out of control slowly, but responds to corrective action quickly. The example examined above serves only to indicate that the behaviour of a control system can be counter-intuitive (many people expect that complete information, although delayed, will always be better for control than only a quarter of the information, even with no delay).

The above naive example of a control system provides some interesting and suggestive ideas, but one should not incautiously apply them to more complicated systems. Bearing this in mind, one should read Jay Forrester's studies of the dynamics of organisations in which he reveals the tendency of industrial systems to be subject to the same kinds of malfunctioning as electro-mechanical systems. He shows that the effect of delay in applying control can be more serious than suggested above because it can induce those quite violent oscillations which are not uncommon in business; Forrester gives many examples of this phenomenon.

The limitations of statistical communication theory

The generality of the statistical theory of communication is remarkable, and it guarantees the theory a central place in the development of our understanding of complex systems – not only engineering systems but also biological and social systems. Cybernetics, the science of 'communication and control in the animal and the machine', as it was defined by Wiener when he coined the term, is a rapidly growing subject, which employs the statistical theory of communication as, perhaps, its most important analytical tool. In the popular discussion of cybernetics, there is a temptation to use analogies suggesting that results based upon communication theory can be applied to social systems with as much justification as to machines. This temptation is perhaps encouraged by the widespread misuse of the term 'information theory' for the statistical theory of signal transmission. This unfortunate confusion dates back to Wiener's classic book which founded cybernetics. The cybernetician, today, should be well aware of the limited validity of the engineering approach and the far wider scope of information theory, but the popular misconception goes marching on.

As we have noted in this chapter, there is no limitation to the kinds of thing or event to which the statistical theory of communication can be applied. Rather, the validity of engineering cybernetics is limited because the theory of signal-transmission upon which it is built applies only to certain sources of messages and communication channels: those with a behaviour capable of strict definition, and of measurement in terms of the relative frequency of events. The ergodic property of an information source guarantees its statistical uniformity; this property is necessary both for the proof of the fundamental theorems (a formal mathematical requirement) and for the existence of operational conditions under which probabilities can be estimated by counting frequencies of actual events.

It would be futile to try building the whole study of information upon the foundation of a statistical theory which presupposes that a host of semantic questions has been resolved before it is invoked. For example, it must be resolved what sets of signs are under discussion, what messages are to be sent and what signals are used in transmission. Only when signs can be identified and distinguished objectively and reliably can the information specialist justifiably employ the apparatus of statistical communication theory. It is no good dragging this method into the study of any economic, social or organisational behaviour which is not capable of as precise and objective definition as the phenomena of natural science and engineering.

In reading about cybernetics, one often encounters an assumption that methods appropriate to understanding a chemical plant are equally appropriate to understanding a large organisation, or even the whole economy. These analogies *may* be appropriate, but you can only assume that they *are* if you are prepared to beg a host of semantic questions. For example, large organisational or social structures often do not retain the same shape long enough for one to gather reliable, relative-frequency data about many aspects of their behaviour. Also, in many cases such as in economics and sociology, the analytical tools being used become absorbed by the material upon which they are brought to bear. The study of social phenomena can be rather like doing anatomy in the laboratory of a strange zoo where the creatures evolve so quickly that their features change before you can picture them; where, as in a painting by Salvador Dali, the scalpel becomes absorbed by, and a living part of, the anatomical structure it was hoped to explore. This surrealist zoo cannot be studied in the same way as the Regent's Park Zoo. But there is every reason to hope that, at the microscopic level, there are organisational patterns and social structures sufficiently stable to permit us to understand them so that we may partly control the evolutionary process. The statistical study of information or *empirics* is relevant at this 'microscopic' level.

These three chapters have explained the most narrowly constrained of the four branches of semiotics. It was shown how signal transmission can be measured in statistical terms, and how the same methods can be applied to human communication when it is sufficiently machine-like. The relevance of this statistical theory to organisational problems was demonstrated in discussions of the processes of modulation and control.

Part Seven

Conclusion

The book has ranged widely, drawing material from anthropology, social psychology, psycholinguistics, philosophy, statistics, probability theory, logic, mathematics, computer science, communications engineering and experimental psychology. It has examined such problems as: What can carry information? How are these sign and signal carriers used by people? By machines? How can their effects be measured? How can reliable information be recognised? Can an organisation, as an information system, be designed?

This final part summarises the major ideas.

21 Summary

Semiotic is thus an interdisciplinary exercise.
In this study we have hardly entered into man's rich symbolic life.
We have been concerned mostly with the language needed to talk about this realm.

Charles Morris, *Signification and Significance*

No corner of man's rich symbolic existence has more practical importance today than the part in which he uses symbols to direct the affairs of government, industry and commerce. As his forbears toiled in vineyard and field, so modern man works in office and committee room; the hoe is replaced by the pen, the even furrows give way to lines of print; and the fruit of his labour springs not from his well-sown seed but from his carefully drafted plans, schedules, proposals and instructions. From words and numbers, man creates his future, and organisation is the name of his task.

We have taken this kind of work as much for granted as the peasant regarded his regular agricultural round. But tractors and computers have changed all that. Quite a new kind of organisation is now possible through the use of technology; to develop it we must understand more exactly what we have been doing unthinkingly for so long. We have been using signs or information to get things accomplished. What signs? How do they inform? How much information do they carry? What carries them? How efficiently?

Semiotics tries to answer these questions. Charles Morris, in his treatment of this subject, places greatest emphasis upon the behavioural sciences and the humanities. I have tried to indicate the relevance of the machine-like use of signs as well, because I am concerned about our failure to use information technology effectively in business and administration.

We fail because we do not understand clearly enough how organisations use information. Too often, elaborate systems are devised by people nurtured on a diet of computer programs, people who have never lifted their eyes from their plates long enou;h to realise that business systems are rather more than 'common sense' or 'mere O. & M.'

We fail because we do not perceive clearly enough what machines can accomplish. Too often, slavish automation of an established clerical system has been demanded by managers and administrators, who have never imagined what might be accomplished by the human intellect and information machines in a new partnership.

The aim of this book has been to place some ideas from the whole of the relevant field of knowledge in a single panoramic display. I should like the reader to feel that, despite their very great differences, all the views are essential to form a complete picture. The whole is semiotics, which I feel sure can help the man facing practical problems if only because it embodies a variety of perspectives rich enough to match the complexities of real life.

All that remains for me to do is to redirect the reader's mind across the whole vista and mention some features that he may have missed because they span too wide an angle. First a review of the key ideas, chapter by chapter.

Pragmatics

What is a sign?

Chapter 3 gave some concepts drawn from anthropology. They exhibit the variety of ways in which people convey messages to one another, not only in words but also silently. The full language is our culture. We communicate it from generation to generation with a great degree of accuracy which depends upon the complex interdependence of one stream of cultural messages upon another. The cultural anthropologists have attempted to describe this interdependence in terms of a syntactic structure,* but it seems to me more like the relationship of mutual information between sources of signals. However it arises, the result is that by pulling on one thread of our cultural web we can convey messages about another. These silent messages communicate emotive information: approval, dislike, threat, allegiance, aspirations. Everything that a person does, what he owns and how he uses things radiates these messages; they are easily mis-read by anyone who does not understand the precise cultural background from which he learnt them.

How do signs acquire their stability?

All our cultural signs, silent or vocal, derive their stability from the social groups in which they are used. Chapter 4 dealt with this topic of norm-formation, which is one of the most important concepts in social psychology. Any departure, by an individual, from the norms of the group will be censured, whereas his conformity will be rewarded by a display

---

* See Lévi-Strauss.

of group approval. Censure and approval are forcefully expressed without words. This mechanism serves to control the individual and to provide the group with the stability essential for effective communication. Norms govern not only our wordless behaviour but also our beliefs, value judgements and even our perceptions, all three of which are usually expressed in words. Thus, deeply embedded in the matrix of a cultural system, language is able to achieve the consistency of usage essential for communication. Although the cultural foundation is slowly shifting, the social mechanism is able to re-align and extend the edifice of natural language to suit the contours of new problems.

How do we respond to language signs?

Most of the information transmitted in organisations is carried by language. Chapter 5 examined our sensitivity to this instrument. There is a great difference between the language we speak and the language we write; the subtle, silent messages from body posture, facial expression and vocal inflexion add a richness to face-to-face communication that makes it indispensable for transmitting affective information. It is almost beyond the power of a human being to refrain from communicating affectively, thereby influencing attitudes, judgements, expectations and morale. When people try to be precisely descriptive, their judgements intrude and modify or even falsify the picture they report. Sensitivity to the affective overtones of language extends to written words; nonsense syllables will acquire an emotive colouring by chance association with expressive words. This colouring of words can be measured using Osgood's method of semantic differentials. Language has power over what we perceive: a word can predetermine how a person will interpret an ambiguous picture or a muffled voice. Even the apparently trivial nods and how-do-you-do's of recognition (phatic communion) serve to establish communication channels which are open to more serious use, should the need arise. The health of an organisation depends upon how its members communicate.

Semantics of Language

What can be done to raise the standard of communication?

Most of our knowledge of signs and how to use them is rooted in the pragmatic level of cultural norms. At this level our linguistic behaviour may be highly sophisticated, but the sensitive interplay between words and thoughts suggests we should exercise caution, lest we should be betrayed by the magic of words. Semantics is a canon of critical methods by which we can establish the legitimacy of the imputed relationships between signs and what they represent. The significations of signs cannot all be established in the same way. Some signs point to what can be observed objectively by many people; these are *designative signs*. Past and future things can also be designated, but the signs which represent them are more difficult to justify than signs for what can be observed at present. *Appraisive signs* convey judgements about things that can be designated; they must be related to expressions of human feelings. Designative and appraisive signs all serve to describe how things were, are or might be in the future, either objectively or as people respond to them; broadly speaking, we can say that *descriptive signs* convey factual information or value judgements. A different kind of information is conveyed by signs that serve to provoke actions, these are *prescriptive signs* and they can be subdivided into *instructions*, which denote the actions to be performed, and others which signify the threat of punishment or the promise of reward. To be effective, instructions must be supported by *inducements* which indicate the power behind them, not necessarily from the same source, perhaps from a centre of authority external to both giver and receiver of instructions, perhaps from the receiver's own conscience. To complete the classification, designations and instructions can be called *denotative information* while appraisals and inducements are called *affective information*. The other chapters on semantics confined their attention to denotative information.

How do words denote things?

Words convey very general information. Words select stable patterns from experience, label them so that they stand out as clear concepts in the mind, and provide handles by which concepts can be shifted to form new patterns that have never been experienced. They are the components from which we construct the imagined worlds of the past, the future and the inaccessible. The patterns which we deem worthy of being named are selected because, by common consent, they are the ones most useful for solving practical problems, getting things done, attaining satisfaction and avoiding discomfort. Apart from their necessary connection with the requirements of the human organism in its social setting, words are somewhat arbitrary. Our language embodies a host of metaphysical assumptions about the nature of the world we live in and the problems we have to solve. In a rapidly changing world we must prevent language from placing a strait jacket on our minds. It is salutary to remind oneself that other cultures, such as the American Indians', have languages which embody radically different assumptions about the world. It is often helpful to introduce subscripts, superscripts, hyphens, etceteras, brackets and inverted commas, as devices to extend our language, and draw attention to the arbitrariness and vagueness of crucial words used in an argument. Starting from words which can be defined ostensively through experience, we can ascend a ladder of abstraction. To construct a secure ladder we must join each conceptual rung to firmer, less abstract rungs below by means of definitions. In the middle of the ladder we can use operational definitions but at the top theoretical definitions will be unavoidable. Unless we are careful to do this, our concepts will be supported only by verbal habits; we may then enjoy a beautiful floating feeling and a kind of mental exhilaration; but when we step off our verbal rung, back into the world of action, we shall fall on our faces.

How should statements be tested?

We use statements to express particular ideas by assembling patterns of general word-tokens. Statements are models of the world as it is, as it was or as it may be. Information about the worlds past and present can be generated from observations, aggregated to a suitable level of abstraction. This information is important in running an organisation but it is not enough. It is the task of managers and administrators to construct the world of the future, so they need also statements about the possible worlds they might create. These are generated in the minds of men. Reasoning begins, always, with a stage of conjecture, creation or *abduction*. This provides an indispensable but neglected input of information to all decisions. Conjectures can be nonsense or they can be sound. How do we distinguish between them? We can test them for logical self-consistency, perhaps with the aid of mathematics. We can apply the aesthetic test of Occam's Razor which pares the statements down to their most economical formulation. This helps to make the empirical tests of the next stage more severe; from the hypotheses being tested, we derive statements which can be checked by observation; if the result is negative we can reject the hypothesis, if it is positive we cannot say that the hypothesis is proven, only that it has been corroborated. Finally, we must inspect the evidence used to check the observational statement; in the natural sciences this can be done by making the observation repeatedly; in other decision-situations it can only be done by checking the reliability of the source of evidence, as a lawyer or historian would. Despite all these tests, it is impossible to make sure that the kinds of statements used for making organisational decisions are segregated into facts and value judgements. Decisions, on the vast scale which is normal in big business and government, are outside the scope of purely rational and objective argument. Operational research, economic and accounting models may look coolly reasoned but they will be based upon assumptions embodying someone's value judgements.

Semantics of Number

How can we check the meaning of numerical information?

Large organisations must use numbers to cope with the scale of their operations. Words can only be aggregated if a person assimilates them and then condenses them into general, subjective conclusions, but numbers can be aggregated arithmetically and objectively. The meaning of the resulting numerical information depends upon the operational procedures by which the numbers are assigned to things: the process of measuring. Some measurements are firmly rooted in structural properties of the real world, these are the *fundamental measurements*. There are *derived measurements* which are obtained by arithmetical manipulations of fundamental measurements. There need be little doubt about the meaning of these in operational terms. Many other measurements used in business are hard to justify. They are the *pointer measurements* which assign numbers to things by an arbitrary procedure or by using an instrument which cannot be calibrated by reference to any fundamental measurement. The key to the distinction between fundamental and pointer measurements is the concept of a scale. When a fundamental measurement is defined, it is *essential* to set up a system of operational relationships among the things being measured; *these relationships do not depend upon the numbers to be assigned* because they can be demonstrated by making empirical tests or by asking a person for his judgements. A scale is then defined which consists of a system of numbers *plus* certain arithmetical relationships, and the measurement is completed by assigning numbers to the things, in such a way that the operational relationships are mirrored by the arithmetical relationships. Pointer measurements have no objective scale because they have to assign numbers *before* any relationship can be defined, instead of the reverse being true. It can be very difficult to justify the use of a pointer measurement, as it can only be done experimentally by showing that the measurement can serve as a predictor. However, if you do not ask awkward questions about the basis of the numerical data (and who does?) it all looks beautifully reliable when garnished with a sprig or two of mathematics!

How do we ascend the ladder of numerical abstractions?

Numbers can be combined in many useful ways that are clearly meaningful, at least when fundamental measurement underlies them: totals, sub-totals, means, medians, modes are well-known. Also statistics provides a host of techniques such as regression, factor analysis, the method of principle components and cluster analysis, which draw attention to apparent patterns in the data. Sometimes one invokes 'objective', statistical tests of the significance of these patterns, dismissing them if the test shows that they might have arisen just by chance. The only adequate test of significance in the final analysis is in terms of their usefulness in solving a practical problem: this is a matter of human judgement; statistical tests can only serve to elect candidates for the accolade of significance.

How do we measure statements?

Clearly, this question could not be evaded in a book on the nature of information. Common sense suggests that 'information' is the name we give to some kind of intrinsic property of statements or messages or signals. A person may be asked to judge how reliable certain statements are as a basis for action, on a scale from 'perfectly' to 'not in the least'. If he is asked first before and then after you give him a message, it is possible to associate the changes in his opinion with the 'information content' of the message. The trouble with this method is that a person will make inconsistent judgements and so make it difficult to attach any clear meaning to the resulting measurement. It is possible to show a person that, to be consistent in his judgements in circumstances where it makes sense to place bets on the statements, he should obey certain rules. These rules are the axioms of probability. Once again you can give him a message and use the change in his subjective probabilities to measure the information in the message. There is yet another improvement. If you can persuade the subject to make probability judgements about all the different messages he might receive, you can impose a further rule of reasonable judgement: the conditional probability rule. This gives rise to another measurement of subjective probability and some better measurements of information, one of them even displaying the precious additivity property:

$$\text{Info}(E_1 \ \& \ E_2) = \text{Info}(E_1) + \text{Info}(E_2)$$

when the messages E_1 and E_2 are 'independent' of one another.

Can information compel 'reasonable' people to reach agreement?

The answer, regrettably, is 'no'. Two people, individually, can remain quite consistent in their judgements and as sharply opposed as ever, even though they adjust their separate opinions to each new item of information in the most reasonable manner. The trouble stems from their very different judgements of the evidence. You may get them to agree on a general rule for interpreting evidence but, when faced with it, each may decide that the only thing proven by the evidence is that their rule for judging it was wrong. It may be better to let both sides believe the evidence to be biassed, provided, thereby, that they are able to feel that it lies within the bounds of credibility. There is another strategy: undermine, separately, the confidence of each in his prepared position before adducing the evidence they must share. Then, as can be shown by the Principle of Stable Estimation, anyone's prior opinion will be irrelevant when confronted by very exact and reliable information provided that he was not too strongly committed in the first place. The process of reaching agreement can be analysed quite precisely using the mathematical model which was discussed informally in chapter 11.

What information counts as truly 'objective'?

People may come to agree how certain evidence should be interpreted, by forming a consensus, through social interaction: as though they were establishing an evaluative norm. This is the only method in many practical situations but, where possible, it is desirable to employ further normative rules which any 'reasonable' man can accept as guides to his judgement. One such principle can be invoked when the evidence can be derived from repeated observations or replicated experiments. Provided that all the processes of sampling and the procedures of observation and experiment can be *randomised*, then, as reasonable men, we are adjured to accept the *relative frequencies* of events as accurate guides to the probabilities we should attach to statements about them. In these very special circumstances the evidence has an objective force that cannot be denied. Provided that enough information can be obtained we can also cast our first, private opinions to the winds and invoke the *maximum likelihood principle* as a basis for our inductive reasoning. Probability based on relative frequency is appropriate in engineering, where it serves as a basis for yet another measurement of information. It is important, however, not to confuse the relative frequencies actually derived from observations with numbers spoken of as though they were relative frequencies, but derived from a mathematical model of a set of possible events. These are logical probabilities, their semantic standing, if any, being derived from the plausibility of the model, not from the observation of relative frequencies.

Parts Three and Four were about *semantic standing* or how to establish the connection between talk and action: the quality control of signs.

Syntactics

What is information processing?

From signs, words, statements, numbers and mathematical expressions, we construct models of the world. How do we assemble them and take them apart? What operations can we perform on these models? Such questions require answers which relate only to the signs; the real world, to which semantics attaches them, we can forget. By doing so, we enter the beautiful clear world of mathematics and formal logic, divorced from the untidy world of action. The only objects of interest are the letters, numbers and other symbols which we shuffle about on pieces of paper and inside computing machinery; there is a limited number of *types* of symbol but an endless supply of *tokens*, should we need them. We distinguish between these *object symbols* from which a formal system is constructed and the *meta-symbols* in which the object system is defined. The bases of these systems are the formal languages, each comprising strings of symbol tokens all produced according to a precise set of rules. Depending upon the kind of production rule, the resulting language is called finite-state, context-free or context-sensitive. From simple languages complex ones can be generated by substitution, from complex ones we can isolate simple component languages that make them easier to understand. All this seems remote from everyday life until we notice that some of these formal languages have grammars like ordinary English and that the production and recognition of sentences can be performed by computers. It is also possible to process information from a multitude of practical problems in exactly the same way by using the rules of a single formal system but with different semantic interpretations. That, as a way of increasing productivity, should gratify the most exacting manager!

How can the procedures of formal logic be used in an organisation?

Bureaucracy is built upon a system of formal procedures for making decisions and taking actions. By using a kind of logic called the propositional calculus, many parts of a bureaucratic system can be cast into the shape of a formal language which can be processed with greater efficiency by computers than by clerks. The propositional calculus is a simple component of our natural language but not a part that most people manipulate with much skill and accuracy. Using decision tables and algorithms (which are like computer programs), the tortuous prose of the bureaucrat can be hammered into neat rows of questions with 'yes' and 'no' answers. If you can assign the answers correctly (a semantic problem) the other procedures can be performed automatically and the tax demand or pension-book can be generated by a machine. It is admitted that the systems-analysis task of translating the rules into logic is much more difficult than the examples of chapter 15 suggest.

Can machines perform more than simple routine work?

They can. They are able to display a kind of rudimentary intelligence by virtue of their power to store thousands of millions of characters of information, any part being within reach in a small fraction of a second. Machine intelligence depends upon the formal manipulation of signs. The first step in building a suitable system is to extend the *propositional logic*, so that each *elementary proposition* is like a simple English sentence with a subject and a predicate. These so-called *basic sentences* form the elementary units of information in another formal language-structure known as *predicate logic*. A computer store, filled with basic sentences, can yield the answers to numerous questions. However, even at a computer's fantastic speed, some questions, which seem quite straight-forward, cannot be answered in a reasonable time if the memory is organised on the basis of a predicate logic. More elaborate *data-structures* are required to enhance the machine's performance. The formal language-structures are all one-dimensional, being based upon strings of symbols, but other data-structures can be multi-dimensional. Despite their greater complexity, they can be accommodated in the structure of a computer store in a form known as a *memory-structure* or *file-structure*. The result is a machine with a memory for detail, with a size and speed of operation able to match the needs of a large organisation.

Does the formal analysis of signs suggest more ways of measuring information?

If a formal system can behave with a degree of intelligence, then it seems natural to use it as an objective standard for measuring information. The simplest way would be to count the numbers of symbols employed in the message; another step would be to count the numbers of basic sentences it contains. In all but the simplest problems these methods are either inappropriate or unworkable. Another method can be developed for a simple predicate logic. It is based upon a set of statements that are the least informative ones which can be made in that logical language; these are the *content elements*. Any message can be translated into a set of content elements; the size of this set can be used to measure the information in the message. This method also gives rise to logical probability measures, emphasising again the close relationship between probability and information. Unfortunately, the method has a serious defect because it takes no account of the processing required to analyse the message; it simply assumes that this can be done instantaneously. There is yet to be discovered a way of measuring information that takes into account the work needed to derive it from a memory structure.

Empirics

Given a communication channel, what limits the information it can carry?

This is an important question which syntactics disregards because it assumes that signs can be re-arranged instantly with perfect precision. Information, in the context of communication, can be regarded as a stream of signs which must be transported from one location to another, regardless of what they mean, but taking account of the speed and accuracy of transportation. Semantic questions can be disregarded, as in syntactics. Instead, attention is directed towards the statistical properties of the events at the source of signals and at their destination. The result is a branch of engineering analysis called the *statistical theory of signal transmission*. It uses measurements of information based upon relative-frequency probabilities. It defines the information generated by a source of signals in terms of its *variety* of actual behaviour, which is measured by a statistic called *entropy*. It measures the capacity of a channel in terms of the variety of its potential behaviour, taking account of the chance corruption of signals or *equivocation*. The theory shows how to measure, in terms of *mutual information*, similarities in the random behaviour of two or more sources, and it guides the engineer in the design of codes which overcome, as far as possible, the effects of *noise* in the communication channel.

Is the engineering theory of communication relevant only to machines?

Not at all. Strictly speaking it is a branch of statistics and it can be applied wherever a sustained pattern of random activity communicates its effects to another place. In fact a person who is speaking, using a keyboard or filling in forms is operating as a channel and his behaviour can be measured statistically. It is found that human channel-capacity is about $2\frac{1}{2}$ bits per stimulus for a very simple task, increasing logarithmically with the complexity of the stimulus. Speed of transmission by a human being can approach 30 bits per second but is normally about 10–20 bits per second, compared with machines which can transmit at ten million times that speed. This engineering analysis is only just beginning to be applied to organisational problems of information-handling.

How might the theory of signal transmission be applied to business?

Two illustrations were given. The first one concerned the idea of *modulation*, the transformation of a signal from one representation to another; it showed how this concept could be used in a qualitative analysis of data acquisition procedures. The second showed how a *control loop* could be analysed quantitatively; the limit of attainable precision was related to the channel capacity of the whole control loop, including the human controller, and the machine being controlled.

Finally it was stressed that the engineering or statistical approach to information has only limited relevance to organisational problems. This is an aspect of the single most important idea in the book: that the four branches of semiotics correspond to quite different kinds of knowledge and yield quite different ways of solving problems. This will be illustrated in the next few paragraphs which link ideas from all four branches of the subject.

Topics which link the branches of semiotics

Design of forms

This is a commonplace task that is much more difficult than first appearances suggest. It poses problems in the design of codes, the use of correlated questions and check-digits for detecting errors; these belong to the field of empirics. Syntactic problems arise in the choice of the sequence of questions, the grouping of forms for clerical operations, and in the use of forms in a filing system. Semantic questions concern the definition of any procedures of observation or measurement, when a form is used as a source of information; they also arise where the information on the documents is to be used for decision-making or for compiling a report. Pragmatic knowledge must be used to decide how people will respond to the form and the instructions for using it.

Decision-making

Repeated decision-procedures such as those used in controlling the quality of a product can be studied by the methods of empirics. Most important organisational decisions are only made once; the result of the decision (the building of a new motorway or the launching of a new product) changes the organisation or its environment to such an extent that the same problem can never occur again. In these circumstances logical models, such as linear programming or critical path analysis, can be used. They are generalised, formal, syntactic solutions but they cannot be employed without a semantic analysis to justify them. Every organisational decision of any importance will involve a number of people arriving at a consensus about values and priorities and sometimes about matters of fact. This process must be understood in terms of pragmatics.

Meaning

Among the threads running right through the book has been the concept of 'meaning'. It is as vague a term as 'information' and it can be interpreted at all four levels of semiotics. 'Meaning' can always be interpreted as a relationship between a sign and a 'thing' or between one sign and another; the 'thing' may be an object, a property, an event, an action or a state of affairs. The relationships can be established in many different ways, resulting in many different kinds of meaning. A few illustrations can be given from each level of semiotics.

At the pragmatic level, almost any object or pattern of behaviour can be invested with meaning by virtue of its regular employment in a social context. Any pair of 'things' which are frequently found in association with one another tends to acquire a meaningful relationship thus: dog–subservience; Fleet Street–newspapers; ceremonial–power; the armchair by the fire–father. Usually the relationship 'x means y' rquires x to be, in a sense, more specific than y. Some of these relationships are rooted in the physical nature of things (storm–trouble; red–danger), others are sustained only by the social process (dark blue–Oxford; handlebar moustache–RAF 1939-45). In all these cases people will come to regard x as a sign for y. This pragmatic meaning will be a kind of mental habit in which they are rehearsed either by observing actual events in nature or by the widespread social use of the habit.

Semantics, as understood in this book, is concerned with meanings established by a chain of *operational procedures* linking a 'thing' and a sign. In a world where pragmatic meanings can be established so easily by the repetition of two things in association with one another, semantic analysis has the important task of sifting the reliable meanings from the unreliable. When using information to organise a business or administer public affairs, it is wise to check that the signs are related or can be

Intention of: SIGNIFICATIONS *mode of:·*	Descriptive signs *represent the world and serve to augment our senses* *'thing' →sign*	Prescriptive signs *are used to provoke actions and serve to extend our grasp on the world* *sign→'thing'*
Denotative signs *are related to the objective world of common experience external to the human organism*	designation *object property* $\Big\}$ *→sign* *event* *'I am showing you this.'*	instruction *sign→* $\begin{cases} action\ to \\ be\ carried \\ out \end{cases}$ *'Don't do that!'*
Affective signs *are related to the subjective world of personal feelings within the organism*	appraisal *feeling about an object, property* $\Big\}$ *→sign* *or event* *'I like it.'*	inducement *sign→* $\begin{cases} feeling\ which \\ will\ result \\ from\ action \end{cases}$ *'You will be hurt if you do.'*

related to 'real' things. The operations through which the relationship is established determine the semantic category of the sign. These categories are shown in the table. It must be remembered that any information used in running an organisation seldom falls into only one category. Words and statements, especially rather abstract ones, have multiple significations.

Information about the hypothetical future is interesting. Its meaning cannot be tested operationally by linking 'things' to signs except by demonstrating that the prospect of doing so is not contrary to our present knowledge. Some justifiable descriptions of the future never come about, others result from the flux of time, and others are brought about through the use of prescriptive information. We generate our future by selecting a suitable description and translating it into instructions and inducements.

Syntactic meanings are relationships between signs at a formal level. If a mechanical process can translate code x to code y or sentence x to sentence y, this can be taken as a definition of 'x means y'. Also at the syntactic level we can associate the word 'meaning' with a system of relationships: imagine a complex file containing details of interrelated jobs, work-in-progress, orders, tools, machine centres and men; the 'meaning' of a message about a machine breakdown could be understood in terms of its effect on the structure of the file.

Meaning at the empirical level can be established by a relationship of cause and effect. You can determine the meanings of the signals received from a communication channel by discovering which input signals might have caused them.

Probability and measurements of information

Spanning many chapters of this book is the important idea that the amount of information conveyed by a statement, signal or message can be measured in many different ways, some of which have scarcely been explored, as yet. One method is by evaluating signs on many scales simultaneously, as in Osgood's technique of semantic differentials. These are intensive measurements; extensive measurements, which have an additivity property, can be obtained by using probability as a fundamental measurement. All probability measurements have the same mathematical structure, which can be used to reflect various empirical structures. By changing the empirical relationships a variety of measurements with different meanings can be obtained. A relationship based upon human judgements of statements gives rise to a subjective probability; formal relationships can be used to generate a variety of logical probability measurements; and observations of the relative frequencies of events provide the objective relationship from which statistical probabilities are derived.

Information measures of various kinds can be obtained from these probability measures in two different ways. There is a measurement, relative to a set of statements, which depends upon the change of opinion caused by the information being measured. There is also a way of measuring a statement, S, directly, in terms of the probability attached to it, using a function such as

$$\text{Info}(S) = 1 - \text{Prob}(S) \quad \text{or} \quad \text{Info}(S) = -\log \text{Prob}(S).$$

Except in the field of communications engineering, very little use has yet been made of information measures, so it will be some years before we learn which ones are important.

Semiotics and four levels of knowledge

Organisation is only possible because we can employ signs to coordinate the work of many hands and eyes. The information systems that we create seem to resemble great machines like communication networks with computers at their nodes; but the analogy is dangerous. It is quite beyond the capacity of men to understand the functioning of an organisation in the same way as a team of engineers can comprehend the functioning of a machine. There may be anything from ten to 100,000 human components in an organisation; each one may respond to signs in his own way, but we cannot describe how a single one behaves, except in performing some simple, repetitive tasks. If we could describe an organisation in detail, our knowledge would be outdated after a few hours because some people working in it would have changed their goals or their perceptions of their tasks. An engineer's kind of knowledge alone will not serve an information specialist. Semiotics, therefore, studies the nature of information on four levels.

Empirics is the engineering level. Some problems in routine, repetitive data-handling will succumb to this type of analysis. Examples are the distribution of the work-load among clerks or machinery, the design of codes, and the optimisation of repetitive decisions.

Syntactics is the computer-programming level. Languages can be designed and used to perform elaborate tasks on computers. These formal systems may be so elaborate that they never do exactly the same thing twice. They depend only upon a knowledge of the structural properties of systems of signs. Examples are the algorithms for scheduling of production or for the storage and retrieval of information.

Semantics is the business analyst's level. Economic analysts, financial analysts, systems analysts and others, in various circumstances, establish the connection between signs and what they signify in the real world.

Examples are the description of a market, the compilation of a budget and the design of an information system.

Pragmatics is the operational level. Everyone in an organisation responds to signs; he must know how to do this intuitively or the organisation would cease functioning. Such knowledge cannot always be made explicit, and some people might not wish to regard it as a part of the knowledge of an information system, but, in practical affairs, it is the most important part.

Limitations of time and resources are enough to force a manager, confronted by a complex and unique problem, to rely upon his pragmatic knowledge. This should be no excuse for failing to use critical semantic analysis, or general syntactic solutions, or even the principles of empirics, where circumstances permit.

Our knowledge resides in the signs we use and how we use them. It would be surprising, therefore, if the study of information did not raise serious philosophical problems. The solution adopted in this book is to acknowledge that we can know about signs in four ways: intuitively, critically, formally and empirically. One must have recourse to all of these when solving a practical problem about the use of information in an organisation.

22 Postscript: Information and Society

Semiotic has for its goal a general theory of signs in all their forms and manifestations.
It provides one more wedge for entering into the tissue of man's symbolic life.

Charles Morris, *Signification and Significance*

We are faced, in the social sciences, with a full and complicated interaction between observer and observed, between subject and object.

Popper, *Poverty of Historicism*

This book has reviewed parts of a number of established disciplines in order to show how they contribute towards a theory of signs. The purpose of the whole study has been to make clearer the nature of the information which is used for running an organisation. The perspective which it gives is a very broad one. By concentrating upon business uses of information, it has been possible to investigate one part of the 'tissue of man's symbolic life', a part which is undergoing rapid changes as a result of the increasing use of information technology. Computers and communication networks are being grafted onto organisations of all kinds. These information machines can be used either to enrich man's elaborate symbolic life, or to tie society to a rack of formal systems which will be tightened in the cause of order and efficiency.

If society is not to disable itself in the name of progress, by thrusting the instruments of information technology into its organs of decision-making and control, then it should stop brandishing the picks and shovels of computer technology as though they were magic surgical instruments. There is a dangerous belief that anyone who can grasp these rudimentary new tools is competent to anaesthetise an organisation with his aura of modern knowledge and tomorrow's jargon and then proceed to rip out the arteries clogged with paper, lance the gathering of committees, loosen the paralysis of indecision, all with the edge of a punched card and a little common sense. Some patients have died and others have suffered agonies recovering from these operations and, moreover, they have paid heavily for the service.

Common sense is not an adequate guide to the anatomy of an organisation. In the days before computers we were only able to administer gentle massage to the stiff parts of a system through management education and some carefully directed personnel work. The advent of the computer has inaugurated the age of organisational surgery. Technology has created machines which can respond to and employ language, behave almost intelligently and supplement the human intellect in areas where it is weakest. These remarkable machines, if they are to serve any useful function, must be grafted with great skill into the tissue of society. We have not yet learnt how to do this. One thing is clear: we cannot leave this job to the machine-makers – there is too great a difference between the functioning of a machine and the functioning of a human information system. We need professional information specialists whose knowledge spans the whole of semiotics, the anatomy of man's symbolic life.

No analogy between the information specialist and the surgeon, no comparison of his work and the work of the engineer or architect, will serve to explain its most difficult characteristic. It is a characteristic shared with all social sciences: 'a full and complicated interaction between the observer and the observed'. The natural scientist, who can make repeated observations under nearly identical conditions, who can regulate the conditions in which he conducts experiments, can plot his field of discourse with a precision denied to anyone surveying our social environment. The Uncertainty Principle in physics forces the investigator to recognise that any attempt to observe a sub-atomic system is likely to be impossible without disturbing it, to such an extent that the process of observation will automatically invalidate its own results. This difficulty can be escaped by investigating gross phenomena. The natural sciences are able, therefore, to underpin the work of the surgeon, the engineer and the architect with a secure framework of objective knowledge, derived from reliable experiments which can be repeated as often as accuracy demands.

The social sciences cannot provide the information specialist with a similar framework of knowledge. Repeated observation and controlled experiment can be used only to a limited extent by social scientists. The information specialist who tries to use these methods to investigate an organisation must recognise their limitations. Social structures, unlike most structures of the physical world, are in a continual state of flux, so that it is difficult to discover about them much that is valid at other times or places. Social structures, unlike physical structures, respond intelligently by deceiving the observer, anticipating his results or changing into something quite different when his conclusions are revealed. There are two problems here: the diversity and flux of social systems, and the interaction of observer and observed that so often nullifies knowledge and action.

The perpetual flux of the universe has been a philosophical problem since Heraclitus, but ordinary language solves it: we *are* able to step twice into the same river provided that we use the word 'river' as ordinary men do; it is when we start to label every drop of water that we go wrong. If we step beyond the operational bounds of our concepts they will not support our understanding but that step must be made. Physics can label the drops of water in the river of Heraclitus without falling in, because it first erects a platform of new concepts; instead of talking about the invariance of the river banks and the cold, wet properties of the water, physics talks about the invariant character of the *process of flowing* and uses a set of hydrodynamic equations instead of the ordinary word 'river'. The flux of a social system does not prevent us from talking about an 'organisation' but trouble arises when we try to label parts or properties of an organisation. We should not expect the micro-structure of an organisation to be capable of being explained in the same way as its macro-structure. We need to find new concepts which correspond to invariant properties of its inner processes, not hydrodynamic equations in this case, but descriptions of the sign-processes through which organisation is accomplished. Semiotics is to organisations as physics is to rivers.

As the engineer can use the hydrodynamics of rivers to design the piers of bridges, so one might expect the information specialist to be able to use the semiotics of organisations to improve their functioning. He can, but not in the same way. The engineer can design a bridge and then assemble the component parts according to his design. The passive materials from which a bridge is built do not question the designer, wilfully change their proportions or reassemble themselves into a boat! The components of an organisation behave in just such perverse ways when anyone tries to force them into a form which they dislike.

Insight into the nature of information should make it possible to exploit information technology to the fullest extent by creating entirely new kinds of organisations. This will only be done successfully if we acknowledge that people, the components from which organisations are built, have the capacity to organise themselves. Information systems will not, then, be imposed upon people; instead, they will be designed to enable social systems to organise themselves more effectively. This can be done at the *empiric level* by matching the capabilities of men and machines; at the *syntactic level* by devising formal languages that are economical and adaptable; at the *semantic level* by showing people how to sustain a firm connection between the symbols they manipulate and the real world; and at the *pragmatic level* by training people to use information with sensitivity.

Organisations create themselves according to their ability to use information. That ability can be enhanced by the use of machines. Semiotics, the general theory of information, is one of the tools we shall need for creating the organisations of the future.

Selected References

ABRAMSON, N., (1963), *Information Theory and Coding*, New York, McGraw Hill.

ALEXANDER, H. G., (1967), *Language and Thinking*, London, Princeton, N.J., Van Nostrand.

ALLPORT, G. W. and POSTMAN, L., (1948), *The Psychology of Rumour*, New York, Holt.

ASCH, S. E., (1951), 'Effects of Group Pressure upon the Modification and Distortion of Judgement', in *Groups, Leadership and Men*, H. Guertzkow (Ed.), Carnegie Press, Pittsburgh.

ASHBY, W. R., (1964), *An Introduction to Cybernetics*, London, Chapman & Hall/Methuen.

ATTNEAVE, F., (1959), *Applications of Information Theory to Psychology*, New York, Holt, Rinehart.

BAR-HILLEL, Y., (1964), 'An Outline of a Theory of Semantic Information', re-printed in his *Language and Information*, Addison-Wesley, Reading, Mass.

BAR-HILLEL, Y. and CARNAP, R., (1953), 'Semantic Information', *Brit. J. Phil. Sc.*, 4, pp. 147–57.

BLAKE, R. R. and RAMSEY, G. V. (Eds), (1951), *Perception—an Approach to Personality*, Ronald Press, New York.

BRITISH COMPUTER SOCIETY, (1970), *Data Organisation for Maintenance and Access*, British Computer Society, London.

CARROLL, J. B., (1964), *Language and Thought*, Englewood Cliffs (N.J.), Prentice Hall.

CARNAP, R., (1950, 1962), *The Logical Foundations of Probability*, (second edition 1962) University of Chicago Press.

CARNAP, R., (1952), *The Continuum of Inductive Methods*, University of Chicago Press, Cambridge.

CARNAP, R. and BAR-HILLEL, Y., (1953), 'Semantic Information', *Brit. J. Phil. Sc.*, 4, pp. 147–57.

CENTRE FOR INTER-FIRM COMPARISON, (1968), *Published Accounts — Your Yardsticks of Performance?*, London.

CHERRY, C., (1957, 1966), *On Human Communication*, (second edition 1966) Cambridge, Mass., MIT Press.

CHOMSKY, N., (1959), Review of Skinner's 'Verbal Behaviour', *Language*, 35, No. 1, (re-printed in Jakobovits and Miron).

CHOMSKY, N., (1956), 'Three Models for the Description of Language', IRE Trans. Inform. Theor., I-T2, pp. 113–24, (re-printed in Luce et al (Eds) *Readings*, 1965).

CHOMSKY, N., (1957), *Syntactic Structures*, The Hague and Paris, Mouton.

CHOMSKY, N., (1965), *Aspects of the Theory of Syntax*, Cambridge, Mass. MIT Press.

CODD, E. F., 'A Relational Model of Data for Large Shared Data Banks', *Communications of the ACM*, Vol. 13, No. 6, pp. 377–87, June 1970.

COHEN, L. J., (1962), *The Diversity of Meaning*, London, Methuen.

CONRAD, R., 'Designing Postal Codes for Public Use', *Ergonomics*, Vol. 10, No. 2, March 1967.

CRAMER, H., (1946), *Mathematical Methods of Statistics*, Princeton U. P.

DEAN, J., (1957), *Managerial Economics*, Englewood Cliffs, Prentice Hall.

DEWEY, J., (1933), *How We Think*, New York, London, Heath.

DEVONS, E., (1958), *An Introduction to British Economic Statistics*, (second impression 1958), Cambridge U. P.

DRUCKER, J. F., (1955), *The Practice of Management*, London, Heinemann.

DUNPHY, D. C., (1966), 'Social Change in Self-Analytical Groups', in Stone et al, *The General Inquirer*.

EDWARDS, W., LINDMANN, H. and SAVAGE, L. J., 'Bayesian Statistical Inference for Psychological Research', *Psychological Review*, 1963, No. 70, pp. 193–242, (re-printed in Luce et al (Eds) *Readings*, 1965).

FAIRTHORNE, R. A., (1961), *Towards Information Retrieval*, London, Butterworths, 1961; Archon, Connecticut, 1968.

FISHBURN, P. C., (1964), *Decision and Value Theory*, New York, Wiley.

FORRESTER, J. W., (1961), *Industrial Dynamics*, Cambridge, Mass., MIT Press.

GALBRAITH, J. K., (1967, 1971), *The New Industrial State*, (revised edition 1971), Boston, Houghton Mifflin.

GALLIE, W. B., (1952), *Peirce and Pragmatism*, Harmondsworth, Penguin.

GARNER, W. R., (1962), *Uncertainty and Structure as Psychological Concepts*, New York, Wiley.

GARVIN, P. L. (Ed.), (1963), *Natural Language and the Computer*, New York, McGraw-Hill.

GELDARD, F. A. (Ed.), *Communication Processes*, NATO Symposium, Washington D.C., 1963; Oxford, Pergamon, 1965.

GINSBERG, S., (1966), *The Mathematical Theory of Context-Free Languages*, New York, McGraw-Hill.

GUETZKOW, H. (Ed.), (1951), *Groups, Leadership and Men*, Pittsburgh, Carnegie Press.

HALL, EDWARD T., (1959), *The Silent Language*, New York, Doubleday.

HALMOS, P. R., (1950), *Measure Theory*, New York, Van Nostrand.

HARTLEY, E. L. and HARTLEY, R. E., (1961), *Fundamentals of Social Psychology*, New York, Knopf.

HAYAKAWA, S. I., (1965), *Language in Thought and Action*, (second edition) London, Allen & Unwin.

HINTIKKA, J. and SUPPES, P. (Eds.), (1970), *Information and Inference*, Dordrecht, Holland, Reidel.

HOLLANDER, E. P., (1967), *Principles and Methods of Social Psychology*, Oxford U. P.

HOOS, IDA R., (1969), *Systems Analysis in Social Policy*, London, Institute of Economic Affairs.

JACOBS, R. C. and CAMPBELL, D. T., 'The Perpetuation of an Arbitrary Tradition through Several Generations of a Laboratory Micro-Culture', *J. Abnorm. Soc. Psychol.*, 1961, No. 62, pp. 649–58.

JAKOBOVITS, L. A. and MIRON, M. S. (Eds.), (1967), *Readings in the Psychology of Language*, Englewood Cliffs, N.J., Prentice-Hall.

JENKINS, J. J. and RUSSEL, W. A., 'An Atlas of Semantic Profiles for 360 Words', *Amer. J. Psychology*, 1958, No. 71, pp. 688–99.

KAHN, R. L., WOLF, D. M., QUINN, R. P., SNOEK, J. D. and ROSENTHAL, R. A., (1964), *Organisational Stress*, New York, Wiley.

KATZ, E. and LAZARSFELD, P. F., (1955), *Personal Influence*, New York, Free Press.

KATZ, E. and KAHN, R. L., (1966), *The Social Psychology of Organisation*, New York, Wiley.

KEAY, F., (1969), *The Numerate Manager*, London, Allen & Unwin.

KHINCHIN, A. I., (1957), *Mathematical Foundation of Information Theory* (Trans. Silverman, R. A. and Friedman, M. D.), Dover, New York and Constable, London, 1957 (1953 and 1956).

KOONTZ, H. D. and O'DONNELL, C., (1955), *Principles of Management* (fourth edition 1968), New York, McGraw-Hill.

KORFHAGE, R. R., (1966), *Logic and Algorithms*, New York, London, John Wiley.

KORZYBSKI, A. (1951), 'The Role of Language in the Perceptual Process', ch. 7 of Blake and Ramsey (eds), *Perception—an Approach to Personality*, New York, Ronald Press.

KOTZ, S., 'Recent Results in Information Theory', *J. Appl. Prob.*, Vol. 3, No. 3, pp. 1–93, June 1966.

KRASNER, L., 'Studies of the Conditioning of Verbal Behaviour', *Psychol. Bull.*, 1958, No. 55, pp. 148–70.

KRASNER, L. and ULLMANN, L. P., (1965), *Research in Behaviour Modification: New Developments and Implications*', New York, Holt, Rinehart.

LAMBERT, W. W. and LAMBERT, W. E., (1964), *Social Psychology*, Englewood Cliffs, N.J., Prentice-Hall.

LEFKOVITZ, D., (1969), *File Structures for On-Line Systems*, New York, Spartan.

LEVI-STRAUSS, C., (1959), *Structual Anthropology*, London, Penguin Press, 1968.

LEWIS, B. N., HORABIN, I. S. and GANE, C. P., (1967), *Flow Charts, Logical Trees and Algorithms for Rules and Regulations*, C.A.S. Occasional Papers, London, HMSO.

348   SELECTED REFERENCES

LIKERT, R., (1961), *New Patterns of Management*, New York, McGraw-Hill.

LITTLE, I. M. S., (1950), *A Critique of Welfare Economics*, (second edition 1957), Oxford U. P.

LOCKE, J., (1689), *Essay Concerning Human Understanding*.

LUCE, R. S., BUSH, R. R. and GALANTER, E., (1963-5), *Handbook of Mathematical Psychology*, 3 vols, New York, London, Wiley.

LUCE, R. S., BUSH, R. R. and GALANTER, E. (Eds.), (1965), *Readings in Mathematical Psychology*, New York, London, Wiley.

LUKASIEWICZ, JAN., (1970), *Selected Works*, (Ed. Bortowski), Amsterdam, North Holland.

MACKAY, S. M., (1969), *Information Mechanism and Meaning*, Cambridge, Mass., London, MIT.

MALINOWSKI, B., (1923), 'The problem of meaning in primitive languages', in Ogden and Richards, *Meaning of Meaning*.

MALINOWSKI, B., (1944), *A Scientific Theory of Culture and Other Essays*, Univ. N. Carolina Press, 1944; Galaxy and Oxford U. P., 1960.

MILLER, G. A., (1967), *The Psychology of Communication*, New York, Basic Books; London, Penguin Press, 1968.

MILLER, G. A., (1953), *Language and Communication*, New York, McGraw-Hill.

MORRIS, C., (1946), *Signs, Language and Behaviour*, New York, Prentice-Hall & Braziller.

MORRIS, C., (1964), *Signification and Significance*, Cambridge, Mass., MIT Press.

MOWRER, O. H., (1954), 'The psychologist looks at language', *The American Psychologist*, Vol. 9, No. 11, November 1954, pp. 660-94.

NEWCOMB, T. M., TURNER, R. H. and CONVERSE, P. E., (1952), *Social Psychology—A Study of Human Interaction*, (revised edition 1966), London, Tavistock Publications.

OGDEN, C. K. and RICHARDS, I. A., (1923), *The Meaning of Meaning*, London, Routledge & Kegan Paul.

OSGOOD, C. E., SUCI, G. J. and TANNENBAUM, P. H., (1957), *The Measurement of Meaning*, Univ. of Illinois Press.

OSGOOD, C. E., 'Semantic Differential Technique in the Comparative Study of Cultures', *American Anthropologist*, 66, No. 3, June 1964, pp. 171-200, (reprinted in Jakobovits & Miron).

PEIRCE, C. S., (1931-5), *Collected Papers*, (6 Vols. ed. C. Hartshorne and P. Weiss), Cambridge, Mass., Harvard U. P.

POPPER, K. R., (1935), *Logic of Scientific Discovery*, New York, Harper & Row, (revised edition 1965).

POPPER, K. R., (1957), *The Poverty of Historicism*, London, Routledge & Kegan Paul.

POPPER, K. R., (1963), *Conjectures and Refutations—The Growth of Scientific Knowledge*, London, Routledge & Kegan Paul.

QUINE, W. V. O., (1953), *From a Logical Point of View*, (revised edition 1961), New York, Harper & Row.

QUINE, W. V. O., (1960), *Word & Object*, New York, MIT Press and Wiley.

RAZRAN, G., 'Semantic and Phonetographic Generalisations of Salivary Conditioning to Verbal Stimuli', *J. Exp. Psychol.*, 1949, 39, pp. 642–52.

RIESS, B. F., 'Semantic Conditioning Involving the Galvanic Skin Reflex', *J. Exp. Psychol.*, 1940, 26, pp. 238–40.

ROSENTHAL, R., (1966), *Experimenter Effects on Behavioural Research'*, New York, Appleton Century Crofts.

RUESCH, J. and KEES, W., (1956), *Non-Verbal Communication*, Berkeley, Univ. California Press.

RUSSELL, B. and WHITEHEAD, A. N., (1910), *Principia Mathematica*, Cambridge U. P.

RUSSELL, B., (1946), *History of Western Philosophy*, (revised edition 1961), London, Allen & Unwin.

SAVAGE, L. J., (1962), *The Foundations of Statistical Inference*, London, Methuen, and New York, Wiley.

SCOTT, W. A., (1957), 'Attitude Change through Reward of Verbal Behaviour', *J. Abnorm. Soc. Psychol.*, 1957, 55, pp. 72–5.

SHACKLE, G. L. S., (1961), *Decision, Order and Time in Human Affairs*, Cambirdge U. P.

SHACKLE, G. L. S., (1955, 1968), *Uncertainty in Economics*, Cambridge U. P.

SHANNON, C. E., 'Prediction and Entropy of Printed English', *Bell Syst. Tech. J.*, 1951, 30, pp. 50–64.

SHANNON, C. E. and WEAVER, W., (1949), *The Mathematical Theory of Communication*, Urbana, Univ. of Illinois Press.

SHERIF, M., 'A Study of some Social Factors in Perception', *Arch. Psychol.*, 1935, 27, No. 187.

SKINNER, B. F., (1957), *Verbal Behaviour*, New York, Appleton Century Crofts.

SOKAL, R. R., and SNEATH, P. H. A., (1957), *Principles of Numerical Taxonomy*, London and San Francisco, Freeman.

STAATS, C. K. and STAATS, A. W., 'Meaning Established by Classical Conditioning', *J. Exp. Psychol.*, 1957, 54, pp. 74–80.

STAMPER, R. K., 'Some Ways of Measuring Information', *Computer Bulletin*, 1971, Vol. 15, pp. 432–6.

STAMPER, R. K., (1971), 'Logical Structures of Files', in *Data Organisation for Maintenance and Access*, London, British Computer Society.

STONE, P. J., DUNPHY, D. C., SMITH and OGILVIE, (1966), *The General Inquirer: A Computer Approach to Content Analysis*, Cambridge, Mass., MIT Press.

STONE, P. J., DUNPHY, D. C., BERNSTEIN, (1966), 'The Analysis of Product Image', in Stone et al, *The General Inquirer*.

SUPPES, P. and ZINNES, J. L., (1963), 'Basic Measurement Theory', in Luce, Bush and Galanter, *Handbook of Mathematical Psychology*, Vol. 1.

TARSKI, A., (1941), *Introduction to Logic*, Oxford U. P.

VERPLANCK, W. S., 'The Control of the Content of Conversation: Re-inforcement of Statements of Opinion', *J. Abnorm. Soc. Psychol.*, 1955, 51, pp. 608–76.

WALLACE, C. S. and BOULTON, S. M., 'An Information Measure for Classification', *Computer Journal*, (1968), Vol. 11, p. 185.

WATERS, S. J., (1970), 'Physical Data Structures', in *Data Organisation for Maintenance & Access*', London, British Computer Society.

WHITAKER, G. (Ed.), (1965), *T-Group Training*, ATM Occasional Paper No. 2, Oxford, Blackwell.

WHORF, B. L., (1938), 'Some Verbal Categories of Hopi', *Language*, Vol. 14, pp. 275–86; re-printed in *Language, Thought and Reality*, Cambridge, Mass., MIT Press, 1956.

WHORF, B. L., (1939), 'The Relation of Habitual Thought and Behaviour to Language', in *Language, Thought and Reality*, 1956.

WITTGENSTEIN, L., (1921), *Tractatus Logico—Philosophicus*, Trans. D. F. Pears and B. F. McGuinness, London and New York, Routledge & Kegan Paul (1961) and Humanities Press.

WITTGENSTEIN, L., (1953), *Philosophical Investigations*, Trans. G. E. M. Anscombe, Oxford, Blackwell.

Index